William Moister

Missionary Anecdotes

Sketches, facts, and incidents relating to the state of the heathen and the effects of the Gospel in various parts of the world. Second Edition

William Moister

Missionary Anecdotes

Sketches, facts, and incidents relating to the state of the heathen and the effects of the Gospel in various parts of the world. Second Edition

ISBN/EAN: 9783337285210

Printed in Europe, USA, Canada, Australia, Japan

Cover: Foto ©Lupo / pixelio.de

More available books at **www.hansebooks.com**

Cape Coast Castle, as seen when approached from the Interior.

MISSIONARY ANECDOTES.

Sketches, Facts, and Incidents

RELATING TO THE STATE OF THE HEATHEN

AND

THE EFFECTS OF THE GOSPEL IN VARIOUS PARTS OF THE WORLD.

BY THE

REV. WILLIAM MOISTER.

AUTHOR OF "HISTORY OF WESLEYAN MISSIONS," "MISSIONARY WORLD,"
"MISSIONARY PIONEERS," "MISSIONARY MEMORIALS,"
"MISSIONARY STORIES," ETC.

Second Edition.

LONDON:
WESLEYAN CONFERENCE OFFICE,
CASTLE STREET, CITY ROAD;
SOLD AT 66 PATERNOSTER ROW.

Ballantyne Press
BALLANTYNE, HANSON AND CO.
EDINBURGH AND LONDON

TO THE

REV. FREDERICK J. JOBSON, D.D.,

ONE OF THE GENERAL TREASURERS OF

THE WESLEYAN METHODIST MISSIONARY SOCIETY,

AND TO

MRS JOBSON,

HIS EXCELLENT AND DEVOTED WIFE,

AND THE COMPANION OF HIS MISSIONARY TRAVELS

IN AUSTRALIA, INDIA, AND THE HOLY LAND,

This Volume

IS MOST RESPECTFULLY DEDICATED

BY THE AUTHOR,

IN ADMIRATION OF THEIR LONG CONTINUED AND FAITHFUL SERVICES

IN THE CAUSE OF METHODISM AND ITS FOREIGN MISSIONS,

AND ALSO

IN TESTIMONY OF SINCERE PERSONAL RESPECT

AND ESTEEM.

PREFACE.

CHRISTIAN MISSIONS to the heathen, in their history, principles, and practical working, have been the favourite theme of the writer's studies and researches for more than forty years, whilst endeavouring to promote the spiritual welfare of his fellow-men both at home and abroad. And having, at an early period, formed the habit of close observation as to the manners and customs of the natives among whom he laboured in Western and Southern Africa, in the West Indies and on the continent of South America, he has accumulated a large amount of information in his journals and note-books. From these, and from hundreds of letters from his devoted missionary associates, which he has carefully preserved, as well as from a good library, he has gathered materials for several missionary works which he has published since his return to his native land, which have met with a favourable reception from the friends of the enterprise.

As the stock of information at his command is far from exhausted, the author ventures to send forth this little volume in the service of the cause to which his life has been devoted. He has endeavoured to make it specially interesting to the large class of young people who are rendering such valuable aid to the mission cause, and he trusts it will also prove helpful to teachers and preachers who are occasionally engaged in advocating missionary enterprise, as well as to general readers. To the divine blessing it is commended, with fervent prayer for its success.

W. M.

WOODBINE COTTAGE,
NEWPORT, ISLE OF WIGHT,
January 27, 1875.

CONTENTS.

SEC.		PAGE
I.	HEATHEN DARKNESS	1
II.	NATIVE GENIUS	41
III.	PROVIDENTIAL OPENINGS	55
IV.	DANGERS AND DELIVERANCES	70
V.	AFFLICTIONS AND BEREAVEMENTS	99
VI.	GENERAL RESULTS OF MISSIONS	116
VII.	REMARKABLE CONVERTS	133
VIII.	HAPPY DEATHS	172
IX.	CHRISTIAN BENEVOLENCE	187
X.	MISCELLANEOUS INCIDENTS	207

ILLUSTRATIONS.

Cape Coast Castle, as seen when approached from the Interior . . . *to face Title*

The Druids preparing to offer Sacrifice . . *to face page* 4

Kaffir Witch-Doctor and Rain-Maker preparing their Incantations 24

Negro Clerk attracting the Admiration of his Employers . 118

Crossing the River Prah between Cape Coast and Kumasi . 148

Street Scene in Demerara, after the arrival of Chinese and Indian Coolies . . . 192

John Woolman, the Quaker Philanthropist, Preaching to the Indians 256

Kama, the Converted Kaffir Chief, addressing his People . 280

MISSIONARY ANECDOTES,

SKETCHES, FACTS, AND INCIDENTS.

I. HEATHEN DARKNESS.

1. Gentile Nations.—The necessity of Christian missions to benighted heathen nations, is the same now as it was in the days of the apostles; and the description which St Paul gives in his Epistle to the Romans of the ignorance, superstition, idolatry, and moral degradation of the Gentiles with whom he had come in contact in the course of his missionary travels and labours, will apply with equal truth and force to the modern pagans of Africa, India, America, and the South Sea Islands. Indeed, some of the heathen tribes with whom we have met, when they had learned to read the Scriptures for themselves, were so struck with the graphic descriptions to which we refer, that they declared their conviction that they must have been written expressly with reference to *them*. But the heathen, when left to themselves, cannot be expected to improve their moral condition. As long as they are left without the light of divine revelation they must necessarily sink deeper and deeper in ignorance and sin. This has been proved by experience and observation in all ages and countries, the faint knowledge which the people once had in some places of the character and claims of the true God having, in process of time, become almost entirely obliterated. The apostle says, "Because that, when they knew God they glorified Him not as God, neither were thankful; but became vain in their imaginations, and their foolish heart was darkened. Professing themselves to be wise, they became fools, and changed the glory of the incorruptible God into an image made like to corruptible man, and to birds, and four-footed beasts, and creeping things. For this cause God gave them up unto vile affections. And even as they did not like to retain God in their knowledge, God gave them over to a reprobate mind, to do those things which are not convenient; being filled with all unrighteousness, fornication, wickedness, covetousness, maliciousness; full of envy, murder, debate, deceit, malignity; whisperers, backbiters, haters of God, despiteful, proud, boasters, covenant-breakers, without natural affection, implacable, unmerciful" (Rom. i. 21-23, 26, 28-31).

2. The Athenians.

With all their learning, philosophy, and civilisation of which they proudly boasted, the natives of Athens, the city of Minerva, were in no way superior to the people of other pagan countries with respect to morality and religion. When the Apostle Paul entered that city, about A.D. 52, he found the inhabitants involved in the densest heathen darkness. They were "wholly given up to idolatry." Almost every object of worship, belonging to every nation, had a niche in its Pantheon. There are said to have been more images and statues here than in all the rest of Greece put together, which gave occasion to one of the humorous satirists to say that "in Athens a god was more easily found than a man."

The moral condition of the people may be inferred from the reception given to the great apostle of the Gentiles on his arrival at Athens in the course of his second extensive missionary journey, and the admirable discourse which he delivered to them on that occasion. "Certain philosophers, Epicureans and Stoics, encountered him, and some said, What will this babbler say? other some, He seemeth to be a setter forth of strange gods, because he preached unto them Jesus and the resurrection. And they took him and brought him unto Areopagus, saying, May we know what this new doctrine, whereof thou speakest, is?" "Then Paul stood in the midst of Mars Hill, and said, Ye men of Athens, I perceive that in all things ye are too superstitious. For as I passed by, and beheld your devotions, I found an altar with this inscription, TO THE UNKNOWN GOD. Whom, therefore, ye ignorantly worship, Him declare I unto you. God, that made the world, and all things therein, seeing that He is Lord of heaven and earth, dwelleth not in temples made with hands; neither is worshipped with men's hands, as though He needed anything, seeing that He giveth to all life and breath and all things; and hath made of one blood all nations of men for to dwell on all the face of the earth, and hath determined the times before appointed, and the bounds of their habitation; that they should seek the Lord, if haply they might feel after Him, and find Him, though He be not far from every one of us; for in Him we live, and move, and have our being" (Acts xvii. 22-28). With many other words did the apostle warn and admonish the proud and haughty idolaters of Athens, and the result was, that whilst "some mocked, certain men clave unto him, and believed: among the which was Dionysius the Areopagite, and a woman named Damaris, and others with them."

3. The Egyptians.

Among all the heathen nations of antiquity, no people were more deeply sunk in idolatry, superstition, and sin, than the inhabitants of Egypt. From sacred and profane history we learn how numerous were their gods, and that they paid divine homage to various kinds of beasts, birds, and reptiles. Their public festivals were, moreover, attended by scenes and circumstances the most shocking and revolting (as viewed from our highly-favoured standpoint). The ancient historian Herodotus, giving an account of a solemn feast which the people of Egypt annually celebrated at Eubastis, in honour of the goddess Diana, says, "To her they offer many sacrifices; and while the victim is burning, they dance and play a thousand tricks, and drink more wine than in the whole year besides. For they assemble to the number of about 700,000 men and women, besides children." It is thought by some learned commentators, that on the occasion of the sad defection of the Israelites, when Aaron made for them the golden calf, the feast celebrated with wild songs and dances was after the manner of that described by Herodotus. How dark and degraded is every country and every people without the light and teaching of Divine revelation!

Although the inhabitants of Egypt are now chiefly Mohammedans, and not pagans, as in ancient times, they are, nevertheless, in a fearful state of spiritual destitution. It is matter of gratitude to God, however, that of late years some efforts have been made to shed forth the light of the ever-blessed gospel in the Valley of the Nile; but much more remains to be done before anything like adequate provision will have been made to meet the pressing necessities of the case.

4. The Assyrians.—In carefully reading the Bible we get some curious glimpses of heathen darkness in ancient times, one specimen of which from the Old Testament may perhaps induce our youthful readers to notice many others. When a considerable number of the children of Israel had been carried away captive to Babylon, the King of Assyria sent a colony of his own people to occupy the cities of Samaria which had been left without inhabitants. These were dark, benighted pagans, who were ignorant of the true and living God, and we have the following notice of their superstitious fears when afflicted by Divine Providence:—"And so it was at the beginning of their dwelling there, that they feared not the Lord: therefore the Lord sent lions among them, which slew some of them. Wherefore they spake to the King of Assyria, saying, The nations which thou hast removed, and placed in the cities of Samaria, know not the manner of the God of the land: therefore He hath sent lions among them, and behold they slay them, because they know not the manner of the God of the land. Then the King of Assyria commanded, saying, Carry thither one of the priests whom ye brought from thence, and let him go and dwell there, and let him teach them the manner of the God of the land. Then one of the priests, whom they had carried away from Samaria, came and dwelt in Beth-el, and taught them how they should fear the Lord." It does not appear that this solitary ancient missionary was very successful in his labours, however, for it is immediately added—"Howbeit every nation made gods of their own, and put them in the houses of the high places which the Samaritans had made, every nation in their cities wherein they dwelt" (2 Kings xvii. 25-29).

5. Ancient Britons.—Surrounded as we now are with numerous and diversified evidences of civilisation, social progress, and religious privileges—railroads, steam-ships, electric telegraphs, and Christian sanctuaries—we can scarcely realise the fact that Great Britain was once as deeply involved in heathen darkness as Africa, India, or any other pagan country in the world. It is nevertheless true—we are informed on undoubted authority—that at an early period of its history the hills and valleys of this beautiful island were covered with impenetrable forests, exhibiting only here and there clearings, on which the natives erected their huts, and where small patches of ground were cultivated in a very rude and superficial manner. Our heathen ancestors wandered about in a state approaching to nudity, painting their bodies, and indulging in other barbarous practices similar to those of the unenlightened Hottentots and Kaffirs of Southern Africa. They were much addicted to the chase, delighted in cruel sports, and the respective clans often waged cruel wars with each other which resulted in much bloodshed, and in the vanquished survivors being reduced to a state of abject slavery.

Nor was there any system of religion among the ancient Britons calculated to raise them from this state of social and moral degradation. Previous to the introduction of Christianity into England Druidism was the only form of worship among the people, and this was a system of superstition, cruelty, and blood, not a whit better than those with which we have met in distant heathen lands in modern times. The Druids were a class of men of high pretensions, but deeply involved in ignorance and sin. They combined in themselves the functions of the priest, the magistrate, the scholar, and the physician ; but in reality they were little, if any, superior in knowledge, or social position, to the witch-doctors, rainmakers, and fetish-men of pagan Africa. They had their high places marked by piles of stones of huge dimensions, the remains of one of which may be seen at Stonehenge, near Salisbury, and other places ; and it is believed that they and their votaries paid divine homage to the rising sun, and that they worshipped other imaginary gods by various superstitious rites, which sometimes involved the offering of human sacrifices. Cæsar says of the Druids of Britain, "They have images of immense size, the limbs of which are framed with twisted twigs, and filled with living persons ; these being set on fire, those within are encompassed by the flames. The punishment of persons apprehended stealing, or doing any injury, they believe to be especially agreeable to the gods ; but when persons of this class are wanting, they do not scruple to destroy even the innocent." Strabo confirms this account of Cæsar, and adds that "animals of all sorts were burned and offered in the sacrifice with the men." He also says that "human victims were sometimes shot with arrows, sometimes crucified, and sometimes slain with the sword, in which last case the Druids made auguries from the quivering of the muscles."

In view of the once heathen state of this highly-favoured land, how thankful we ought to be for the gospel of Christ! If Christianity has produced such a change in Great Britain as we now behold, we may be assured it can do the same for other countries to which it may be sent by the friends of the missionary enterprise.

6. Ancient Gauls.—That part of the European Continent which in ancient geography was included under the general name of Gallia, or Gaul, included those countries now known as Spain, Portugal, France, Germany, and some others. The inhabitants of these extensive regions, in their original pagan state, were remarkable for their savage, ferocious, warlike character. Cæsar tells us that the petty nations and various tribes into which the population was divided were constantly at war with one another, and that not only their cities, cantons, and districts, but almost all their families, were frequently at variance among themselves, and divided and torn by factions. They were, moreover, so

The Druids preparing to offer Sacrifice.

cruel and void of human feeling, that when their relatives and friends became incapable of action, through old age, infirmity, wounds, or chronic diseases, they were wont to put them to death in cold blood. In the numerous wars in which they were engaged with the Greeks and Romans, they exhibited a remarkable recklessness of human life. When they found themselves straitly besieged in their cities, and could hold out no longer, instead of thinking how to obtain honourable terms of capitulation, their chief care very often was to put their wives and children to death, and then to kill one another, to avoid being led into slavery. Their contempt of death, according to Strabo, very much facilitated their conquest by Cæsar; for, pouring their numerous forces upon such an experienced enemy as the one with which they had to contend, their want of discipline soon proved their ruin.

The inhabitants of the various countries of modern Europe are now, to a large extent, professed Roman Catholics, or avowed infidels, the number of consistent Protestant Christians being in the minority. The true people of God, of every name, who are so nobly struggling on the Continent against sin and error in their various forms, are deserving of our sympathy and aid; and the genuine friends of evangelical truth may there find a grand field of missionary labour in their midst.

7. Romish Infatuation.—During the prevalence of distressing poverty in Calais, a Protestant lady from England, who was visiting the place, relieved, according to her ability, several necessitous cases. One of these was a poor Frenchwoman, apparently in a state of extreme destitution. On receiving a small silver coin, the haggard-looking pauper expressed the most fervent gratitude; and, with a countenance lighted up for the moment with an expression of unwonted joy, she prayed that the blessing of the "Holy Virgin might rest upon her benefactor." The lady was astonished at this manifestation of gratitude for such a small gift, and said, "You are very thankful for a trifle, for I only gave you a shilling," when, with tears of joy, the poor woman said it was precisely the sum she had been anxious to obtain for three months. Just three months previously she had lost a child by death, whose soul she declared had been in purgatory ever since, because she had not the means of procuring its deliverance; but that she should now take that shilling to the priest, and her child would be released from its torment. Nor could anything the lady was able to say induce the poor woman to purchase the bread she so much needed, and leave her infant to the care of Him who said, "Suffer little children to come unto me, and forbid them not," and who had doubtless taken it to Himself. Surely France, and other Roman Catholic countries, stand in need of the pure gospel of Christ, as preached by Protestant missionaries.

8. Popish Charms.—The Roman Catholics of Ireland and Scotland have sometimes discovered as much ignorance and superstition as the pagan natives of Africa; and it is a remarkable circumstance that they have shown it in the same manner, by trusting in greegrees, amulets, or charms for safety in times of danger. With a view to expose this kind of superstitious folly, and, if possible, make the people ashamed of it, Dr Anderson took occasion to ridicule it in a lecture he delivered in the City Hall,

Glasgow. As recorded in Dr Alexander Macleod's "Reminiscences" of his friend, the lecturer, having obtained some real specimens, "held up the charms themselves—pieces of calico shaped like hearts. He told his audience how, if they wished to be safe, they should buy one of these, and put it on the naked breast; but if they had plenty of means, and wished to be safer still, they should buy two, and put one on the breast above, and one on the back beneath the heart. Then came the climax. 'We have heard of many ways and means of salvation. There is in the oldest dispensation of all, salvation *by works;* and in the Mosaic dispensation, salvation *by works of the law.* And in the new dispensation we have salvation *by grace;* and we have had, since that new dispensation was set up, many comings and goings between the old and the new —salvation *by pilgrimages,* salvation *by priests,* salvation *by the Church;* but this is the first time in the history of the world that we have been offered *salvation by clouts!*" The effect of this ludicrous exposure of the wicked and foolish practice of the lower order of Papists in Scotland convulsed the audience in such a manner that it was some time before the learned lecturer could proceed with his address. It was hoped also that this mode of treating the subject would have a better effect upon the minds of those whom it chiefly concerned than a graver line of argument.

9. The Feast of Arafat.—The extent to which foolish and ridiculous superstition prevails both in Mohammedan and pagan countries which have never been visited with the light of the gospel, is truly astonishing. The following illustration may serve as a specimen:—The wife of a missionary labouring in Syria, observing a Moslem feast going on near Beyrout with great noise and merriment, asked a native female what was the object of its celebration. "Oh," said the woman, "it is to commemorate Adam's reconciliation with his wife." The missionary's wife never having heard before of family jars of such an ancient date, was curious to know something more about an oriental legend relating to such a curious subject, and made further inquiry about it, when the woman proceeded to relate the substance of it as follows :—Eve was one day admiring a beautiful figure which was reflected from a looking-glass as she stood before it, when Satan made his appearance, and assured her that Adam, her husband, loved the lady she saw in the glass more than he loved her. On hearing this, Eve was offended, and ran away from Adam, and wandered about in the world for several years. At length she met Adam on the top of a mountain called Arafat (knowledge) near Mecca, where they knew each other, and were reconciled. "Therefore," concluded the woman, "this feast is called Arafat, to commemorate the joyful event." The missionary's wife took the woman aside, and read to her from the Bible the interesting story of Adam and Eve as therein recorded, and explained to her the fall of man and the need of salvation. With this she was so much pleased that she thanked the lady for her kindness, and promised to come to her again, and to bring with her other women to be instructed, which led to the formation of a Christian school in that place soon afterwards.

10. A Ghost Story.—The following incident is illustrative of the spiritual darkness and gross superstition in which many parts of Ireland were involved before Protestant missionaries went forth to diffuse the light of the gospel among the people :—The Rev. Mr Lambe was travelling to a town called Headford in the county of Galway, on the 14th of April 1829, when his attention was attracted by an extraordinary-looking building on the roadside. On asking what it was intended for, he was informed that it was erected as a place of shelter for a ghost! He had no idea that spiritual beings required such accommodation, and was curious to know something more about such a strange theory. On inquiring further into the matter, he was gravely told that some time before a man had died in that neighbourhood, and that, for some reason not explained, his spirit could not rest, but was seen roaming about, especially on stormy nights. His son, therefore, as an act both of religious duty and filial affection, erected this shed to shelter the troubled spirit of his departed father from the inclemency of the weather, whenever he might have occasion to revisit the earth.

11. American Indians.—When the continent and islands of America first became known to Europeans, they were inhabited by numerous tribes of aborigines whom the discoverers called Indians. They appeared almost destitute of clothing, with their heads ornamented with the feathers of wild birds, and their lank black hair floating upon their shoulders, or bound in tresses round their heads. Their complexion was of a dusky copper-colour; and although not tall, they were well shaped and active. Their faces, and several parts of their bodies, were painted with glaring colours, which gave them a strange appearance. The social and moral condition of these wild Indians of the Western World was low and degraded in the extreme. They were very ignorant, and appeared to have strange and confused ideas of the Supreme Being, whom they regarded as represented by the sun in the heavens, to which they paid divine homage. Some indeed appeared to be almost entirely destitute of any idea of a great First Cause. They were, moreover, warlike, cruel and revengeful in their temper and spirit, and almost total strangers to all kind and humane feelings.

Many changes have taken place of late years in the position and circumstances of the North American Indians. As the country once claimed by them as their ancient hunting-grounds became settled by European emigrants, they were driven westward; and in some of their locations, where lands have been assigned to them by Government, many have been brought to a pleasing state of civilisation, through the labours of Christian missionaries. But those tribes which have not yet been brought under the influence of Christianity are as ignorant and degraded as were their savage ancestors. As a people who have at different periods suffered from their contact with white men, and who have given evidence of their capability to receive and appreciate religious instruction, the American Indians have a strong claim on the sympathies and efforts of the friends of Christian missions.

12. Cruel Practices.—Adverting to the cruel and savage habits of the North American Indians, and writing from near Cedar Lake, the Rev. Mr Bontell says :—" Before I returned to our tent, which was pitched but a few yards from two graves, the greater part of the Indians had collected here, and began the scalp-dance. It was led by three squaws, each bearing in her hand one of the recent scalps. Two or three men sat beating drums and singing, while old and young, male and female, all joined in the song. Occasionally all would become so animated, that there would be one general hop, and all at the same time throwing their heads back, would raise a most horrible yell, clapping the mouth with the hand, to render it, if possible, more terrific. Here were seen little boys and girls, not six years old, imitating their fathers and mothers, and participating in their brutal joy. Thus early do they learn by precept and example to imbibe the spirit of revenge and war which is thus fostered in their bosoms, and which in after-life stimulates them to go and perform some deed of daring and of blood, which shall gain for themselves the like applause.

"A circumstance which rendered the scene not a little appalling, was its being performed around the graves of the dead. At the head of one of these graves hangs an old scalp, some ten feet above the ground, which the winds have almost divested of its ornaments and its hair. The grass and the turf, for several yards round, are literally destroyed, I presume, by their frequent dancing there. One of the scalps I examined; the flesh side had apparently been smoked, and rubbed with some material till it was pliant, after which it had been painted with vermilion. A piece of wood is turned in the form of a horse-shoe, into which the scalp is sewed, the threads passing round the wood, which keeps it tight. Narrow pieces of cloth and ribands of various colours were attached to the bow, and were ornamented with beads and feathers. A small stick, which serves as a handle to shake it in the air when they dance, was attached to the top of the bow by a string. While examining it, a lock of hair fell from it, which the Indian gave me, and which I still preserve." Verily "the dark places of the earth are full of the habitations of cruelty."

13. A Recent Instance.—So recently as 1873, in a communication from the Rev. Mr Hinman, missionary to the Indians at Santee, we find the following statement, illustrative of the present condition of the wild red men of the West :—
" At Four Bears' Camp, ten miles above the Agency, the Indians have built a village of log-houses. There are seventy of them, and their town is laid out in the form of a parallelogram stockaded between the houses, with a grand entrance to the enclosed square at the east end, adjoining the house of the chief, Drag-the-Stone. In the centre, I am sorry to say, I saw when there the tall black and white pole, or ensign of war, and around it a scalp-dance going on. Indians with blackened faces, looking like very demons, attended by young women (tattooed also with black), as singers and chanters. The son of the Sans Arc Chief had been scalped by the Mandans, during an attack on them, and they, to add shame to sorrow, had sent his scalp back to his father, with a message of derision. A large party of some two hundred warriors, started off to avenge the insult, but finding no Mandans outside the defences, and hearing the thunder of the big gun, discharged at them from the fort, they thought it safest to return home without attacking their enemies. They say, however, that they do not think it fair for the Whites to interfere with their private quarrels and disputes. The prompt measures now adopted by the military authorities will, I

think, soon put an end to these barbarisms among themselves; but in this village they want a missionary also. Here a white man who has an Indian wife promises to build us a good school-house, at his own expense, if we will provide a teacher. I hope some one will volunteer."

14. Extreme Ignorance.—In the far-distant regions of the cold and cheerless north, it would appear that the natives are still more ignorant and debased. Captain Ross, in his account of the Arctic Expedition which he commanded, gives the following account of the Esquimaux with whom he came in contact:—
"Ervick, being the senior of the first party that came on board, was judged to be the most proper person to question on the subject of religion. I directed Sacheuse to ask him if he had any knowledge of a Supreme Being; but after trying every word used in his own language to express it, he could not make him understand what he meant. It was distinctly asserted that he did not worship the sun, moon, or stars, or any image or living creature. When asked what the sun or moon was for, he said 'to give light.' He had no knowledge or idea how he came into being, or of a future state; but said that when he died, he would be put into the ground. Having fully ascertained that he had no idea of a beneficent Supreme Being, I proceeded, through Sachense, to inquire if he believed in an evil spirit; but he could not be made to understand what it meant. The word 'angekok,' which means a conjuror, or sorcerer, was then pronounced to him in the South Greenland Esquimaux language. He said 'they had many of them; that it was in their power to raise a storm or make a calm, and to drive off seals, or to bring them; that they learned this art from old angekoks when young; that they were afraid of them, but they had generally one in every family.'

"Meggack, another native, gave precisely the same answers, and had the same notions, but he was not so intelligent as Ervick. Finding that Otooniah, the nephew of Ervick, a lad of eighteen years of age, was a young angekok, I got him into the cabin by himself, and, through Sachense, asked him how he learned this art. He replied 'from an old angekok; that he could raise the wind, and drive off seals and birds.' He said that this was done by gestures, and words; but the words had no meaning, nor were they said or addressed to anything but the wind or sea. He was positive that in this incantation he did not receive assistance from anything, nor could he be made to understand what a good or evil spirit meant. When Ervick was told that there was an omnipotent, omnipresent, and invisible Being, who had created the sun and land, and all therein, he showed much surprise, and eagerly asked where He lived. When told that He was everywhere, he evinced much alarm, and became very impatient to be upon deck. When informed there was a future state, and another world, he said that 'a wise man, who had lived long before his time, had said they were to go to the moon, but that it was not now believed, and that none of the others knew anything of this matter; they believed, however, that birds and other living things came from it.'"

15. Notions of God.—The lamented Sir John Franklin, in the narrative of his second expedition to the shores of the Polar Seas, when describing the moral condition of the natives, says, that "on Mr Dean questioning some of the elderly men as to their knowledge of a Supreme Being, they replied, 'We believe that there is a Great Spirit, who created everything, both us and the world for our use. We suppose that he dwells in the land from whence the white people come, that he is kind to the inhabitants of those lands, and that there are people who never die; the winds that blow from that quarter (the south) are always warm. He does not know of the wicked state of our country, nor the pitiful condition in which we are.' To the question, 'Whom do your medicine-men address when they conjure?' they answered, 'We do not think they speak to the master of life; for if they did, we should fare better than we do, and should not die. He does not inhabit our lands.'"

Since then many of the poor degraded Esquimaux have been made acquainted with the character of the true God, and Jesus Christ whom He has sent, through the efforts of Christian missionaries; and it is hoped that many more will yet be gathered into the fold of the Redeemer.

16. The Poor Indian's Offering.

—It is recorded of a young Indian chief, with a wife and family, in Upper Canada, that on one occasion he left the camp of his people, and retired to a considerable distance in the forest for the purpose of hunting. Shortly after reaching his new place of abode, his supply of provisions having become exhausted, he went forth, as usual, in quest of game, but soon discovered that his former good fortune had deserted him; the animals, as if apprised of his intentions, retiring to a safe distance out of the reach of gun-shot. Foiled in his purpose, the poor Indian renewed his exertions; but failure attended every attempt. Discouraged after long and persevering efforts, remembering his isolated condition and the pressing necessities of his family, which had been living for more than three days on wild roots, he paused, weary and faint, and taking his seat on a log of wood out of sight, but so that he could hear his little children playing around the wigwam, he fell into a train of meditation. He looked upwards to the blue arch above him, and beheld the beautiful sky and the bright sun, and casting his eyes around him, he saw the green grass, the waving trees, and the flowing water, and he said to himself, "These things come not here by their own bidding; there must be a cause for them; they could not produce themselves, and therefore they must have been created! and who is their Creator? Surely He must be the Great Spirit! I wish the Great Spirit would bless poor Indian, that his famishing wife and family might not starve."

Then he thought that perhaps he must give the Great Spirit something, so that He might bless him. And what had he? There was his blanket: though it had done him good service, and was still much needed, he would give it up to Him if He would bless him. So he took the blanket in his hand and laid it on a log, and with upturned eyes said, "Here, Great Spirit, accept this blanket, and bless poor Indian, that he may find food, and that his wife and family may not starve." The anguish of his heart was unabated. No manna fell from heaven to afford relief. The offering did not suffice. What must he now do? A tomahawk hung in his belt; could he spare that? Yes, if that was what the Great Spirit required, he thought he could. He advanced as before, and laid it upon the log, and said, "O Great Spirit, take my tomahawk; it is all poor Indian has,

He has nothing else to give; take it and bless me, and give me food for my children." But alas! no answer came. The burden rests still on his bosom. And what can he do now? There was his gun, his only means of obtaining game, his sole support, and hitherto his unfailing friend. How could he spare that? Must he part with that also? He paused, but pressed down by his forlorn condition, almost hopeless, he took the gun in his hand, and laid it on the log, and sobbed out, "O Great Spirit, take my gun too! it is all poor Indian has: he has nothing more. Take it, and bless poor Indian, that his wife and children may not starve." Still the messenger of love came not. Almost broken-hearted, he started to his feet, a ray of light flashed through his mind. He would go to that rude altar again and offer *himself* up to the Great Spirit. So he sat down on the log with his blanket, his tomahawk, and his gun by his side, and said. "Here, Great Spirit, poor Indian has given up all that he has: he has nothing more; so take poor Indian too, and bless him, that he may find food for his famishing family, that they may not starve."

In a moment a change comes over the scene, and everything seems smiling and joyous. His soul is filled with happiness such as he had never felt before. As he contemplates, lo! a deer comes bounding towards him from the thicket; he raises his gun and secures him. Thus was his offering accepted and his prayer answered, and he was ever afterwards successful in hunting. On returning to his family the poor Indian told them what had happened; and, thinking that if he left the blanket, the tomahawk, and the gun on the log, they would be of no use to any one, he took them with him, and told the Great Spirit that he would take care of them for *Him*, and use them subject to His will, and that henceforth he would regard himself, and all that he had, as belonging to Him.

When the hunting season was over, the young chief returned to his tribe; and soon afterwards, hearing for the first time the teaching of a Christian missionary, while seated with his red brethren and sisters, and listening attentively to the speaker as he told them they must *give up themselves to Christ*, and remembering what had occurred in the forest, he could contain himself no longer, but jumped up, and shouted, "Yes, that's me! that's me!" Then he related to the missionary and those around him how he had offered *himself* up to God in the time of his trouble; and with clearer views of the way of salvation through faith in Christ Jesus, he henceforth became a faithful and consistent Christian, exemplifying the beauty and blessedness of entire consecration to God.

"Jesus, all-atoning Lamb,
 Thine, and only Thine I am;
 Take my body, spirit, soul,
 Only Thou possess the whole."

17. Mexicans. — When Mexico was first discovered by the Spaniards in the fifteenth century, the native inhabitants were found to be in a much more advanced state of civilisation than the aborigines of North America generally. The native chiefs or kings, from the great Montezuma downwards, were living in a style of wealth and splendour, the account of which, as given by Robertson and other historians, reads more like a fairy tale than a narrative of real facts. But notwithstanding this outward array of splendour and barbarous magnificence, the Mexicans were as deeply involved in idolatry, superstition, and sin, as any other pagan nation in the world. They performed their heathen rites and ceremonies in or around massive temples, built for the purpose in honour of the host of heaven which they adored. And among other barbarous and cruel practices, they are said to have offered human sacrifices on a scale which surpasses anything we ever heard of before. According to Gomara, there was no year in which twenty thousand human victims were not offered to the Mexican divinities; and in some years they amounted to fifty thousand. The skulls of these unhappy creatures were arranged in order, in a building erected for the purpose, and two of Cortes's officers who declared that they counted them, informed Gomara that they amounted to a hundred and thirty-six thousand. The account given by Herrera is still more extravagant; but, admitting that there may have been some exaggeration in these statements, there can be no question that the religious system of the original Mexicans was of an appalling character, and that in their heathen state their moral condition was fearful to contemplate.

Since the conquest of the country by the Spaniards, the population of Mexico has undergone a remarkable change. The Spanish settlers have become, to a large extent, amalgamated with the native Indians, and whilst the original pagan superstitions may be found still existing in some places, in the country generally they have given way to a low and debased species of Roman Catholicism introduced by the conquerors of the country. This mongrel form of Christianity, largely imbued with the grossest ignorance, and exhibiting a strange mixture of popish and pagan superstition, has for many years been the dominant religious system of the Creoles, and indeed of the population of Mexico generally. Of late years, however, attempts have been made, and, for the shortness of the time, with marvellous success, to propagate among the people evangelical and Protestant Christianity, and there is reason to believe that still greater changes may ere long be witnessed in Central America.

18. South Americans.—When the Spaniards pushed forward their conquests in the Western World to the sunny regions of South America, they found a country fully peopled and cultivated, presenting an appearance of industry which excited their surprise. The natives were decently clothed, and possessed of habits far surpassing in civilisation any of the aborigines which they had previously seen. This was the case especially with the Peruvians, Chilians, and Brazilians. The *Incas*, or sovereigns, lived in a style of wealth and splendour equal, if not superior, to that of the Mexicans; and gold and silver were everywhere seen among the people, and regarded as comparatively common metals. But, with all this, the social and moral condition of all classes was on a par with that of most other pagan nations. Their system of religion and politics, which generally prevailed, was a strange combination of superstition and regal despotism. The precepts of the Inca, or supreme ruler, were received, not merely as the injunctions of a superior mortal, but as the mandates of a deity. To those *children of the sun*, for that was the appellation bestowed upon the offspring of the first Inca, the people looked up with a reverence due to a being of a superior order. The policy of thus superstitiously combining religion with civil government is evident, inasmuch as obedience to the ruling power became a sacred duty, and disobedience not only rebellion against the state, but impiety towards heaven.

The idolatrous rites and ceremonies of the Peruvians, and of the aborigines of South America generally, appear to have been of a milder type than those of the Mexicans. The sun, as the great source of light, joy, and fertility in the creation, attracted their homage. The moon and the stars, as co-operating with him, were regarded as entitled to secondary honours. They offered to the sun a portion of those productions which his genial warmth had called forth from the bosom of the earth and reared to maturity. They sacrificed, as an oblation of gratitude, some of those animals which were indebted to him for his influence in their nourishment. They also presented to him choice specimens of those works of ingenuity which his light had guided the hand of man in forming. But, so far as we can learn, their altars were never stained with human blood, nor could they conceive that their beneficent father, the sun, would be pleased with such horrid victims.

The same process of amalgamation between the first European settlers and their descendants and the aborigines, has for generations been going on in the respective states of South America, which we find in Mexico, and the moral and social results have been similar in both cases. The Romanism of Brazil and other places is of a very low type, and blended with much of pagan superstition. Many of the priests themselves are illiterate men, and evangelical truth, as taught by Protestant missionaries, is much required.

19. **Patagonians.**—The extreme southern peninsula of the American Continent, embracing the dreary regions known as Terra del Fuego and Cape Horn, is inhabited by a race of aborigines called Patagonians. The early voyagers who visited this country brought home strangely exaggerated accounts of the appearance and character of these people. They represented them, for instance, as of gigantic stature, and as in many other respects differing from the rest of their species. A more intimate acquaintance with them in modern times, through the visits of missionaries and others, has proved to us that the Patagonians are ignorant, wild, savage, and degraded in the extreme; but that in no respect do they materially differ from many of the pagan tribes of Indians in the north. In the narratives of the early voyagers we find no tangible account of the religious ideas or superstitions of this wild and uncivilised race of men; but from modern accounts we gather that they are almost entirely destitute of any definite notions of a Supreme Being, or a future state, and that no people in the world stand more in need of the blessings of the gospel. Repeated and praiseworthy attempts have been made at different times to introduce Christianity into Patagonia; but the results have not as yet been very encouraging. When it is remembered, however, that nations and tribes equally savage and debased have been subdued, civilised, and evangelised, by the influence of divine truth, we must not despair of the ultimate conversion of the wild Patagonians to the faith of Christ. Let us pray for God's blessing upon every effort put forth in this and other parts of the American Continent, to bring the people to a saving knowledge of the truth.

20. **West Indians.**—Most of the

West India Islands, when first discovered, were inhabited by a race of people resembling in many respects the aborigines of the American Continent, to which the Spaniards gave the general name of Indians or Caribs. The treatment which these simple-minded and unoffending natives received at the hands of the pale-faced strangers is shocking to contemplate. They were robbed, enslaved, compelled to work in the mines beyond their strength, and ground down with cruelty and oppression till they gradually sunk beneath the heavy burdens imposed upon them by their tyrannical taskmasters. It has been stated on good authority, that the native population of St Domingo and Jamaica, amounting to nearly two hundred thousand, literally melted away in the presence of their oppressors in the course of fifty years, and that the colonists were left without labourers to till the soil, work the mines, or to perform for them any other kind of service. Speaking of the early Spanish settlers in Jamaica, Abbé Raynal says:—"These barbarous wretches never sheathed their swords while there was one native left to preserve the memory of a numerous, good-natured, plain, and hospitable people."

The rapid decrease, and ultimate extinction, of the aborigines in most of the West India Islands, under the cruel treatment of the Spaniards, left the planters almost destitute of labourers, and they scarcely knew what to do. At length, to meet the pressing want, the cruel and inhuman plan was adopted of bringing negro slaves from Africa. These hardy sons and daughters of Ham were found better adapted for continuous labour than the delicate Carib Indians, and by them and their descendants were the islands, in process of time, gradually peopled. As cargoes of fresh slaves were constantly being brought over from Africa to increase the population, and to supply the waste involved by the mode of their treatment, the social and moral state of these poor miserable creatures at an early period may be more readily imagined than described. The negroes brought with them from their pagan fatherland, in addition to their general ignorance, numerous superstitious notions and practices, which, when added to the vicious habits which they learned from their European masters, sunk them to the lowest depths of moral degradation. From the people thus introduced the present population of the West Indies have chiefly sprung; but a wonderful change has taken place in their social and moral condition since the advent of freedom, and the introduction of Christian missionaries among them. An intelligent and respectable class of coloured persons has, moreover, risen up, the religious portion of which would in many respects bear a favourable comparison with Christian people occupying a similar position in Europe.

21. **Negro Witchcraft.**—When Christian Missionaries first entered upon their labours in the West Indies, they found the negro slaves, to whom they were more especially sent, in a very low and degraded condition. In addition to the gross ignorance and stupidity which was no doubt the result of their long-continued bondage and oppression, they had brought with them from Africa many superstitious notions and usages, which proved serious barriers to their religious instruction. The principal of these was a species of witchcraft known as obeism and myalism. Connected with these was the practice of numerous foolish and senseless magical rites, ceremo-

nies, and incantations, by professed obei-men, the influence of which on the popular mind was extensive and powerful. These systems of witchcraft were employed avowedly to revenge injuries, and as a protection against theft or disease, &c., and were almost identical with *fetish* as practised on the western coast of Africa. The materials employed, after they had been consecrated by various magical rites, were generally a calabash or gourd containing pieces of rag, cats' teeth, parrots' feathers, toads' feet, egg-shells, fish bones, snakes' teeth, lizards' tails, and such like. These were hung on trees in the gardens, or attached to the doors of the parties against whom the spells were directed. Terror and dismay immediately seized the individual who first beheld this array of well-known rubbish for the practice of obeism, and when he regarded himself as the victim, he would frequently give himself up to a feeling of fear and despondency, and pine away till he died, from the influence of imagination, if poison was not secretly administered through the agency of the obei-man to hasten his death, which it is feared was often the case. We have sometimes known a whole village or estate, where the gospel had been but recently introduced, thrown into confusion by the discovery of obei-matter, and it has required our utmost influence to induce the people to resume their work and attendance on divine worship. In proportion as the people became spiritually enlightened and established in religion, however, these superstitious notions lost their influence, and gradually died away.

22. Spiritual Destitution.—The inhabitants of the West Indies, of all classes and complexions, were in a fearful state of spiritual destitution towards the close of the last century when Christian missionaries were first sent out to attempt their evangelisation. The social and moral condition of the negro slaves was as low and degraded as it could possibly be. It scarcely seemed to have occurred to their owners that they were possessed of immortal souls, and no kind of provision was made for their religious instruction. Nor was the condition of the white portion of the population much, if any, better. "Many of those," says Mr Long the historian, "who succeed to the management of estates in Jamaica, had much fewer good qualities than the slaves over whom they were set in authority, the better sort of whom heartily despised them, perceiving little or no difference from themselves, except in sin and blacker depravity." The practice of profane swearing, gambling, drunkenness, and sensuality, was awfully prevalent among the Whites at an early period, and the Sabbath was desecrated in the most awful manner. Whilst the poor slaves were attending the Sunday market, the managers and overseers were visiting, smoking, drinking, and carousing at each others houses from morning till night. It is doubted whether, previous to 1789, when Dr Coke paid his first visit, a Sabbath had ever dawned on Jamaica, on which five hundred persons assembled in all the places of worship put together, out of a population of nearly four hundred thousand. There was never a louder call in any country for missionary effort.

23. Strange Superstition.—One of the first Wesleyan missionaries who laboured in the republic of Hayti, having received an invitation to visit one of the mountain districts in the neighbourhood of Port-au-Prince, set off from that city early in the morning, and after winding his way up the sides of the mountain for the space of about three hours, arrived at the place of his destination. On his arrival he entered into conversation on religious subjects with the colonel, a native of Africa, to whose house he had been invited, and with others who had assembled to meet him. After many questions had been asked and answered, the colonel, who was the most intelligent person in the company, observed, "Minister, they tell me a strange thing about you: they tell me *you never eat.*" This rather startled the missionary, who, having left home with the dawn, and finding himself without breakfast within a short period of the hour of noon, began to fear that, if his new friends entertained such an idea, he might be kept fasting the whole day, and he answered energetically that it was a great mistake, that he must eat to live, like other people. The colonel assured him that it was a common opinion in that neighbourhood that the ministers never ate; but having spread before his visitor a homely repast, he had soon an opportunity of dismissing from his mind such a silly and erroneous notion.

We smile at the absurdity; but let us not forget the destitution of gospel light which gave rise to it, and that if many of our fellow-creatures are thus superstitious, it is because they are without the blessings of Christianity which we enjoy. Let us then do our utmost to send the light of divine truth to those who are sitting in darkness, and in the region of the shadow of death, that ignorance and superstition may give way before the beams of the Sun of Righteousness.

24. Africans.—The natives of Western, Southern, and Central Africa, estimated at 110,000,000 in number, and occupying as they do such an extensive area, differ considerably in their personal appearance, as well as in their language, manners, and customs. When we look at them from a missionary point of view, however, and consider their social and moral condition, and their need of the gospel of our Lord Jesus Christ, they stand much upon the same level, and possess many features of character in common with each other. They are divided into numerous nations and petty tribes, and are governed by their own chiefs, paramount or subordinate, as the case may be, and in their modes of living, building, dress, ornaments, &c., they differ according to locality and circumstances. But whether we read of the natives of Africa as negroes, including Mandingoes, Jolloffs, Ashantis, Fantis, Dahomans, Yarubans, and others; as Kaffirs, embracing the tribes known as the Amakosa, Anagaliku, Amatembu Amaponda, Amazulu or Amafingu; as Bechuanas, Namaquas, Hottentots, or Malays, we must remember that from their extreme spiritual destitution, they have all strong claims upon our Christian sympathy and effort.

It is almost impossible in words to convey an adequate idea of the ignorance, superstition, and moral degradation of those nations and tribes inhabiting the coast and interior of Africa, who have never yet been favoured with the light of divine revelation. To understand it fully, a person should visit the country, mingle with the people, and witness their idolatrous, cruel, and sinful practices as we have done. The heathen darkness in which they are involved not only entails upon them a large amount of temporal privation and personal suffering, but it exposes them to the displeasure of God in this world, and to everlasting perdition in the world to come; for "the wages of sin is death, but the gift of God is eternal life, through our Lord Jesus Christ."

25. Slavery and the Slave Trade.

Africa is pre-eminently and emphatically a land of slaves, slavery, and the slave trade; and in this circumstance especially we see the moral degradation and misery in which its inhabitants are involved. Every traveller who has visited the coast, or passed through the interior, testifies to the general prevalence of slavery. When Colonel Nicholls appeared before the West African Committee of the House of Commons, to give evidence on the subject, he said, "I know no other characters in Africa than master and slave." And Mr M'Queen, on a similar occasion, said, "Slavery and the slave trade form the general law of Africa; these two evils reign acknowledged, sanctioned, known, recognised, and submitted to by her population of every rank and degree, throughout all her extended borders." According to the computation of Mungo Park, three-fourths of the entire population of Western and Interior Africa, through which he travelled, was in a state of bondage. In his first journey through the town and district of Kanu, Captain Clapperton, estimating the inhabitants at 40,000, records his opinion that at least one-half of the population were slaves. At a subsequent visit to the same place, however, he ascertained that his first impressions had been too favourable, for he was now informed that there were no fewer than thirty slaves for every free man. The same traveller incidentally mentions a village in the neighbourhood of Sakatu, where only one in seventy of the inhabitants was free. As illustrative of the number of slaves, and the manner in which they were sometimes employed, Major Denham states that the Sultan of Bornu had at one time in his service 70,000 armed slaves as native soldiers, whilst Sir Fowel Buxton calculated that 500,000 slaves were annually shipped from Africa to various places in the Western World.

It is freely admitted that these estimates were formed, and these statements made, when the African slave trade was in the height of its prosperity, and that since then the traffic in human flesh has been declared piracy by England and some other nations. But it would be a grand mistake if we were to jump to the conclusion that the crying evil has been annihilated. It has no doubt greatly diminished on the western coast, but there is ample evidence that it exists in the east, and that tens of thousands of wretched slaves are still annually dragged away from their homes to distant lands through Mozambique, Zanzibar, and other places, whilst domestic slavery still exists in Africa on an extensive scale as a standing institution, as asserted by Dr Livingstone and others.

It is, moreover, a curious but appalling fact, that a well-to-do slave in Africa, who, by the indulgence of his master, has acquired a little property, no sooner finds himself in a position to do so, than he himself is ambitious to purchase a slave, whom he commands and controls in a manner which is truly surprising. This strange anomaly is not discouraged by the original slave-owner, inasmuch as he considers himself the lawful proprietor both of his slaves and the slaves of his slaves, with all that they possess. We can testify to the general accuracy of this humiliating representation from personal observation, having often had occasion to weep over the miseries of the poor Africans while labouring among them. The grand remedy for these complicated evils is the universal diffusion of the benign influence of Christianity, for "whom the truth makes free, they are free indeed."

26. Slave Hunting.—Domestic slaves, even in Africa, are not generally sold to foreigners to be transported to other lands, unless they have incurred the displeasure of their owners by the commission of some crime. The foreign slave trade was supplied ostensibly by the sale of criminals and negroes taken captive in war; but the demand at length became so great, that war among the petty tribes of the interior has been encouraged to an alarming extent, and it has been frequently waged, not so much for avenging wrongs and insults, as for the purpose of procuring captives for the supply of the slave market. This fearful state of things at length led the way to the organisation of regular slave-hunting expeditions, for the capture of innocent and unoffending natives, who were unceremoniously dragged away into hopeless bondage. The following is a picture of one of these diabolical scenes, from the fascinating pen of an eye-witness to what he so graphically describes:—

"While daylight lasts, the robbers remain hidden in the thicket, trying the edges of their swords, and making slave-forks. When night comes on, spies are sent out, and on their return the time of attack is fixed for daybreak. The nomads allow themselves a short rest, and then the attack commences. The dogs give the alarm, and, amidst the bellowing and lowing of cattle, the robbers spring over the low thorn hedges into the irregular streets of the village, to which they set fire, thundering forth the cry, 'There is no god but God, and Mohammed is His prophet!' Terrified, the inhabitants run out of their huts as the heavy swords of their assailants come down upon their shoulders and naked heads. At first none are spared, old and young fall beneath the murderous strokes of the cruel tyrants; only a few blacks have the presence of mind or the courage to seize their weapons, and the defence does not last long. The village is soon taken, the survivors beg for mercy, the riders dismount and bind the men, women, and children, to the slave-chain or forks, as the case may be, and drive them off towards the market. With bent heads and painful, tottering steps and parched lips, the unhappy captives move on with heavy loads upon their heads; and the little children, having their hands tied behind them, trotting by their sides. The whips of the cruel drivers fall mercilessly on the bleeding backs of the prisoners if they attempt to loiter. Thus they wend their way to the coast, tens of thousands perishing in the wilderness, whilst the few wretched survivors are transported to distant lands."

Here we let the curtain fall without attempting to describe the horrors of the middle passage, or the cruel treatment which the hapless victims frequently received in the lands of their exile. These we have witnessed with feelings of deep emotion in the dark and gloomy days of negro slavery in the West Indies; but, thank God, those days are past and gone for ever, and we sincerely pray that the time may soon come when the last vestiges of slavery and the slave trade shall be swept away from the face of the earth.

27. Little Benomê.—The method of capture and the treatment of African slave-children is touchingly illustrated by the story of little Benomê, a liberated African girl, as related by herself many years afterwards, when an inmate in the writer's family as a free domestic servant.

Benomê was born in the interior of Africa, at a place called Radda, in the Ebo country. When about seven years of age, she went one morning with another little girl to the well for water, and on looking round they saw a neighbouring village on fire. This was evidence of the approach of a slave-hunting party, of which there had been some rumour before. The girls ran home and reported what they had seen; and the people of Radda, knowing what to expect, fled into the woods for safety, cherishing a faint hope that their enemies might perhaps pass up the country in another direction. It was not long, however, before they saw their own village on fire, and were themselves pursued by the merciless man-stealers. Little Benomê, with her mother, brother, and elder sister, together with many others, were captured by the ruffians, tied together two and two, and marched off towards the coast like a flock of sheep for the market, whilst nothing was heard on every hand but mourning, lamentation, and woe.

The sufferings endured by the poor captives while travelling through the desert, as related by little Benomê, were distressing in the extreme. On coming to a large river which crossed their path, the sister of Benomê was one of the last to ford the stream, being occupied with a little child which she carried in her arms. Annoyed with her delay, the cruel monster in charge of the slaves came and snatched the infant from the arms of its mother, and threw it into the jungle, where it was left to perish; and with oaths and curses urged the poor captives onward in their march. After travelling for several weeks in succession, they came in sight of the "great salt water," which they beheld with dismay, knowing well that they were to be carried beyond the foaming billows to some unknown country. When they reached the coast, all the little people were sold to a certain "black lady," by whom they were kept for a length of time, till they were considered old enough for the foreign slave market. They were then resold, and shipped for the West Indies.

Long before the period of embarkation, little Benomê had been separated from her mother, sister, and brother, whom she was never again permitted to see in this world. When the vessel in which they sailed got out to sea, according to the account of Benomê, the slave children were occasionally allowed to come on deck to dance and "straight their legs." One night, when they had finished their exercises and gone below again, before they went to sleep, they heard strange noises on deck, with the trampling of feet, and the firing of guns, the meaning of which they were at first unable to comprehend. Next morning, however, the hatches were removed, and when the slaves looked up from the hold in which they were confined, they saw several strangers, "gentlemen with fine blue coats and caps, with shining gold lace and bright buttons." These were the officers of the British man-of-war who had captured the slaver during the night, and who called upon the negroes to come up on deck, assuring them that they were now all free.

The liberated slaves were brought to the Island of Trinidad, where the writer laboured as a missionary, and where little Benomê was introduced into his family to be trained in knowledge and industry, by an arrangement with the government authorities. The little negro girl soon learned to read and write a little, became pious, was baptized by the name of Betsy, and grew up an affectionate, honest, and industrious servant. She continued with us for nine years, till we returned to England, after which she faithfully served other missionaries till her marriage in 1854. She never forgot the kindness shown to her in her youth, and occasionally sent us letters full of affection and love, telling us how her first-born son was called "*William*" after her dear old master, and her little daughter *Jane*, after her loving mistress." In 1873 we received a letter from her bereaved husband, informing us that Betsy had died in peace, June 12th, 1872, leaving him with one son and two daughters, one of whom also wrote a beautiful letter, which showed not only that she had been taught to remember her mother's benefactors, but also that she had received a good education in the mission-school.

28. Objects worshipped.—The entire population of Western Africa was no doubt pagan at no very remote period; but in modern times the religion of the false prophet has extensively prevailed, having been zealously propagated with fire and sword by the northern tribes of Arab descent. But there is not so much difference between the Mohammedanism and the paganism of the negroes as many suppose. The distinction is rather nominal than real, so far as the moral conduct, and many of the superstitious rites and ceremonies of the people, are concerned. All profess to believe in the existence of God, if a confused notion of a higher power may be so designated; but all are entirely ignorant of the character of the Divine Being, and of the spiritual nature of the worship which He requires. This is evident from the eagerness with which they resort to their *greegrees* and *fetish* in times of difficulty and danger, and the confidence which they place in them for protection, safety, and success. They are, moreover, in the habit of noting lucky and unlucky days, and of performing numerous foolish rites and ceremonies on going to war, or commencing a journey, which seem to partake of the nature of sorcery or witchcraft.

But some of the superstitious notions and practices of the negro race partake more of the nature of open idolatry than any of those we have yet mentioned. For instance, they pay divine homage to certain lakes, rivers, and mountains, which they regard as sacred, believing them to be favourite abodes of their gods. They also adore various animals and reptiles, especially certain kinds of monkeys, serpents, and crocodiles, which they believe to be inspired or possessed by the spirits of their ancestors. These creatures are often kept tame in houses, or places set apart for them, and are carefully fed and kept by the fetish priests at the expense of the people, who offer sacrifices to them, and regard them with superstitious reverence. The priests, moreover, make little wooden images, which they anoint and consecrate for their votaries, when bereaved of their children or friends, persuading them that they have brought back the spirits of the departed to inhabit the said wooden images, &c. One of these is now before the writer, which was given to a poor woman who had lost her only child, and which she caressed with all parental fondness, believing that the spirit of her babe was thus restored to her, till she was brought to a saving knowledge of the truth, and taught to look to the only real source of comfort in trouble, when she gave up her idol to the missionary. It stands about nine inches high, is of a very uncomely countenance, and bears evident marks of its consecration. But the most awful kind of worship which we have witnessed among the pagan Africans is that which is openly offered to the devil himself, for the alleged reason that nothing can injure them but the great wicked spirit. They therefore offer sacrifices to him, to propitiate his favour, that he may do them no harm!

29. A Sacred Crocodile.—At Dix Cove, on the western coast of Africa, a few years ago, there was a large crocodile kept in a pond or small lake near the fort, to which the superstitious natives offered sacrifices, and paid divine honours as to a god. This they did under the strange notion that it was possessed by the spirit of one of their great chiefs, who since his death had in this form returned to the earth for the benefit of his people in some way. The ugly creature was in charge of a fetish priest, who fed it regularly, and who presented to it the people's offerings, always reserving an ample share for himself, which he claimed for his support. Any person visiting the place might see the sacred crocodile, whether one of his votaries or not, if he took him a white fowl for his breakfast, and a bottle of rum as a present for the priest. The fetish man takes the offering, and proceeds to the pond, where he makes a peculiar whistling noise with his mouth, on hearing which the monster comes splashing to the shore to receive his share of the present. The priest throws to him the fowl, and appropriates the spirits to himself.

On one occasion Captain Leavens and Mr Hutchen, on landing at Dix Cove, asked to see the sacred crocodile, when they were exposed to considerable risk from a little accident which occurred. On the fetish man calling the animal to receive the offering, the fowl escaped into the bush; when the disappointed and enraged crocodile, seeing the white men, made towards them, and pursued them so closely, that, had not a dog crossed the path, of which he made his morning's meal, one of them would most probably have fallen a victim to his rapacity. This was a narrow escape, and taught the visitors a lesson of caution for the future.

30. The Idol-room.—The Rev. R. Smith, a missionary stationed at New Calabar, Western Africa, describing a visit which he paid to a native king, says:—"The whole of his front door was covered with *charms*. I spoke to him about these, and his room of idols, that was open to our view. He replied that they were his medicines, and kept him from harm and witchcraft. This gave me an opportunity of speaking to him about the one living and true God, His care over us, and love to us, and how we ought to love and trust Him. He said both he and his people would understand these things by and by; that they very much wanted missionaries to live among them to teach them. I asked for permission to look at his idol-room, which he immediately granted; and oh, what a strange scene it was! In the middle and on either side were small figures resembling Egyptian mummies. These were decorated, and held various things in their hands. In the corner were a number of boxes. These contained 'sacred things'— old and dirty pieces of stick, and other things that looked fit only for the dust-cart. A short distance from these were a number of skulls of various animals, and, I think, only one human skull. Beyond the idols or figures were three small pyramids of earth, with holes in the top, either for water or fire, or for the offering of incense in sacrifice. The whole place and the rubbish were held sacred."

31. Human Sacrifices.—One of the darkest and most dreadful features in African superstition is the practice which prevails among some of the tribes on the western coast, of offering human sacrifices. These are generally connected with the death or funeral ceremonies of natives chiefs, or other important personages. On these occasions multitudes of slaves are put to death, with the foolish idea that they will thus be able to attend and wait upon the departed in the spirit-land to which they go. Or if a chief wishes to send a message to a deceased friend or relative, he will call into his presence a trustworthy slave, give him the message, charge him to deliver it carefully, and then have him immediately beheaded by the executioner, who is always in attendance. As an illustration of the extent and character of these horrid "customs," we may cite an incident which came under the personal notice of a devoted native missionary, who was brought to God and raised up to labour in the Lord's vineyard, on one of our mission stations in the West Indies. Having offered himself as a missionary to Africa, and been appointed to Kumasi, the capital of Ashanti, he wrote us a long and interesting letter from that notorious and blood-stained city. After giving a minute account of the circumstances connected with his reception by the king in the presence of ten thousand of his warriors, caboceers, and others, he says:—

"One incident I must not omit to mention; being the first of the kind I had been called to witness, I shall not easily forget it. Whilst waiting to receive the respects of the king and his councillors, two men about to be sacrificed were marched along near where I was sitting. They were in a state of complete nudity. Their arms were closely tied behind their backs. Long spear-knives were thrust through their cheeks, from which the blood flowed copiously, and curdled on their breasts. The moans of one of the victims were heartrending. Never till that moment did I feel myself really to be in miserable, pitiless Africa. In all, eight human beings fell under the sacrificial knife in honour of the deceased Queen of Jabin, in Coomassie alone. The number already slaughtered in Jabin itself must be immense. I have since heard from a captain who was present at the 'custom' in Jabin, that upwards of three hundred were sacrificed in that town. Human sacrifices are almost of daily occurrence in Coomassie. I have witnessed several decapitations, and have seen as many as twelve headless human bodies scattered along the public streets. The constantly witnessing such cold-blooded murder has almost paralysed my efforts, and I am sometimes led to think that human sacrifices will never be done away in Coomassie. Then again, my gloomy thoughts are dispelled when I remember what has been done in other places by the regenerating power of the gospel."

32. Barbarous Practices.—Fearful accounts of the prevalence of human sacrifices among the Ashantees and Dahomans in the interior of Western Africa, have frequently reached us, but we were not prepared to hear that the horrid custom obtains among the smaller tribes along the coast, which for many years past have had frequent intercourse with Europeans. It appears nevertheless to be a fact. So recently as March 1873, accounts were brought by the mail steamer *Senegal* of the barbarous custom observed a short time ago in the ratification of a treaty of peace between the chiefs of Opobo and Bonny. On this occasion, it is said, a slave was sacrificed to the heathen deity "Ju Ju," attended by circumstances of a most appalling character. After being marked by a sharp knife from the crown of the head down the front of the body, the poor creature was chopped in halves. The Opobo "Ju-Ju-man" and the Bonny "Ju-Ju-man" each took half of the body and threw it into the ebbing tide. The victim showed the greatest indifference to his fate, solacing himself, it is said, with the belief that he should meet again in the spirit-land those who were going to kill him, and that then they would be the victims and he the slayer. It is due to King George of Bonny to state that he tried to have a cow or a goat substituted for a human being as a sacrifice; but was obliged to yield to the gross superstition of the people, who, prompted by the heathen priests, clamoured for the usual custom. "Truly the dark places of the earth are full of the habitations of cruelty."

33. South African Legend.— When travelling in Namaqualand, South Africa, we heard the following curious legend, which was commonly believed in former days by the degraded inhabitants of that country, and which is still taught by some of the heathen to their children. It shows what strange ideas were entertained by the Namaquas of a Supreme Being, and of a Saviour, before the missionaries came among them. It is evidently a corruption of the story, handed down by tradition, of the life and death of Jesus Christ.

A distinguished person named Achie Abiss, the son of a great chief, when a youth, was taken sick and died. His mother laid the corpse behind a bush, and going to look at it again, weeping, she met him coming from the bush where she had laid him, he having risen from the dead. After his resurrection he was immortal, and became ruler of all things. The people now invoked his favour by erecting conical piles of stones to his honour, each person bringing a stone for the purpose. These heaps, in course of time, became common in the neighbourhood of all the principal fountains in Namaqualand, as seen at this day. As the people wished their cattle to increase, they thought it might be best accomplished by constantly adding to these heaps of stones, piled up in honour of Achie Abiss. Every man going on a journey also threw a stone on the heap, that he might be prosperous in what he had in view. Good luck in hunting was also thought to be secured by each man casting a stone as he passed these piles.

Achie Abiss was supposed to be a benevolent being, and all his acts were believed to be for the good of the people. The reason why the people were not always prosperous in their undertakings, was accounted for by the fact that there was another being ever intent on frustrating the designs of Achie Abiss. The name of that being was Ickänap, the name now used in Namaqua for the devil. Achie Abiss, having often been thwarted in his plans by Ickân-ap, fell upon him one day to punish him. In the contest he received a wound in his knee, from which time he was called Tshe-Kwap, a name now used in Namaqua for God. This name was not given in derision, but as a mark of respect, because he was wounded in defending the cause of the people. The word Achie Abiss signifies existence before all things. It is translated by some, "double and double the first," signifying, not only priority of existence, but an existence very long before any other beings. It sounds somewhat ludicrous to hear the converted Namaquas addressing in prayer "him with the sore knee;" but it is even so, for they have no other word for God than Tshe-Kwap. Through the labours of Christian missionaries hundreds of the natives have now, however, enlightened views of the being and character of Jehovah, and of Jesus Christ their Saviour and Redeemer, so that the lack of a more appropriate name for the Supreme Being is of minor consequence.

34. Kaffir Superstitions.—The Kaffirs of Southern Africa have, properly speaking, no religious system of their own, and consequently no temples, or idols, or sacred days set apart for public worship. They have, in fact, no forms of worship of any kind, unless we regard a certain homage paid to the departed chiefs and heroes, whose spirits they think still live, as such. They are, however, extremely superstitious. They believe in lucky and unlucky days for engaging in any enterprise; and on commencing a journey, they make it a practice to cast a stone on a heap which has accumulated from similar offerings previously made near the cattle-kraal of the chief's great place.

All misfortunes, diseases, and sudden deaths among men or cattle are attributed to the influence of witchcraft, in the power of which they have unbounded confidence. Their ideas of the existence of God and a future state of being, are very vague and confused, and when Christian missionaries first entered their country it was not without difficulty that they could be made to comprehend the nature of spiritual and eternal things.

35. Witch-doctors and Rain-makers.—The only priests, or sacred persons, known among the Kaffirs in South Africa, are the witch-doctors and rain-makers. When any untoward circumstance, as sickness or death, occurs in the family of a chief, or other person of importance, the first question that is asked is, "Who is the witch?" and as the person implicated is always liable to have his property confiscated, or, in Kaffir phrase, to be "eaten up," the wily witch-doctor, who has been summoned to the scene of action, is sure to fix upon some one possessed of wealth. At the command of the chief the suspected parties are cited to appear before a great meeting convened for the purpose, and various rites and ceremonies are performed, with a view to "smell out" the culprit. When a declaration is made by the witch-doctor implicating some one present, the unhappy victim is at once seized, and subjected to the most revolting cruelty, to make him or her confess the crime, and divulge all the particulars as to where the bewitching matter has been concealed, &c. Sometimes the suspected person is bound with cords, besmeared with grease, and placed upon an ant-hill to be tormented by the stinging insects; at other times hot stones are applied to the feet, and other sensitive parts of the

Kaffir Witch Doctor and Rain Maker preparing their Incantations.

body, producing the most excruciating pain, and thousands have been actually put to death by burning at the stake, strangulation, and in various other ways, under this appalling system of superstition.

The same person who acts as witch-doctor is, when occasion requires, a rain-maker; when drought has prevailed for some time, he is sent for, however distant his place of residence. On his arrival, surrounded by a large concourse of people, he goes through sundry antics, attended by the slaughter of cattle and the drinking of Kaffir beer, to make rain, always contriving to lengthen out the ceremony with a hope that a shower may fall, when he claims to have succeeded in his art.

36. Ignorance of God and Spiritual Things.—Describing the extreme ignorance of the Bechuanas of South Africa before the introduction of the gospel, the Rev. R. Moffat says:—" Inquiring one day of a group of natives whom I had been addressing, if any of them had previously known the Great Being which had been described to them, among the whole party I found only one old woman who said she remembered hearing the name Morimo (God) when she was a child, but was not told what the thing was. Indeed, even in the towns, the general reply on that subject is, that these are things about which the old people can speak; but as they are not in the habit of instructing the rising generation on such topics, it is easy to see how even these vague notions become extinct altogether, as they have done in many parts of the country. Nor is it surprising that a chief, after listening attentively to me while he stood leaning on his spear, should utter an exclamation of amazement that a man whom he accounted wise should vend such fables for truths. Calling about thirty of his men who stood near him, he addressed them, pointing to me, ''There is Ra-Mary (Father of Mary), who tells me that the heavens were made, the earth also, by a beginner whom he calls Morimo. Have you ever heard anything to be compared with this? He says that the sun rises and sets by the power of Morimo; as also that Morimo causes winter to follow summer, the winds to blow, the rain to fall, the grass to grow, and the trees to bud;' and, casting his arm above and around him, added, ' God works in everything you see and hear! Did you ever hear such words?' Seeing them ready to burst into laughter, he said, ' Wait, I shall tell you more. Ra-Mary tells me that we have spirits in us which will never die; and that our bodies, though dead and buried, will rise and live again. Open your eyes to-day; did you ever hear fables like these?' This was followed by a burst of deafening laughter; and on its partially subsiding, the chief man begged me to say no more on such trifles, lest the people should think me mad."

37. Heathen Estimate of Life.—The following illustration of the manner in which the heathen regard human life is given by the Rev. R. Moffat. When describing what he witnessed at the great place of a noted African chief, he says:—" The following morning was marked by a melancholy display of the so-called heroism which prefers death to dishonour. A feast had been proclaimed, cattle had been slaughtered, and many hearts beat high in anticipation of wallowing in all the excess of savage delight; eating and drinking, dancing and singing the victor's song over the slain, whose bones lay bleaching on the neighbouring plain.

Every heart appeared elate but one. He was a man of rank, and what was called an *Entuna* (officer), who wore on his head the usual badge of dignity. He was brought to head-quarters into the presence of the king and his chief counsel, charged with a crime for which it was in vain to expect pardon, even at the hands of a more humane government. He bowed his fine elastic figure, and kneeled before the judge. The case was investigated silently, so far as the spectators were concerned, which gave solemnity to the scene. Not a whisper was heard among the listening audience, and the voices of the counsellors were only audible to each other and the nearest spectators. The prisoner, though on his knees, had something noble in his mien. Not a muscle of his countenance moved, but his bright black eyes indicated a feeling of intense interest, which the moving balance between life and death only could produce. The case required little investigation; the charges were clearly substantiated, and the culprit pleaded guilty. A pause ensued, during which the silence of death pervaded the assembly.

"At length the monarch spoke, and addressing the prisoner, said, 'You are a dead man, but I shall do to-day what I never did before. I shall spare your life for the sake of my father and friend the missionary. I know his heart weeps at the shedding of blood; for his sake I spare your life. He has travelled from a far country to see me, and he has made my heart white; but he tells me that to take away life is an awful thing, and never can be undone again. He has pleaded with me not to go to war, nor destroy life. I wish him, when he returns to his own home again, to return with a heart as white as he has made mine. But,' continued the king, 'you must be degraded for life: you must no more associate with the nobles of the land, nor enter the towns of the princes of the people, nor ever again mingle in the dance of the mighty. Go to the poor of the field, and let your companions be the inhabitants of the desert.' The sentence passed, the pardoned man was expected to bow in gratitude to the king; but no! holding his hands clasped on his bosom, he replied, 'O king, afflict not my heart! I have merited thy displeasure; let me die like the warrior. I cannot live with the poor,' and, raising his hand to the ring he wore on his brow, he continued, 'How can I live among the dogs of the king, and disgrace these badges of honour which I won among the spears and shields of the mighty? No, I cannot live; let me die, O Pezoolu!' He was forthwith executed."

38. Heathen Cruelty.—Adverting to the cruel practices of the heathen in South Africa, the Rev. R. Moffat says:—"During my stay at Kongke an instance occurred confirming the view of Dr Burchell. A man was quarrelling with his wife about a very trifling affair, when, in a fit of rage, he grasped his spear and laid her at his feet a bleeding corpse." Here there were no coroners to take cognisance of the fact, and he walked about without a blush, while the lifeless body was dragged out to be devoured by the hyæna. When I endeavoured to represent to the chiefs with whom I was familiar the magnitude of such crimes, they laughed, I might say, inordinately, at the horror I felt for the murder of a woman by her husband."

The same missionary further remarks:—" A custom prevails among all the Bechuanas whom I visited, of removing to a distance from the towns and villages persons who are ill or have been wounded. Two young men, who had been wounded by the poisoned arrows of the bushmen, were thus removed from the Kuruman station. Having visited them to administer relief, I made inquiries as to the cause of such treatment, and could learn no reason except that it was a custom. This unnatural practice often exposes the helpless invalid to great danger; for if not well attended during the night, his paltry little hut, or rather shade from the sun and wind, would be assailed by the hyæna or lion. A catastrophe of this kind occurred a short time before my arrival among the Baralongs. The son of one of the principal chiefs, a fine young man, had been wounded by a buffalo; he was, according to custom, placed on the outside of the village till he should recover, a portion of food being daily sent to him, and a person appointed to make his fire for the night. One night the fire went out, and the hapless man, notwithstanding his piteous cries, was carried off by lions and devoured."

39. Superstitions of South Sea Islanders.—The religious rites and superstitions of the inhabitants of Polynesia in their heathen state, before the arrival of Christian missionaries, differed considerably in the various islands, but they were almost all dark and sanguinary, and marked with cruelty and blood. In the character of their gods, the nature of their worship, their ideas of a future state, and the means they adopted to secure final happiness, there was, however, with few exceptions, a general sameness which deserves a passing notice.

The *objects of their worship* were of three kinds—their deified ancestors, their idols, and their *etus*. In most of the islands departed chiefs, and other celebrated ancestors, were deified, and worshipped for real or supposed benefits which they had conferred upon the inhabitants. Various superstitious notions existed with reference to the part which their progenitors had taken in the creation of the world. One had made the sun to give light, another the moon and stars, &c., and for these benevolent acts divine homage was paid to them. Others were believed to have been famous as warriors, fishers, husbandmen, navigators, and robbers, and were consequently held in high esteem, and worshipped by those who followed those professions, in hope of securing their aid. Various superstitions were practised by pregnant women, to secure their becoming the mothers of great warriors. Then they had their idols, which were different in almost every island and district. Some were large, and others small; some were beautiful, and others hideous; some were in the form of human beings, and others of various shapes. The god-makers do not seem to have followed any particular pattern, but to have acted according to their own fancy. The *etu* consisted of some bird, fish, or reptile, which each native adopted at pleasure, and in which he believed some spirit resided, and worshipped it accordingly. In addition to these superstitious ideas, some of the natives had a vague and confused notion of a Supreme Being, whom they regarded as the creator of all things, and whom the Samoans called Tangaloa.

The *worship* which was offered to these deities consisted of prayer, incantations, and sacrificial offerings of pigs, fish, vegetable food, native cloth, canvas, and other valuable property on great occasions. To these must be added, in some of the islands, human beings, to an extent which is perfectly appalling.

The *ideas of a future* state which the Polynesians had formed were very peculiar. They believed in its existence, but were ignorant of the value and immortality of the soul, and knew not that eternity would be the measure of its sorrows or its joys. They regarded it as consisting of scenes and exercises entirely sensual and earthly, and attended by circumstances the recital of which was painfully ludicrous.

The *terms of entrance* into this paradise, and of exclusion from it, were entirely ceremonial, and monstrously absurd. The natives appeared to have formed no conception of moral fitness for future blessedness. They relied entirely on the superstitious ceremonies performed over the dead, most of which are unfit for record. Connected with their religious observances, were the fearful rites of cannibalism, infanticide, mutilations, and other cruelties, more particularly noticed elsewhere.

40. Heathen Customs in the Friendly Islands. — Missionaries had not been long in the Friendly Islands, when they discovered that in their heathen state the inhabitants were not so *friendly* after all as they had been led to expect. They were found to be frequently at war among themselves, and their numbers were rapidly decreasing, and the whole race wasting away, in consequence of the cruel and degrading customs to which they were addicted. They actually murdered two or three of the first party of missionaries who landed upon their shores, and the rest had to flee for their lives, and the mission was abandoned. When a second and more successful attempt was made to evangelise these barbarous people, more than twenty years afterwards, it was not without much difficulty that they were induced to listen to the truths of the gospel; and a more intimate acquaintance of the missionaries with the natives, revealed a fearful state of things, and might well constrain them to exclaim, "The dark places of the earth are full of the habitations of cruelty."

One of the most revolting and awful crimes prevalent in the Friendly Islands when the missionaries arrived was infanticide. If the new-born child were a girl, or deformed, or made its advent on an unlucky day, or weak and sickly in its appearance, it was, in many instances, immediately put to death. After their conversion, scores and hundreds of mothers confessed, with aching hearts and streaming eyes, that they had strangled many of their children as soon as they were born. One woman stated that she had thus murdered with her own hands no fewer than seven of her own infants.

Another barbarous practice was that of maiming their children in honour of their idol-gods. If a friend or relative were ill, or if success in war or any other important undertaking was ardently desired, it was a common practice to cut off the little finger of a favourite child, and offer it in sacrifice to their principal god. The finger was amputated at the first or second joint with a chisel, or some other sharp instrument. The finger, when taken off, was carried in solemn procession to the temple, and offered to the idol, the priest muttering his foolish incantation, after which the people returned to their homes rejoicing. If the object sought was not immediately gained, another joint or a whole finger was sometimes cut off, and offered in a similar manner; so that grown persons might often be seen with their hands fearfully mutilated, having been subjected to this cruel treatment when children.

The king and queen of Tonga, and many other Friendly Islanders who grew up in heathenism, but who have since been converted to the faith of Christ, carry these marks of their former degraded state, and they sometimes point to them with feelings of deep humility when speaking of their former heathen degradation, and with sincere gratitude to God for His abundant mercy in sending them the gospel which has produced such a wonderful change in all the islands.

41. Infanticide in Polynesia.—

The extent to which infanticide was carried in Tahiti and the Society Islands previous to the introduction of Christianity is almost incredible. The Rev. John Williams declares that during the many years that he spent there, he never conversed with a female that had borne children while in her heathen state who had not destroyed some of them, and frequently as many as from five to ten. Proceeding to give instances of the fearful prevalence of this horrid vice, he says:—"During the visit of the Deputation, our respected friend, G. Bennett, Esq., was our guest for three or four months; and on one occasion, while conversing on the subject, he expressed a wish to obtain accurate knowledge of the extent to which this cruel system had prevailed. Three women were sitting in the room at the time, making European garments under Mrs W.'s direction; and after replying to Mr Bennett's inquiries, I said, 'I have no doubt but each of these women has destroyed some of her children.' Looking at them with an expression of surprise and incredulity, Mr Bennett exclaimed, 'Impossible! such motherly, respectable women could never have been guilty of so great an atrocity.' 'Well,' I added, 'we will ask them.' Addressing the first, I said to her, 'Friend, how many children have you destroyed?' She was startled at my question, and at first charged me with unkindness, in harrowing up her feelings by bringing the destruction of her babes to her remembrance; but on hearing the object of my inquiry, she replied, with a faltering voice, 'I have destroyed *nine;*' the second, with eyes suffused with tears, said, 'I have destroyed *seven;*' and a third informed us as she had destroyed *five.* Thus, three individuals, casually selected, had killed one-and-twenty children! but I am happy to add that these mothers were, at the time of this conversation, and continued to be so long as I knew them, consistent members of the church under my care." "On another occasion," he says, "I was called to visit the wife of a chief (*in dying circumstances*). She had professed Christianity for many years, had learned to read, and was an active teacher in the adult school. On entering her apartment, she exclaimed, 'O servant of God! come and tell me what I must do.' On inquiring the cause of her distress, she said, 'I am about to die, I am about to die! O my sins, my sins!' I then inquired what the particular sins were which so greatly distressed her, when she exclaimed, 'Oh, my children, my murdered children! I am about to die, and I shall meet them at the judgment-seat of Christ!' Upon this I inquired how many she had destroyed, and, to my astonishment, she replied, 'I have destroyed *sixteen*, and now I am about to die!'" After visiting her frequently, and directing her thoughts to that blood which cleanseth from all sin, I succeeded, by the blessing of God, in tranquillising her troubled spirit, and she died happy in the pardoning love of God."

42. Methods of Destroying Children.—The fact of the prevalence of infanticide in many of the South Sea Islands, affords a fearful illustration of the statement of an inspired writer, that "the dark places of the earth are full of the habitations of cruelty." Nor is the case made any better by an examination of the modes by which these deeds of darkness were perpetrated by the savage and deluded inhabitants. Sometimes they put a wet cloth upon the infant's mouth as soon as it was born; at others, they pinched their little throats until they expired; a third method was to bury them alive; and a fourth was, if possible, still more brutal. The moment the child was born, they broke the first joints of its fingers and toes, and then the second. If the infant survived this agonising process, they dislocated its ankles and the wrists; and if the powers of endurance still continued, the knee and elbow joints were then broken. This would generally terminate the tortures of the little sufferer; but if not, they would resort to the second method of strangulation. One of the modes of infanticide was to put the babe in a hole covered with a plank, to keep the earth from pressing it, and to leave it there to perish.

A touching story is told by the missionaries, of a father who was from home in the mountains at the time of his child's birth in Tahiti, and on his return he found that the poor little infant had been interred in the manner we have described. As soon as it was dark he hastened to the spot, unseen by any one, opened the grave, and finding that the babe was still alive, he took her up, and gave her in charge to his brother and sister, by whom she was conveyed to the isle of Eimeo, about seventy miles distant, where she was brought up. The husband died without having informed his wife that their daughter was still alive. After the advent of Christianity, the mother was on one occasion bewailing most bitterly the destruction of her children, when a woman who happened to be present, and who was acquainted with the fact of the child's disinterment, astonished and overwhelmed her by the announcement that her daughter had been saved, and was then living in Eimeo. She immediately embarked for the place, and found that it was even so; she embraced her long-lost child with ardent affection, and thanked God for the light of the gospel, and for the preservation of even one of her offspring.

43. Hervey's Island—Heathen. —Speaking of Hervey's Island in its heathen state, the Rev. John Williams says:—"I visited it in 1823, intending to place a native teacher there, as I expected to find a considerable population; but on learning that, by their frequent and exterminating wars, they had reduced themselves to about sixty in number, I did not fulfil my intention. Some six or seven years after this I visited the same island again, and found that this miserable remnant of the former population had fought so frequently and so desperately, that the only survivors were five men, three women, and a few children! and at that period there was a contention among them as to which should be king!"

Dark as is this picture of heathen cruelty, it is only a specimen of what was found in many other islands when first visited by the missionaries. In reference to Mauke, an island about fifteen miles in circumference, belonging to the same group, Mr Williams says:—"By an invasion of a large fleet of canoes, laden with warriors from a neighbouring island, three years prior to our arrival, the population, previously considerable, was by the dreadful massacre that ensued reduced to about 300." Indeed, many of the South Sea Islands appear to have been on the eve of being entirely depopulated by the cruel wars and heathenish practices which prevailed, when, in the providence and grace of God, Christianity came to their rescue.

44. Female Degradation in India.—A missionary's wife gives the following touching account of the condition of Hindu females in their heathen state:—"Had we skill to paint in colours sufficiently strong the mental darkness and degradation in which females in India are at present found, we imagine the Christian women of England would be more importunate at the throne of grace on their behalf, and more self-denying in their contributions for the purpose of promoting 'Female Education in the East.' From the young bride of six or eight years, to the bald-headed widow of sixty or seventy, they may be said to 'groan, being in bondage.' The Hindu wife is never regarded as a companion to her husband, and the following remarks, made by an intelligent Christian native on the subject, will serve to exemplify this fact. 'We go,' said he, 'into the house of an European, and we find him advising with his wife about his various concerns, and by this interchange of confidence unburdening his mind. We return to our own homes, and we painfully feel that the females to whom we are and must be united cannot be made acquainted with our affairs; we cannot ask their advice, or make them our confidantes.'

"The case of a Hindu widow is still worse: she is among the most unfortunate of beings, the loss of her husband being considered as a punishment for sins committed in a former state, and she is accordingly regarded with horror and detestation by all her friends. Never again permitted to mix with her relations and acquaintance as formerly, after having her head shaved, and the marriage token cut asunder, she is appointed to the most menial work in the family. Her children are placed under the guidance of her deceased husband's nearest male relative, and the only food she receives is what the others leave. The following are some of the lamentations frequently uttered by those unfortunate ones:—'My beloved, you have left me; you have left me, and I stand desolate among the jovial women! The time is come when I must be cast out! The hair which was once decked with flowers must now be covered with dust! The string of the marriage token is snapped asunder, and I must stand desolate in the streets! Who will my children call father? I am a solitary sinner; what shall I do? Why have you departed, my king, the apple of my eye? Why have you left me alone? The marriage cloth is not creased; the flowers with which my hair was decked are unfaded; the wreath of flowers adorning my neck are still in their beauty; the jessamines have lost none of their odour; but you have left me alone, and I have no more pleasure in life!' What breast is there that will not heave a sigh at the recital of such miseries? What heart is there that will not beat with pity, and what lips which will not utter the prayer—

'Thy kingdom come with power and grace
To every heart of man'"?

45. Degradation of Hindu Women.—The Rev. Mr Osborne,

one of the early missionaries to India, thus describes the degraded state of native females in that country:—" The first thing that attracted my notice relative to this subject was, that the men were employed in work which in England is done by the women, and the women in that which is there done by the men. Soon after my arrival at Point-de-Galle, I went to the house of an English gentleman, and on entering the verandah, saw a brawny man sitting on a mat, making muslin dresses. This appeared to me so feminine, that I could not forbear expressing my astonishment at seeing a hand formed for hard labour employed in adjusting the trimmings of a lady's dress; while I passed several delicate females in the streets, who were engaged in a drudgery better suited to the athletic mantua-maker in the verandah than to them. I have also frequently been grieved by seeing poor slender females bending beneath the heavy loads of fruit, rice, &c., which they were carrying to market, while stout and indolent men were walking before them at their ease; not unfrequently the poor woman, besides the load upon her head, has had her infant astride upon her hip. After she has sat all day in the bazaar to vend her goods, and her husband has been enjoying his betel and tobacco, she takes home what she has not sold; then first prepares rice and curry for her lord and master; and when he has done eating, and not till then, is allowed to refresh herself. Washing, ironing, and clear-starching, are all done by the men, as the lighter work; while women are sitting at the mill or working in the fields."

46. The Great Mela of Divi Pathan.—Writing from Tulispore in India in March 1874, the Rev. B. H. Badley gives the following account of the great *mela* annually held at that place, and which he had just attended, along with two native helpers, to circulate portions of Scripture, and to preach the gospel to the deluded idolaters who were congregated in vast numbers on the occasion:—

"Divi, as the Hindus believe, is the goddess who thirsts for blood; and hence at this *mela* much profit is supposed to be gained by making her blood-offerings. The whole process of worship and sacrifice is disgusting in the extreme, and as we have looked upon it during the past fortnight, our hearts have been greatly moved, and we have longed for the power to vividly pourtray the scene before the Church at home. It is enough to say that sheep, goats, lambs, pigs, and even chickens, are brought and slaughtered to propitiate the goddess. The deluded devotee brings his offering, and after washing it and himself in a pool of dirty water, he presents himself before the temple, where stand two butchers (priests they can hardly be called), with bloody hands and knives. A rope is slipped over the head of the struggling victim, the butcher's knife suddenly descends, and in an instant the head is off, and falls to the ground. The man who brings the offering quickly gathers up the bleeding head, and rushes with it into the temple, to sprinkle with blood the image of the goddess. A relative or friend takes up the quivering body and carries it away, to be eaten by the family. Other members of the family buy cocoanuts, sweetmeats, flowers, &c., and present these before the goddess. Others bring young pigs, and, holding them by the hind legs, they dash out their brains upon a certain stone, and then smear with the blood another idol near at hand. This horrible work is accompanied by the beating of drums, ringing of bells, and singing, and continues with great enthusiasm from sunrise to sunset.

"It was with peculiar feelings that we stood up in the midst of all this, and sang of Jesus as the world's mighty Saviour, and proclaimed, day after day, that the blood needed for the remission of sins had been shed, and that through faith in Christ all may have everlasting life. It was a delightful duty to point the thousands crowding about us to the 'Lamb of God which taketh away the sin of the world.' The people gave very good attention, and we had scarcely any interruptions. Questions would be asked, but we invariably came off best. Numbers heard the gospel message for the first time, and it was very encouraging to see the many bands of mountaineers who listened most attentively. We hope they may have carried the message hundreds of miles over the mountains, where as yet the missionary cannot go."

46. Cruel Superstitions of the Hindus.

—"One evening," says the widow of a missionary, "as I was walking with my husband by the river-side, we saw two respectable natives carrying a woman in their arms. We asked them what they were going to do with her. They very coolly answered, 'We are going to put her into the water, that her soul may go to heaven; for she is our mother.' I asked them if she was ill. They said, 'She is not very ill, but she is old and has no teeth, and what is the use of her living?' I felt a great deal on hearing this, and said, 'What! have you no compassion on your mother? will you drown her because she is old?' The woman instantly fixed her eyes on me, and said, 'What sort of a woman are you?' I told her I was an English woman, and wished to prevent her children drowning her, and if they did I would acquaint the governor with it. They said, 'Never mind,' and proceeded towards the river. Mr R. then ran down the bank, and taking hold of the woman, insisted on their taking her home. They did so; but they brought her again the next evening; and Mr F. Carey saw them throw her into the water, without performing the usual ceremony of giving her water to drink in the name of their gods."

Another instance is equally striking:—"A man who was working in the paper-mill at Serampore was bitten by a snake. His companions immediately took him to the river to throw him in, without knowing whether it was a poisonous snake that had bitten him or not. When Mr R. and Mr F. Carey got to them, they found the poor creature between two men; one had hold of his shoulders, the other of his legs, and they were about to throw him into the river. Mr Carey said he thought the man was not dead, and made them put him down. Medicine was sent for, and a spoonful given him. He had no sooner taken it than he spoke and said, 'It is very strong: I will sooner die than take any more.' Mr Carey well understood the nature of the bite, and said it would be necessary to repeat the medicine every twenty minutes during the night. Mr R. asked those around if any one would stay with him all night. They all answered, 'No, we cannot lose our sleep, it would be much better for him to die than for us to be deprived of a night's sleep.' My husband stayed all night, and the poor man continued to get better. In the morning he was so far recovered as to be able to walk home. The next day he came to our house, and fell down at my husband's feet, and said, 'I am come to worship you, Sahib, for saving my life; and I will work for you as long as I live.' He proved a faithful creature, and was working on the mission premises when I left Serampore, and attended the preaching in Bengalee regularly."

47. Burning of Widows in India.—In the month of November 1822, a shocking case of immolation occurred at Hourah, near Calcutta, of which a writer in a Madras newspaper gives the following affecting account:—"I beg leave to inform you that, opposite to Fort William, on Monday morning, at gun-fire, a widow, the mother of a large family, was put on a pile of combustibles, and burned to death, attended with circumstances of cruelty at which human nature shudders, and which I shall endeavour to describe, partly as seen by myself, and partly as informed by others.

"On Friday the 11th instant, about noon, an old Brahmin died. At the time of his death he was possessed of considerable riches, and had two wives, one of whom was many years younger than the other, and by each of these wives he had a large family of children, boys and girls, now living. The moment this man expired, his eldest son, heir to all his property, posted off to Allypore, and applied to C. R. Barwell, Esq., magistrate of the suburbs of Calcutta, for a licence to burn his own mother and his step-mother with the body of his deceased father; but it appears that Mr Barwell then granted a licence for one wife only, the eldest, to be burned. Confident, however, that by another application leave would be granted to burn the other wife also, the pile was raised, and every preparation made to burn them both the next day at noon; but at the hour of noon on Saturday no licence from Mr Barwell for the destruction of the youngest woman had arrived, and no such licence was granted through the whole of the day. The news of this rather novel circumstance soon spread through the neighbourhood; thousands of people assembled to learn the particulars, and to me the family and Brahmin friends of the deceased voluntarily confessed that either both wives must be burned, or neither of them could be burned, as the one of them for whom the licence was obtained declared that she would not be burned alone. On Sunday circumstances remained just the same as on Saturday, for Mr Barwell was inflexible, and no licence to burn the youngest woman could be obtained from him.

"Great hope began now to be entertained by the humane that Mr Barwell's firmness would save both the women; but the poor creatures were all this time, from the moment at which their husband had breathed his last—on Friday at noon—kept locked up, and not allowed to taste a morsel of food of any description, and the hope that had been entertained of their being saved from the flames was greatly damped by the fear that both would be starved to death by their merciless keepers.

"On the following morning, Monday the 14th instant, at gun-fire, notwithstanding the repeated declarations of the family and friends of the deceased that they would not burn the one wife alone, at that selected period when they thought that few eyes would be open to view their proceedings, the elder woman was dragged from her prison of starvation, made to mount the pile, and clasp the putrid carcass of her deceased husband in her arms, the stench of which at that time was intolerable. Two thick ropes, previously prepared, were then passed over the bodies, and two long levers of bamboo crossing each other were likewise employed to pinion her down, the unconsumed ends of which are still to be seen on the spot. All things being thus arranged, the eldest son and heir, who was to succeed to the property, set fire to the pile, which speedily burned and consumed his own mother; and at this act it is said that he triumphantly exulted. The other poor woman, being still kept in confinement, and no nourishment supplied, is now seized with delerium, and in a few hours more will no doubt end her existence also, she being actually starved to death." Such is a picture of heathenism. Truly "the dark places of the earth are full of the habitations of cruelty."

48. Whither shall I go at last?—Many of the heathen priests in India teach their followers that the soul, after it has worn out one body, passes into another. They say if a person has not attended to the worship of the gods, or neglected the priests, then the soul at death will go into a deformed and afflicted body; or, if he has given much money to the idol-temples, then he shall be again born into the world of a beautiful form, and shall be rich and happy. A soul, they say, may pass into the body of a bird, beast, or insect, and be punished in its new state for the sins of a previous one; so that it may dwell in a buffalo or a butterfly, a fierce tiger or a gentle dove, according to its character in this life. And after many millions of changes, the highest state of perfection will be when it passes into the body of a white elephant.

A Hindu was lying upon his bed, expecting soon to die. He was full of thought where his soul would go after death. He had been wholly given to idolatry, and now he felt he was not happy. A priest came to see him, when the dying man exclaimed, "What will become of me?" "Oh," said the priest, "you will inhabit another body." "And where," said he, "shall I go then?" "Into another; and so on through thousands of millions." The mind of the poor sufferer darted across the whole period of changes as though it were only an instant, and cried, "Where shall I go then?" The priest could not reply, and the unhappy idolater died in the dark as to his final destiny. There was no one near to tell him that "the wicked shall go away into everlasting punishment, but the righteous into life eternal." Happy they who can do anything to dispel the darkness from the minds of poor deluded heathens, and be the means of pointing them to Christ and heaven!

49. Worshipping the Peacock.—The peacock is a wild bird in the woods of India, and flies about unmolested, the Hindus regarding it with superstitious reverence. Even when it visits the cultivated fields, it is allowed to feed upon the rice and other grain without let or hindrance. It matters not how much mischief it does; the natives say it is a *sacred bird*, a favourite with many of their gods, and so they will not frighten it away. When they make images of their god *Kartikeya*, they represent him as riding on a peacock, with his beautiful tail sparkling with green and gold, spread out behind, forming a sort of canopy or tent over him. Once a year great festivals have been held in honour of this god at Calcutta and other places. Sometimes on these occasions as many as five thousand images of Kartikeya and his peacock have been made, some of them twenty-five feet high. After the people had worshipped them, they were all cast into the river Ganges. This is one of the hymns they have often sung to this peacock-god :—

"Let us ascribe praises to the six faces of Scanda,
Who resides under the mango-tree at Conjeveram;
Praise to the grace proceeding from these six faces;
Praise to his twelve arms,
Praise to the cock and peacock, his ensign and chariot,
And to the divine and living spear in his hand."

They say that one day he went to play in the grove, when all the gods were assembled together to wait upon Siva, his father. Kartikeya began to destroy all the flowers and plants. The keepers of the garden, thinking him a naughty boy, beat him for it, upon which he fell into a passion, and running at the gods, he put all he could reach to death. Those who escaped began to pray for mercy, on which he restored them all to life. The keepers seeing this, were very sorry, saying they thought he was only a little boy. But to show that he was a god, he suddenly swelled himself so as to fill the sky and the earth, and then at their prayer again became a little child.

Such silly tales are but the wicked inventions of the heathen priests to deceive the people, and to keep them from the knowledge of the true God. Many of them not only worship the images of that idol, but they also treat the living peacock itself as a god, worshipping it as if it could hear prayer. Oh, when will the Hindus learn to adore the only living and true God, and Jesus Christ whom He has sent!

50. Perpetual Fires of the Brahmins.—The *Friend of India*, a paper published at Serampore, says :—"Every Brahmin is directed to keep alive, to the day of his death, the fire used in sacrifice on his investment with the poita, that it may be employed in reducing him to ashes. This is rather an expensive ordinance, it is true; but still it is commanded in the shasters, which have not, however, told us how the man who is too poor to keep a servant is to attend to the fire and his secular employment at the same time. Some in the higher walks of life have done this. In the family of Rajah Krishna-Chundra-Roy, one fire has now been burning for *seventy years*, and we hear it has not yet been suffered to go out. It has served three generations in the manner above described. It is, however, kept in a distinct house, and has a regular establishment of priests to keep it perpetually alive." How much more important it is for us who profess to be Christians, to keep the fire of heavenly love and zeal for the mission cause burning upon our hearts, that it may never go out!

51. Chinese Temple Service.—Although the Chinese are decided idolaters, they only attend their temple services on New Year's Day and a few other special occasions. For their ordinary worship they have small idol-gods in their closets at home, before which they burn candles, offer incense, and make their prayers. Their mode of proceeding when they congregate at their gorgeous temples on great festival-days, is thus described by the Rev. Mr Slater, who was present on one occasion in 1819:

—" Within the temple-yard, which prevents the idol being seen from without, is a high stage, on which the Chinese players perform their exploits, to the astonishment of the crowd below. On passing this, we were struck with the gaudy appearance of golden ornaments, and various-coloured paper cut in shreds; but principally by the quantity of painted candles burning in front of the idol, the smoke of which, together with the incense, is intolerable at first entering. The candles are about one hundred in number, of various sizes, from one foot to three feet high, and measuring from two to six inches in circumference. These are kept burning during the time of worship; but as every worshipper brings two candles, they are constantly changing them, so that I suppose the whole number is changed every twenty minutes. Two men are employed to keep a few places vacant, that no one may be prevented from placing his candles, and that the worship may go on without impediment. The candles, which are removed, are for the benefit of the temple, and a great sum they must produce, as the smallest of them are bought at a dollar a pair.

"Every worshipper, on his entering the temple, presents his light, and receives six sprigs of incense; three of these, after bowing to the idol, to intimate that he is about to worship, he places close to the image, and the others at a short distance, and returning to a cushion in the front of the idol, pays his homage, which consists in kneeling down, and bowing his head to the ground three times; and this also is repeated three times. When this is done, he goes to a large table on the left side of the temple, where there are persons to receive his contributions and enrol his name. Oh! with what apparent gladness do they contribute their rupees, as though anxious to exceed each other in the sum they give for this abominable worship!

"During all this, our ears were almost stunned by a large drum and a gong, used to rouse the idol; and these are beat with unusual vehemence when any person of celebrity comes to worship. Several females, richly dressed, brought offerings of fruit and sweetmeats; these, I was informed, were the wives of the rich Chinese, who gladly embraced that opportunity of appearing abroad, which probably had not been the case since they visited the temple last year on a similar occasion."

52. **Paper Gods.**—The Rev. Mr Ince gives the following description of heathen superstition, which he witnessed at a Chinese festival in Pulo Penang :—" When we arrived at the temple, it was surrounded by a vast concourse of people, the appearance of which was very like that of a fair in England. Opposite the temple there was a stage erected for play-actors. On one side of the temple there was a large paper idol called *La sze yay*, I suppose fourteen feet in height, a most distorted figure, painted various colours, with uncommonly large glass eyes. Immediately before this idol was a long table, set out with all kinds of provisions, interspersed with small paper idols. At the end of the table furthest from the idol were a number of carpets spread on the ground, on which sat half a dozen priests worshipping the god, chanting an unintelligible jargon, and bowing themselves to the ground. There were many other smaller paper idols represented as riding on animals, also made of paper. The whole scene was illuminated by a profusion of lanterns and candles. Behind the great idol was a large quantity of

pieces of paper, the most valuable of which were covered with gold leaf. These papers the idolaters burn, and most firmly believe that they become money in the world of spirits.

"This feast is considered as one of pure benevolence, being celebrated on behalf of those poor bereaved spirits who have no relatives to mourn for them, to supply them with clothes or money, to rescue them from Tartarus, and exalt them to higher and brighter regions. I told some who stood around me that there was one true God, who was not pleased but angry at such things as these. I asked what their god was made of? They replied, 'Paper.' I expressed surprise at their worshipping a piece of painted paper, adding, that the god they were worshipping had eyes indeed, but could not see; ears, but could not hear; hands, but could not handle; feet, but could not walk. They replied, 'Certainly not.' I then inquired what they would do with their god when the feast was over? They answered, 'Burn him.' I rejoined, surely he was a god of no strength, or he would not suffer that; but the true God was almighty, and infinite in every perfection. Truly 'darkness hath covered the earth, and gross darkness the people.'"

53. A Chinese Threatening his God.—The Rev. G. S. Owen, a missionary of the London Society, in order to show that the people of the "Celestial Empire" are losing their confidence in their gods, writes as follows:—"Let the following story, for the truth of which I can vouch, serve as a specimen. The wife of a man living at Chuen-sha, a city near Shanghai, had a severe attack of madness. At night she became especially wild, foaming and raging terribly. The husband went at once to the temple of the city god, presented various sacrifices and made vows; but his wife remained mad as ever. He went again and again; but to no purpose, the woman grew worse. The man got furious; he had half beggared himself by making offerings to the city god, yet his wife was no better. He would have his revenge. Away he went to the temple, and thus addressed the city god—'You call yourself the city god, while in reality you are an evil, money-loving, unjust demon. It was my ancestors who built you this fine temple, and I have been most regular and devout in my worship; in return you have made my wife mad, and refuse to cure her. Well, now, mark what I say: if she is not better within three days, I will pull you down from that pedestal, and throw you into the first ditch I can find, and there you shall rot.' The woman got better within the prescribed time, and thus the god escaped the threatened punishment."

54. Story of Jung Chuo.—Infanticide is fearfully prevalent in China, although there are some localities where it is not practised. This is true of most of the northern provinces, but there are others where not more than one or two girls in a household are suffered to live. The history of Jung Chuo will illustrate that of many a mother in China. This woman belonged to the class of large-footed or working women of the "Celestial Empire." She had been accustomed from her earliest years to gather fuel upon the mountain-sides, to plough, sow, and reap. All that hard labour which we are accustomed in this favoured land to see the stronger sex perform, fell to the share of poor Jung Chuo and her sisters of the same class. Yet all the rude toil, and the hardening, degrading influence of heathenism, had failed to crush out the love and tenderness of her heart.

Coming into the presence of a missionary's wife just at the time when she was mourning the loss of a darling child, Jung Chuo, with evident sympathy of feeling, said, "Sing, sing, niong (teacher's wife), I know just how you feel, and the great grief you carry." She then proceeded to give the following account of her own history :—" My family was very poor, and I have always worked very hard. When I was young, I was married to a man I did not know. As is the custom, my husband and I prayed to the gods for a son. My first child came, but alas! it was a girl. Oh, how I loved it! It was a beautiful child, so large and bright-looking, that my heart was full of love for it; but my husband was very angry because it was not a boy, and said he would not have it. He went out and brought in a tub of water, placed it close to my bed, and then he came to take my little girl away from me to drown her. Oh, how I besought him not to kill her! I held her tight, fast in my arms, reasoning with him, and telling him if he would let her live, we could sell her for a wife; but he would not heed me, and was very angry. He took her from me, and put her head down into the water. I heard the gurgling sound in her throat; I shut my eyes and stopped my ears, but heard the dreadful sound. He pushed her head down, once, twice, thrice—then all was still, and I had no little girl. Oh, how heavy was my grief! I then made larger offerings to the gods, that the next time they might give me a son. A second child came, and it was a girl. Again my husband was angry, and again the same thing happened, the drowning of my child. My third child came, and this time it was a boy. Oh, how glad I was! How happy that I had a child that I might keep! My husband and his friends rejoiced much, and presented thank-offerings to the gods. But when my little boy was so high (measuring with her hand), he died, and I had no child. O sing, sing, niong, my grief is great!"

55. The Dyaks of Borneo.—Borneo is the largest island in the world except Australia, and its native population is estimated at four or five millions, irrespective of a number of Chinese and Malays who inhabit the east coast, and the mouths of some of the rivers. The aborigines are called Dyaks, who live in various tribes or clans, under their respective chiefs, and are said to be in a fearful state of barbarism and moral degradation. They delight in war, and to obtain the head of an enemy is the great ambition and passion of a Dyak. The women encourage this diabolical propensity to such an extent, that no girl will marry until her future bridegroom has shown his prowess by bringing home at least one human head to ornament his house. Mr Brooke describes how, after the heads are brought home in triumph, dried, and hung up, the men chant nightly addresses to them such as the following :—" Your head is in our dwelling, but your spirit wanders to your own country." "Your head and your spirit are now ours; persuade, therefore, your countrymen to be slain by us."

The ideas of the Dyaks with reference to religion vary with the different tribes, but they are all dark and confused in the extreme. They have imaginary gods, but they have no temples, no idols, no priests, no sacrifices, nor do they appear to offer any formal prayers. Indeed, it is difficult to say what kind of homage, if any, they pay to the spiritual beings, concerning whose existence they seem to have some strange, confused, superstitious notions. They give the name of Tupa to an invisible power, whom they regard as the author of thunder, lightning, and rain. They have also gods whom they call Battara and Iowata—names which appear to have been derived from the Hindus. They speak of a place of future happiness, which they call Sabyan; and of another place, to which they appear to give no name, where departed spirits will not be happy.

Thus the interior of Borneo presents itself to our view as an important and inviting field of missionary labour. Something has been done by a few Dutch and English missionaries; but, as yet, little impression has been made upon the mass of its savage inhabitants. Many more zealous and devoted evangelists are needed to engage in a work of so much hazard and difficulty.

56. Similarity of Heathen Systems.

—Great diversity exists among dark, benighted heathen people in different countries with respect to language, complexion, features, dress, manners, and customs; but there is a striking resemblance between many of their superstitious notions, rites, and ceremonies. They all exhibit the same ignorance of the spiritual nature of the Divine Being, and His claims on His rational, intelligent creatures. They have "gods many, and lords many," but all their worship is characterised, not by love and gratitude, but by fear and dread. The things which they sacrifice they offer to demons, and not to God. Open and avowed devil-worship is common in Africa and India. The poor deluded Singalese in Ceylon will dedicate part of his rice-field to the devil, that the rest may not be blighted! And yet he cannot see reflected in the widespread harvest the goodness of God, "who maketh His sun to shine upon the evil and the good, and causeth the rain to descend upon the just and the unjust." Idolatry in every age and country has been much the same in its general features. The gods of the heathen are the same now as in ancient times, and exactly answer the description of the Psalmist—"Their idols are silver and gold, the work of men's hands. They have mouths, but they speak not: eyes have they, but they see not: they have ears, but they hear not: they have hands, but they handle not: feet have they, but they walk not: neither speak they through their throat. They that make them are like unto them; so is every one that trusteth in them" (Ps. cxv. 4–8). The superstitious folly and trickery of the fetish-man on the western coast of Africa is identical with that of the witch-doctor and rain-maker in Kaffraria; and the horrors of infanticide are the same in China, India, Polynesia, and other countries. As children were offered to Moloch in times of old, so they are now frequently sacrificed to demons. In fact, a striking resemblance in the main features of paganism, as practised in different ages and countries, is very perceptible, and reminds us how deeply fallen and degraded man is everywhere, and how much he stands in need of a revelation from heaven, and of that glorious gospel which it is the object of missionary societies to send to every nation and people and kindred and tongue.

"Lord over all, if Thou hast made,
 Hast ransomed every soul of man,
Why is the grace so long delayed?
 Why unfulfilled the saving plan?
The bliss for Adam's race designed,
 When will it reach to all mankind?"

II. NATIVE GENIUS.

57. Unity of the Human Race. Notwithstanding the diversity of language, complexion, manners, condition, and general appearance of the inhabitants of different countries and climes, we have abundant evidence that they have all one common origin, and that they are possessed of the same nature, sympathies, and high destiny. This is clearly stated in Scripture, and corroborated by the facts of history and the teachings of sound philosophy. Nor is it difficult to find ample reasons in locality, climate, soil, food, water, and other conditions affecting the growth and development of the human species, to account for all the varieties which appear in the different nations of men which inhabit our globe. This unity of the human race must ever be regarded as one of the fundamental principles on which the missionary enterprise is based; because, if the doctrine were not true, or if it were even doubtful, one of the most powerful motives to exertion for the benefit of our fellow-men would be weakened, if not entirely paralysed, and we should be left in a perfect maze as to the character of our work. But, as the matter now stands, we behold in the whole human family one common brotherhood. The objects of our sympathy, prayer, and efforts, of every nation, people and kindred and tongue, are our brethren and sisters, bone of our bone, and flesh of our flesh, created by the same almighty power, preserved by the same kind Providence, and redeemed with the same precious blood.

Enlightened and converted heathens are well aware of their proper place in the human family, and sometimes ground their claims upon it in a very emphatic manner. An amusing instance, illustrative of this, occurred at the Gambia, Western Africa, in 1833. A mission party had just arrived from England, who were highly interested and delighted with the evidences of intelligence and progress which they beheld among the native converts on the station. The missionaries and their wives gladly embraced every opportunity of conversing with our school children and domestics, to test the extent of their knowledge and the capacity of their intellects. One day, while sitting at her work, Mrs D. was talking with Matty our servant-maid, a liberated African girl, and, with a view to teaze her, humorously said of the garments she was making, "Oh, they will do very well, they are only for black people." "Don't say, 'only for black people,' missy," replied Matty, "black and white all de same, only de skin different." "How do you know," said Mrs D., "that white and black are the same?" "Because," rejoined the negro girl, "I read in my Testament, 'God hath made of one blood all nations of men to dwell upon all the face of the earth." "Then you think," inquired Mrs D., "that the blood of white and black is the same?" "Yes, ma'am," said Matty. "Then," said Mrs D., holding out a pen-knife which she had in her hand, "suppose we each of us cut a finger, to see if the blood is the same." "Yes, ma'am," replied Matty with an arch smile, "if you will cut yours first!" This was enough. Mrs D. came running to Mrs M., and declared that she had never met with superior wit and smartness among any people in any country.

58. The Negro's Defence.—At different periods from the days of Hume and Gibbon downwards, persons of a sceptical turn of mind have ventured to insinuate doubts as to the manhood of the negro race, and other degraded tribes of the human family; but it was left to professed philosophers of modern times, and to the members of an institution called the "Anthropological Society," systematically and publicly to proclaim this kind of infidelity. These learned gentlemen have plainly and unblushingly asserted that the aborigines of Australia, the negroes of Africa, and other poor miserable outcasts, are not members of the human family at all, but merely a superior kind of baboon, ourang-outang, or gorilla; and that, consequently, they have no souls, and require none of that sympathy and care which the friends of missions are anxious to extend to them.

At a recent public meeting of gentlemen connected with the said "Anthropological Society," these silly views were propounded with a great show of eloquence and earnestness, when the best refutation was given of them that we have ever known. There happened to be present an intelligent negro youth, who had come to England to study at one of our colleges. Immediately after one of the speakers had dwelt, very learnedly, as he thought, on the subject in question, arguing from the awkwardness of his gait, the thickness of his skull, and the curly character of his hair, the great improbability that the negro belonged to the human species, the young African requested permission to address the meeting. The chairman having given his consent, the black man arose, and all eyes being fixed upon him, with a dignified mien and an unfaltering voice, he spoke substantially as follows:—"Mr Chairman, ladies, and gentlemen,—The speaker who has just addressed the meeting thinks that I and my brethren of the negro race are not men because we have curly hair, our craniums are thick, and we have a shuffling gait when we walk. I have lately been down in Dorsetshire, where I observed the farm labourers have a shuffling gait; and I thought that my countrymen, who generally walk much better, might be tempted to laugh at them for their awkwardness if they saw them, but I do not think they would doubt their humanity on that account. And as to our curly hair, I think that need be no disparagement to us, as I have known persons of fair complexion try to make theirs curl without success. With regard to the thickness of our skulls, I may observe, that I suppose our Almighty and All-wise Creator knew what He was doing when He made us so. Our home is in a very hot and sultry climate, where the fiery rays of the sun have great power, and where the inner region of the cranium no doubt requires such a defence. If by any mistake in our conformation, we had been made with skulls as frail as that of the learned gentleman who last spoke, our brains, under the influence of the heat, might have become as thin and addled as his appears to be, judging from the foolish and unphilosophical statement which he has made, and then it might have been reasonably doubted whether we were men worth listening to."

The young negro resumed his seat amid thundering applause; and for once, at least, it appeared to be the general opinion that the black was as clever as the white man.

59. Eminent Characters.—After many happy years of labour among them, with a view to their improvement, both in their original home in Africa, and in the lands of their exile in the West Indies, and on the American Continent, we claim for the negro race, not only their proper place in the human family, but mental ability for progress and advancement in general knowledge, and improvement according to their opportunities. In schools, congregations, and workshops, we have found the sable sons of Ham possessed of a capacity to receive instruction which would compare favourably with that of any other people, making due allowance for the climate in which they live, their long years of oppression, and other circumstances not very favourable to mental development. We have, moreover, found among them some eminent Christians, clever tradesmen, and trustworthy friends. For life, cheerfulness, zeal and earnestness in the cause of Christ, and for love to God's house, and affection for their ministers, our negro converts are worthy of the highest commendation, and we have often wished that in these respects they were more generally imitated by their brethren and sisters of fairer hue.

Nor are there wanting among them instances of superior mental excellency where fair opportunities have been afforded for study and improvement. Both in Africa, America, and the West Indies, we have black and coloured gentlemen who, by dint of their own persevering efforts, have risen to the honourable position of respectable merchants, government officials, members of parliament, physicians, barristers-at-law, and to the sacred office of the Christian ministry; and these stations have been reached, in some instances, amid difficulties and prejudices which would have crushed and disheartened persons of less ardour and perseverance. We may further add, without hesitation, that when men of African descent have been raised to positions of respectability, honour, and trust, they have generally acquitted themselves well, and proved themselves worthy of their elevation. If there have been occasional failures, they have been as few in number as could reasonably be expected, all circumstances considered; and if there has sometimes been in the appearance and carriage of those thus elevated a manifestation of French dash, rather than a partiality for the plain, unassuming manners of John Bull, allowance may well be made for difference of temperament, climate, and circumstances.

60. Self-taught Astronomer.—We have a very pleasant recollection of an intelligent young man of colour on one of our mission stations in the West Indies, who by dint of his own persevering efforts, with the aid of such books as he could obtain from the missionaries and others, acquired a respectable knowledge of astronomy, with its kindred sciences.

Considering the slender means at his command, in the way of books and instruments for the prosecution of his studies, the progress which he made was perfectly astonishing. He not only obtained a general knowledge of the character, dimensions, and motions of the heavenly bodies, but by means of an ordinary telescope he made several remarkable astronomical observations during the period of our personal acquaintance with him. Among other achievements, he traced the track of the comet which appeared in the West Indies in the month of September 1844, and from night to night noted its precise position in the heavens with an accuracy truly remarkable. The result of these observations was communicated by the young astronomer to the *St George's Chronicle* in an article of rare merit and scientific skill. It was printed and published by a native typographer; and to make the subject as interesting as possible, it was illustrated with diagrams drawn by the author, and engraved by a self-taught native artist. This little incident was altogether a remarkable feat of native genius.

To enable the self-taught native astronomer to prosecute his studies with greater facility, and in testimony of their respect for him, his friends subscribed among themselves a sum sufficient to purchase a first-rate achromatic telescope, which they presented to him in due form. This instrument was ordered from London, where it was selected and tested by the late Dr Dick, author of the "Christian Philosopher" and other scientific works, previous to its being sent out to the island of Grenada. The doctor took a lively interest in the native astronomer, and in a long and interesting letter which he addressed to the writer, he expressed his admiration at the accuracy of the observations made with such slender means, and his grateful recognition of such instances of native genius as the collateral results of Christian missions. This communication of the celebrated astronomer we preserve among the precious mementoes of bygone years, and gratefully call to mind the pleasing instances we have witnessed in the mission-field of genuine native genius.

61. **Native Poets.**—Both in Africa and in the West Indies we have met with numerous instances of real talent among the natives. On leaving one station where we had laboured with much happiness and some success, we felt specially anxious for the continued steadfastness of the new converts. Consequently, in a farewell sermon, we admonished them to guard against the temptations to which they were exposed, and to persevere in their Christian course even to the end. Among other things, the preacher said, "For my part, I have made up my mind to go to heaven, and I charge you to meet me there." This sentiment made such an impression on the mind of a young man of colour, that on going home he wrote the following lines, which he handed to us before our embarkation.

To my dear Pastor, after hearing his Farewell Sermon.

"Meet you there! there is something both awful and sweet,
In those words of your charge, 'Meet me there;'
'Tis so truly sublime, and with love so replete,
And comes from a heart so sincere.

"Meet you there! and why not? shall the trammels of sin
Ever fetter me down to vile clay?
No, no, I shall mount! the great prize I *must* win;
I cannot stop short in the way.

"Your Saviour a mansion for you did prepare,
Still travel to heaven, I shall meet you there."

Another young native Christian had lost a little infant, and to soothe his sorrows he wrote the following lines, which he afterwards, by request, transferred to our scrap-book.

On the Death of my Infant Daughter.
"I once possessed a rosebud dear,
  So lovely, delicate, and fair;
It seemed as if its nature were
  Ethereal — destined for another sphere.
A cherub from the realms on high
  My tender Germin did espy,
And thought it wrong such purity
  Should stay on earth to fade and die.
Ere through its short ephemeral day,
  My beauteous flower had striven,
The cherub came and plucked it up—
  Then flew away to heaven."

62. A Negro's Logic.—In the days of negro slavery in the West Indies, we, who laboured among the poor outcasts, found it very difficult to impress their minds with correct views of right and wrong on some subjects. For instance, if they took anything belonging to an estate with which they were not connected, they admitted at once that that was stealing; but they could scarcely be made to feel and acknowledge that it was wrong to appropriate to their own use anything belonging to the estate to which they were attached as slaves, as they regarded themselves with all that they possessed as belonging to "massa," in common with all his other property. An amusing instance of these confused notions with regard to pilfering occurred on an estate in the island of St Vincent at an early period.

A slave returned from the field one day very hungry, and, going into his master's yard to speak to one of the domestics, his attention was attracted to the meat-safe, which stood outside on a poll, to keep it from the ants and other insects. The temptation was too strong for him, and, watching his opportunity, and finding it open, he went and helped himself to a slice or two of ham. Whilst in the act he was detected by some of the other servants, who, to clear themselves, informed their master when he came home who was the real culprit. Quashy was accordingly called into the presence of the planter to answer to the crime laid against him. He could not deny the fact that he had taken the ham, but he stoutly denied that he had stolen it. In his defence he became quite earnest, if not eloquent. He said, "Ham belong to massa, ebery ting belong to massa, me, poor neger, belong to massa. Me ben work for massa long time. Now me feel bery weak. Dat dare salt-fish cannot make strong for work, so me just take one little piece massa ham to make me strong, to work good for massa." Notwithstanding the apparent plausibility of this reasoning, Quashy was punished for the offence, and given to understand that his logic would not do. It is a pleasing fact, however, that since the introduction of the gospel among them, and especially since the advent of freedom, more enlightened views prevail among the people of the West Indies; no one would now affect to doubt the sinfulness of pilfering in any form, whilst the most ignorant know that, in every respect, "honesty is the best policy."

63. Ingenious Escape.—After the abolition of slavery in 1834, British ground everywhere became free, and it was no uncommon thing for slaves in the French colonies of the West Indies to attempt to make their escape to one of the English islands. Whilst resident there, many daring attempts of this kind came under our notice, some of which were successful, and others ended in sad disaster. In the absence of boats or canoes, we have known slaves venture out to sea on old doors, window-shutters, or pieces of plank, hoping almost against hope that the winds and waves might be propitious, and that they might be wafted across in safety to the nearest British isle. The plans resorted to by the poor negroes to accomplish their object were sometimes ludicrous and sometimes appalling, and not unfrequently discovered considerable smartness of intellect, as well as courage and daring, as the following instance will show:—

On one occasion, five slaves in the French island of Guadeloupe formed the project of escaping to Antigua. Two of them arrived at the appointed place of meeting rather too late, and had the mortification to behold their three associates already on the sea at some distance, in a small canoe provided for the occasion; for they had embarked at once without waiting for the rest, for fear of treachery. The two poor fellows thus left behind had to set their wits to work to devise a plan to make their escape also, and to avoid the punishment consequent on making the attempt without success, if discovered. At length they resolved on a desperate experiment. They ran in breathless haste to the great house, and called up Mr M., their owner, crying out, "See, master, three negroes are making their escape in a canoe which they have stolen!" Mr M. was much obliged by this timely notice, and having hastily dressed himself, and given a glass of rum to each of his faithful informers, he threw himself into a boat, and with the two men as rowers, set out with all speed in pursuit of the fugitives. But with all their efforts they could only just keep the chase in sight, without gaining any considerable advantage. Of course the two negroes knew how to manage this part of the business, and as an excuse for making no greater headway, reminded their master that there were three pulling in the canoe against two in the boat. On hearing this remark Mr M. threw off his coat, and applied himself to the oar. At length they all arrived at Antigua. The three slaves with the canoe landed first, however, and Mr M. and his party followed in their turn. Instead of helping their master to capture the fugitives, the two slaves who had accompanied him, turned round and coolly said, "Good master, we did not know how to rejoin our friends in the canoe, who had left us behind; and as you have brought us over yourself in your boat, we give you many thanks. Good-bye, master, we are now in a free country." They then fled from him, and left him in the lurch. The French planter felt indignant at the loss of his slaves, and more especially at the idea of having been thus befooled by his own negroes; but there was no help for it. He applied to the British authorities for redress, but without avail, and on the following day he was obliged to hire men to row his boat back to Guadeloupe, reluctantly leaving his five slaves behind to breathe the free air of Antigua.

64. **The Negro Post-boy.**—A ludicrous story is told in Jamaica of a negro boy named Benjie and his mule Juno, which, nevertheless, shows a measure of native wit and

NATIVE GENIUS.

smartness such as we have often witnessed among this class of our fellow-men. It was usual with a planter, on the arrival of the monthly mail from England, to despatch one of the most intelligent boys on the estate to town for his letters and papers. In this instance the important office of post-boy was held by little Benjie, who mounted his mule Juno, and started off post-haste at the bidding of his master, vigorously blowing a cow's horn which hung by his side, to give notice to the neighbouring estates that the English packet was in. As he galloped along, he passed a traveller, whom he scarcely noticed, but who watched the manœuvres of the negro post-boy with great interest. On coming to a river which was not very deep or difficult to ford, Miss Juno turned mulish, and refused to take the water. Benjie vigorously applied the spur which he carried on his naked heel, and the tamarind switch which he used as a whip, but to no purpose. Juno rushed furiously from one side of the road to the other, and threw up her heels in defiance of her rider's authority. Whilst the contest was going on the traveller came up, and witnessed the amusing scene. Benjie, as is common with the negroes, commenced a conversation with the mule in the way of remonstrance. "So Miss Juno, you no want to carry me to town to fetch massa's letters from de post-office." The mule gave a snort, as if to say, "That is assuredly my determination." "Bery well, Miss Juno, den we mus' see."

After a moment's hesitation, during which little Benjie appeared to be thinking over the best plan to adopt to extricate himself from the dilemma in which he was placed by the stupidity of his mule, he resumed the dialogue, "You no go, eh? Now, Miss Juno, me bet you one fippenny (about threepence sterling) me make you go!" The mule gave another snort, probably of defiance, but which the boy chose to interpret as a signal of acquiescence. "Bery well, you say done, you see now wedder me no make you go, and carry me to town; you stan' here one little piece." He then threw himself from the saddle, and pulling the rein over the animal's head, made it fast to a bush. This done, he went to the margin of the river, and filled his pockets with little pebbles. He then drew out from among the bushes a few green withs, and returned to the mule, which he found standing quietly enough. "Now, Miss Juno," he said, showing his glittering teeth, "me see who sall win de bet." He then filled both ears of the mule with the pebbles, and tied them close with the withs he had procured for the purpose. "Now Juno," he triumphantly exclaimed, as he gathered up the reins and vaulted nimbly into the saddle, "we sall see who is de massa, Juno or Benjie," giving her at the same time a touch with his spur and switch. Juno shook her head, and hearing the strange rumbling noise in her ears, forded the stream without hesitation, and cantered along without stopping again till she reached the post-office.

Some time afterwards the traveller also reached town, and seeing little Benjie playing marbles with some other negro boys, he beckoned him, to inquire how he had got on with the restive mule. Benjie was rather shy with the stranger at first, but on learning that it was the same gentleman who had seen him contending with Juno at the river, and on receiving the promise of a fippeny if he would tell him, and an assurance that the planter should not be made acquainted with the circumstance, the boy relaxed somewhat, and he assured the traveller that he won the bet. "But how did you make Juno pay?" inquired the stranger. "Oh, bery well," said Benjie; "you see mass gibe me two fippenny to buy grass for Juno, and when Benjie win one fippenny from Juno, he take it from de grass money, and only gibe Juno one fippenny grass." The gentleman gave the boy what he had promised, and turned away convulsed with laughter at this specimen of negro shrewdness.

65. The Sagacious Judge.—On the 15th of August 1863, a very singular case was brought before Quaw Dade, the native king of Aquapem, in the Fanti country, Cape Coast, Western Africa, in the decision of which he showed considerable skill and sagacity of mind. A man from a neighbouring town called Date, and another man from the small village of Amanokurom, met in the bush towards sunset, not far from the place last named. They did not salute each other according to custom; but the man from Amanokurom, instead of saluting, cried out to the Date man, "You are a murderer; we have heard that you have killed somebody, and are now running away." (A man had killed his wife in a neighbouring town the same week, and had run away.) The man from Date answered, "No, I am not a murderer; I have been working for a friend of mine, and I am now looking for a few sticks to build a hut for myself and family, who are living on a farm not far from here: but I have lost my way, and as it is now getting dark, I am going to the village from which you come to sleep for the night, and I intend to return to my family to-morrow morning." Says the other man, "I too am going to cut some palm-branches to repair the roof of my hut; but I do not believe you, you are telling a lie." With these words he gave him a cut on his head with his bush-knife. The Date man returned the blow, and both were wounded in a fearful manner, and were conveyed soon afterwards to the nearest village.

When the matter was brought before the court of the native king or chief of Aquapem, the grandees found it very difficult to decide, as each in relating his version of the story asserted that the other struck the first blow. In the course of the investigation the men were asked if they knew each other before, and whether they had ever quarrelled previously. But it appeared that they were entire strangers to each other, and had never met before. Now the whole court was in great perplexity. There were no witnesses, and each accused the other as the aggressor. Some members of the court said, "Let us count each man's wounds, and see who has the most." Others said, "No, that cannot help us to a decision." At length the king, who sat as judge, decided the case in a very clever manner, if not with the wisdom of Solomon. He said, "I have seen that each man's account is as sweet as honey; but none of us was there, and you cannot produce any witnesses. You all know that we are under the protection of the British government, and I being the native king of this district, am responsible for all that is done against the English laws. You know that some years ago a subject of mine murdered an Acraman and hid him in the bush, and the Acras said I myself had killed him. Had the murderer not been found out, the governor would have punished me. Now suppose you two had wounded each other in the bush in such a way that both had died on the spot, who had to give an account before the English court but myself? Therefore this folly which you two have committed has been done against me, and my good name, before the English government. Now you both deserve a severe punishment; but I will wait till your wounds are healed before I tell you how I will punish you. In the meantime I shall see how you behave yourselves," and so he dismissed them for the time being.

66. The Zulus in England.— A few years ago, a party of Zulu Kaffirs were taken from Natal to England, for the purpose of public exhibition in their war-dances and other savage exploits. If the experiment failed to remunerate the silly projector of the enterprise, it gave the party of natives an opportunity of seeing and forming their opinion of the "white man's country," of which they were not slow to avail themselves. When the survivors returned to Natal—for we are sorry to say that some of them died in this strange land—they were immediately surrounded by crowds of their countrymen, asking for the news from the other side of the great "salt water." A set time having been appointed for a hearing in the presence of the chief of the tribe to which they belonged, and a large concourse being assembled to hear what their friends had seen in England, a young man stood up to speak on behalf of himself and his companions. The following is a literal translation of the principal points in his address, and it may serve to show that these degraded Africans had their wits about them. After telling of the voyage, and how frightened and sea-sick they were for some time on board the ship, he said :—

"In the third moon we saw England. Then we were told we were in the mouth of a river, and soon after that London was before us. Those who knew London saw it; our eyes, however, saw nothing but a cloud of smoke, then houses, and presently poles standing out of the water like reeds in a marsh, and these were the masts of the London ships. We went in among them, and our ship stood still, and we found ourselves in London, the great place of the English. The place is very large. We never saw the end of it. We tried hard to find it, but we could not. We ascended a high building like a pole (the Monument) to see where it ended, but our sight was filled with houses and streets and people. We heard that many people born and grown old there never saw the end of it, and we said, 'If such is the case, why should we who are strangers look for it?' We gave it up. The people are so many, that they tread on one another. All day and night the streets are crowded. At first we thought some great thing had happened, and said, 'Let us wait till the people have passed on,' but they never did pass. The surface of the earth is too small for the people, and some live under the earth, and even under the water (alluding to the shops in the Thames Tunnel).

"When we left London, we travelled in a fine waggon, drawn by another waggon, but how, I never could understand. I could only make out that the first waggon is like a large kettle on wheels, full of water, with a fire under it to make it boil. But before it boils other waggons, loaded, are tied on behind it; for the moment it does boil it runs away on its own road; and if it were to boil before the waggons were tied to it, I do not

D

know where it would go. We saw a number of oxen, but the oxen in England do not draw the waggons; they ride in them, and are drawn along altogether by the big thing with the boiling water in it. We saw many other strange things, more than we can tell you. We saw men ascend into the skies, and go higher than the eagle. The men did not go up with wings, but in a basket. The basket was tied to a large round bag filled with smoke. It looked like a large calabash, with the mouth downwards, and the basket hung beneath. In this two people sat, and when the bag was let go, it went up with them. I looked at it till my eyes were tired, and it became smaller than a bird. They took up sand with them, and poured it on the people beneath, and some fell on us. We likewise saw dogs carrying letters, and monkeys firing off guns. We saw a horse dance to a drum; and when he had finished, he made a bow to the people who were looking at him. We saw elephants, sea-cows, tigers, and crocodiles, living in houses, and snakes handled by human hands; we saw men standing on their heads and walking on their hands for money, and we paid our own money to see them do it."

After a minute and intelligent account of an interview with the Queen with which they were honoured, and a description of her palace, guards, and equipage, the young Kaffir concluded his address amid loud applause and clapping of hands on the part of his countrymen. The young people were delighted with what they had heard, and many expressed a wish to go and see the "white man's country;" but the old men shook their heads in mute astonishment, declaring that they could believe almost everything they had heard, except the account which had been given of oxen riding in waggons instead of drawing them.

67. The Negro Bishop.

Many pleasing instances have come under our notice of natives of Africa, and other heathen countries, who have been instructed, and raised to the important office of the Christian ministry, after their conversion to the faith of the gospel; but the most remarkable case we have known was that of Samuel Crowther, a liberated African of pure negro blood, whose history is one of thrilling interest.

One morning, in the year 1821, the inhabitants of Oshugum, a town about 100 miles inland from the Bight of Benin, were attacked by a slave-hunting party. The town was captured and burnt. Among the prisoners was a boy named Adjai, about eleven years of age, with his mother, his two sisters, and one of his cousins. The relatives were soon separated and divided among the conquerors, Adjai, whose story we have briefly to relate, being allotted to the principal chief, who almost immediately bartered him for a horse. He was next sold in the slave-market to a Mohammedan mistress, by whom he was again disposed of for some rum and tobacco. From his new owners little Adjai experienced barbarous treatment. With 186 fellow-captives he was bound with fetters, and thrown into the hold of a slave-ship, where their sufferings were most intense. The vessel was, however, captured by a British ship-of-war and taken to Sierra Leone. The captured slaves were now free, and placed in circumstances to receive instruction and to earn their own living.

Adjai, together with a little girl named Asano and several other children, were placed under the care of the Rev. Mr Weeks, of the Church

Missionary Society, in Freetown. The little negro boy displayed, from the beginning of his emancipated life, a remarkable degree of natural talent, intelligence, and industry. Not content with two hours' teaching daily in the school, he begged a copper from some of his countrymen, purchased a lesson-book, and engaged one of the more advanced school-children as his teacher. In three days he had learned the alphabet pretty well, in six months was able to read the New Testament, and had shown such a desire for improvement that he attracted the special notice of the missionary and his wife. Three years of kind and faithful teaching were more than rewarded by remarkable progress, and by bringing Adjai to renounce heathenism and embrace the religion of Jesus Christ. He was consequently baptized on the 11th of December 1825, and received the name of Samuel Crowther, a well-known and excellent English clergyman. After visiting England in 1826, he returned to Sierra Leone, and became the first student in the Fourah Bay Institution, which was founded in order to prepare pious Africans for the work of evangelising their countrymen. In 1829 he married Asano, the companion of his boyhood, who was now a mission-school teacher. In 1841 Mr Crowther accompanied the first Niger expedition, when he saw what a grand field of missionary labour was opening up in the interior, to which he resolved to devote his life. Having again visited England to complete his studies at the missionary college in Islington, he was ordained by the Bishop of London as a missionary to Abbeokuta. On reaching his appointed station he was delighted to meet with his mother and relatives, after a separation of five and twenty years. On the 29th of June 1864, the Rev. S. Crowther was still further promoted by being consecrated Bishop of the Niger, where he has since laboured in preaching, teaching, and translating, with a measure of zeal, diligence, and success which has excited the admiration of the friends of missions, and proved to a demonstration that Africans, when favoured with opportunities of improvement, are capable of rising in the scale of being.

68. First Native Kaffir Minister.—The introduction of the gospel among the warlike Kaffirs of Southern Africa was attended with many difficulties; but when the work was once established, it advanced in a very pleasing manner. Among the converts to the faith of Christ, many have been raised up as teachers of others, and a few have been promoted to the high and holy office of the Christian ministry, who have given evidence of considerable native talent. The most remarkable of these was Tiyo Soga, the first of his countrymen who were thus distinguished. He was born at the Chumie mission-station in 1829. Of his parents his mother only was a Christian; but, by the blessing of God upon her humble efforts, young Tiyo's mind was early brought under a gracious influence, and he was noticed by the missionaries as one likely to be made useful to his degraded fellow-men. With a view to this he was trained and instructed, first at the common mission-school at the Chumie, afterwards at the training academy at Lovedale, and finally at the Glasgow University in Scotland. At the place last mentioned the young Kaffir student not only made rapid progress in learning, but he gained the respect and esteem of all with whom he came in contact; and on his departure for his native land he was presented with an address and testimonials which were highly creditable to his mental and moral character.

Having been ordained to the sacred office, Mr Soga returned to Africa, and entered upon his missionary work in Kaffraria in 1857, when everything was in a state of confusion in consequence of the late Kaffir war. By his intelligence, the mildness of his natural temperament, and the respect in which he was held by all parties, he was singularly adapted to take a prominent part in the work of re-organisation. He was consequently appointed to Magwali, as a missionary to his own tribe, and soon succeeded in rebuilding the mission premises, and in restoring everything to order. At this station he spent ten years in earnest labour for the conversion and elevation of his countrymen, itinerating far and near through the Gaika district, faithfully preaching at heathen kraals the glorious gospel of the blessed God, and that with the most gratifying results.

A new station being then proposed for Kreli's country, Mr Soga was unanimously invited by his brethren to go forth as the pioneer evangelist to that centre of heathenism, because of his peculiar adaptation for the work. When, after several years of useful labour at this place, his health and constitution began to give way, his brethren would gladly have relieved him from pulpit and pastoral work, that he might devote his entire attention, as strength would permit, to the translation of the Scriptures and other works into the Kaffir language, for which he was so admirably qualified; but the devoted missionary absolutely declined to be relieved, and continued to preach with all his might, whilst at the same time he pursued, as he had opportunity, his literary studies. After years of careful toil, he finished a beautiful translation of the *Pilgrim's Progress*, which has been greatly admired by competent judges. He also composed several charming Kaffir hymns, which will help to keep his memory green in the hearts and minds of his grateful countrymen. Having been much exposed, in the course of a long missionary journey, in June 1871, Mr Soga was seized with an illness which terminated his valuable life in the course of a few weeks. On hearing of the attack, his friend, the Rev. J. Longden, of the Wesleyan Missionary Society, hastened to the side of his dying bed to console and comfort him in the trying hour, and was favoured to see him pass away peacefully to his eternal rest. Among his last utterances were these impressive words :—" The will of the Lord be done. His will is best. Weep not for me, for I am leaning with my whole strength on Jesus Christ."

69. Bartimeus, the Blind Preacher.—A wonderful man was Bartimeus, the blind preacher of Hawaii, one of the Sandwich Islands. His native name was Puaaiki, and he was born in East Maui, about the year 1785, a few years after the death of Captain Cook. And so dark and barbarous were the people at that time, that it is said he would have been buried alive by his mother, but for the intervention of a relative. The inhabitants were then wasting away under the influence of the most abominable vices; and, as he grew up, he became as vicious and degraded as the rest of his countrymen. When the missionaries came to Kailua in 1820, Puaaiki was there in the king's train, playing the buffoon for the amusement of the queen and chiefs, having been taught the practice of rude, lascivious songs and dances. In this way he obtained the means of a scanty sustenance, and dragged on a miserable life.

When the royal family removed to Honolulu in 1821, the blind dancer made part of their wild and noisy train. There he suffered from illness and neglect; and during his affliction he was visited by John Honolii, one of the early native converts, who told him of the Good Physician. These visits were made a blessing to him, and as soon as he could walk he accompanied his friend to hear the missionaries preach. At that time he was a miserable object to look upon, of diminutive stature, bowed down by sickness, bereft of eyesight, with no clothing but a piece of bark cloth thrown round his loins, a long black beard, and dark soul. No one could behold him without a feeling of pity; yet he was a chosen vessel, and the Lord Jesus was just such a friend as he needed. Led by a heathen lad, he came often to the place of Christian worship, gave up his intoxicating drinks, and other heathenish practices, and sought to conform to the rules of the gospel as he understood them. His heart was gradually opened, and the Spirit took of the things of Christ and revealed them unto him. When the chiefs now called upon him to sing and dance for their amusement, he said, "No, that service of Satan is ended; I intend to serve Jehovah, the King of Heaven." About this time the queen came under the influence of the gospel, and the blind convert earnestly exhorted her to persevere in seeking salvation, and she happily attended to his counsel.

In the spring of 1825 Puaaiki was admitted into the Church by baptism, when he received the name of Bartimeus. His progress in religious knowledge was remarkably rapid. His blindness seemed to favour his studies; for although he could not read, he had a wonderful memory, and treasured up the substance of every sermon he heard; and from this storehouse, as a Christian teacher, he brought forth things new and old for the edification of the people. For eighteen years Bartimeus laboured as a native preacher, despite his blindness, with amazing power and success, till, on the 17th of September 1843, he died happy in God, at Honolulu, sincerely regretted by the missionaries and their people.

70. **Mission-Schools.**—Any unprejudiced person might soon be convinced of the capability of the natives of the respective countries to which missionaries are sent to receive instruction, if they could only pay a visit of inspection to some of our mission-schools. We have a very pleasant recollection of many excellent institutions of this kind in foreign lands where we have laboured—institutions which would bear a favourable comparison with similar establishments in any country. We have never seen a common school anywhere to surpass the mission day-school in Port of Spain, Trinidad, in 1841. The pupils were all black and coloured children, and the progress which they made under the able instructions of Messrs Cleaver, Jordan, and other teachers in succession, was truly astonishing. At the first annual examination of the school the more advanced boys and girls showed an acquaintance with arithmetic, grammar, geography, Scripture, and general history, the histories of England and of Trinidad, the Conference Catechisms, and with various other branches of secular and religious knowledge, which elicited the high commendation of His Excellency Lord Harris, the Governor, and others who were present.

The following honourable testimony, in reference to another negro mission-school, was spontaneously given by a gentleman who was present at the anniversary:—"I witnessed the examination of the children in the lower classes with peculiar pleasure and interest; but the elder children in the upper classes truly filled my mind with wonder and admiration. After reading portions of the Holy Scriptures and the history of Greece, they were very minutely interrogated on those portions, and their answers were so correct, that I could scarcely help blushing at my own ignorance. Their facility in arithmetic was surprising; sums in reduction, proportion, practice, fellowship, and vulgar fractions, were worked with such rapidity, that the examiner could scarcely keep pace with them. In the sciences of geography and astronomy the whole school appeared enthusiastic; the whole world, as it were in a moment, was divided into continents, islands, oceans, seas, and lakes: zones, longitudes, and latitudes, the twelve signs of the zodiac, motions of the earth, and its distance from the sun, were all described with an expertness and accuracy I could scarcely have believed. Upon the whole, it far surpassed all that I ever saw in England."

We add the following remarkable feats of memory and penmanship exhibited in another school, with a view to vindicate the Africans from the oft-repeated charge of want of mental capacity:—"One little school-boy repeated 136 hymns and 3 chapters from the Bible, comprising 66 verses, almost without a mistake or hesitation. A little girl recited, with equal facility and correctness, 49 hymns and 8 chapters, containing 240 verses. At the same examination two negro boys exhibited beautiful specimens of penmanship, and maps of their own construction." The teachers of the two schools last mentioned had both been slaves, and had raised themselves to the honourable position which they occupied as instructors of others, chiefly by their own persevering exertions, aided by the kind attentions of their friends the missionaries. Verily the sable sons of Ham are men of like powers and passions with ourselves.

"Is he not man, by sin and suffering tried?
Is he not man, for whom the Saviour died?
Belie the negro's powers:—in headlong will,
Christian! *thy* brother thou shalt prove him still."

III. PROVIDENTIAL OPENINGS.

71. Providence of God.—From the beginning to the end of the Sacred Scriptures, there is no doctrine more clearly stated, or more constantly recognised, than the providence of God over all His works; and certainly next to that of the Atonement itself, there is no doctrine better calculated to afford comfort and encouragement to all who are engaged in the missionary enterprise. The great Jehovah is represented as "King of kings, and Lord of lords," and as ruling, governing, and controlling all things in heaven and on earth by His wisdom and power. The elements of nature are absolutely under His control, and as we say in our infantile prayers, "The darkness goes away, and the daylight comes at His command." The hearts of all men are represented as in His hands, and He can turn them as He pleases, to prepare the way for the promulgation of His truth, or to provide for the defence or the deliverance of His people. It is in this great and glorious truth, in connection with the revelation which God himself has given of His moral character, and of His gracious and merciful purposes in reference to our lost and sinful race, that we find our greatest encouragement to prayer, and our most sure ground for hope of success in the work of the Lord in all its departments.

When about to engage in an important and hazardous foreign mission in the year 1830, we were favoured to hear a most excellent sermon by the great and good Richard Watson, relating chiefly to the providence of God, which left an impression never to be obliterated. His subject was Ezekiel's vision, and the substance of the discourse was afterwards published in his works (vol. iv. p. 256). When expatiating on the "wheel" which Ezekiel saw, and the "eyes in the wheel," the remarks and appeals of the preacher were most pointed and touching. His representation of the ceaseless and watchful care of their heavenly Father over His children by night and by day, when exposed to danger by sea and by land, in sickness and in health, in life and in death, were often recalled afterwards in foreign lands, with much consolation in seasons of peculiar trial and difficulty; and we were enabled to exclaim with David, "This God is our God, for ever and ever; He will be our guide even unto death."

Nor is the doctrine of Divine Providence less encouraging when viewed in connection with the means which He employs to open the way for the introduction of the gospel into regions previously closed against the light of divine truth. In the past history of the Christian

Church we have many remarkable instances of divine interposition for the advancement of the cause and kingdom of the Redeemer. Often has the Almighty made the wrath of man to praise Him, and the remainder of wrath has He restrained.

72. Openings in Sundry Places.—From the very commencement of the missionary enterprise, the hand of Divine Providence has been clearly seen in the raising up of suitable agents for the work as occasion required, and in so controlling the hearts of men, and overruling passing events, that the way has been opened for the introduction of the gospel among nations and tribes of people who had long been sitting in darkness and in the shadow of death. We trace it in the days of the Apostles, in the time of Reformation in Europe, and especially during the great religious movement in which the Wesleys, Whitefield, and others, took such a prominent part. Nor is the finger of God less clearly discernible in more recent events which have transpired in various parts of the mission-field. Time was when the friends of the enterprise were most anxious for the opening up of fields of labour; and in some instances, after missionary societies had been organised, their agents waited for years before they could commence their operations, in consequence of the difficulties which beset their path. But of late years, in answer to the united fervent prayers of the people of God, obstacles have been removed, and countries previously closed against the truth have been thrown open, with a rapidity and in a manner truly wonderful, and we are constrained to exclaim, "It is the Lord's doing, and it is marvellous in our eyes." In this circumstance we have great encouragement for continued prayer and earnest effort, that the men and means may be provided for entering the openings which, in the providence of God, present themselves on every hand. Having often said, "Thy kingdom come, Thy will be done on earth, as it is in heaven," and prayed that doors of usefulness might be opened before the servants of the Lord, we are pledged to follow up the work with corresponding efforts, that His way may be made known upon earth, His saving health among all nations.

73. In Europe.—From the exclusive and despotic character of Popery, and the prevalence of infidelity on the continent of Europe, the work of evangelisation appeared to be almost a hopeless task a few years ago. Every effort to circulate the Scriptures, and to diffuse among the people a saving knowledge of the truth, was jealously watched and vigorously opposed, both by priests and people. But in the order of Divine Providence a wonderful change has recently taken place in this respect. Various disturbing forces have been at work, and the social and political systems of several kingdoms on the Continent have been upheaved and shaken to their very centre. Wars and rumours of wars have done their deadly work; but, in the midst of all, there has been a guiding and controlling power, directing the course of events in a manner which was little expected by the principal actors in the bloody scenes which have been witnessed. The tendency of every change has been in the direction of civil and religious liberty. In almost every part of the European continent the way is now open for the promulgation of the gospel, to an extent which was never known before. This is especially the case in France, Spain, Portugal, and Italy. Not only have civil and political difficulties, which had for ages impeded the progress of the truth, been removed, but the minds of the people have been graciously prepared, by an unseen but real influence, for its cordial reception. Occasional opposition to evangelistic efforts may still be witnessed; but, as a rule, it emanates, not from Government authorities, as formerly, but from the watchful jealousy of the priesthood, of a system which is evidently becoming weaker and weaker at its centre, whatever may be the case at the extremities. Happy will it be for the Christian Church if it promptly take advantage of the present favourable openings on the Continent, and go up at once and possess the good land in the name of the Redeemer.

74. In Rome.—Never was the hand of God more clearly seen in the history of the Church or of the world, than in the course of events which have led to the opening of Rome to the reception of the gospel. After ages of determined and despotic exclusivism, by means and in a manner entirely unexpected, and which no mortal man would have ventured to predict, the temporal power of the Pope has been destroyed; his Holiness and his conclave have had quarters assigned to them in the neighbourhood of the Vatican, while the "Eternal City" has been claimed and taken by Victor Emanuel as the capital of Italy, amid the enthusiastic plaudits of the entire nation. The result of this was the extension of the religious liberty, which had for some time existed in other parts of Italy, to Rome also, and the opening of the city to the free proclamation of the gospel of Christ. Promptly and energetically did various agents of the Christian Church step in and avail themselves of the glorious privilege. In the course of a few months places of religious worship were opened in connection with the Wesleyan and Baptist Missionary Societies, as well as those of the Waldensian and other Churches, and Christian people may now worship God according to the dictates of their own conscience, none daring to make them afraid.

75. In Turkey.—As a system of religion, Mohammedanism is noted for its exclusivism; and within the memory of living men, Turkey, which is its home and headquarters, was most intolerant of any other form of faith. So zealously did the followers of the false prophet guard against any attempts at proselytism, that they would not allow a "Christian dog," as a European or American was called, to enter their principal mosques on any account whatever. All efforts at evangelisation were strictly prohibited; and, if by any means a Turk was induced to abandon Islamism for the faith of the gospel, he was not only regarded as an outcast, but he was actually in danger of losing his life. All this is changed now. For several years past, and especially since, in her feebleness and trouble, Turkey stood in need of the aid of England and other European powers for the maintenance of her very existence as a nation, more liberal ideas have prevailed among the people. Intercourse with Christian countries has been more free and untrammelled; the arts and sciences have been more generally cultivated; and if persecuting laws have not been entirely abrogated, they have certainly not been enforced as formerly. Consequently, Christian missionaries, especially those of the Presbyterian Churches of Scotland and America, have entered the country in considerable numbers, and by the preaching of the gospel, the establishment of schools, and the circulation of the Scriptures in the vernacular language of the people, they are doing much to dispel the spiritual darkness in which the deluded natives have been so long involved. Some fruit has already been realised among the bigoted Mohammedans themselves, at Constantinople and other places, and a work of great interest has commenced, and is going on among nominal Christians, professed members of the corrupt and decayed Greek and Armenian Churches, in various parts of the Turkish Empire.

76. The Village of Hazark.—

There is a village on a mountain-top near the Euphrates called Hazark, about twelve miles from Erzingan, which has been often heard of, but never visited till lately, when the Rev. Mr Pierce and Miss Patrick of the Eastern Turkey Mission found their way to it, and met with a most cordial reception from a people who had become acquainted with the good news of salvation in a very remarkable manner. Adverting to this circumstance, Mr P. says:—"You will be interested to know how the truth first found its way into that mountain village. I will tell the story as I heard it from the lips of an old man, in whom we became much interested, and who may be regarded as the first preacher of the gospel in that region. Twenty-five years ago he was learning a trade somewhere near Broosa, and accidentally got hold of a Turkish New Testament, which he read secretly for a long time. After a while he returned to his native village, and began to preach the truth as he understood it. Then several others, who were trading in different parts of Western Turkey, also became partially persuaded. Finally three young men were received into one of the Protestant churches near Broosa, and on their return to their village five families separated from the old church, and formed themselves into a Protestant community. No missionary teacher or preacher had ever visited them, but they had the Bible and hymn-book, and the Holy Spirit was their teacher."

Speaking of the journey to Hazark, Mr P. says:—"Our road lay along the valley of the Euphrates, or rather wound up and down its steep, sandy banks. A timid, nervous woman would hardly enjoy a path six inches wide, thirty or forty feet above a swift-running river, knowing that the slightest accident would be likely to send horse and rider sliding into its muddy waters; but Miss P. is not one of the kind to be easily frightened, and if you were to ask her, I think she would say she positively enjoyed that ride. We were now only one hour from the village, but to reach it we must climb. We were fortunate in having a native for a guide, for no one but a native would suspect the existence of a path or a village in such a place. After a continued series of windings and climbing we reached the top, and there, literally upon the mountain-top, was the village of Hazark. We were met by a crowd of men, women, and children, each one anxious to welcome and do us honour. We were soon located in a house belonging to the brethren; then followed a series of salutations and welcomes. As we were the first foreigners that had ever visited their village, every one was curious to get a look at us, and all wished to do us some little favour. On Sabbath morning, before we had time to take breakfast, a congregation of more than sixty gathered in our room, and we spent an hour in preaching to the most attentive audience I ever saw in Turkey. Similar services followed each other in rapid succession, Miss Patrick meantime holding several meetings with the women, so that altogether we had no less than *seven* preaching services with these villagers in one day, and their singing was lively, earnest, and hearty.

77. In America.—The simple story of the introduction of Methodism into America, however often told, will never lose its interest. This event, so important in its consequences to the entire continent, was not brought about by a grand array of ecclesiastical arrangements, but by the providential arrival in New York, in 1760, of a few humble emigrants from Ireland, some of whom had been brought to a saving knowledge of the truth, through the instrumentality of Wesley and his preachers, before leaving home. The most distinguished of these were Philip Embury and Barbara Heck, who were honoured to be the chief agents in the good work at its commencement. Some time after the arrival of the party alluded to, it would appear that several of them had suffered declension in their religious experience, and that some of them even had fallen away so far as to give themselves up to worldly amusements. It is said that, one evening in the autumn of 1776, Mrs Heck entered the house of one of them, where she found a party playing cards. Burning with indignation at their sin and folly, the good woman seized the cards and threw them into the fire, and at the same time administered a scathing rebuke to all concerned. She then went to the residence of Mr Embury, and told him what she had done, adding, with great earnestness, "Philip, you must preach to us, or we shall all go to hell, and God will require our blood at your hands." The backsliding professor, who had formerly officiated as a local preacher in his own country, was somewhat confused by this startling appeal, and he endeavoured to excuse himself by saying, "How can I preach, when I have neither a house to preach in, nor a congregation to preach to?" "Preach," said this noble, earnest Christian woman, "in your own house and to your own company;" and before she left she elicited a promise from Mr Embury that he would endeavour once more to speak to the people in the name of the Lord.

A few days afterwards Mr Embury redeemed his pledge by preaching the first Methodist sermon ever delivered in America, in his own hired house, to a congregation of *five* persons. The number attending the services rapidly increased, so that there was not room to accommodate them. This led to the erection of a place of worship, and to the sending out by Mr Wesley, in 1769, of two missionaries, the Revs. Joseph Pilmoor and Richard Boardman, the preachers at the Conference in Leeds, at which they received their appointment, generously contributing the sum of £50 to help on the good work. In this humble manner was the foundation of Methodism laid in America, and the way prepared for the organisation of a Christian Church which was destined, in the order of Divine Providence, to become the largest and most influential religious body in the Western World, and which is already spreading its branches to the ends of the earth, numbering millions of persons, of all classes, among its adherents.

"See how great a flame aspires,
 Kindled by a spark of grace!
Jesu's love the nations fires,
 Sets the kingdoms on a blaze."

"Saw ye not the cloud arise,
Little as a human hand?
Now it spreads along the skies
Hangs o'er all the thirsty land."

78. In the West Indies.—Few incidents in the history of missions more clearly show the special interposition of Divine Providence than those connected with the introduction of the gospel among the degraded inhabitants of the West Indies. In 1758 Nathaniel Gilbert, Esq., a respectable lawyer, and Speaker in the House of Assembly in Antigua, when on a visit to England, heard Mr Wesley preach, and was brought to a saving knowledge of the truth. On returning to the West Indies, he at once made known to his friends what a treasure he had found; and, pitying the destitute condition of the poor negroes, he began to hold meetings especially for their benefit. His labours, in connection with those of his devoted wife and family, were greatly owned and blessed of God, and he was favoured to see multitudes of his sable hearers, with a few whites, reclaimed from the error of their ways, and united in religious societies, after the manner of the Methodists in England. When Mr Gilbert was called to his heavenly rest, there was no one in Antigua to take his place as instructor and friend of the poor slaves; but, in 1778, additional shipwrights being required in H.M. dockyard at St John's, Providence opened the way for the appointment of Mr John Baxter, a Wesleyan local preacher at Chatham, to go out to Antigua. There he found a sphere of spiritual usefulness which he had not anticipated, but on which he entered with a ready mind, whilst, at the same time, he laboured diligently in his worldly calling.

Mr Baxter had established religious services in different parts of the island, erected a chapel in St John's, and was beginning to feel that the work was expanding beyond his ability to do it justice, when God in His providence arranged for its support and extension in a very remarkable manner. Dr Coke, the father and founder of Methodist missions, embarked for the American continent with three missionaries, intended for Nova Scotia, in the autumn of 1786. The voyage was the most stormy and uncomfortable that the doctor ever experienced, although he crossed the Atlantic eighteen times in the prosecution of his holy calling. When they had been to sea several weeks, the ship sprung a leak, and the captain was reluctantly obliged to alter her course, and steer for the West Indies, having no hope of reaching his original destination. After being tossed about for three months, the shattered bark, with the weather-beaten missionaries, put into the harbour of St John's, Antigua, early on the morning of Christmas Day. Dr Coke and his party immediately went on shore, intending to inquire for Mr Baxter, with whose name and character they were well acquainted. As they walked along the street, however, they met the good man himself, on his way to the chapel, to hold early morning service. The feelings produced in the minds of all concerned by this unexpected meeting may be more easily imagined than described. They all proceeded to the sanctuary to return thanks to Almighty God for having delivered His servants from the dangers of the deep, and for bringing them in safety to a land where their labours were so much required. Dr Coke immediately ascended the pulpit, and preached with his wonted zeal and energy to a large and attentive congregation.

The hand of God was so manifest in this event, that the zealous doctor concluded at once that it was his duty to enter the field of labour which was opening out before him in such a remarkable manner. He therefore set out on a tour of observation among the islands, stationed his missionaries where they were most required, returned to England by way of America with all speed, sent out more men, from time to time, according to circumstances; and thus a work was commenced and carried on throughout the length and breadth of the West Indies which, for prosperity and success, and its results in the conversion of tens of thousands to the faith of the gospel, has scarcely a parallel in the history of the Church since the days of the Apostles.

79. In Mexico.

The introduction into Roman Catholic countries of the pure gospel of Christ, as believed and taught by Protestant Christians, has ever been regarded as a difficult if not a hopeless task. But nothing is too hard for God to accomplish. Of late years some remarkable instances have occurred in which Divine Providence has prepared the way before His servants in countries that were considered entirely closed against evangelical truth. One of these is Mexico, where, after a series of struggles between contending parties, involving the principles of civil and religious liberty, a wonderful religious movement has commenced which bids fair to change the moral aspect of the whole empire. Copies of the Scriptures in Spanish had at different times been circulated by agents of the American and British and Foreign Bible Societies, which no doubt led the way to that decided action which was at length taken for the diffusion of the gospel; but the work was accelerated by the zealous efforts of Christian ladies and gentlemen, chiefly from the United States of America, who engaged in the work of education and religious instruction generally. There were also found within the dominant and corrupt Romish Church of Mexico, parties who were prepared, by the secret workings of Providence and grace, to throw off the shackles with which they had so long been bound.

In 1869 a Roman Catholic presbyter, named Aguilar, was induced, through the study of the Word of God, to abandon the Church of Rome, and to protest against the evils of the superstitious system of religion in which he had been trained. Having been brought to a saving knowledge of the truth himself, Aguilar proceeded to proclaim the good news of salvation to his fellow-countrymen; and, in the face of much opposition, he succeeded in establishing an evangelical congregation in the city. He died in extreme poverty, but bravely struggled on behalf of the gospel. The good seed sown by him and others has sprung up with a rapidity unequalled in the history of Christian work in Spanish America, there being now over fifty evangelical congregations in the city and neighbourhood. Several dilapidated Roman Catholic churches have been purchased and fitted up as Protestant places of worship, chiefly by the benevolent aid of Christian friends in America. The blessing of God has accompanied the faithful preaching of the Word, and multitudes have been gathered into the fold of the Redeemer.

For some time an attempt was made to avoid anything like denominational distinctions in the prosecution of Christian work in Mexico, and the congregations collected, and the societies formed, were all described as belonging to the

"Church of Jesus." But the success of this attempt was but very partial. It soon became evident that the wide field which Providence was opening up for the spread of the gospel in various parts of the empire would call forth all the efforts which the leading missionary societies of Christendom could put forth to supply the growing demand for religious instruction. Nor has there appeared any lack of disposition, on the part of those most immediately concerned, to engage in the work. Already promising missions have been established by the Presbyterians, Methodists, and other religious bodies; and it is hoped that ere long, by the blessing of God on their labours, the whole country will be permeated with the leaven of genuine Christianity.

80. **A Wonderful Change.**—The Missionary Society of the Methodist Episcopal Church of the United States of America entrusted the commencement of a new mission in Mexico to the superintendence of the Rev. Dr Butler, a gentleman who was well qualified for the enterprise, by his large experience in India, as well as by his learning, piety, and zeal. On reaching the scene of his labours, he set about his work with an earnestness which gave good hope of success. In the first place, he obtained the use of some convent buildings, which were soon fitted up for divine worship and general missionary purposes. Mrs Butler, writing under date of March 25th, 1873, gives the following account of the establishment and the commencement of the mission:—
"It was finished last week, and opened on Sabbath. We had a high day. The little church is narrow, long, and lofty, the windows also being small, and up near the roof. The roof has three domes, and from the centre of each depends a light. The altar is carpeted with crimson, and the pulpit-table, &c., draped with crimson cloth. On Sunday morning we had Spanish Sabbath-school at 10 o'clock, and Spanish preaching at 11. At 3 P.M. we had English preaching, and Sabbath-school after. The congregations were very large,—the largest Protestant congregation ever assembling in Mexico being ours that Sunday. My daughter on the harmonium, assisted by our young friends, led the singing, in which we all most heartily joined, making those old domes and arches ring with

"All hail the power of Jesus' name," &c.,

We had Spanish preaching again in the evening. These are some of the joys of missionary life, and God gives us even more, as the work is opening well. We had a class-meeting of twenty-five last week, and openings are occurring in various places."

Mrs Butler then adverts to the doctor's visit to "Puebla los Angelos (the City of Angels), to look after the deeds of a property he has purchased there for the mission. It is part of the convent of San Domingo, and was the headquarters of the Inquisition. When the Inquisition was abolished, an old gentleman purchased the property for a trifle. From him we buy. He has shown Dr B. the cells where the victims of the Inquisition were immured, and he has stood in them. Some of them were about six feet high, and three wide, having a little hole where the martyr might put his hand out for food. Others had a contrivance for causing a drop of water to trickle on the head until the brain became diseased, and so on. These cells were discovered in the wall when this gentleman wanted to make some alterations. They were filled with the remains of those who perished under the tender mercies of the Inquisitors, and we have some of their skulls. One of them is near me now. How little these demons imagined that a Methodist preacher would come here and find out these iniquities, and establish the preaching of a pure gospel in the very halls they polluted by their presence!" Verily the hand of God is opening the way, and is leading His servants forward into the high places of the mission-field, which were in former times considered effectually closed against the light of the gospel.

81. In Africa.—At the close of the American War of Independence, a considerable number of free blacks were taken to the British colony of Nova Scotia, and located at a place called Cape Negro, where they received considerable attention from the Wesleyan missionaries. Nor were their labours in vain in the Lord. Several were brought to God, and united in Christian fellowship at an early period. In the success of this unique settlement Wesley himself showed great interest. In a letter to Mr R. Barry, dated London, January 11th, 1790, he says:—"As a town of negroes in America is almost without a precedent, I was struck to hear of a society there. It is worthy of your particular care and attention. I am glad our preachers visit them regularly." The founder of Methodism little thought in this free negro settlement the pioneers of the work in Africa were being prepared by Divine Providence; but so it was. The cold regions of British America proving unsuitable for these liberated slaves, most of them were ultimately taken to Sierra Leone on the western coast of Africa, where a new settlement was being formed. These sable children of Ham, several of whom had been torn from their native homes many years before, carried back with them to their fatherland a knowledge of the true God, and of Jesus Christ His Son, whom they were not ashamed to acknowledge in the sight of the heathen. They erected a place of worship in Freetown, and one or two of the most intelligent of them ministered to the rest as local preachers and exhorters. As the work expanded, they wrote to Dr Coke, requesting that a missionary might be sent from England; and when the Rev. George Warren arrived in Sierra Leone in 1811, as the first Wesleyan missionary to Africa, he found about one hundred of them who were in the habit of meeting together for public worship and mutual edification, a fair proportion of whom were living in the enjoyment of true religion. Thus was the way prepared for that great and glorious work which afterwards took place among the liberated slaves and others on the western coast, where the Wesleyan Missionary Society alone now numbers upwards of eight thousand converts, to say nothing of the multitudes who have passed away to the better country from the respective stations, since the work was first commenced.

82. The Unexpected Meeting.—When the Rev. Barnabas Shaw, the founder of Wesleyan missions in Southern Africa, arrived at the Cape of Good Hope, he found strong prejudices still existing in the minds of Government officials, and the colonists generally, against missionary operations. In Capetown and neighbourhood there were thousands of slaves, both pagans and Mohammedans, who stood in great need of religious instruction; but their owners seemed to prefer their remaining in ignorance, and did all in their power to prevent the missionary from getting access to them. Annoyed with the impediments which were thus thrown in the way of his usefulness at the Cape, Mr Shaw longed for an opportunity to preach the gospel to the dark, benighted heathen in the far-distant interior. At length the way opened. He purchased a travelling waggon, a span of oxen, stores, and everything necessary for the journey; and with his devoted wife, and a missionary and his party belonging to the London Society, he set out for Namaqualand.

When the devoted missionary had pursued his toilsome journey for about a month, a remarkable incident occurred which fixed the scene of his future labours. He had set out with the intention of entering the first favourable opening which might present itself, but without any idea as to the locality in which he would settle, trusting that, in answer to prayer, God would direct his steps. After crossing the Elephant River, on the 4th of October 1816, Mr Shaw and his party actually met with the chief of Little Namaqualand, accompanied by four men, on his way to Cape Town to seek for a missionary to instruct him and his people, being aware of the advantages which other tribes had realised by the reception of the gospel. Both parties, struck with the coincidence, for they might easily have passed each other, encamped for the night, and spent the evening around the camp-fire in conversation, prayer, and praise. The result was that Mr Shaw became so deeply affected with the story of the Namaqua chief, and his earnest plea for a teacher, and so thoroughly convinced of the guidance of Divine Providence, that he consented to accompany him to his mountain home at Lilly Fountain on the Khamisberg, which he ultimately reached after travelling about two hundred miles further. There the devoted missionary pitched his tent, built a dwelling-house and chapel, cultivated the ground, and established the first Wesleyan mission-station in Southern Africa. The Lord prospered the efforts of His servants, and that station became the spiritual birthplace of many precious souls, and has continued for more than half a century to be a centre of light and influence and blessing to all around.

83. In Australasia.—A detail of facts and incidents connected with the openings of Divine Providence for the introduction and spread of the gospel in Australia and Polynesia, including the various groups of islands which stud the Southern Pacific Ocean, would fill many pages, and would, at the same time, clearly show the finger of God beckoning forward His servants at every stage of the enterprise. A century or two ago these extensive regions were scarcely known to the civilised world, and as the numerous islands of the South Sea were discovered from time to time, they were found inhabited by races of men so savage, warlike, and cruel, that they became the dread of navigators who had occasion to call for supplies of wood, water, and other necessaries, in the course of their long voyages. At length Christian missionaries reached their shores, whose hearts God himself inspired with courage and fortitude which fitted them for the work they had to do. The wild and savage natives were disposed to look with favour on the white strangers who had come to them without weapons of war, but with books to instruct them, and good news for all men. The Holy Spirit applied the Word to the hearts of the people, and multitudes were savingly converted to God. Many of the native converts learned to read the Scriptures, and soon became, not only the teachers of their fellow-countrymen, but the pioneers of the gospel to other lands. The news spread from island to island that the *lotu*, or Christianity, was coming; and in some instances, as in the Sandwich Islands and others, idolatry was abolished before the arrival of the missionaries on their shores, and the people were waiting to be taught how they must worship the true and living God. Numerous instances occurred in the Friendly and other islands, in which the natives erected Christian sanctuaries long before they could obtain teachers to tell them how they ought to worship in them. Thus was the way opened and prepared, by Him who has the hearts of all men in His hands, for the overthrow of idolatry in the Southern World, and for the general spread of His everlasting gospel among the degraded inhabitants of these distant islands in the Pacific Ocean.

84. The Long-expected Answer.—When the Wesleyan Mission in the Friendly Islands began to extend its influence all around, and the work had become somewhat established in Tonga, it was considered exceedingly desirable to commence a new station in the Haabai group. As the expense involved in this new enterprise would be considerable, the missionaries did not feel at liberty to move forward till they had obtained the sanction of the Committee in London. They therefore sent home a full statement of the case, and anxiously awaited the answer. Month after month passed, but no intelligence came, and the missionaries were perplexed to know what to do, especially as the chief of Haabai earnestly desired a missionary, and had already built a chapel at Lifuka, the capital of the group. At length the question was solved in a manner quite unexpected, but which clearly showed the hand of Divine Providence. A small box or packet was one day washed on shore at Tonga, near to Nukualofa, and was picked up by one of the natives. It was immediately taken to the missionary, the Rev. N. Turner, and on being opened it was found to contain the long-expected answer of the Missionary Committee, giving permission for the commencement of a new station in Haabai. The anxiety of the missionaries was thus relieved, and the work was commenced without delay. The vessel which bore that package containing the precious letter, a schooner from Sydney, had foundered at sea, and all on board were lost. It is said that neither vessel nor crew, nor any of the goods with which she had been freighted, were ever seen or heard of again. The package containing that letter alone, the messenger of mercy to a people waiting for the law of the Lord, guided by Him "whom winds and sea obey," escaped the general wreck, and was cast on shore at the right place, and at the right time, to relieve the minds of the missionaries, and to authorise them to go forward in the name and strength of their Divine Master.

85. Opposition Subdued.—When native teachers first landed on the island of Mangaia, one of the Hervey group, to instruct the people in the knowledge of Christianity, their well-meant offers were not only rejected, but they and their wives were so cruelly treated by the savage natives, that they barely escaped with their lives. Soon after the departure of the teachers,

E

the natives of Mangaia were visited with an epidemical disease which proved exceedingly fatal, the infant and the aged, the chieftain and the peasant, falling alike beneath its deadly influence. Ascribing this calamitous visitation to the vengeance of the "God of the strangers," whose teachers they had rejected and robbed, the natives were greatly alarmed, and proceeded to collect all the property they had taken from them, and cast it into an immense cavern in one of the mountains, making a vow to the "God of the strangers," that if He would suspend the execution of His vengeance, and conduct His worshippers to their island once more, they would treat them kindly, and give them food to eat. At this juncture the plague was stayed, and shortly afterwards their promises were put to the test. Without knowing anything of what had transpired, Davida and Tiere, two unmarried members of the church at Tahaa, offered their services to carry the gospel to the barbarous island of Mangaia. On reaching the place they leaped into the sea and swam to the shore, taking nothing with them but the light dresses which they wore, and a portion of the New Testament in the Tahitian language, which was carefully wrapped up and tied upon their heads. Contrary to expectation, they were kindly received, Divine Providence having prepared the way before them, and the island was soon evangelised.

86. Bereavement overruled for Good.—When the gospel was beginning to take effect in Aitutaki, the old grandfather of the chief Tamatoa continued firm in his determination to adhere to his heathen superstitions. While he was busily engaged in celebrating an idolatrous feast, however, a beloved daughter was taken ill. The priests were immediately on the alert, presenting numerous offerings, and invoking the gods from morning to evening, day after day, in order to induce them to restore the child to health. The disease, however, increased, and the girl died. The chief was so much affected at the death of his daughter, that he determined at once to abandon the gods who were so ungrateful as to requite his zeal with such manifest unkindness, and therefore sent his son next morning to set fire to his marae or heathen temple. Two other maraes near it caught fire also, and were consumed. From thence the son, enraged with the gods for destroying his sister, proceeded to a large marae before which the people were presenting their offerings, and attempted to set it on fire, but was prevented by the worshippers, who seized and dragged him away.

Adverting to this and similar incidents, the devoted John Williams remarks, "By such circumstances does God, in numberless instances, work upon the minds of men, to prepare the way for the reception of His truth." He then proceeds to narrate how in Tahiti also the chiefs and people were induced to abandon idolatry and embrace the gospel, partly in consequence of the death of the beloved and only daughter of Tenania, on whose behalf they had sought aid in vain from their heathen priests, and at length believed that they were being deluded and deceived by their idol-gods, and consequently relinquished them entirely, and destroyed their temples.

87. In India.—A remarkable change has taken place in India during the last half century, with regard to facilities for making known to its teeming millions the "glorious gospel of the blessed God." For many years after the country came under British rule, the religious instruction of the natives by Europeans was proscribed, whilst their idolatrous and superstitious practices were patronised and encouraged. The first Christian missionaries to India were not allowed to go out in the Company's ships, and were glad to avail themselves of the greater liberty afforded by foreign nations, and to sail in their vessels. They were thus obliged, in a certain sense, to smuggle themselves, and that blessed Book which they wished to teach, into the country. All this is changed now. Infanticide, the burning of widows with corpses of their deceased husbands, and the practice of many other cruel heathen rites and ceremonies, have been abolished by the ruling powers; British law has been made more generally to prevail, and every hindrance to the propagation of Christianity has been entirely removed. Christian missionaries can now go wherever they please, and faithfully proclaim to the people the unsearchable riches of Christ. They may be seen and heard, not only in the numerous churches and chapels which have been erected, but also in the lanes, streets, and bazaars of the villages and crowded cities, and even on the steps leading into their splendid idol-temples, no one presuming to interfere with them for thus boldly speaking in the name of their Divine Master. And who dare venture to say that this wonderful change has not been brought about by the special providence of God, in answer to the fervent and faithful prayers of His people? Infidels may laugh, and sceptics may sneer, but the humble disciples of the Lord Jesus will gratefully recognise the hand of God in so controlling and overruling events as to remove obstacles, subdue evil passions, and open the way for the free promulgation of His truth among the populous and idolatrous nations of the East. May the churches of Britain have the zeal, courage, and benevolence to enter the open doors which are presenting themselves in various places, and go up at once and possess the good land in the name and strength of the "King of kings and Lord of lords!"

88. The Garrows of Assam.—Up among the mountains of Assam, in a region where a white man was a wonder, and where a white woman had never been seen, lived a tribe known as the Garrows. For forty years they had remained an unsolved problem to their English rulers. Fond of making raids into the plains, and securing bloody heads as proofs of their bravery, fond of beads and brass ornaments, and of puppies roasted alive, but *not* fond of much clothing; knowing nothing of God, worshipping the stars, the rivers, the spirits of the hills; sacrificing liquor, rice, flowers, white cocks, sometimes beautiful fat bulls, and on very great occasions human beings, but hardly knowing to what they sacrificed them; enjoying no feast so well as one eaten from the skull of an enemy—they were a class of subjects the English Government preferred to ignore, except when they forced themselves upon its consciousness by their plundering raids.

The way was opened for the introduction of the gospel among these wild mountaineers in a very remarkable manner. Two Garrows, Omed and Ramkhe, who had enlisted into the British army as sepoys, were awakened by tracts left at Gowalpara by an English missionary. "Is there no missionary for *my* people?" was the first question asked by Omed after his conversion. There was none. Months passed, and the Garrow converts grew stronger in the faith, and with their increasing knowledge, their love for their countrymen became intensified. At length, in 1864, they were liberated from military service, and went at once as missionaries to their heathen countrymen, the wild Garrows of the hills. "I am glad to see any one who is willing to attempt the reformation of these bloodthirsty savages; I hope you will succeed," said the Lieutenant-Governor of Bengal to one of the missionaries, in a tone indicating the profoundest incredulity. Soon there came an appeal for help from eight Garrows awakened by the preaching of Omed and Ramkhe, the two converted discharged sepoys. This led to the appointment, first of Mr and Mrs Scott, and afterwards of Messrs Bronson, Stodard, and Comfort, and to the commencement of a good work among the Mirkers, as well as the Garrows. At the close of 1869 there were five Garrow churches, with a membership of 176 native converts, as the result of this small beginning.

89. **In China.**—The extensive and populous empire of China had been for ages shut up against the commerce, science, literature, and religious influences of the West, when a circumstance occurred which ultimately led to the opening of the country to foreign intercourse, to an extent which had never been seen before. It became known to the Chinese that the tea-plant, so famous among themselves, was beginning to be appreciated and desired by the inhabitants of Europe, and the civilised world generally. The prospect of gain arising from this and other branches of commerce caused the "Celestials" to relax somewhat the habits of exclusiveness in which they had enshrouded themselves.

Then came the opening of certain ports to foreign ships, the formation of treaties with the governments of Europe and America, the breach of treaties, wars, and tumults, all of which were overruled by Providence for the opening up of China to the influence of Christianity. Since the way has thus been prepared, missions and schools for the religious instruction of the natives have been established by the agents of different societies in various cities and provinces of the empire, and the results already warrant the hope that the faithful preaching of the gospel will ultimately be as successful here as in other lands, notwithstanding the difficulties with which it has had to contend. The evangelisation of China will, moreover, probably be further aided by the extensive emigration of the Chinese which is now going on to other lands, as many of the emigrants will return to their own country with enlightened views on religious matters, which will tend to hasten the spread of Christian truth. In all these things we see the hand of God working for the accomplishment of His own purposes of love and mercy towards our lost and ruined world.

90. **In Japan.**—Until a comparatively recent period the empire of Japan was, if possible, more effectually closed against the entrance of foreigners, and the influence of Christianity, than India and China in former times. The misconduct of certain Romish missionaries, who gained a footing in the country in a clandestine manner, in the early part of the last century, resulted in their expulsion from the empire, and the persecution, even unto death, of many of their deluded followers. Henceforth Christianity was not only interdicted, but foreigners

were prohibited from entering the country for purposes of commerce, or under any pretence whatever. This attitude of exclusiveness was maintained for many years, and every effort made by Europeans and Americans to cultivate commercial intercourse and friendly relations was in vain. At length, however, the Japanese began to take an interest in what was passing in the outer world. The accounts which they heard of railroads, electric telegraphs, and the general progress of science, awakened their curiosity, and ambassadors were sent to inspect and examine the results of modern improvements in different countries. The consequence was that the Mikado, or Emperor of Japan, and his principal courtiers, conceived an earnest desire for the arts, sciences, education and social improvement of the West, concerning which the ambassadors brought such wonderful accounts. The country was forthwith opened to European and American skilled artisans, mechanics, and instructors of various kinds, whose services were in great demand; steamships were purchased, a railroad constructed, telegraphic wires laid, schools and colleges established, and other modern improvements adopted, with a rapidity and on a scale truly surprising. At the same time, Christian missionaries of different societies promptly entered the door which Divine Providence had so mysteriously and unexpectedly opened; and although the persecuting edicts against professing Christians were not immediately abrogated, no serious opposition to the preaching of the gospel was manifested; and, according to the testimony of the Rev. J. Goble, who arrived in Yokohama early in 1873, "evangelical efforts in Japan are now as free and unrestricted as in Great Britain or America."

"Sons of God, your Saviour praise,
　　He the door hath opened wide;
　Jesus gives the word of grace,
　　Jesus' word is glorified."

IV. DANGERS AND DELIVERANCES.

91. The Watchful Care of the Almighty.—The ever-watchful care of Divine Providence over the interests of the Church of Christ is clearly seen, not only in the removal of difficulties, and in opening the way for the spread of the everlasting gospel, but also in the preservation of the agents employed in the work. The Sacred Scriptures abound with precious promises and divine declarations calculated to comfort and encourage the faithful servants of God, when exposed to danger and trial in the prosecution of their important duties. The ninety-first Psalm, especially, is one continued song of triumph and assurance of safety for those who "abide under the shadow of the Almighty." Speaking of the watchful care of the Almighty, David says:—"Surely He shall deliver thee from the snare of the fowler, and from the noisome pestilence. He shall cover thee with His feathers, and under His wings shalt thou trust: His truth shall be thy shield and buckler. Thou shalt not be afraid for the terror by night; nor for the arrow that flieth by day; nor for the pestilence that walketh in darkness; nor for the destruction that wasteth at noonday. A thousand shall fall at thy side, and ten thousand at thy right hand; but it shall not come nigh thee. Only with thine eyes shalt thou behold and see the reward of the wicked. Because thou hast made the Lord, which is my refuge, even the Most High, thy habitation; there shall no evil befall thee, neither shall any plague come nigh thy dwelling. For He shall give His angels charge over thee, to keep thee in all thy ways. They shall bear thee up in their hands, lest thou dash thy foot against a stone. Thou shalt tread upon the lion and adder: the young lion and the dragon shalt thou trample under feet. Because He hath set His love upon me, therefore will I deliver him: I will set him on high, because he hath known my name. He shall call upon me, and I will answer him: I will be with him in trouble; I will deliver him, and honour him. With long life will I satisfy him, and show him my salvation." Again, the Lord says by the prophet Isaiah:—"When thou passest through the waters, I will be with thee; and through the rivers, they shall not overflow thee: when thou walkest through the fire, thou shalt not be burned; neither shall the flame kindle upon thee, for I am the Lord thy God, the Holy One of Israel, thy Saviour." Oh, how often have the Lord's missionary servants proved the truth and the sweetness of His blessed word!

DANGERS AND DELIVERANCES. 71

92. Paul's Shipwreck.—The earliest record which we have in history of the shipwreck of a missionary was that of Paul the great apostle of the Gentiles, which occurred in the Mediterranean Sea, on the coast of Malta, under circumstances peculiarly affecting. He was on his voyage to Rome a prisoner, when the ship in which he sailed was overtaken by one of those dreadful storms or hurricanes which are still common in those parts. The wind blew, the sea roared, and the sky was densely beclouded, so that neither sun nor moon appeared for several days; and to lighten the ship, both cargo and tackling were thrown overboard into the sea. After two weeks of perplexity and distress, the depth of water, as indicated by soundings, having decreased from twenty to fifteen fathoms, the mariners suspected, about midnight, that they were approaching land, but where they knew not. Fearing that the ship might be dashed to pieces upon the rocks, "they cast four anchors out of the stern, and wished for the day." Some of them now formed the plan of escaping on shore in the small boat, and of leaving the rest to their fate; but Paul prevented them by declaring to the centurion that their continuance in the ship was necessary for the safety of the whole party. As the day dawned, the apostle, having had a vision from the Almighty, assured his fellow-voyagers of the safety of all on board, if they would adopt the means which he recommended, and he encouraged them by his exhortation and example to partake of refreshment, and trust in God.

"And when it was day, they knew not the land: but they discovered a certain creek with a shore, into the which they were minded, if it were possible, to thrust in the ship. And when they had taken up the anchors, they committed themselves unto the sea, and loosed the rudder bands, and hoised up the mainsail to the wind, and made toward shore. And falling into a place where two seas met, they ran the ship aground; and the forepart stuck fast, and remained unmoveable, but the hinder part was broken with the violence of the waves. And the soldiers' counsel was to kill the prisoners, lest any of them should swim out, and escape. But the centurion, willing to save Paul, kept them from their purpose, and commanded that they which could swim should cast themselves first into the sea, and get to land; and the rest, some on boards, and some on broken pieces of the ship. And so it came to pass, that they escaped all safe to land" (Acts xxvii. 30–44).

93. Left for Dead.—One of the most violent attacks ever made by the heathen upon Christian missionaries, was that of the people of Lystra and Lyconia, on the occasion of the visit of Paul and Barnabas, to make known to them the good news of salvation. When the apostles, in the course of their first great missionary journey through Syria and Asia Minor, came to Lystra, the people for a time almost idolised them. Having witnessed a miracle wrought by Paul, restoring to perfect health a cripple who had never walked before, they thought the gods had come down in the likeness of men. They called Barnabas Jupiter, and Paul Mercurius, because he was the chief speaker. Then the priests of Jupiter brought oxen and garlands into the gates of the city, and would have done sacrifice with the people. But the apostles wished not for divine honours, but to win souls for Christ, and rushing into the crowd, they exclaimed, "Why do ye these things? we also are men of like passions with you, and preach unto you that you should turn from these vanities unto the living God, which made heaven and earth, and the sea, and all things that are therein," and with many other words scarcely restrained they the people from sacrificing unto them. Yet, strange as it may appear, the very men who would have thus idolised the apostles, were soon stirred up by certain wicked Jews, who came from Antioch, to deeds of cruelty and blood; for having stoned Paul, they drew him out of the city, supposing that he had been dead. But whilst the disciples stood around him, bemoaning with tears his unhappy fate, he was inspired, as if by a miracle, with new life and vigour; and, to the surprise of every one, "he rose up and came into the city." The next day Paul and Barnabas, not wishing to provoke further opposition, took their departure for other scenes of missionary labour (Acts xiv. 20).

94. Peter's Escape from Prison.

—It was a miraculous interposition of Divine Providence by which the Apostle Peter was delivered from prison just before his intended execution. He was guarded by four quaternions of Roman soldiers; and, to make his imprisonment still more secure, he was required to sleep between two of them, to whom he was bound with chains. But what is the use of such precautions, when opposed to Omnipotence, moved by the power of prayer? While Peter was sleeping in prison, prayer was made for him without ceasing by the members of the Church, and in answer to their supplications, God sent a messenger to deliver him. "Behold, the angel of the Lord came upon him, and a light shined in the prison: and he smote Peter on the side, and raised him up, saying, Arise up quickly. And his chains fell off from his hands. And the angel said unto him, Gird thyself, and bind on thy sandals. And so he did. And he saith unto him, Cast thy garment about thee, and follow me. And he went out, and followed him; and wist not that it was true which was done by the angel; but thought he saw a vision. When they were past the first and the second ward, they came unto the iron gate that leadeth into the city; which opened to them of its own accord, and they went out, and passed on through one street; and forthwith the angel departed from him. And when Peter was come to himself, he said, Now I know of a surety, that the Lord hath sent His angel, and hath delivered me out of the hand of Herod, and from all the expectation of the people of the Jews. And when he had considered the thing, he came to the house of Mary, the mother of John, whose surname was Mark; where many were gathered together praying" (Acts xii. 7-12).

95. Wesley's Rescue from Fire.

—John Wesley was born at Epworth, in Lincolnshire, on the 14th of June 1703. When he was about six years of age, he had an almost miraculous escape from death. One night it was discovered that the parsonage was on fire; and when the rest of the family had fled for their lives from the flaming mansion, they were distressed to find that little John was missing, he being asleep in one of the chambers to which all access was now cut off by the rapid spread of the flames. In this terrible emergency he awoke, and fled to the window, where his appearance excited the strongest sympathy in the hearts of the gazing multitude. What can be done to save the darling little boy? There is no time to procure ladders, so one man stands under the window on the ground, another mounts up on his shoulders, the child drops into his arms, and he is safe! Just then the roof of the burning house fell in, so that had his deliverance been delayed a few minutes, he must have perished in the flames. Thus did a kind and gracious Providence watch over and preserve one who was destined to be an instrument of good to tens of thousands both at home and abroad. The father, witnessing this singular instance of divine compassion, and finding himself at length surrounded with his wife and children, called upon all present to kneel down and unite with him in sincere thanksgiving to Almighty God. "Let the house go," said he, "I am rich enough," alluding to the deliverance and safety of all his family.

96. Remarkable Deliverance.

—The Rev. Richard Boardman, one of the first missionaries sent to America by Mr Wesley, was heard to relate the following instance of a remarkable deliverance from danger which he experienced on one occasion, some time before he left his native land. It was written down in the words of the speaker by Mr Owen Davies, who thought it worthy of being preserved as illustrative of the special providence of God. "I preached," said Mr Boardman, "one evening at Mould in Flintshire, and next morning set out for Park Gate. After riding some miles, I asked a man if I was on my road to that place. He answered, 'Yes; but you will have some sands to go over; and unless you ride very fast, you will be in danger of being enclosed by the tide.' It then began to snow to such a degree that I could scarcely see a step of the way; and my mare being with foal, prevented me from riding so fast as I otherwise should have done. I got to the sands, and pursued my way over them for some time; but the tide then came in, and surrounded me on every side, so that I could neither proceed nor turn back, and to ascend the perpendicular cliffs was impossible. In this situation I commended my soul to God, not having the least expectation of escaping death. In a little time I perceived two men running down a hill on the other side of the water; and by some means they got a boat, and came to my relief just as the sea had reached my knees as I sat upon the mare. They took me into the boat, the mare swimming by our side, till we reached the land. While we were in the boat, one of them cried out, 'Surely, sir, God is with you!' I answered, 'I trust He is.' The man replied, 'I know He is;' and then related the following circumstance. 'Last night I dreamed that I must go to the top of such a hill. When I awoke, the dream made so deep an impression upon me that I could not rest. I went and called upon this my friend, and desired him to accompany me. When we came to the place, we saw nothing more than usual. However, I begged him to go with me to another hill at a short distance, and then we saw your distressing situation.'

"When we got on shore, I went with my two friends to a public-house not far from the place where we landed, and as we were relating this wonderful providence, the landlady said, 'This day month we saw a gentleman in your situation; but before we could hasten to his relief, he plunged into the sea, supposing (as we conjectured) that his horse would swim with him to the shore; but they both sunk, and were drowned together.' I gave my deliverers all the money I had, which, I think, was about eighteen-pence, and tarried all night at the public-house. Next morning I was not a little embarrassed how to pay my reckoning. I therefore apologised to my landlord for the want of cash, and begged that he would keep a pair of silver spurs till I should send to redeem them. But he answered, 'The Lord bless you, sir, I would not take a farthing of you for the world.' After some serious conversation with the friendly people of the house, I bade them farewell, and recommenced my journey, rejoicing in the Lord, and praising Him for His great salvation." Thus was the life of this good man providentially preserved for future usefulness in the missionfield.

97. Shipwreck and Robbers.—When the Rev. William Jenkin was proceeding to the West Indies as a missionary, in 1799, he was both shipwrecked and robbed on the coast of Ireland. On reaching his station at St Kitt's, on the 2d of March, he gave the following account of his disasters in his first letter to England :—"I am at length, by the blessing of God, arrived at the place of my destination, after enduring some considerable hardships. We embarked on board a ship at Bristol, and put to sea. But after five days beating to windward, we were obliged to bear up again for Bristol, where we waited for some time longer for a fair wind. We made two attempts more without success. But trying a fourth time, and getting some distance from Bristol, a heavy gale of wind came on, which split our foretopsail, and obliged us to put into Milford Haven. Having repaired our damages, we set sail again, with the intention of going to Cork, and joining the West India fleet. But a terrible storm overtook us on the Irish coast, which carried away our foretop-mast, broke our rigging, and rent most of the sails in pieces; in consequence of which we were driven on shore at a place called Old Head of Kinsale. The ship bilged and filled with water almost as soon as she touched the ground. One sea struck in the cabin dead-lights, while the succeeding tremendous waves beat on us with such violence that we expected the vessel would quickly fall to pieces. When the ship first struck, I betook myself to the shrouds; but, apprehending that the mast would soon give way, I came down, and resolved to take my station on the deck with the rest, and wait the event. Our sufferings were very great for the space of four hours, while the sea made a constant way over us, and threatened to wash us off the wreck. The upper works of the ship gave way, and piece after piece was washed into the sea. In this extremity the cold seized upon our limbs, and I found myself exceedingly stiff; but on rubbing and beating myself as much as possible, I found much benefit, and immediately called out to the rest of the men to do the same. They followed my example, which, I believe, was a great means of saving our lives.

"When the water ebbed, the vessel was left almost dry, and so we escaped to land. By this time a great number of robbers were assembled on the shore, and attempted to board the vessel. Having observed that the captain had secured some silver spoons in his pocket, they endeavoured to cut off the skirt of his coat, in order to obtain the property, but were prevented. But when we got to our quarters, they plundered us of every article we had carried on shore with us. I was apprehensive that the robbers would have murdered us, but providentially a party of soldiers came to our assistance; they fired upon the plunderers, and killed four of them, which intimidated the rest, and they dispersed. Next day we set off for Kinsale, where we found a small society, who gave us every help in their power, and assisted us to travel to Cork, where we were supplied with everything necessary for our voyage. There we embarked again, in a vessel called the *Mary*, for the West Indies, and arrived in safety, by the good providence of God."

98. Danger from Fire.—Writing from the capital of Turkey in 1872, the Rev. H. O. Dwight, an American missionary, says:—" We have again occasion to record our gratitude to God for His care over us. This time we have been saved from *fire*, the scourge of Constantinople. Our house stands on the crest of a hill looking off upon the Bosphorus. The fire commenced upon the shore in front of us, and, driven by a tremendous north wind, swept up the valley, entirely destroying the Jewish quarter of Kouzkoun-juk, and then taking the Armenian and Greek houses along the road leading into the valley, until it had carried every house as far as to our street. Then the wind veered a little, and kept the flames from touching our block, and the fire soon died out on reaching the wide open ground between us and Mr Hitchcock's quarter. But for four hours or more the heavy gale of wind kept our house in the midst of a storm of firebrands, whirling, eddying, and drifting up in heaps, like the snow in one of your New England storms; and it was only the most constant labour upon the roof with water and wetted carpets, and upon the front with a small fire-engine, which kept our house from going long before the flames had reached our vicinity. Once it did take fire, but water soon quenched it. Friends kindly came to our aid; and when it seemed as if our house must go, we were able to get everything out into the garden, where we made a great pile of furniture and household goods, covered with wet carpets; but when the danger was passed, we returned to our humble abode, thankful to God for a shelter whilst thousands were homeless and destitute."

99. John Wesley Overboard.—On one occasion during his sojourn in America, Mr Wesley had a narrow escape from drowning, concerning which he makes the following entry in his journal, under date of April 4th, 1736:—" About four in the afternoon I set out for Frederica in a flat-bottomed barge. The next evening we anchored near Skidoway Island, where the water at flood was twelve or fourteen feet deep. I wrapped myself up from head to foot in a large cloak, to keep me from sand-flies, and lay down on the quarterdeck. Between one and two I awoke under water, being so fast asleep that I did not know where I was until my mouth was full of it. Having left my cloak, I know not how, upon the deck, I swam round to the other side of the barge, where a boat was tied, and climbed up by a rope, without any more harm than wetting my clothes." And then he piously ejaculates, " Thou art the God of whom cometh salvation: Thou art the Lord by whom we escape death!" The troubles and discomforts of this journey did not end here. During the whole of the following week the frail bark was tossed about with contrary winds, and she was at one time exposed to considerable danger by a fearful thunderstorm, attended by loud thunder and vivid lightning; but in the midst of all, the faithful servant of God was preserved by His special providence, and on reaching Frederica, he preached with his wonted zeal and earnestness.

> "I would the precious time redeem,
> And longer live for this alone,
> To spend and to be spent for them
> Who have not yet my Saviour known;
> Fully on these my mission prove,
> And only breathe to breathe Thy love."

100. Shipwrecked among the Ice.—On their voyage homeward to Copenhagen in 1804, after a missionary service of twenty-six years in Greenland, the Rev. C. Rudolph and his wife experienced a merciful deliverance from a watery grave and from starvation among the ice. After being at sea about three days, a hurricane drove mountains of ice to the immediate vicinity of the vessel in which they sailed. The ship struck against the ice, filled with water, and in a few minutes only the larboard gunwale rose above the waves. The captain and crew took to their boats, and carried off several companies to the floating field of ice. The missionary and his wife were the last who were removed, and by that time the water was up to their knees, and fast gaining upon them. They steered for the nearest island, but it turned out a rough and naked rock. The provisions which they had endeavoured to save from the wreck were swept away by the rolling sea. Rain fell during the night, and turned the miserable resting-place into a pool of water. After waiting for two days, the captain and part of the crew endeavoured to leap from one mass of ice to another till they gained the shore. Mr and Mrs Rudolph were so enfeebled by want of food and exposure to the cold, that they could not risk such an experiment, and therefore remained on the rock. The captain and crew promised, that if they succeeded in reaching the shore, they would immediately send a boat for their deliverance. On the ninth day they were still unrelieved, and with no support but the small pools of fresh water which they found in the chinks of the rock.

Painful and perilous as was the situation of the shipwrecked missionary and his wife, they maintained their confidence in God, and with failing strength and feeble voice sang hymns in anticipation of an immediate removal to the world of spirits. Towards evening on the ninth day Mrs Rudolph saw and hailed two Greenlanders in their kajaks or canoes, who had been searching for them during the entire day, and were just about returning home, under the conviction that they must have perished. Thus providentially were the missionary and his wife delivered from their perilous position, when reduced to the last extremity. Most of the rest were also saved, for it is a remarkable fact that only one man perished by this shipwreck. Mr and Mrs Rudolph passed the winter at Lichtenau, and returned to Europe the following year.

101. Danger from the Snow.— The missionaries in North America have often been exposed to danger from the intensity of the cold, and the prevalence in the winter season of dreadful snow-storms, whilst prosecuting their extensive journeys to preach the gospel among a scattered and spiritually destitute population. On one occasion the Rev. James Mann was travelling on foot from Port-Mutton to Liverpool, Nova Scotia, a distance of about ten or twelve miles, when he found the snow so deep on the ground that he was ready to faint from sheer fatigue.

Having lost his path, and night coming on, he became discouraged, and concluded it was in vain to make any further attempts to reach his destination. With these gloomy impressions he sat down under a tree, having little or no hope that he should be able to endure the cold until morning. In this melancholy situation he endeavoured to resign his soul to God, and calmly wait the issues of His divine will, pouring out his feeble prayers to the Almighty either to interpose and spare his life, or to receive him to Himself. Instantly, as if by the force of lightning, the thought "Rise up and go forward," passed through his mind, electrifying, as he expressed it, his whole system. His spirits revived, his strength was restored, and his soul was happy. He sprang to his feet, feeling as if inspired with supernatural vigour, and, pressing forward with all his might through the snow, he succeeded in reaching Liverpool about an hour afterwards, where his friends united with him in praise to God for his providential deliverance from the danger to which he had been exposed.

102. Danger from a Thunderstorm.—Describing a missionary visit which he had recently paid to Grand Turtle Key, one of the Bahama Islands, in 1821, the Rev. John Turtle says:—"There I was called to witness the effects of a terrible thunderstorm, which happened on this key on the night of the 1st of August, eight days after we left Nassau. This storm was the most awful the inhabitants had ever witnessed. The only building struck and damaged by the lightning was the mission-house, which was the only house unoccupied at the time. The electric fluid completely destroyed the north-west end of the building, burst open the windows and doors, carried off part of the roof, and split the partition which divides the chamber from the hall. It is generally believed by all who witnessed the ruins, and examined the course of the lightning, that if the house had been full of people at the time, they would in all probability have been hurried in a moment into an awful eternity. We had so recently left the premises, that I could not but feel the liveliest gratitude to our great Deliverer and merciful God, for His kind providence exercised over us in the hour of danger."

103. Another Thunderstorm. —Writing in the month of May 1796, the Rev. John Brownell, a missionary in Nevis, says:—" Yesterday, being at the estate of John Taylor, Esq., there fell in the afternoon a heavy shower of rain, accompanied by thunder and lightning. The negroes took shelter in a windmill, the top of which was struck at the time by a large ball of fire. The destructive fluid shivered the neck-beam, descended among the terrified negroes, killed two of them on the spot, and burned, scorched, or wounded thirty more. It also penetrated into the dungeon under the dwelling-house, where was a small cask of gunpowder, and thus exposed Mr Taylor, his lady, and me, to the danger of being involved in the sulphurous flame. Had the gunpowder taken fire, we should in all probability have lost our lives. The cries of the negroes were dreadful beyond description; and it would have pierced the hardest heart to have seen many of them, to all appearance, dead with fear, and others who had been deprived of the use of their limbs. One of them was so severely burnt that she died soon afterwards. The day after this melancholy occurrence, I buried the two men who were instantaneously killed, and then preached on the following impressive text of Scripture:—'At this also my heart trembleth, and is moved out of his place. Hear attentively the noise of His voice, and the sound that goeth out of His mouth. He directeth it under the whole heaven, and His lightning unto the ends of the earth. After it a voice roareth: He thundereth with the voice of His excellency; and He will not stay them when His voice is heard. God thundereth marvellously with His voice; great things doeth He, which we cannot comprehend'" (Job xxxvii. 1–5).

104. African Fevers.—The fevers which prevail on the pestilential coast of Western Africa are a source of much suffering and mortality among the few Europeans resident there. From the manner in which the missionaries are exposed in the discharge of their duties, they are often obliged to succumb to the wasting influence of the marsh miasma. In the course of two or three years, when stationed at St Mary's, on the River Gambia, the writer was prostrated by African fever more than one hundred times, and as often raised up again to pursue his beloved work among the people of his charge. The first attack, generally known as the "seasoning fever," was the most protracted and dangerous. Few survive the fifth day without intermission. In my own case the evening of the fourth day came, and the burning heat still continued. Considerable anxiety was felt by all classes of the community, as I was the only Christian minister of any denomination in the country, and my predecessor had died on the fifth day. About midnight, being quite conscious, my attention was attracted to a strange murmuring sound as of distant singing, wafted in at the open window of the sick chamber. On inquiring what it meant, my dear wife, who was bending over me, said, "It is the prayer-meeting which the people hold every night for your recovery." This intelligence seemed to inspire me with new life, and I faintly whispered, "Then I shall not die, but live to declare the wonderful works of God." It was even so. The crisis came, and before daylight the fever broke, and in ten days afterwards, I was ministering in the sanctuary, raised up from the brink of death in answer to the prayers of a loving people.

"Oft from the margin of the grave,
    Thou, Lord, hast lifted up my head;
Sudden I found Thee near to save;
    The fever owned Thy touch and fled."

105. Wreck of the "Haidee."—On Tuesday, the 30th of January 1838, the writer, with his wife and four other missionaries, embarked at Calliaqua, in the island of St Vincent, on board the schooner *Haidee*, for Trinidad, where the annual district-meeting was about to be held. Everything being ready for sea, and all the passengers on board, we weighed anchor, never more comfortable in our arrangements, or more happy in prospect of the future. We had not proceeded many hundred yards, however, and had scarcely cleared the point of land at the entrance of the harbour, when our noble little vessel struck upon a coral reef, and was dashed to pieces in an hour, and our luggage was scattered in every direction. As the wreck occurred in the daytime, and in sight of the shipping in the harbour, assistance was promptly rendered; and although there was much sacrifice and damage of property, no lives were lost, for which we were thankful. As the vessel went to pieces soon after she struck, as soon as we had got the passengers on shore or on board the ships at anchor, we turned our attention to the baggage, most of which was ultimately saved, though in a damaged state, from being saturated with salt water.

Thankful to God for our providential deliverance, on the following day we hired another vessel, collected our scattered luggage, got it on board, and in the evening weighed anchor and put to sea again, sailing close past the wreck of the previous day. All went well till towards midnight, when all the passengers being sea-sick below, I was pacing the deck, when I made the discovery that our captain and crew, who were strangers to us, were all more or less intoxicated; and to make the matter worse, we were sailing along to the leeward of a number of rocky little islets known as the Grenadines, where the navigation is extremely precarious. Soon afterwards I heard the rumbling sound of breakers on our "larboard bow," and feeling convinced that we were keeping too near the land, I took upon myself the responsibility of giving directions, and I called out to the steersman, "Put the helm hard down," a command which he instantly obeyed, and our little vessel veered off, and just cleared the rocks which were now visible above the foaming waters. We thus providentially escaped from the danger of a second shipwreck, which, occurring in the night-time among these rocky islets, far from human aid, might have been much more disastrous than the former one. When the captain and his men had slept off the fumes of the drink, they returned to their duty, and on the following day we happily reached our destination in safety.

"Oft hath the sea confessed Thy power,
And given me back at Thy command;
It could not, Lord, my life devour,
Safe in the hollow of Thy hand."

106. Death Averted.—One of the most remarkable interpositions of Divine Providence which is recorded in the history of modern missions occurred to the writer himself, whilst labouring in the Island of Trinidad, in the West Indies, a brief account of which may perhaps be considered worthy of a place here. The statement of the particulars, written soon afterwards, was substantially as follows:—"On the 5th of August 1846, I had occasion to visit Couva in the discharge of my ministerial duties. This station is situated midway between the capital and San Fernando, being about fifteen miles from each. I left my home in Port of Spain at six o'clock in the morning, in an open boat, accompanied by two native boatmen, John Ovid and William Woodford. The morning was fine, and we glided down the smooth and placid waters of the Gulf of Paria, with the tide in our favour, never more happy in our missionary labours. Having reached our destination in safety, inspected the mission-school, united a couple in marriage, and performed other duties, we set out on our return voyage, in the course of which the sad disaster occurred.

"We started from New Day at half-past two o'clock P.M. The weather had become showery, but not by any means more threatening than usual at that season of the year. A light breeze filled our sails, which were all set, and the use of the oars was unnecessary. After proceeding for about an hour very pleasantly, and when off the coast of the Carapichima district, we observed signs of a thunderstorm gathering to the eastward. Dense masses of black clouds gathered in rapid succession, and in a short time the face of the sky assumed a wild and threatening aspect. The rain descended in torrents, the wind blew with great violence, the thunder roared, and in a moment—in the twinkling of an eye—the lightning-flash struck the highest part of the vessel, which was the boom-yard that crossed the masthead to support the lug-sail. This was completely shattered to pieces, and hung down like a bundle of straw. The electric fluid then descended the mast, against which William was reclining, with the halliard rope in his hand, ready to let go in case the squall should increase. The poor man was struck dead in a moment. The lightning set his clothes on fire, and evidently passed through the bottom of the boat, as it began rapidly to fill with water. In the same instant John, who was at the helm, was laid prostrate at my feet. I felt the shock myself, which produced an awful sensation; but, through mercy, it did not for a moment deprive me of my reasoning faculties. I was wonderfully self-possessed, and able to consider what was best to be done. The concussion sent the boat nearly over; but she soon righted again, though half full of water.

"At this perilous moment I commenced baling the water out of the sinking boat with one hand, whilst I attempted to rouse up John with the other. After a few wild expressions of surprise, John recovered from the shock, and came to my assistance. He began to throw out the stones from the bottom of the boat which had been placed there as ballast, whilst I continued my fruitless attempts to bale out the water, which increased with alarming rapidity. As to William, he remained just where he had fallen upon his face, with his arms extended, and never spoke, or moved, or groaned.

The fire on his clothes was soon extinguished by the flowing in of the water, and the danger which now seemed to threaten us was a grave in the mighty deep. We soon found that our efforts to keep the boat afloat would be entirely ineffectual, as she was rapidly filling with water, which poured in through the holes made in her bottom by the escape of the electric fluid. I now saw the necessity of making strenuous efforts for life by swimming or otherwise, and I commenced pulling off my boots and coat simultaneously; but when I had got one boot off, and my coat just thrown over my shoulders, the boat went down, and we were completely submerged in the waves of the sea. Providentially, the weight of the dead man's body, which hung partly over the gunwale, caused the boat to capsize in its descent; so that, being emptied of its contents, it came to the surface of the water again, and floated with the bottom upwards.

"On emerging from the deep, I and the surviving boatman made an effort to regain the wreck. We could both swim, but I found myself much impeded by my coat, which, being partly off and partly on, acted as a pinion to my arms. How I cleared myself from this difficulty I know not; I think I tore it asunder under the water, as I never saw any portion of it again. I only remember being free from this impediment when I reached the wreck. Although both John and I succeeded in generally keeping our heads above the water after we got to the wreck, we found great difficulty in clinging to it, in consequence of its rolling motion, and we were repeatedly thrown off, and had to swim to it again. At length the storm subsided somewhat, and we anxiously scanned the horizon to ascertain if there was any vessel in sight. When almost all hope was taken away, I observed a small white speck in the distance. It was the schooner *Atlanta*, which God in His providence was sending for our deliverance. We were no sooner seen by the men on board, than Captain Dwyer manned a boat and sent it to our assistance, and we were taken from the wreck, when we felt incapable of much further effort, from exhaustion, and received every attention on board the schooner.

"The *Atlanta* was bound for Port of Spain, and after a night of anxious watching, prayer, and praise for our great deliverance, we reached home on the following day, and were received by our families and friends almost as persons raised from the dead, various exaggerated reports having already been circulated as to the nature and extent of the accident. I endeavoured humbly to consecrate myself afresh to the service of my Divine Master, and with a view to benefit others also, I attempted to improve the visitation by preaching on the following Sabbath evening, to a crowded congregation, from the impressive passage, 'I will sing of mercy and of judgment; unto Thee, O Lord, will I sing'" (Ps. ci. 1).

107. Danger from Hurricanes.—In the prosecution of their important work in foreign lands, Christian missionaries are frequently exposed to danger and discomfort from hurricanes. This is especially the case in the South Sea Islands and in the West Indies. Persons unaccustomed to a tropical climate can scarcely form an adequate idea of the power of the wind, and the fury of the tempest, at certain seasons in these countries, when ships are wrecked, houses blown down, trees torn up by the roots, provision-grounds destroyed, and the land turned into a waste, a howling wilderness in the course of a few hours. The most destructive hurricane ever witnessed by the writer occurred in the Island of Barbadoes on the 3d of September 1835, a brief notice of which may give the reader a faint idea of the character of these visitations.

The station occupied was Providence, about six miles from Bridge Town, and somewhat elevated in its position. On the morning of the day mentioned, we observed the wind to begin to blow fresh from the east, and the clouds collecting in dense masses towards the north, with frequent gusts, which increased in violence about ten o'clock A.M., and excited our apprehension that a storm was gathering. In order to secure, if possible, the mission-house and chapel, both of which had been destroyed on a former occasion, we made fast all the doors and windows, and used every other necessary precaution. It was not long before we saw that a hurricane was regularly set in. The wind became furious beyond expression, and the rain fell in torrents. Through the gloom which enveloped our dwelling, we saw several small cottages blown down, and the poor destitute inhabitants fled to us for shelter, terror and dismay being seen in every countenance. Knowing that a valuable horse was killed in a hurricane on this station in 1831, I made my way across the yard to liberate ours from his stable, and I had only just returned to the house when the roof of the kitchen and one wing of the main building and chimney-stack were carried away, a considerable portion of which fell with a tremendous crash, a few feet from the place where we stood. As other parts of the building were lifted with every blast of wind, we found it necessary to flee for our lives. We therefore left the house to its fate,

F

and with considerable difficulty I and my dear wife, and a young lady who was paying us a visit, made our way to the most sheltered place we could find, by the side of a canefield. There we stood ankle-deep in mud and water, watching and waiting the result of this awful visitation, one part after another of the roof of our house being blown away in rapid succession. We were thankful, however, to observe that the walls stood the fury of the tempest, and the chapel, which was also strongly built of stone, also stood well.

In the course of the afternoon the hurricane began to abate, when we ventured to return to the house, which we found flooded with water, and in a sad state of desolation. We began to put things in order as best we could, and to make arrangements for lodging in the rooms which had suffered the least damage, the family of a kind planter, whose house escaped destruction, considerately sending us a portion of their dinner for our refreshment. And in our turn we tried to show kindness to our poor neighbours who were left destitute, by opening the chapel for their accommodation, where several lodged and lived till their frail tenements could be rebuilt for their reception. We employed workmen without delay, who soon repaired our house; and this trial, like many others, passed over, and we saw abundant cause for gratitude to God for His preserving goodness, and that we had suffered so little compared with hundreds and thousands in various parts of the island, who had been left without a shelter.

108. Prayer Answered.—The sanguinary King of Dahomey, in Western Africa, declared to Commodore Wilmot, that he had bound himself by an oath to avenge the defeat of his father in 1851, before Abbeokuta, and that for twelve years preparations had been made for the intended expedition. In the month of May 1868, the arrangements were completed, and the Dahoman army marched forward, under the command of the king himself, and encamped on rising ground in sight of Abbeokuta, at a distance of about six miles. For sixteen days an attack was hourly expected, and the people of Abbeokuta, many of whom were professing Christians, felt great anxiety as to the result. Whilst they made every preparation in their power to repel the enemy, they were instant in prayer to God for His protection. Nor were their supplications in vain. On looking out one morning, they were surprised to find that the Dahomians had suddenly decamped during the night, leaving their huts standing along a ridge, to the extent of two miles, to cover their retreat. The sudden and unexpected departure of this formidable army was regarded by the native Christians as an answer to prayer.

Adverting to the occurrences of this eventful period, a missionary stationed at Abbeokuta writes as follows:—" One evening a false alarm was spread that the Dahomans were approaching. It was after nine o'clock P.M., and every fighting-man ran to the walls, and the rest of the people, missionaries, the aged, the women, and the children, betook themselves to prayer. That evening I heard a female member pray with a fervency which affected me to tears. I could not help thinking, if only this one prayer were offered up in sincerity, the Lord would not refuse a gracious answer. The following is almost a literal translation: —' O Lord Jesus, lift up Thine arm; lift up, lift up, O Lord, Lord Jesus our Redeemer, lift up Thy holy arm, and deliver us from the cruel Dahomans. O Lord Jesus, remember what they have done to Thy saints in Ishagga, how much innocent blood they have shed. O Lord, our God, deliver us, that we may not fall into their hands. Thou hast sent Thy messengers to us with Thy holy Word; we trust in Thee, O Lord our God, do not forsake us. Thou didst deliver Thy people Israel from the hand of Pharaoh, and didst overthrow his army; Thou didst deliver Hezekiah and his people from the hand of Sennacherib, who blasphemed Thy holy name. Do also remember us, O Lord; remember Thy Church, remember Thy servants, remember our children. O Lord, deliver us for Thy dear Son's sake, Amen.' I sat in a quiet, dark place, many hundreds of warriors passing along without observing me; but I overheard several saying aloud, 'God will deliver us.' I consider the retreat of the Dahomans from before Abbeokuta, as one of the greatest victories that the Church of God has obtained by prayer. The King of Dahomey has not come into the city, nor has he shot an arrow here, nor has he come before it with shields, nor has he cast a bank against it; by the way that he came, by the same has he returned, and has not entered into the city."

109. **Danger from Lightning.**— In the year 1843 the Rev. William Shepstone and his family were providentially delivered from the danger to which they were exposed, in a thunderstorm which proved fatal to many in that part of Southern Africa where they were stationed. It was on Tuesday the 10th of October that Mr Shepstone met the members of the Dutch class in his parlour, the new chapel not being quite finished. Mrs Shepstone had retired to the bedroom with the children to be out of the way; but as soon as the meeting was over, she returned with her family and the servant-girl to the sitting-room, while Mr S. took a walk in the garden, till the members of a Kaffir class were assembled which he had still to meet. Just at this moment the thunderstorm commenced with heavy rain and vivid flashes of lightning. The missionary had only walked about twenty yards from the house when he was struck by the electric fluid on the left temple, and over the left eye, and was severely shaken all over, but more especially in the left side and arm, in the hand of which he was at the time carrying a bright table-knife, which probably attracted the lightning. He reeled and staggered, but did not quite fall or lose his recollection. On turning to regain the house, he saw the cloud of dust arise from the falling in of the bedroom gable, into which the main force of the electric fluid had entered, taking the whole of the centre, from top to bottom, about four feet wide, entering the bedroom, and smashing all to pieces, or burying beneath its fall bedsteads and other furniture on the very same floor which Mrs Shepstone and her children had only just left. The missionary's son also received a powerful shock, as did also two natives, who were standing near a large saw. They were instantly struck to the earth, and the saw was powerfully acted upon. A mason who was on the scaffold, working at the new chapel, was also struck senseless, whilst the tools by which he was surrounded were scattered in every direction, some of them to a distance of forty feet. His arm, in which he held a spade, was much burnt, leaving a blue stripe nearly two inches broad from the hand to the bend of the forearm; but he afterwards recovered.

Those who were inside the house

were mercifully preserved amid the scene of desolation. The rush of dust, mixed with the electric fire, as it swept from the bedroom to the parlour, where the mission family were assembled, was said to be terrific, powerfully shaking several but seriously injuring none. In making its escape the electric fluid passed through a large chest full of linen and wearing apparel, to a small tin case, burning holes through everything in its way, as though red-hot irons had been run through the chest and its contents. Thus a heavy loss was sustained by the damage done to the mission-house furniture and other property; but every heart was filled with gratitude and praise to God, that, by His good providence, no lives were lost, nor any one seriously injured on the station.

110. Danger from a Deceiver.—During the short time that Dr Vanderkemp spent in Kaffirland attempting to form a mission-station at the commencement of the present century, the native magicians of Gaika, the paramount chief, having failed in their attempts to make rain in a season of drought, the chieftain sent two milch cows and their calves as a present to the missionary, earnestly soliciting his interference. The doctor replied that he could not make rain, but that he could and would pray to God for it. He did so, and his prayers were heard. Rain fell abundantly; but the doctor refused to accept the cattle sent by the chief, as he wished to labour for the good of the people on the principle of pure, disinterested benevolence. There were living at that time in Kaffirland several renegade Europeans of abandoned character, who pronounced Vanderkemp a fool for declining the chief's present. One of these, named Buys, sent to Gaika in the missionary's name after the manner of wicked Gehazi of old, to say that the cattle offered as a present were not sufficient for the rain, which induced him to send more, all of which, like the prophet's servant, he appropriated to his own use, and thus exposed the doctor to misconception and peril in a heathen land. But through a kind Providence, the thing was brought to light, and the missionary escaped the evil consequences.

Adverting to the depredations and the fate of this deceiver and his compeers, the Rev. S. Kay says, many years afterwards:—" It does not appear that any of this party died a natural death. Faber was afterwards hung in the Colony as a rebel. Buys wandered about among the tribes, murdering and plundering until he himself was murdered. Botha was killed by the Kaffirs, at the instigation of his companion. The hut in which Bezuidenhoud slept was one night fired by the natives, and he was burned to death. The Irishman (a deserter connected with the band), with one of his children, was also burned to ashes while asleep by one of the native women with whom he had lived; and Lochenberg, whom 'vengeance suffered not to live,' was literally cut to pieces by the Amakwabi about the middle of 1829."

111. Restitution.—The Rev. Mr Nott, a missionary in Tahiti, preached on one occasion from the text, "Let him that stole, steal no more," and the word made a powerful impression on the minds of his congregation. Nor were the appropriate fruits lacking. The next morning, when the missionary opened his door, he saw a number of natives sitting on the ground before his dwelling, with tools and other articles by their side. He requested an explanation of this circumstance. They answered, "We have not been able to sleep all night; we were in the chapel yesterday. We thought, when we were pagans, that it was right to steal when we could do it without being found out. Hiro, the god of thieves, used to assist us. But we heard what you said yesterday from the Word of God, that Jehovah had commanded that we should not steal. We have stolen, and all these things that we have brought with us are stolen goods." One man then lifted up an axe, a hatchet, or a chisel, and exclaimed, "I stole this from the carpenter of such a ship; others held up an *ume ti*, or a saw, or a knife; indeed almost every kind of movable property was brought and exhibited with similar confessions. Mr Nott proposed that they should take the plundered property home, and restore it, when an opportunity should occur, to its lawful owners. But to this they objected. They all said, "Oh no, we cannot take the things back; we have had no peace ever since we heard it was displeasing to God to steal them, and we shall have no peace so long as they remain in our dwellings. We wish you to take them, and give them back to the owners whenever they come."

112. Timely Supply.—Describing an incident which occurred in the course of one of his missionary journeys in South Africa, the Rev. R. Moffat says:—"As the sun arose above the horizon, the heat became excessive; and if we had been nearly frozen in the night, we were almost scorched during the day; and before we reached water the following evening, we would have given a crown for a bottle of that in which we had washed in the morning. Our return was little different to our outward journey, 'in fastings oft.' A kind Providence watched over us, however, and in some cases remarkably interposed in our behalf, which the following incident will show. We had passed the night without food; and after a long day's ride, the sun was descending on us, with little prospect of meeting with anything to assuage the pains of hunger, when, as we were descending from the high ground, weak and weary, we saw, at a great distance on the opposite ridge, a line of dust approaching with the fleetness of the ostrich. It proved to be a spring-buck, closely pursued by a wild dog, which must have brought it many miles, for it was seized within two hundred yards of the spot where we stood, and instantly despatched. We, of course, thankfully took possession of his prize, the right to which the wild dog seemed much inclined to dispute with us. I proposed to leave half of it for the pursuer, 'No,' said one of my men, 'he is not so hungry as we are, or he would not run so fast!'"

113. Lost in the Desert.—The Rev. Barnabas Shaw, with whom the writer was associated in missionary labour in South Africa, gives the following account of the danger to which he was exposed whilst lost in the desert, when on his way from Cape Town to Namaqualand, accompanied by a young Dutchman and an African boy:—"On the 7th of January 1827, Captain Aam put us on shore some miles south of Spoog River. Having supplied us with some ship's provisions, and each a bottle of water, he sailed for the place of his destination. About nine A.M., we commenced our journey in the wilderness, with the expectation of finding the first farm-house before the setting of the sun. We travelled onward till mid-day, and then sat down to rest, and ate a little biscuit; the sands being very deep, we had already begun to feel weary. Towards evening, having discovered no dwelling-house, as we expected, we agreed to lie down for the night. Our water being nearly exhausted, we were faint with thirst. Before laying down, a fire was made on the top of the hill, in hope that if any human beings were near they would come to our aid; but, alas! it was a land not inhabited. Having scratched holes in the sand, we commended ourselves to God in prayer, and lay down to rest; but the jackals screamed loud in the night, and drove away our six marino sheep, which his Excellency General Bourke had sent with us as a present to the station. On the 8th I awoke my companions early, in order that we might travel in the cool of the morning. We tried to eat a little biscuit, but could not, our supply of water being exhausted, except a little we had saved to moisten our parched lips. Our sheep were gone, and we were too weak to search for them, and therefore we set off again over hills of sand and straggling bushes; but our exertions greatly increased our thirst, and filled us with anxiety as to the future. Again and again we sat down to rest; repeatedly we climbed the tops of the hills to try if we could discover any flocks or herds, or the smoke of distant fires, but all in vain.

"Though I had been in that part of the country before, and at the farmer's house we were in search of, yet we were so completely bewildered among the sand-hills, that I was constrained to acknowledge myself lost. It was a trying season, and in this dilemma I opened my Bible and read the account of Hagar in the wilderness. This seemed to encourage us to trust in Divine Providence, and we had not proceeded far when I discovered several bullocks at a distance. Our hopes were now raised, and we ascended the top of a hill, hallooing as loud as we were able, and waving our hats; but there was no person to answer us, and, to our great sorrow, the oxen disappeared, and we saw them no more. This circumstance greatly depressed us, and the wilderness became more solitary than before. Whilst thus dejected, I again saw some distant objects, which proved to be a flock of sheep and goats. By this time my strength had completely failed, and I fell to the ground faint and helpless. My African boy, William, was also quite exhausted. Mr M. being the strongest, pushed forward till he came up with a Hottentot in charge of the flock, who informed him that the farmer's house we were seeking was at no great distance. The man went at once to inform his master of his discovery, and the kind-hearted boer, Mr Engelbrecht, sent horses to convey us to his place, and we were thus mercifully delivered from our perilous position.

"When we reached the farmer's place, he exclaimed, 'It is the Lord who has wonderfully delivered you this day. In the morning, when I arose, it was my intention to send my sheep to the northward, but the Hottentot had taken them away to the southward. I therefore reserved my orders till to-morrow. But had the sheep been sent to the north, instead of in the direction in which you found them, nothing could have saved you from perishing, as you were going into a country where there is no water, and which is destitute of inhabitants. The Lord kept me asleep *half an hour longer than usual this morning to save your lives.*' On hearing this Mr M. cried out, '*De Heere heeft ons ver lost!*' 'The Lord has delivered us!' and engaged as long as he lived to keep the 8th of January as a day of thanksgiving to God, and surely I may sing with the poet,

'Through hidden dangers, toils, and death,
He gently cleared my way.'"

114. Missionary attacked by a Serpent.—It is recorded of a Moravian missionary labouring in Guiana, on the continent of South America, that he had a fearful encounter with a boa-constrictor, a serpent of the largest class, and narrowly escaped with his life. Feeling ill one day, the missionary resolved to go into his hut and lie down in his hammock. Just as he entered the door, a large boa-constrictor lowered itself from the roof and entwined itself round him. He struggled manfully with it, and the creature bit him three times; but happily the bite of this kind of serpent, though painful and dangerous enough, is not poisonous like that of several others of a smaller size. The chief danger from the boa-constrictor lies in the fact that it is in the habit of strangling its victim. This seemed to be the aim of the ugly creature that attacked the missionary on this occasion. At last it twisted itself so firmly round his neck that he almost relinquished the hope of deliverance. And fearing it might be supposed that the Indians had murdered him, he had the presence of mind to write on the table with a piece of chalk, "A serpent has killed me." Then the words of Christ suddenly coming to his mind that His disciples should tread upon serpents and not be hurt, the poor man was inspired with new vigour, and began again to struggle with his terrible enemy. After some time, exerting all his strength, he succeeded in tearing it loose from his body and in casting it out of the hut, and so by the good providence of God, made his escape to his friends, who soon came and despatched the ugly monster.

115. Poisoned Water.—In the course of one of his missionary journeys in Southern Africa, the Rev. R. Moffat had a narrow escape from death by drinking poisoned water. He thus describes the incident:— "On one occasion I was remarkably preserved when all expected that my race was run. We had reached the river early in the afternoon, after a dreadfully scorching ride across a plain. Three of my companions, who were in advance, rode forward to a Bushman village, on an ascent some hundred yards from the river. I went because my horse would go towards a little pool on a dry branch, from which the flood or torrent had receded to the larger course. Dismounting, I pushed through a narrow opening in the bushes, and lying down, took a hearty draught. Immediately on raising myself I felt an unusual taste in my mouth, and looking attentively at the water, and the temporary fence around, it flashed across my mind that the water was poisoned for the purpose of killing game. I came out, and meeting one of our number, who had been a little in the rear, just entering, told him my suspicion.

At that moment a Bushman from the village came running breathless, and apparently terrified. He took me by the hand, as if to prevent my going to the water, talking with great excitement, though neither I nor my companions could understand him; but when I made signs that I had drunk, he was speechless for a minute or two, and then ran off to the village. I followed; and, on again dismounting, as I was beginning to think for the last time, the poor Bushmen and women looked on me with eyes which bespoke heartfelt compassion. My companions expected me to fall down every moment: not one spoke. Observing the downcast looks of the poor Bushmen, I smiled, and this seemed to operate on them like an electric shock, for all began to babble and sing, the women striking their elbows against their naked sides, expressive of their joy. However, I began to feel a violent turmoil within, and a fulness of the system, as if the arteries would burst, while the pulsation was exceedingly quick, being accompanied with a slight giddiness in the head. We made the natives understand that I wanted the fruit of the solanum, which grows in these quarters nearly the size and shape of an egg, and which acts as an emetic. They ran in all directions, but sought in vain. By this time I was covered with a profuse perspiration, and drank largely of pure water. The strange and painful sensation which I had experienced gradually wore away, though it was not entirely removed for some days."

116. Exposed to Wild Beasts.—The dangerous proximity of wild beasts of different kinds at one of his halting-places, when travelling in Southern Africa, and when afterwards pursuing his journey through the desert, is thus described by the Rev. R. Moffat:—"We had eaten a small portion of meat that morning, reserving only enough for one single meal, lest we should get no more, and drank freely of water, to keep the stomach distended, and felt tolerably comfortable. At night we came to some old huts, where were the remains of tobacco gardens, which had been watered with wooden vessels from the adjoining river. We spent the evening in one of these huts, though, from certain holes for ingress and egress, it was evidently a domicile for hyænas and other beasts of prey. We had scarcely ended our evening song of praise to Him whose watchful care had guided and preserved us through the day, when the distant and dolorous howls of the hyæna, and the no less inharmonious jabbering of the jackal, announced the kind of company with which we were to spend the night; while from the river the hippopotami kept up a blowing and snorting chorus. Our sleep was anything but sweet. On the addition of the dismal notes of the hooting owl, one of our men remarked, 'We want only the lion's roar to complete the music of the desert.' 'Were they as sleepy and tired as I am,' said another, 'they would find something else to do.' In the morning we found that some of these nightly scavengers had approached very near to the door of our hut.

"Having refreshed ourselves with a bathe and a draught of water, we prepared for the thirsty road we had to traverse; but before starting, a council was held whether we should finish the last small portion of meat (which any one might have devoured in a minute), or reserve it. The decision was to keep it till evening. We travelled on the whole day as quickly as our jaded horses could carry us. When evening drew on, we had to ascend and descend several sand-hills, which was very fatiguing. Some of our party lagged behind. Concerned for their safety, we halted, and fired our guns, but were only answered by a lion, apparently close to the place where we stood. The ravenous beast roared repeatedly, and the horses trembled with fear; but we pressed on, and were providentially delivered from our perilous position."

117. Baboon Annoyance.—In

the course of our missionary travels in Africa, we have often been brought into close contact with different varieties of the monkey tribe. They have sometimes proved amusing, and sometimes annoying; but seldom dangerous, unless when encountered in large companies and much irritated. The Rev. R. Moffat gives the following account of his adventures with a tribe of baboons, which assumed a very threatening attitude:—"Turning to descend the mountain, I happened to cough, and was instantly surrounded by almost a hundred baboons, some of gigantic size. They grunted, grinned, and sprang from stone to stone, protruding their mouths, showing their teeth, and drawing back the skin of their foreheads, threatening an instant attack. I kept parrying them with my gun, which was loaded; but I knew their character and disposition too well to fire, for if I had wounded one of them, I should have been skinned in five minutes. The ascent was very laborious, but I would have given anything to be at the bottom of the hill again. Some of the impertinent animals came so near as even to touch my hat while passing projecting rocks. It was some time before I reached the plain, when they appeared to hold a noisy council, either about what they had done, or intended doing. Levelling my piece at two that seemed the most fierce, as I was about to touch the trigger, the thought occurred, I have escaped, let me be thankful; therefore I left them uninjured, perhaps with the gratification of having given me a fright."

118. Burning Thirst.—Describing one of his perilous journeys in the wilds of Africa, the Rev. Robert Moffat says:—"We continued our slow and silent march for hours. The tongue cleaving to the roof of the mouth from thirst, made conversation difficult. At last we reached the long-wished-for 'waterfall,' so named because when it rains, water sometimes falls from a rock, though in small quantities; but it was too late to ascend the hill. We allowed our poor worn-out horses to go where they pleased, and having kindled a small fire, we sat around it and talked about our lost companions, who happened for their comfort to have the only small quantity of meat we possessed, and who, as Jantjie thought, would wander from the position in which we left them towards the river. We bowed the knee to Him who had mercifully preserved us, and laid our heads on our saddles. The last sound we heard to soothe us was the distinct roar of a lion, but we were too much exhausted to feel anything like fear. Sleep came to our relief, and it seemed made up of scenes the most lovely, forming a glowing contrast to our real situation. I felt as if engaged, during my short repose, in roving among ambrosial bowers of paradisaical delight, hearing sounds of music, as if from angels' harps: it was the night wind falling on my ears from the neighbouring hills. I seemed to pass from stream to stream in which I bathed and slaked my thirst, at many a crystal fount, flowing from golden mountains enriched with living green. These Elysian pleasures continued till morning dawn, when we awoke speechless with thirst, our eyes inflamed, and our whole frames burning like a coal. We were, however, somewhat less fatigued, but wanted water, and it was some time before we could articulate a word.

We once more saddled our jaded horses, which, though they had picked up a little grass, looked miserable beyond description. We now directed our course towards Witte

Water, where we could scarcely hope to arrive before afternoon, even if we reached it at all, for we were soon obliged to dismount, and to drive our horses slowly and silently over the glowing plain, where the delusive mirage tantalised our feelings with exhibitions of the loveliest pictures of lakes and pools, studded with beautiful islets, and towering trees moving in the breeze on their banks. This optical delusion was produced by the highly rarified state of the atmosphere, or the reflected heat of the sun's rays on the sultry plain. After resting a while under a bush we pressed forward, and reached the pool late in the afternoon. Oh what a relief! we drank, and though moving with animalculæ, muddy and nauseous with filth, it was to us a reviving draught.

119. Danger from Lions.—When travelling in the interior of Africa, missionaries have often been exposed to danger from lions. Describing his encampments in Namaqualand, the Rev. R. Moffat says:—"At one of these places I had slept on the ground near the door of the hut in which the principal man and his wife reposed. I remarked in the morning that it appeared that some of the cattle had broken loose during the night, as I had heard something moving about on the outside of the thorn fence, under which I lay. 'Oh,' he replied, ' I was looking at the *spoor* this morning, it was a lion;' adding that a few nights before it sprung over on the very spot on which I had been lying, and seized a goat, with which it bounded off through another part of the fold.' On asking him how he could appoint me to sleep on that very spot, he replied, 'The lion would not have the audacity to jump over *you*.' This remark produced a laugh from me, in which the man and his wife joined most heartily; and he reminded me of a circumstance in his own history, with which I was well acquainted; for he had been in the jaws of a lion. One night he and about a dozen more hunters were fast asleep with a circle of bushes placed around their fire. When the blaze was extinguished, a lion sprang into the midst of the sleeping party, seized my host by the shoulder, and with his *caross*, dragged him off to some distance. The others, aroused by the scuffle, snatched up their guns, and not knowing one of their number had been carried off, shot in the direction whence the noise proceeded. One ball happened to wound the lion, and in trying to roar, it let the man drop from its grasp who instantly ran off, leaving his mantle, and bolted in among his companions, crying out, 'Do not shoot me,' for they supposed for the moment that he was the lion. He showed me the ugly marks of the lion's teeth on his shoulder."

The same missionary remarks on another occasion:—" In the morning we unyoked the waggons, and proceeded to the water, which lay far to the right; and on arriving there, we saw, to our astonishment and instruction, that we had been led by a way that we knew not, for there had been several lions about the water-pool apparently the whole night. Had we arrived at the time we expected, in all probability the oxen would have taken fright, and occasioned some serious accident, or even worse consequences might have followed."

120. Another Lion Story.—Describing one of his journeys in the interior of Africa, the Rev. R. Moffat says:—"The two Baralongs had brought with them a young cow, and I recommended their making her fast also, as we had done the oxen; but they humorously replied that she was too wise to leave the waggon, even though a lion should be scented. We took a little supper, which was followed by our evening hymn and prayer. I had retired only a few minutes to my waggon to prepare for the night, when the whole of the oxen started to their feet. A lion had seized the cow only a few steps from their tails, and dragged it to a distance of thirty or forty yards, where we distinctly heard it tearing the animal and breaking the bones, while its bellowings were most pitiful. When these were over, I seized my gun, but as it was too dark to see my object at half the distance, I aimed at the spot where the devouring jaws of the lion were heard. I fired again and again, to which he replied with tremendous roars, at the same time making a rush towards the waggon, so as exceedingly to terrify the oxen. The two Baralongs engaged to take firebrands, advanced a few yards, and threw them at him, so as to afford me a degree of light, that I might take aim, the place being bushy. They had scarcely discharged them from their hands, when the flame went out, and the enraged animal rushed towards them with such swiftness, that I had barely time to turn the gun and fire between the men and the lion, and, providentially, the ball struck the ground immediately under his head, as we found by examination next morning. From this surprise he returned, growling dreadfully. The men darted through some thorn-bushes with countenances indicative of the utmost terror. It was now the opinion of all that we had better let the lion alone if he did not further molest us.

"Having but a scanty supply of wood to keep up a fire, one man crept among the bushes on one side of the pool, with the hope of obtaining some, while I proceeded for the same purpose on the other side. I had not gone far, when, looking upward to the edge of the small basin, I saw four large lions. I crept gently towards the man on the other side of the pool, to inform him of our danger, when to my surprise I found him earnestly looking in another direction, where there were two more full-grown lions and a cub eyeing us in a very threatening manner. We were now glad to retreat to the waggon, where we kept a fire burning during the night, and on the following morning, although it was the Sabbath, we felt it to be our duty to move forward to a little village which we saw on the heights, thankful to leave a place that was haunted with something worse than ghosts."

121. A Double Danger.—Adverting to his travels in the interior of Southern Africa, the Rev. R. Moffat says :—" In one of my early journeys, I had an escape from an African tiger and a serpent truly providential. I had left the waggon, and wandered to a distance among the coppice and grassy openings in quest of game. I had a small doubled-barrelled gun on my shoulder, which was loaded with a ball and small-shot; an antelope passed, at which I fired, and slowly followed the course it took. After advancing a short distance, I saw a tiger-cat staring at me between the forked branches of a tree, behind which his long, spotted body was concealed, twisting and turning his tail like a cat going to spring on its prey. This I knew was a critical moment, not having a shot of ball in my gun. I moved about as if in search of something on the grass, taking care to retreat at the same time. After getting, as I thought, a suitable distance to turn my back, I moved somewhat more quickly; but in my anxiety to escape what was behind, I did not see what was before, until startled by treading on a large cobra de capello serpent, asleep on the grass. It instantly twirled its body round my leg, on which I had nothing but a thin pair of trousers, when I leaped from the spot, dragging the venomous and enraged reptile after me; and while in the act of throwing itself into a position to bite, without turning round, I threw my piece over my shoulder, and shot it. Taking it by the tail, I brought it to my people at the waggon, who, on examining the bags of poison, asserted, that had the creature bitten me, I could never have reached the waggon. The serpent was six feet long.

122. Deliverance from the Jaws of a Lion.—Writing under date of December 2d, 1829, in Kaffirland, South Africa, the Rev. S. Kay says:—" When divine service was over, I visited a poor sick Hottentot, who recently experienced one of the most providential deliverances that I ever heard or read of. I found him in great pain from the shocking wounds he had received on the occasion; and in the course of conversation he furnished me with the following particulars of his escape from the jaws of a lion, which he ascribed wholly to the gracious interposition of the Father of mercies, and which is, therefore, worthy of being recorded to His glory.

"About three weeks or a month ago, he went out on a hunting excursion, accompanied by several other natives. Arriving on an extensive plain, where there was abundance of game, they discovered a number of lions also, which appeared to be disturbed by their approach. A prodigiously large male immediately separated himself from the troop, and began slowly to advance towards the party, the majority of whom were young men, and altogether unaccustomed to rencontres of so formidable a nature. When droves of timid antelopes or springbucks only came in their way, they made a great boast of their courage; but the very appearance of the king of the forest made them tremble. While the animal was yet at a distance, they all dismounted to prepare for firing, and, according to custom on such occasions, began tying their horses together, by means of the bridles, with the view of keeping the latter between them and the lion, as an object to attract his attention, until they were able to take deliberate aim. His movements were at length too swift for them. Before the horses were properly fastened to each other, the monster made a tremendous bound or two, and suddenly pounced upon the hind-parts of one of them, which in its fright plunged forward, and knocked down the poor man in question, who was holding the reins in his hand.

"His comrades instantly took fright, and ran off with all speed; and he of course rose as quickly as possible to follow them. But no sooner had he regained his feet, than the majestic beast, with a seeming consciousness of his superior might, stretched forth his paw, and striking him just behind the neck immediately brought him to the ground again. He then rolled on his back, when the lion set his foot upon his breast and lay down upon him. The poor man now became almost breathless, partly from fear, but principally from the intolerable pressure of his terrific load. He endeavoured to move a little to one side, in order to breathe; but feeling this, the lion seized his left arm, close to the elbow, and after once laying hold with his teeth, he continued to amuse himself with the limb for some time, biting it in sundry different places down to the hand, the thick part of which seemed to have been pierced entirely through. All this time the lion did not appear to be angry, but merely caught at his prey, like a cat sporting with a mouse that is not quite dead; so that there was not a single bone fractured, as would, in all probability, have been the case had the creature been hungry or irritated. Whilst writhing in agony, gasping for breath, and expecting every moment to be torn limb from limb, the sufferer cried to his companions for assistance, but cried in vain. On raising his head a little, the beast opened his dreadful jaws to receive it, but providentially the hat, which I saw in its rent state, slipped off, so that the points of the lion's teeth only just grazed the surface of the skull. The lion now set his foot upon the man's arm, from which the blood was freely flowing; his fearful paw was soon covered therewith, and he again and again licked it clean! The idea verily makes me shudder while I write. But this was not the worst; for the animal steadily fixed his flaming eyes upon those of the man, smelt first on one side and then on the other of his face, and having tasted the blood, he appeared half inclined to devour his helpless victim.

"'At this critical moment,' said the poor man, 'I recollected having heard that there is a God in the heavens who is able to deliver at the very last extremity, and I began to pray that He would save me, and not allow the lion to eat my flesh and drink my blood.' Whilst thus engaged in calling upon God, the beast turned himself completely round. On perceiving this, the Hottentot made an effort to get from under him; but no sooner did the creature perceive his movement than he laid terrible hold on his right thigh. This wound was dreadfully deep, and evidently occasioned the sufferer most acute pain. He again sent up his cry to God for help; nor were his prayers in vain. The huge animal soon afterwards quietly relinquished his prey, though he had not been in the least interrupted. Having deliberately risen from his seat, he walked majestically off to the distance of thirty or forty paces, and then lay down in the grass, as if for the purpose of watching the man. The latter being happily relieved of his load, ventured to sit up, which circumstance immediately attracted the lion's attention; nevertheless, it did not induce another attack, as the poor fellow naturally expected, but, as if bereft of power, and unable to do anything more, he again rose, took his departure, and was seen no more. The man seeing this took up his gun, and hastened away to his terrified companions, who had given him up for dead. Being in a state of great exhaustion from loss of blood, he was immediately set upon his horse, and brought to the place where I found him.

"Mr Gaulter, surgeon, son of the Rev. John Gaulter, being stationed at a military post in the neighbourhood, and hearing of the case, hastened to his relief, and has very humanely rendered him all necessary attention ever since. Mr Gaulter informs me, that on his arrival the appearance of the wounds was truly alarming, and amputation of the arm seemed absolutely necessary. To this, however, the patient objected, having a number of young children whose subsistence depends upon his labour. 'As the Almighty had delivered me,' said he, 'from that horrid death, I thought, surely He is able to save my arm also.' And, astonishing to relate, several of the wounds are already healed, and there is now hope of his complete recovery. 'Oh that men would praise the Lord for His goodness, and for His wonderful works to the children of men!'"

123. Danger from a Puff-Adder.—We remember hearing the Rev. Barnabas Shaw give the following account of the danger to which he was once exposed from a puff-adder: "Having suffered for several weeks from severe pain, I went to the sea for a short time for the benefit of bathing. While there our mattress was laid under a bush, where we were accustomed to sleep, as being the best lodgings we could procure on the spot. Towards the evening of one of those days, as I rose up from the mattress, the wind having changed, Mrs Shaw said, 'We will remove our bed to another place.' She immediately began to take away some of the bedding from the place where we had lodged, when to her great surprise a puff-adder was curled up under the end of our bolster. I had been sitting within a few inches of this venomous creature more than an hour, this being the place where we had always slept. Had the wind not changed one or both of us would doubtless have felt, during the night, the sharpness of the serpent's teeth, of which there were two formed after the manner of fish-hooks. We could not, therefore, but acknowledge the providential care of Him, who said, 'Even the very hairs of your head are all numbered.'"

124. Danger from Crocodiles.—Many of the rivers, both in Western and Southern Africa, abound with alligators or crocodiles, and we have often ourselves been brought into close and uncomfortable proximity to them. They are very savage and dangerous creatures, and many a poor fellow has been seized, dragged down, and devoured by them. But the most remarkable instance of providential deliverance from one of these monsters of the deep, with which we are acquainted, was experienced by the Rev. Mr Butler, an American missionary labouring in Natal. This devoted servant of God was on one occasion crossing the Umkumas River on horseback, when a large alligator seized his leg. He held on for life to his horse, and dragged the savage beast ashore. Happily for him a number of Kaffir women were near, who ran to the rescue, and beat the horrible creature off him. The wound, after a long time, was healed; but the missionary never fully recovered from its effects. With his health seriously impaired, he some time afterwards returned to America.

125. Bitten by a Serpent.—Missionaries are frequently exposed to danger, from coming in contact with snakes or serpents in the course of their travels in foreign lands. The Rev. Henry Tindall gives the following account of an incident of this kind, which occurred to himself when labouring with his father in Namaqualand, South Africa, in 1852:—"I left Nisbet-Bath on horseback, to visit Hoole's Fountain, where I arrived on the following evening. I took up my lodgings in the dilapidated preacher's room, which is merely an enclosure of walls without door or window, and a roof in several places open to the sky. Being wearied with my journey of seventy-five miles, I took such refreshment as my saddle-bags afforded, with some milk, and sought repose in one corner of the room, my attendant imitating my example in the opposite corner. I lay down without my clothes, and wrapped myself in a blanket of sheepskin. I had not slept long before I awoke with a sharp pain in my side, to which I at first paid little attention. However, it soon became so sharp as to awaken my suspicion. I consequently arose, and awoke my attendant, when, having procured a light, we at once discovered a serpent of a very venomous character. We immediately rushed out of the hut, and fled to the house of Klass Afrikaner, who lost no time in applying a plaster of blue vitriol to the wound, and in administering a solution of the same as a strong emetic. The pain I suffered was intense, and I could see by the alarm of the people that they thought my life was in danger. The serpent, which had taken refuge among my clothes, was then destroyed by the people who had come to my aid.

"Messengers were immediately despatched to the Bath to acquaint my father and mother with the occurrence, and to Kamis River to hasten the arrival of a snake-doctor, in whom great confidence was placed. On the following day I was full of pain, and too weak to walk. The blue vitriol was now changed for tobacco oil. I also found relief from some sweet oil, which one of the natives possessed. In the evening the snake-doctor arrived. He pronounced the remedies that had been employed good, and only added a filthy handkerchief, which had been worn next his person, and which he said possessed great virtue from having absorbed his perspiration! On Sunday night my dear parents came, having travelled night and day in great alarm. The poison appeared subdued throughout my system; but the wound was in such a state of inflammation as to threaten almost immediate mortification. However, by the blessing of God, this was prevented, and in a few days I was removed to the Bath, preferring the pain occasioned by the jolting of the waggon to the almost insupportable heat of the native hut in which I was accommodated. I was greatly reduced, and it was some time before I fully recovered. I feel I have great cause to thank God for sparing my life. Had the accident occurred during the previous night, when I slept in the open field, or had not my parents arrived soon, in all human probability my course would soon have been finished. I add with a grateful heart that the time of affliction was to me a time of spiritual profit."

126. **Snakes in Tasmania.**—So recently as 1866, although the clearing and cultivating the land had been carried on to a great extent in the island of Tasmania, two instances of encounters with snakes occurred which appear to be well authenticated. In the first case, Mrs Hayes, the wife of a storekeeper at a place called Jericho, was sitting in the shop sewing, when she felt several rather smart blows applied to her back. She put her hand once or twice in the direction of the knocks without feeling anything; but as the act was repeated, she at last turned round, and to her horror discovered, in a crookedly erect attitude, a large snake with flaming eyes and protruded fangs, which had evidently been her assailant. Without moving, she called for her husband, who fortunately was at hand, and who promptly killed the reptile; which measured within a few inches of seven feet. It is a matter of gratitude that, with the exception of the fright, the woman received no injury.

The scene of the second story was in the neighbourhood of Mansfield. Two men were in a hut, one of whom was half asleep, reclining on a mattress thrown carelessly against the wall. Suddenly he felt an uneven mobile substance beneath his shoulders, the nature of which he failed to detect by putting his hands on the place. His mate's attention was attracted by his uneasiness, and after keeping his eye upon him for a minute or two, was rather taken aback by observing a large black snake wriggle out from between his friend's shoulders and the mattress on which he was lying. The snake made for the door, but was not allowed to reach it alive, being despatched before it made its escape.

127. Saved from Drowning.—
Adverting to the danger attending his landing on one occasion at the island of Atiu, one of the Hervey group in Polynesia, the Rev. John Williams says:—" On my next visit to this island my life and labours had nearly terminated. On reaching the reef we perceived that the sea was not breaking with its usual violence, and I therefore determined to land in the boat. This was effected without much difficulty; but on returning, before we could get a sufficient distance from the shore, another billow rolled in and overwhelmed us, and the boat with her crew was dashed upon the reef. Unfortunately I fell toward the sea, and was conveyed by the recoil of the wave to a considerable distance from the shore, where I was twirled about in a whirlpool, and sank to a great depth. Being so long under water, I began to fear that I should rise no more. At length, however, I rose to the surface; and finding that there was time for me to reach the reef before the next wave burst upon it, I swam in that direction. On perceiving my situation, two natives sprang into the sea, and, as a considerable time elapsed before the next billow arrived, I succeeded, by their assistance, in escaping its fury. The people were standing upon the reef, weeping bitterly, under the apprehension that I was lost; and on reaching the shore they gathered around me, and demonstrated their great joy at my preservation, by touching my clothes or kissing my hands. Thus, for the sixth time, was I rescued from a watery grave."

128. Deliverance from Wicked Men.—
While the Rev. John Williams was labouring in Raiatea, the progress of the work of civilisation was hindered by a number of dissolute young men and others, who, when heathens, had been accustomed to live by plunder, and who did not like the restraints which Christianity imposed upon them. They at length determined to overturn the newly-formed government of the island, and for that purpose they entered into a regular and organised conspiracy. In order to effect their wicked designs, they resolved to murder the missionaries and the chief; but were providentially thwarted of their purpose by means very simple, but effectual in the hands of God. "I was in the habit," says Mr Williams, "of spending every second or third Sunday at the island of Tahaa, which was about eight miles from our settlement, but always went on the Saturday. The four men who had volunteered their services to convey me were among the conspirators, and had engaged, when about half way, to throw me into the sea, while their associates despatched Mr Threlkeld and Tamatoa. An apparently trivial circumstance prevented my going on that day. I had repaired and painted the boat on the preceding Wednesday, and not having sufficient paint-oil, was under the necessity of using a considerable proportion of a sub-

stitute made from the cocoa-nut, which prevented the paint from drying according to my expectation; so that when we prepared to launch the boat, we found her unfit for the voyage, and were thus prevented from taking the journey. The young men came to me several times during the day, and appeared exceedingly anxious that we should go; but I told them that, as the paint was not dry, it was utterly impossible. I was not aware at the time what induced them to be so urgent, and as little imagined that the simple circumstance alluded to was to be the means which Providence employed to preserve me from an untimely death and a watery grave.

"Thwarted in their plans, they determined, on the following day, to carry them openly and at once into execution; and while we were sitting at dinner one of them was sent to our house for that purpose. He was dressed in a most fantastic manner, having his head decorated with leaves, and wearing a pair of trousers with his arms through the legs as a jacket, &c. He came brandishing a large carving-knife, and danced before the house, crying, 'Turn out the hog, let us kill him! turn out the pig, let us cut his throat!' Annoyed with his conduct, and not apprehending any danger, I arose from the table, to desire him to desist. On opening the door, one of the deacons, almost breathless with running, met me, thrust me back, and exclaimed. 'Why do you go out? Why do you expose your life? You are the pig he is calling for: you will be dead in a moment.' The deacon then informed me of the danger I had escaped, and the plot which had been discovered. Thus two days in succession had I been in most imminent danger, and yet was preserved by the good providence of God."

129. Mr Pitman's Narrow Escape.—The Rev. Messrs Williams and Pitman were engaged, with a large number of natives, in the erection of a new chapel at Rarotonga, when the missionary last named had a narrow and most providential escape from being killed by the fall of a large piece of timber. One of the chiefs having requested Mr Pitman to go and instruct him how to fix one of the window-sills, he went accordingly, and was thus employed when a man on the thatch, unobserved by him, was dragging a heavy piece of wood which slipped, and falling upon Mr Pitman's head, levelled him to the ground. He was taken up senseless, and conveyed home. "I examined the bruise," says Mr Williams, "and was truly thankful to find that no bone was broken, no material injury sustained; for, providentially, the heavy end of the log reached the ground before Mr Pitman was struck, otherwise his work on earth would have been finished." In mentioning this event to his friends, the devoted missionary says, "Thus it hath pleased the Lord to spare me a little longer in His vineyard. Oh that my life may be more than ever devoted to His service!"

130. Danger from Dogs.—The number of half-famished dogs kept in many heathen villages is very remarkable, and a stranger no sooner approaches than they are ready to pounce upon him. If not held in check by their almost equally savage owners, the consequences may be serious; and in any case, the horrid noise which they make by their united and continuous howls is perfectly deafening. We have often been annoyed by this kind of greeting on approaching a native village in Africa, and we have known some narrow escapes from danger, as mad dogs are frequently suffered to go at large in heathen lands.

On the 29th of April 1872, the Rev. Mr Cardwell, while engaged in a missionary excursion by boat on the Po-Yang Lake in Central China, had encountered many dangers and difficulties from rapids, shallows, and unfaithful boatmen, when he was assailed from a quarter and in a manner which he little expected. Having gone on shore to sell copies of the Scriptures and other good books, he says:—" I was invited by a respectable man to go to his house. I accepted the invitation, and had quite a gathering of people, to whom we sold some books, and exhorted them to leave the worship of idols and serve the only one true God, believing in Jesus Christ the only Saviour. My host, after treating me to tea and sweatmeats, provided a wheel-barrow for my return, as the road was very muddy. It was quite dusk before we arrived at the boat; and having alighted from the barrow to walk through the village, a dog seized me by the leg. I shook him off, but the bitten part pained me much. Getting a light, we quickly examined the leg, and were thankful to find the skin was not broken, and after a little time the pain ceased, though I felt it again the next day. The Lord is my keeper."

Thus does the God of Missions preserve and protect His servants, when exposed to danger by sea and by land, in the prosecution of their important duties in foreign lands, and thus does He give encouragement to all His faithful people to be instant in prayer for those who, like St Paul, are "in perils in sea, in perils in the wilderness, in death oft."

" In all my ways Thy hand I own,
  Thy ruling providence I see;
Assist me still my course to run,
  And still direct my paths to Thee."

V. AFFLICTIONS AND BEREAVEMENTS.

131. Mysterious Dispensations.—Considering the number of agents employed in mission-work, the unhealthy climates in which many of them are called to labour, and the peculiar dangers to which they are often exposed in travelling by sea and by land, we can only attribute their general preservation, and the comparative fewness of the casualties which occur in their ranks, to the watchful care of the Almighty. Verily the God of Missions is mindful of His servants, and His ear is ever attentive to the prayers of His people for their protection. And yet, the history of missions has been occasionally marked by afflictions and bereavements of a very painful character which are worthy of a passing notice, and which we cannot contemplate without being deeply impressed with the strong claims which the missionaries and their families have upon our sympathy and prayers. Able missionaries have sometimes been smitten down with fever, and called away by death in the prime of life, and in the midst of their usefulness, after they had learned the language of the people among whom they laboured, and when their friends were anticipating for them many years of successful service. Men of God have also been called to mourn the death of beloved partners or dear children, and to commit them to the silent grave in distant lands. And in a few instances missionaries and their wives have been lost at sea under circumstances peculiarly trying and afflictive.

These and similar mysterious dispensations of Divine Providence are no doubt intended for the trial of our faith, and to humble us beneath the mighty hand of God, that we may be led to depend more implicitly on Him, who can work with or without means as He thinks best, and who sometimes sees fit to bury His workmen while at the same time He carries on His work. Or He may intend by these afflictive visitations to remove those whom He loves from the evil to come, and to admonish us for our lack of earnestness in prayer for the preservation of useful lives, and our general want of interest in the work of God. In any case we may be quite sure that a God of infinite wisdom and goodness can do nothing wrong; and we may confidently ask with the patriarch, "Shall not the Judge of all the earth do right?" "Clouds and darkness may be round about Him; but righteousness and judgment are the habitation of His throne."

"With even mind thy course of duty run:
God nothing does, or suffers to be done,
But thou wouldst do thyself, couldst thou but see
The end of all events as well as He."

132. The Missionary's Orphan.

—One of the most affecting cases of affliction and bereavement which has come under our notice in the mission-field, was the sickness and sudden death by yellow fever of both the Rev. James M'Mullen, and his devoted wife, soon after their arrival at Gibraltar in 1804. On landing at their appointed station, they found the fell disease raging among the wasted population with fearful violence. It had invaded almost every family, and there was scarcely a house in which there was not one dead. The missionary's child, a beautiful little girl, had scarcely breathed the tainted air when she was seized with the malady. On the 10th of October her anxious father, fatigued with constant watching by the couch of affliction, was himself prostrated with fever, and on the 18th he was a corpse. Mrs M'Mullen had borne up during these days of woe with wonderful fortitude, being sustained by her unwavering faith in the goodness and mercy of God; but at the hour which ended the life of her dear husband, she was herself smitten with the shaft of the pestilence, and followed him in a few days to the tomb. Contrary to all expectation, the orphan child survived, and as soon as possible, was sent under suitable care to England. In His kind providence, the God of her parents gave her a home in the family of good Dr Clarke. That fatherly man and his excellent wife brought up the little Gibraltar orphan-girl as their own daughter, and had the satisfaction of seeing her rise into life well-educated, amiable, and pious. She at length became the wife of an eminent Methodist minster, the Rev. John Rigg, and lived to see her children the subject of divine blessing in providence and grace; one of her sons being the Rev. James H. Rigg, D.D., the esteemed Principal of the Westminster Training College. She finished her course in peace at Southport, on the 3d of June 1869, in the seventy-third year of her age.

133. A Missionary Overboard.

—Additional labourers being required to minister to the scattered settlers of the British Provinces of North America, missionaries were occasionally sent from England to strengthen the hands of the brethren already there. In 1830 an intelligent and devoted young minister, the Rev. Robert J. Snelgrove, was appointed to a station in the New Brunswick district, and he embarked for his new sphere of labour in good health and spirits, anticipating a long and useful career in that part of the wide field for which he was designated. In the mysterious but all-wise providence of God, however, he was not permitted to engage in the work on which his heart was set. He never reached his destination, but found a watery grave in the wide Atlantic. The ship in which the young missionary sailed had reached the banks of Newfoundland when she was overtaken by a severe gale of wind. The passengers were advised to remain below as much as possible; but Mr Snelgrove, feeling the need of a little fresh air, ventured on deck when the ship was contending against a rough sea and a contrary wind. He had seated himself for a moment on a hen-coop, when, seeing a tremendous wave approaching, he arose to return to the cabin; but before he reached the companion-way the wave swept over the ship and washed him overboard. From the tempestuous state of the weather, and the speed at which the vessel was surging along, no help could be rendered, and the young missionary was seen no more; but from his acknowledged piety and zeal, he was no doubt prepared for the sudden change. When the intelligence of this sad disaster reached his friends at home, and the people of the station where his arrival was expected, the effects which it produced may be more readily imagined than described. This mournful event occurred on the 19th of August 1830.

134. Missionary Prisoner of War.—At an early period of the missionary enterprise, and especially in war-time, the missionaries were exposed to trials and difficulties such as their successors have happily but seldom experienced. On reaching his appointed station in Antigua, and writing home under date of May 3, 1798, the Rev. B. M'Donald gives the following account of the adventures of his voyage to the West Indies:—

"The first Sabbath after we sailed from Liverpool was spent in warlike preparations, as we met with a French privateer, which kept us two days in continual readiness for fighting: but she durst not engage us, and at last parted from us in a gale of wind. For three weeks we met with continual storms and foul winds, after which the weather became more favourable. On the 6th of November, when about ten leagues from Antigua, we fell in with another French privateer. We made all preparations in our power to receive her. I thought it my duty on this occasion not to remain an idle spectator; but commending myself to the protection of the Almighty, I took my station in a place which I judged would be most serviceable to the common cause. The enemy did not fire till she was almost within pistol-shot of us, and then commenced a close fire for about an hour. Our captain being wounded in the thigh by a four-pound shot, was unable to stand any longer. However, we continued the engagement till they boarded us. We had twelve guns, and 21 men and boys. The French ship had 10 guns, and 136 men, 50 of whom were marines. I was plundered of everything except the clothes I had on. All my religious books were torn in pieces. During the engagement the French had 30 men killed and wounded; we had a few men wounded, but no lives lost. Three days after I was landed in Guadaloupe, and cast into a filthy prison with the bare floor for my bed, among a number of unhappy wretches of all kinds, particularly some French negroes, who lived worse than beasts.

"I was happily released in a few days from this horrible situation, through the kind intercession of a French nobleman, likewise a prisoner, but who was indulged with a lodging in the jailer's house. He procured me the same favour, and I resided with him till my removal to Bassaterre. In this place I was confined in an old church, which the French had converted into a prison. My fellow-prisoners were mostly Englishmen. They were given up to drunkenness and swearing. However, I preached to them, and some seemed attentive to the Word. I likewise found some Methodist negroes, to whom I often read the Bible, and had serious conversation with them. No beds were allowed us, but we slept upon the flags or boards. Our allowance was one pound each of coarse bread, and five ounces of salt fish. After remaining three weeks in this prison, I was exchanged, and sent on board an English man-of-war. The captain, understanding that I was a Methodist preacher, treated me with the greatest kindness, and desired that I would continue with him as chaplain in his ship; but my previous engagements prevented me from accepting this kind offer, and he landed me on the Island of Dominica; from thence I went to Port Royal in Martinico. Here I found myself in a forlorn condition, destitute of money, food, or friends, and among strangers, most of whom were French, and no probable method presented itself of procuring a passage to Antigua. As I was walking through the streets, looking up to the Lord for deliverance, I met a strange gentleman, and had the boldness given me to acquaint him with my embarrassment. The Lord opened his heart—and he lent me ten pounds to pursue my voyage to Antigua.

"After taking a little refreshment, I sailed in a boat to St Piers, a good trading-town, where I hoped to obtain a passage to the place of my destination. Here also the Lord raised up another friend: a strange gentleman took me to his house, and gave me clean linen, which I was greatly in want of. From St Piers I sailed in a sloop, under convoy of an English privateer of 14 guns. Next day we were becalmed close under Guadaloupe. The French sent out two privateers to take us, one of 16 guns, and the other of 6, both full of men. Our privateer fought them, while we lay by looking on, having no arms, nor any oars to effect our escape from the danger; and consequently I expected in a short time to fall into the enemy's hands again, and to be lodged in the same jail I had so lately been liberated from. In about an hour our privateer beat off both the French vessels, and drove them home in a very shattered condition. Immediately the enemy sent more ships after us, but the Lord gave us wind, so we got safe into St John's in Antigua on Sunday the 9th of December.

"In Antigua I have met with an affectionate people, and am happy in my work. Notwithstanding the difficulties I have met with in my voyage, I do not regret coming here; but am amply repaid for all my toils by a sense of God's goodness, and by being made a happy witness of the revival of His work in this island."

135. A Missionary Plundered.

—The Rev. William Burns, Presbyterian missionary in China, in the course of a journey in the interior, was lying awake one night in anxious thought, when suddenly he became aware of two muffled figures approaching his bed-side, with blackened faces and stealthy steps. They stood over him with naked swords held to his breast! "Do no violence, my friends," he said calmly, "and you shall have all." Accordingly the robbers released their victim, but took with them all he possessed, save only the contents of a loose bag, which seemed to contain nothing but useless papers. Beneath these papers, however, lay a few *shreds* of under-garments, of which the poor missionary contrived to make for himself an outlandish costume, in which he found his way back to the sea-coast, and thence to Hong Kong, waiting under cover in the boat until the return of a messenger supplied him with the means of appearing among his friends in a more appropriate garb.

Whilst the thieves were plundering the apartment of the missionary, they came upon a strange article, the use of which they could not divine. This was a hone. One of the fellows had the audacity to come with it to Mr Burns to ascertain its use, when the dear man of God patiently taught the robber the mode of sharpening a razor upon it! The next morning, when his landlord came to his plundered guest to condole with him in his sufferings, the only answer he received was, "Poor fellows, let us pray for them."

136. Loss of the "Maria" Mailboat.

The mail-boat called the *Maria* was a beautiful little schooner employed chiefly in the service of the Government among the Leeward Islands of the West Indies. At the close of the annual district meeting held in St Kitts in February 1826, five Wesleyan missionaries, the Rev. Messrs White, Truscott, Hillier, Oke, and Jones, with Mrs Truscott, Mrs Jones, four children, and two servants, embarked on board this vessel for Antigua, after having in vain attempted to reach the island in another schooner in which they first set sail, and which was driven back by contrary winds. Captain Witney, who commanded the *Maria*, was an experienced mariner, and as his vessel appeared superior to the one which they had left, the missionaries hoped to reach their destination on the following day. They had not been on board long, however, before they were again overtaken by stormy weather and adverse winds. During the night of Monday the 27th, the day on which they embarked, the vessel was tossed about with great violence; and although the passengers had turned into their berths, it was impossible for any one to obtain much sleep, although no special danger was as yet apprehended. On the following morning it was found that the gale had increased in violence, and on attempting to go on deck, the missionaries were driven back by the waves which were washing over the bulwarks, and all was confusion and dismay among the seamen.

Considerable alarm now prevailed on board, which was for a time allayed by the cheering sound of "Land ahead! Antigua in sight!" Mr Hillier, who had succeeded in reaching the deck, called to his friends below to be of good cheer, as they would soon be on shore.

Shortly after land had been sighted, and hope was entertained of soon reaching the harbour of St John's, the *Maria* struck upon a reef of rocks, and became a total wreck. The vessel parted about midship, and broke up by degrees as the waves of the sea continued to roll over her. This continued for three days and three nights, during which the sufferings of the seamen and passengers were indescribable. One after another they succumbed to the cold and wet and literal starvation, and all on board perished in the waves except Mrs Jones, who was found insensible, and only just alive, on the morning of Friday, March the 3d, when the wreck was discovered, and assistance was sent from the shore. By the kind attentions of Messrs Kentish and Ashford, and Dr Peddie of St John's, Antigua, Mrs Jones, the only survivor of the mission party, was restored to health, and spared to tell the touching story of what she and her companions endured on the occasion of this mysterious dispensation of Divine Providence. Thus suddenly were five devoted missionaries hurried out of time into eternity, and nearly three thousand church-members deprived of their beloved pastors. Truly the ways of God are a great deep which we cannot fathom with our present feeble finite minds; but "what we know not now we shall know hereafter."

137. Death of Mr and Mrs Wrigley, and Mr and Mrs Harrop.

The climate of the

Western Coast of Africa is proverbially unhealthy, especially to Europeans, and it is not without a cause that it has been designated "*the white man's grave.*" The mortality has been great, both in the army and navy serving there, as well as in the ranks of mercantile adventurers, and among the agents of different missionary bodies; the Wesleyan Missionary Society having lost by death sixty-eight missionaries and missionary wives in the course of about half a century, to say nothing of the scores who have returned to their native land with their health seriously impaired. Some of these devoted servants of Christ have been called away under circumstances peculiarly affecting, an instance or two of which may be given as specimens, to show the claim which those who still labour there have upon the sympathy and prayers of the friends of missions.

To meet the necessities of the new station at Cape Coast, left vacant by the death of the Rev. J. R. Dunwell in 1835, the Rev. G. O. Wrigley and his excellent wife were sent out the following year, and arrived in safety on the 15th of September 1836. Four months afterwards, on the 15th of January 1837, they were joined by the Rev. Peter and Mrs Harrop, who were sent out to strengthen the mission, and to provide against the casualties to which the work had so often been subject in Western Africa. With this efficient staff of labourers it was hoped that the good work, which had assumed such an encouraging aspect, would be prosecuted with great success. But how frail and weak and short-sighted is mortal man! In a few short months the whole party was swept away by fever, and the people were again left as sheep without a shepherd. Indeed, Mr and Mrs Harrop died in three weeks after their arrival, having been attacked with fever soon after they landed. They finished their course, and were called to their reward in the following order:—Mrs Harrop on the 5th of February, Mr Harrop and Mrs Wrigley on the 8th of February, and Mr Wrigley on the 15th of November 1837. We may imagine the feelings of the poor bereaved missionary, Mr Wrigley, the last survivor of the four, when he was called to close the eyes of his beloved wife, and those of his dear colleague, in the same hour, and that within three days of the death of the first victim of the fell destroyer. In writing to the Missionary Committee shortly afterwards, he says:—"Life indeed, in my circumstances, has no charms; nor could I support myself beneath the weight of such a stroke, were it not for the hope of ere long joining the glorified spirit of my devoted partner, and in the meantime following up those victories of the cross of our Emmanuel, which together we have been enabled to achieve to His glory, since we arrived on these inhospitable shores." This hope of meeting in heaven with the glorified spirits of the dear departed, was soon realised by the removal of the writer to the better country, and the station was once more left vacant. It is a pleasing fact, however, that others were soon found ready to hazard their lives in the noble enterprise, and Western Africa has never been without volunteer missionaries to fill the vacancies caused by the death of those who have fallen at their posts of duty.

138. Death of Mr and Mrs Parkinson.—The Rev. James and Mrs Parkinson, having been appointed by the Wesleyan Missionary Society to labour in Western Africa, arrived at St Mary's, on the River Gambia, on the 13th of December 1838; and being in every respect, to all human appearance, well adapted to the work which they had undertaken, they entered upon it with cheering prospects of success. For some time they continued to labour without interruption, and their letters to the Committee and to their personal friends were most encouraging; but when the first rainy season set in, their troubles commenced. Mr Parkinson was attacked with fever one Sunday evening after preaching; and such was the rapid progress of the disease, that he sank beneath its influence on Sunday morning following, the 8th of September 1839. Mrs Parkinson had been seized with the same disorder in the meantime, and being dangerously ill at the time of her husband's death, from a mistaken feeling of tenderness, as we think, the friends in attendance kept her in ignorance of the mournful fact, fearing the intelligence of her sad bereavement might be more than she could bear.

At length the attention of the sufferer was attracted by a strange noise, which she could not reconcile with the wonted stillness of the Sabbath morn. She inquired what it meant. It was the native carpenters at work on her husband's coffin, at a short distance from the mission premises; but the friends evaded her question, and tried to pacify her. Two days after the death of her husband, Mrs Parkinson gave birth to a daughter. Again she asked about her husband's health, as she had repeatedly done before, and she was told that "he was doing very well indeed." "If he is doing so very well, and is so much better," said the poor invalid, "why does he not come to see me and the dear babe?" On being told that, "although doing well he could not be removed," she became almost frantic, and exclaimed, "Then if he cannot come to see me, I must go to him, *and I will!*" and suiting the action to the word, she was with difficulty kept in bed: nor could she be pacified, till a gentleman present took in his hand a cup of coffee, with her kind love, and went out of the room to that at the opposite end of the house, where she supposed her husband was! The sequel is soon told. On the following day, September 12th, she gently breathed her spirit into the hands of that God who gave it, and joined her husband in the "better country;" and then the mystery was unravelled, and the declaration of David emphatically verified, "I shall go to him, but he shall not return to me."

This affecting story does not end here, however. The little orphan babe was sent to England, under the care of a kind friend; but she died on the passage, and so escaped from this world of sin and sorrow, to join her parents in the skies. Then was the happy mother in a better position than the Shunammite woman of old, to whom the threefold question was put, "Is it well with thee? Is it well with thy husband? Is it well with the child? And she answered, It is well."

139. Affecting Funeral.—Many touching instances of affliction and bereavement have come under our notice at different times and in different countries, but the case of the first mission family that settled in Kaffirland, South Africa, was peculiarly affecting. Some time after the zealous but eccentric Dr Vanderkemp had failed in his attempt to establish a mission-station among the warlike Kaffirs, the directors of the London Missionary Society appointed the Rev. Joseph

Williams and his devoted wife to that part of the wide field. They had laboured there about two years, and a good impression had been made, when, in the month of August 1818, the useful career of the zealous missionary was cut short by sickness and death. Mrs Williams watched by the death-couch of her beloved husband till the flickering lamp of life was quenched in darkness, and was left a lonely widow under circumstances peculiarly trying. The station, on the upper part of the Kat River, was far away from the abodes of civilised men, and she had no kind friend at hand to render her assistance in this the hour of her great sorrow. The natives were very attentive, however, and showed a cheerful readiness to do everything in their power to comfort and aid the poor bereaved widow. Under her direction they made a rude coffin and dug the grave; and when all was ready for the funeral, they bore the remains of their dear departed missionary silently and sorrowfully to their last resting-place in the wilderness, followed by the lonely mourner with an infant in her arms and a little child led by the hand. When they reached the place, there being no one sufficiently advanced as yet to read, or perform any religious service on the solemn occasion, Mrs Williams knelt on the margin of the grave, and made her requests known to God, whilst the natives, in sympathy and sadness, committed the body to the ground in "sure and certain hope of a joyful resurrection to eternal life through our Lord Jesus Christ." The Father of the fatherless and the Judge of the widow did not forget the bereaved ones in the wilderness; He provided for them friends and home, when their case became known to the supporters of the enterprise, but many years passed away before the people were favoured with another teacher.

The Rev. S. Kay, of the Wesleyan Missionary Society, on travelling through that part of the country eleven years afterwards, makes the following touching observations:—
"The day being oppressively hot, I was obliged to travel very slowly; nevertheless, about an hour's ride brought me to the spot where lie the remains of the Rev. Mr Williams. I rode a short distance out of the way in order to see the field in which he toiled, and the place where he expired. Having with me one of the Kaffirs who resided with him, witnessed his death, and assisted at his funeral, I was enabled to collect various particulars, the interest of which was, of course, greatly enhanced by the circumstance of our being in the very vale where they transpired. The grave of our departed brother is distinguished from others only by a larger pile of stones, one of which, somewhat bigger than the rest, is placed in an upright position at the head. From hence I was led to the tree under which Mr Williams preached; to the field that he had ploughed, the furrows of which are still visible; to the garden he had cultivated; to the dam that he designed for the irrigation of his grounds; and to the precipice whence he had rolled many a huge mass, with the view of turning the course of the river below, so as to render the complete inundation of his land practicable when necessary. This was a gigantic scheme; in attempting which he lost one of his fingers: a large stone falling upon it, entirely severed it from the hand. We next proceeded to the building that was intended for a place of worship, and to the dwelling-house, which was partially completed. 'In that corner,' said Cota, 'our *umfundis* (teacher) expired, and there did I

140. Missionary Martyrs of Namaqualand.—The Rev. William Threlfall was a zealous young missionary, who, having failed in an attempt to establish a Wesleyan mission at Delago Bay, in consequence of the failure of his health and other untoward circumstances, proceeded to the Khamiesberg Station, South Africa, in 1825, to assist the Rev. Barnabas Shaw in the good work in which he was engaged. It had long been in contemplation to endeavour to carry the gospel into the regions beyond the Orange River known as Great Namaqualand, where the people were in a fearful state of moral degradation. The mission at Khamiesberg having been recently reinforced, it was thought a favourable time to enter upon the new enterprise; and Mr Threlfall, in the ardour of his zeal, and with improved health, having offered his services, with the sanction of his superintendent he set out on a journey of discovery, accompanied by two native teachers, Jacob Links and Johannes Jager. They were mounted on trained oxen, after the fashion of the country, and travelled without molestation till they got two or three days' journey beyond the Orange River.

At this point they came in contact with troublesome wandering tribes of Bushmen. Although they had with them, on a pack-ox, a few goods for barter, they suffered much from want of food, the people being unfriendly and unwilling to supply them with what they required at a fair price. On proceeding some distance beyond the Warm Bath, they obtained a guide at a Bushman village; but he and his associates, instead of conducting the travellers in safety through the wilderness, formed a cruel plot for the destruction of the whole party, that they might take possession of their effects. Accordingly the following night, while Mr Threlfall and his companions were sleeping under a bush, as usual, without the slightest apprehension of danger, their foes came upon them, and murdered them all in cold blood. Jacob Links and Johannes Jager were first despatched, by repeated blows from assagis and large stones. Mr Threlfall was awoke by the commotion in the camp, and seeing his danger he fled to a short distance, pursued by his enemies; when, finding his escape impossible, he fell upon his knees under a bush, and received the fatal blows of the assailants in the attitude of prayer. As the murderers confessed afterwards, he appeared to be "talking with God" when he was thus mercilessly hurried out of time into eternity. The principal criminal was afterwards apprehended, tried, condemned and executed, and the writer looked upon his solitary grave in the desert many years afterwards with peculiar feelings. As several months elapsed before the sad fate of the martyred missionaries was known to the nearest stations, their remains were never recovered; but they will be forthcoming in that day when "the dead, small and great, shall stand before God." In the meantime their souls no doubt rest in peace, and, having been faithful unto death, they will each of them at last receive "a crown of glory that fadeth not away."

141. Murder of the Rev. J. S. Thomas.—The Rev. J. S. Thomas was a zealous and devoted Wesleyan missionary to the warlike Kaffirs in

South Africa, and had lived and laboured for many years in Kaffirland, when, in 1856, his useful career was suddenly cut short by a painful and mysterious dispensation of Divine Providence. He had just removed from Clarkebury to Beecham Wood, and the country was in a very unsettled state. Some of the people who had joined him on his new station had recently been quarrelling and fighting with a party of natives belonging to another tribe. In the fight three men had been killed, and their friends declared that they would not rest till they had taken the life of the man who had led on the attack.

In the middle of the fourth night, after Mr Thomas had arrived at Beecham Wood, there was a cry, "We are attacked by the Pondas." He immediately arose and ran out of the house. He returned for a minute just to arrange as best he could for the safety of his family, and the women and children who were flocking to his dwelling in confusion and dismay. He then went to speak to the enemy, with the hope of appeasing their rage and preventing bloodshed, as he had often done before. When he reached the cattle-fold he found the enemy in strong force, and apparently bent upon plunder. He cried out, "I am your missionary! Why do you attack me?" As soon as he had said this, one of the enemy cried out to another repeatedly, "Stab! stab!" When Mr Thomas heard this he said to the man who was with him. "Let us return, they will do us mischief." They turned to go back; but alas! it was too late: one of the men threw a spear which struck Mr Thomas, and he fell, upon which the enemy rushed upon him, and struck him several times with their assagais till life was extinct. Hearing the noise of the tumult, the missionary's wife handed her child to a Kaffir girl, and rushed out of the house towards the cattle-kraal, whence the savage yells of the cruel natives came; but before she reached the place, she met a party of natives carrying her husband a livid corpse! She was indeed severely crushed and sorely afflicted by this sad bereavement; but she tried to gather some consolation from the facts that her beloved husband had laboured long and faithfully in the mission-field, and that he was found prepared for his Master's call, and had written a short time before his lamented death the following striking lines.

"For me a victor's crown
Of glory is prepared,
And when I lay this body down,
This shall be my reward."

142. Loss of the Steamship "London."—The Rev. D. J. Draper and his excellent wife were about to return to Australia in the early part of the year 1865, after a very pleasant visit to England, when they were unexpectedly called to the "better country," under circumstances peculiarly affecting. They had taken their passage in the steamer *London*, a first-class ship, 260 feet in length, and of 200 horse-power in her engines. On the 1st of January they took leave of their friends in the metropolis, and proceeded to Plymouth to be ready for embarkation, the ship having gone round to that port from Gravesend. In her passage down the Channel, the *London* experienced boisterous weather, and came to anchor at intervals, both at the Nore and at Spithead; and it was not without difficulty, and even the loss of the pilot's life, that she was brought within the breakwater at Plymouth, about noon on Friday the 5th. In the evening Mr and Mrs Draper went on board in good health and spirits. Having been inspected by the emigration agent, who found all right, and who gave the usual certificate, a little after midnight, when the remainder of the passengers had embarked, and all was ready for sea, the vessel steamed out of the Sound, and proceeded on her eventful voyage, the weather being now moderate, with a light wind ahead.

At the time the ship left the port the barometer had fallen considerably; yet, as the wind and sea had moderated, no serious consequences were apprehended, and it was not deemed necessary to detain her. During the whole of Saturday the vessel had full steam on, and she proceeded on her way satisfactorily. On Sunday morning the 7th, although the wind had freshened somewhat, there was nothing to excite alarm in the mind of any one, and divine service was held in the chief saloon, the Rev. Dr Woolley, Professor of Sydney University, and the Rev. D. J. Draper, Wesleyan missionary, being associated in conducting it. On Sunday night, however, the wind increased to a strong gale, and the sea rose considerably. On Monday the ship was well clear of land, and had reached the open Bay of Biscay. The heavy swell continuing and the storm rising still higher, the captain stopped the engines and set his topsails, with a view to steady the motion of the vessel. On the following day the wind increased to a perfect hurricane; the sea ran mountains high, and broke over the vessel, and carried away one of the lifeboats. The long and dreary night which followed, was a time of gloomy apprehension to many on board; but at length it wore away, and as the storm gave no signs of abatement, the captain ordered the ship to be put about, intending to run back to Plymouth for repairs. Within half an hour from the time when her course was altered, the full fury of a heavy sea struck the ship, swept away the starboard lifeboat, and stove in the starboard cutter. The *London*, with her passengers and crew, was now about two hundred miles south-west of the Land's End.

About half-past ten o'clock on Wednesday night, January the 10th, a "mountain of waters," as described by the survivors, fell suddenly on the waist of the ship, swept away the main hatchway, flooded the engine-room, extinguished the fires, and filled the lower decks until the engineer was up to the waist in water. Soon after this the awful crisis came. The ship went down with her crew and passengers, 252 in number, all of whom found a watery grave except nineteen, who were saved as by miracle, in a boat which they entered at the last moment. The survivors described Mr Draper as incessantly engaged in praying with and exhorting the passengers to look to Christ, the only Saviour of sinners, in the hour of peril, and there is reason to believe that he was made the means of comfort and salvation to many. Thus were the shipwrecked missionary and his devoted wife found at the post of duty, when they and the whole congregation were in the same moment called into the presence of the King eternal.

143. A Missionary Murdered in Prison.—The missionaries of the Wesleyan Society have, from the commencement of the enterprise, cheerfully ministered to all classes of persons with whom they have come in contact in foreign parts, whilst at the same time they paid special attention to the heathen to whom they were more especially sent. At an early period the convicts of Australia were greatly indebted to them for religious instruction and pastoral oversight, and long after the termination of the convict system the missionaries frequently ministered to poor unhappy prisoners. It was whilst engaged in service of this kind that the Rev. William Hill lost his life. On the 14th of May 1869 he went to see a criminal under sentence of death, in the prison at Melbourne, with the hope of leading him to a sense of his awful condition. On entering the cell of the unhappy man, the missionary perceived a strange wildness, and an indescribable something in his appearance and manner; but, unmoved by fear, he proceeded to discharge the important duty which was before him. Little or no impression appeared to be made upon the mind of the prisoner by the faithful exhortations and solemn appeals of the zealous minister, but he proceeded as usual to ask God's blessing upon him. When bowed in the attitude of prayer, the wretched criminal watched his opportunity, pounced upon his victim like a tiger, and with a piece of iron which he had torn from his cot, and apparently prepared for the purpose, he murdered the missionary in a moment, and the turnkey, attracted by the dying cries of the man of God, hastened to the cell to find him a mangled corpse. How mysterious that a devoted minister of Christ should thus be ignominiously smitten down in the midst of his days and usefulness by the hand of violence in a criminal's cell, when in the very act of ministering to his spiritual welfare!

144. Shipwreck of Mr and Mrs Cross.—The Rev. William Cross was a zealous and devoted Wesleyan missionary, who laboured long and successfully in the Friendly and Fiji Islands, at an early period of the enterprise, when many hardships and privations had to be endured. In the month of January 1832, when on their way from Tonga to Vavau, Mr and Mrs Cross suffered shipwreck under circumstances peculiarly afflictive, inasmuch as Mrs Cross lost her life in the struggle, and her bereaved husband was left in loneliness and sorrow. The mournful story forms one of the saddest pages in the history of the South Sea Mission, and we shall endeavour to give it as briefly as possible, that our readers may see and feel the claim which the missionaries and their families have upon their sympathy and prayers.

It was on Saturday morning, the 7th, that Mr and Mrs Cross embarked on board a large canoe at Nukualofa, with a considerable number of native sailors and attendants. The plan was to proceed as far as a small island called Namuka, one of the Haabi group, and after spending the Sabbath there in religious service, proceed to Vavau. For some time the weather was fine and the wind favourable ; but before noon the breeze and the swell increased, and soon afterwards, first a yard and then a mast were carried away. As evening approached, the sailors were anxiously looking out for land, supposing they were not far from Namuka. Night, however, came on, and no land appeared. The men having toiled hard all day, and provisions being scarce, many of them slept through weariness ; and those whose anxiety for the safety of the vessel kept them awake, were unable to manage her. Consequently she made no progress, but drifted hither and thither till the break of day. The condition of Mr and Mrs Cross during this long and gloomy night was one of extreme discomfort, and not unattended with apprehensions of danger. About an hour after sunrise on Sunday morning, an island appeared in sight which all on board hoped might be Namuka, at which they wished to call, as already stated. As the wind was still favourable, another sail was set to accelerate the progress of the vessel, and they steered towards the land, which proved to be a small uninhabited island called Hunga Haabi, where they were unable to go on shore on account of the steepness of the rocks.

Finding themselves quite out of their proper track, the missionary and his men were perplexed to know what to do for the best. At length they resolved to return to Tongataboo, and make a fresh start. They accordingly stood away on the new course just decided upon; and in order to lighten the canoe, which laboured much from the heavy swell on the sea, they threw the mast and part of the broken yard overboard. The motion of the vessel being now less violent, the missionary and his wife availed themselves of the opportunity of taking a little refreshment, as they began to feel very weak, Mr Cross having taken nothing for upwards of thirty hours, and Mrs Cross only a little cocoa-nut milk during that time. The lady was, moreover, delicate at best, and had been very unwell since Saturday. The wind continuing favourable, the canoe made fair progress, and before sunset they sighted an island called Atata, one of the Tonga group, and only seven miles from Tongataboo. The native sailors hoped soon to reach that place, and proceed homeward on the following day. At nine o'clock they were not more than three or four miles from land; but as the moon went down the wind changed, and blew furiously against them. As the storm increased, the men made haste to take in sail; but they had scarcely done so, and seized their paddles, when the canoe was driven with fearful violence on a coral reef, and immediately began to break up. Joseph, a native teacher, came to the missionary, and said with trembling, in his native tongue, "Mr Cross, be strong our minds towards God: we are all dead!" They endeavoured to commit themselves to God in prayer; and in a few minutes they were all washed off the wreck into the sea, and the frail vessel was entirely dashed to pieces. Mr Cross had his arms round his dear wife when they first went down, nor did he lose his grasp. Several times they rose to the surface, but were as often again overwhelmed with the surf. Whilst thus buffeting with the waves, the missionary continued to hold his precious burden with his right arm, whilst his left hand was employed in catching at some poles and broken pieces of the canoe which were floating about, and by means of which their heads were for a time kept above the water, so that they could breathe occasionally. No word of complaint or alarm escaped from the lips of the frail sufferer in this fearful time of trial. She only called upon the name of the Lord for help, and was encouraged by her husband to look to Jesus. A few more seconds and she spoke no more. Her spirit had taken its flight to the mansions above. In this appalling wreck, in addition to Mrs Cross, fourteen adults and five children lost their lives, and Mr Cross and the rest of the men narrowly escaped a watery grave by constructing a rude raft from pieces of the broken canoe, on which, by the good providence of God, they were floated on shore.

The survivors at length reached Tongataboo; and when Mr Cross had walked along the beach about two miles towards his former home, he was overtaken by a messenger from Hihifo, to inform him that the body of his dear wife had been washed on shore. Mr Cross was kindly received by his missionary brother, the Rev. J. Thomas, who sincerely sympathised with him in his sad bereavement. Having committed the remains of his beloved wife to the grave in a foreign land, and rested for a few days, the bereaved missionary embarked once more for his new sphere of labour in Vavau, where he ultimately arrived in safety, and addressed himself to his important work as best he could in his sorrow and loneliness.

145. The Rev. John H. Bumby.

—The Rev. J. H. Bumby was a talented Wesleyan minister who had occupied important circuits for several years at home, when he felt it upon his heart to offer himself for the foreign department of the work. His offer was accepted, and in 1838 he received an appointment as a missionary to New Zealand. As Mr Bumby was unmarried, his sister accompanied him to his new sphere of labour, where he arrived in safety, and entered upon his work with a pleasing prospect of success. He had only been in the country about fifteen months, however, when his labours were suddenly cut short by a melancholy event, which plunged the churches at home and abroad in sorrow, and deprived the Wesleyan Missionary Society of one of its most faithful and devoted servants.

In the prosecution of his important duties, as chairman of the New Zealand district, Mr Bumby found it necessary to take extensive journeys both by sea and by land, and in the course of one of them he was suddenly and unexpectedly hurried out of time into eternity. In this instance the missionary had occasion to cross an arm of the sea known as the Bay of Thames, on his homeward journey, after an absence of two or three weeks. The weather was remarkably fine as he sailed along in a large canoe, accompanied by eighteen natives. No danger was apprehended from any source. When one of the men stood up to set the sail with a view to accelerate their progress, a gentle breeze having just sprung up in their favour, at the same moment several of the other natives rose from their seats, with eager haste to assist, and the canoe being deeply laden, was upset, and the whole party submerged in the mighty deep. It was a moment of intense consternation; but as soon as the natives recovered themselves a little—for most of them were excellent swimmers—they made a strenuous effort, not only to save their own lives, but also that of their beloved missionary. They soon succeeded in righting the canoe, and in getting Mr Bumby, who was unable to swim, into it; but when partly baled out, and hope was entertained of success, the frail vessel was upset again, by the rush towards it of several of the men who were struggling in the water. Again they got the drowning missionary lifted on to the canoe, capsized as it was, and again he was washed off by the waves. As there was no other vessel in sight, all hope of deliverance was taken away, and the devoted missionary and twelve of the natives sank to rise no more, only six escaping on shore to carry to their friends the news of the sad disaster.

This mournful event occurred on Friday the 26th of June 1860, and when the intelligence was conveyed to the mission-station of Mangungu, it produced a scene of mourning, lamentation, and woe never to be forgotten by those who witnessed it. The mortal remains of the dear departed missionary were never washed on shore, and could not therefore be honoured with those funeral rites which are sometimes a source of melancholy satisfaction to surviving friends; but his redeemed spirit was no doubt conveyed to the paradise of God, and his body will be forthcoming when the "sea shall give up the dead that are therein."

146. The Martyrs of Erromanga.

The life and labours of the Rev. John Williams, of the London Missionary Society, will ever be associated with the history of Christianity in Polynesia. Mr Williams and his noble band of associates and native assistants had succeeded in planting the gospel in many of the islands of the South Seas, where the name of Christ had never before been heard, when their attention was directed to the New Hebrides, the inhabitants of which were noted for their savage cruelty. The reception of the pioneer and his companions at the first two islands of the group which they visited was favourable; but when they landed on the shores of Erromanga, they witnessed signs of distrust and treachery which developed themselves in acts of violence when it was too late for the peaceful strangers to make their escape. Mr Harris, an English gentleman who accompanied Mr Williams on this occasion, was seen to fall under the clubs of the infuriated savages as he walked along the shore, whilst Mr Williams was smitten down after he had entered the water, and while attempting to reach the boat. The melancholy intelligence of the missionary martyr's doom was the cause of sincere mourning and lamentation both in Polynesia and in England; but having been found faithful unto death, his redeemed spirit was no doubt received into that happy place where the "wicked cease from troubling and where the weary are at rest." This mournful event occurred in 1838, soon after Mr Williams' visit to England. Some portions of the remains of the murdered missionary and his companion were afterwards recovered and conveyed to the island of Upola, where they were devoutly interred near to the spot where the zealous pioneer first landed when he took that gospel to the Navigator's group which has produced such a moral revolution among the natives.

In 1872 another missionary martyr fell in unhappy Erromanga. After the death of Mr Williams, the friends of missions were anxious to convey the gospel to a people so savage and degraded, and the station was at length occupied by missionaries of the Presbyterian denomination, who succeeded in bringing a few of them to the knowledge of the truth. The Rev. J. D. Gordon was a medical man as well as a minister, and was therefore peculiarly adapted for his position. One of the natives had sent a request that the missionary should visit his sick children. He promptly responded; but on arriving at the place he found that the children were dead. The native charged Mr Gordon with being the cause of his bereavement, and in a rage of passion tomahawked him on the spot. This tragedy is rendered the more distressing from the fact that Mr Gordon's brother and his sister-in-law were both killed by the natives of Erromanga about twelve years ago. Verily "the dark places of the earth are full of the habitations of cruelty."

147. Missionary Martyrs of Fiji.

Missionary-work had been

carried on for several years among the savage cannibals of Fiji with remarkable results, and with comparatively little sacrifice of health and life, when an event occurred which involved the brethren of the district, as well as the Society at home, in grief and sorrow. This was the barbarous murder of the Rev. Thomas Baker and his companions in the interior of one of the larger islands called Viti Levu. The station occupied by Mr Baker at the time was Davuiluvu, in the Rewa Circuit, about twelve miles from the mouth of the river; but several native teachers having been appointed to interior stations, among tribes who had recently abandoned their idols and embraced the *lotu*, it was thought desirable to pay them a visit of inspection. With this object in view Mr Baker left home, accompanied by a few native youths, on Saturday, July the 20th 1867, and ascended the river in his boat to a place called Natoaika, where he preached on the Sabbath. The following week was spent in visiting various out-stations and scattered tribes higher up the country, with which he had been more or less acquainted before.

When they reached Dawarau, Mr Baker seems to have resolved to attempt to cross the country to the northern coast, an object which he had long secretly cherished, as he wished to penetrate to the interior regions of Viti Levu, with the hope of inducing other tribes to embrace the *lotu*. From this place he wrote a letter to his wife, stating his intention, and the probability of his returning home by sea. On proceeding forward, Mr Baker and his party, which now consisted of a native missionary, two teachers, and six young men from the Training Institution, came in contact with a tribe of savage heathens at a place called Navosa, the chief of which wickedly plotted their destruction. They were allowed the use of a hut to lodge in on Saturday night; and, having cooked their supper, and united in their evening devotion, they retired to rest. But the noise and confusion which were kept up outside made sleep impossible, and from what they heard they had reason to believe that mischief was intended. This circumstance hastened their departure from the town next morning; but they had not proceeded more than a hundred yards when they were attacked by a band of armed men, with the chief at their head, and were all murdered in cold blood, with the exception of two of the young men, who escaped as by miracle, and fled with all possible speed to communicate to the missionary of the nearest station the mournful intelligence of the sad disaster.

148. Missionary Martyrs of Melanesia.—Since the lamented and tragic death of John Williams, no event has caused more sorrow to the friends of missions, than the murder of Bishop Patteson by the savage natives of Melanesia. He was one of the most earnest and devoted missionary labourers in the South Sea Islands, and his loss will be deeply felt, and sincerely deplored by all with whom he was associated. As an able and talented clergyman of the Church of England, he had fair prospects of promotion in his own country; but he left them all to engage in missionary-work among the heathen, first in New Zealand, and afterwards in the different islands of Melanesia; and he at length fell a sacrifice, not so much to the savage instincts of the heathen tribes among whom his lot was cast, as to the brutal treachery of his own countrymen, for it is admitted on all hands that white men had committed fearful depredations in connection with what they called the "labour traffic," and had dragged away hundreds of natives by force, to toil in Queensland and other places. Knowing the confidence of the people in Bishop Patteson and his missionaries, these marauders were in the habit of alluring them on board their vessel, by trying to make them believe that it was the mission-ship in which he was wont to travel. They went so far as to perform mock religious services on deck, one of them personating the good bishop in his canonicals! The consequence was, that the natives of certain Melanesian islands, in retaliation for the depredations committed, resolved to murder the first white men who ventured to approach their shores. Shortly afterwards, towards the close of 1871, Bishop Patteson paid his usual visit; but the natives refused to believe that it was really he, and as soon as he and his party attempted to land on the island of Santa Cruz, one of the Queen Charlotte group, the savages fell upon them and murdered the good bishop, the Rev. Mr Atkin, his companion, and a native teacher who was with them. Surely it is time for the British Government to put a stop to the system of kidnapping the helpless natives of the South Sea Islands which has so long been carried on under the flags of America and England.

"God moves in a mysterious way,
　His wonders to perform ;
He plants His footsteps in the sea,
　And rides upon the storm.
Deep in unfathomable mines
　Of never-failing skill,
He treasures up His bright designs,
　And works His sovereign will."

VI. GENERAL RESULTS OF MISSIONS.

149. Temporal Advantages of Missions.—The commercial value of Christian missions to the respective countries by which they have been sent forth and sustained, is evident and beyond question, although not often a subject of remark. The introduction of the gospel among a degraded heathen people everywhere tends to promote civilisation and social improvement; and consequently, in addition to the direct spiritual benefits which it confers, it creates a demand for European and American merchandise to an extent truly astonishing. We have no means of knowing the exact amount of the commerce which Christian missions have created in different countries, but it is quite clear that the gains of trade with once heathen countries are many times greater than the cost of the missions. The increase of our exports to Africa, Australasia, India, China, and other countries since Christianity began to prevail, is something marvellous. These exports have brought increased business-profits to our manufacturers; they have given work and competence to our mechanics; they have added to the business of railroads, steamships, and sailing vessels, increasing the wealth of individuals, companies, and nations. Nor must the value of our imports be overlooked. It has been estimated that for every pound England spends in missions she receives *ten* back in trade. We are sending to mission-fields for the natives, in sufficient quantities to be noticed, farming implements, machinery, furniture, household utensils and conveniences, clothing, books, and various other articles; and we receive from them importations of various productions. These increase commerce, and commerce enriches a nation by its transportation, by the sale of its exports and imports, by revenue on imported articles, and by its competition giving better articles on cheaper rates. So that in a temporal point of view it is evident that Christian missions pay even now, and every year their commercial value shows an increasing ratio.

150. Progress of the Gospel in Turkey.—Although we hear but little of it in this country, a great and good work has been going on for several years past in various parts of the Turkish Empire, generally known as the "Lands of the Bible." The honoured agents in this movement are chiefly missionaries from Scotland and America. Those from the country last named have been remarkably successful. According to a recent report, up to the present time the Americans have established in Turkey 222 common schools, have founded 78 churches, have educated and licensed 110 pastors and teachers, have opened 200 preaching-stations, have founded 4 theological colleges, have set up 12 girls' schools, and around these various institutions have gathered a Protestant population of over 20,000 souls. They have, moreover, circulated in the various languages of the empire 400,000 copies of the Sacred Scriptures, besides 500,000 other religious and useful books, many of them translations of European favourites and classics, and many college and school books, such as grammars, and works on arithmetic, astronomy, algebra, philosophy, mental science, and domestic economy.

These stupendous labours have been carried on, not so much among the Mohammedan population, who are extremely difficult of access, as among nominal Christians of the decayed and heterodox Greek and Armenian Churches. The moral and social change which has been produced in the neighbourhood of the respective stations has attracted the favourable notice of the Sultan, who now smiles on the efforts of the missionaries. The intellectual influence of these Transatlantic strangers begins at length to assert itself even in Constantinople. On the lofty shores of the Bosphorus, precisely on the spot where the Persians under Darius passed into Europe, the Robert College has been erected for the higher education of Turks, Armenians, Jews, Catholics, and Protestants alike, founded by the princely liberality of a New York merchant, whose name it bears. It accommodates 250 students, who are all taught English, as well as various branches of knowledge in their native tongues. A similar college at Beyrout, where Arabic—the language of 100,000,000 of mankind—is the common tongue of the institution, is occupied in spreading sound medical science and Christian knowledge over the whole of Syria. And the College of Aintab, now in progress, is expected to carry on the good work of civilisation in the Turkish language over the vast extent of Karamania and Armenia in the interior. The Americans expend £50,000 a year on their Turkish Missions, besides the sum of £100,000 which they have invested in the permanent institutions which we have described. Every true friend of missions must sincerely wish them success in their noble enterprise.

151. Mission to the Wyandot Indians.—As early as the year 1823, John Johnson, Esq., United States Agent for Indian Affairs, bore the following honourable testimony to the success of the mission of the Methodist Episcopal Church to the Wyandots at Upper Sandusky, under the superintendency of the Rev. J. B. Finley, in a letter to Bishop M'Kendree:—"The farm is under excellent fence, and in fine order, comprising about one hundred and forty acres in pasture, corn, and vegetables. Sixty children belong to the school, of which number fifty-one are Indians. These children are boarded and lodged at the mission-house. They are orderly and attentive; and comprise every class, from the alphabet to those that read in the Bible. I am told by the teacher that they are apt in learning, and that he is entirely satisfied with the progress they have made. They attend with the family regularly to the duties of religion. The meeting-house on the Sabbath is numerously and devoutly attended. A better congregation in behaviour I have not beheld; and I believe there can be no doubt that there are very many persons of both sexes in the Wyandot nation who have experienced the saving effects of the gospel upon their minds. Many of the Indians are now settling on farms, and have comfortable houses and large fields. A spirit of order, industry, and improvement appears to prevail with that part of the nation which has embraced Christianity—and this constitutes a full half of the whole population.

"I do not pretend to offer any opinion here on the practicability of civilising the Indians under the present arrangements of Government; but having spent a considerable portion of my life in managing this description of people, I am free to declare that the prospect of success here is greater than I have ever before witnessed,—that this mission is faithfully and ably conducted, and has the strongest claims upon the countenance and support of the Methodist Church, as well as on the Christian public at large."

152. Change in the West Indies.—Having laboured as a Christian missionary in the West Indies in the dark and gloomy days of negro slavery, during the transition period of the apprenticeship, and for several years after the glorious emancipation, the writer can testify to the wonderful change which was wrought by the power of the gospel among all classes at that early period,—a change which has scarcely a parallel in the history of the Church since the days of the apostles. And it is pleasing to know that the good work still goes on. A missionary, recently writing from Jamaica, bears testimony to the continued improvement of the people in every respect since the advent of freedom. He says:—
"In their houses, dress, manners, customs, personal appearance (complexion excepted), general deportment, wealth, morals, and religion, many of the black and coloured population are on equality with the most respectable of the whites. Nor are they less so in the higher attainments of the mind. There are now to be found among them men of talent, learning, and accomplishments, who would do honour to any community. They fill the public offices, practise as solicitors and barristers in the courts of law, and are found among our tradesmen, merchants, and estate proprietors, and directors of our civil institutions, are enrolled among our magistrates, and have even obtained seats and influence in the senate.

"The generosity of the females of colour has ever been proverbial, and their kindness to strangers suffering from the diseases of the country has won for them universal gratitude and admiration. Neither are they less remarkable for their social and domestic qualities. There have always been found among them some who in no respect suffered by a comparison with the most respectable of the whites. This number is increasing, and soon, by the possession of equal advantages, everything like characteristic distinction between these two classes will be lost."

"Children we are all
Of one Great Father, in whatever clime
His providence hath cast the seed of life,—
All tongues, all colours! Neither after death
Shall we be sorted into languages
And tints—white, black, and tawny,
Greek and Goth,
Northman and offspring of hot Africa.
The all-seeing Father—He in whom we live and move—
He, the indifferent Judge of all—regards
Nations and hues and dialects alike;
According to their works shall they be judged."

153. Eagerness of Negro Slaves to Learn to Read.—The Rev. Joseph Fletcher, a Wesleyan missionary to the West Indies, says:—"I

Negro Clerk attracting the admiration of his Employers.

" From isle to isle the welcome tidings ran;
The slave that heard them started into man:
Like Peter sleeping in his chains he lay,—
The angel came, his night was turn'd to day:
' Arise!'—his fetters fall, his slumbers flee;
He wakes to life, he springs to liberty."

MONTGOMERY.

witnessed the great desire of the negro slave-children and young persons to learn to read in all the colonies; but in Demerara and Trinidad, where, if possible, opportunities were most scarce, the desire to learn led to the greatest exertion, proving how they valued the opportunity, by the distance they would travel to the Sunday-school, for an hour or two on the Sabbath, walking six, seven, or more miles; and their progress was often cheering, when one doubted if they could learn at all with such scanty means. In Trinidad, in 1831 and 1832, a little girl about seven or eight years of age regularly attended at the Sunday-school, though she had to come a distance of about seven miles. Her mother was a slave, and a member of our society. They would start sufficiently early to reach Port of Spain by the time of opening the Sunday-school. The mother carried the child part of the way, but she was generally present at the beginning. The mother would attend preaching and class-meeting, and the child another hour at the school in the afternoon. Mother and daughter would then return home, making a journey of fourteen miles.

"Some of the young people would persevere in a highly praiseworthy manner, and learn to read in the midst of the greatest difficulties. Frequently would they have a spelling-book about them, and when opportunity offered, would call at the mission-house and ask my child, 'Will missy please tell me what t-h-a-t spells?' and repeating the word a few times, would leave, musing upon it, till fixed in the memory; and at the next opportunity, another word would be proposed to myself or some one belonging to the mission. We had constant proof of the negro children, though slaves, being as capable of learning as European children."

To the correctness of this representation we can testify from personal experience, having frequently witnessed the same eagerness at the stations mentioned, and other places. Nor was the anxiety to learn to read confined to children and young persons. Men and women of forty, fifty, or sixty years of age attended the Sunday-schools, especially in Demerara, and many of them, with the aid of spectacles, learned to read the Scriptures for themselves; so that, at the time of emancipation, when the British and Foreign Bible Society generously presented to each liberated slave who was able to read a copy of the New Testament and Psalms in large type, *ten thousand* were required for the colony of Demerara alone.

154. Negro Love-feast.—On the arrival of the Rev. Mr Alexander in the West Indies in 1794, he was very favourably impressed with the results of the labours of his predecessors in the work of the mission. Writing from St Kitts on the 22d of August, he says:—"On the 13th inst. we had a love-feast. It was the best I ever was at. Indeed it was a heaven upon earth to hear the converted negroes declare the goodness of God with such artless simplicity. Their attitude was very expressive, while in broken accents, and with tears running down their black faces, they spoke of the goodness of God to them in such words as these—'No fader; no moder; no sister; no broder; no friend! But Jesus is all in all.' And when they blessed God that they had been taken from their native country, and brought to hear the sound of the gospel, they frequently concluded with this short prayer—'May God bless my dear massa ministers from first to last. Bless my leader. Bless my broders and sisters. May we join heart and hand together to travel to de new Jerusalem.' If you had been there, it would have made your heart to dance for joy. The congregations are very large, and I think they are the most loving people I ever saw."

155. Elevation of Africans.—
Traders and travellers visiting the Western Coast of Africa now see a marked change in the moral and social condition of the natives, as compared with former times, when the horrors of slavery shed a blighting influence on all around. Then the entire population were found in a state of nudity, and addicted to the most barbarous and cruel superstitions. The few words of English which those learned who came in contact with white men visiting their shores, were generally words of blasphemy and cursing, and the people were in a fearfully degraded condition. Whilst there is still sufficient of heathen darkness to be seen in many places, it is nevertheless a fact that, in the neighbourhood of the mission-stations, and along the entire coast, a wonderful change has been effected since the introduction of the gospel to a few favoured localities. At the Gambia, Sierra Leone, Gold Coast, Liberia, and at several places in the Bight of Benin, Christian communities have been raised up which would be a credit to any country. Many of those who have become converted to the faith of the gospel have themselves been educated and called to the work of the ministry, and a large majority of the missionaries of the respective societies now at work for the Christianisation of Western Africa are natives of the country, and themselves the fruit of missionary labour. The civilising influence of Christianity has, moreover, been felt among the coast population generally, who are now anxious to procure European clothing, to speak the English language, and to learn to read and write after the fashion of white men. This advancement in social progress is not only calculated to encourage the friends of missions to persevere in their good work, but it exercises a wonderful influence on trade and commerce, which mercantile men know how to appreciate. From official returns recently published, it appears that for the year 1872 the exports to our West African possessions amounted to £1,500,000, and imports reached £1,000,000.

156. Change in South Africa.—
In no country have the general and miscellaneous results of Christian missions been more remarkable than in the colony of the Cape of Good Hope, and in the interior of South Africa beyond the colonial border. To say nothing, in this connection, of the spiritual blessings connected with the numerous flourishing mission-stations which have been established, the native churches which have been organised, the places of worship which have been erected, and the Christian schools which have been opened, no one can travel through the land without being impressed with the fact that the diffusion of the gospel has created a sense of security to life and property unknown before. In former times, within the recollection of living men, the traveller and the trader moved from place to place at the hazard of his life, and had to arm himself to the teeth, to be ready to resist the attacks, not only of wild beasts, but of savage men, and horrid tales may still be heard of instances of murder, cruelty, and blood. But by the blessing of God on the labours of the

missionaries, a wonderful change has taken place in this respect. In the colony generally, and far away into the interior for a thousand miles, the traveller may pursue his journey without any serious apprehensions of danger. If he conduct himself in a pacific and proper manner towards the natives, he will generally receive from them the aid which he requires, so far as it is in their power to give it; and at many a smiling mission-station he will meet with a kind and hospitable reception, such as ought to convince the most incredulous of the manifold blessings which follow in the train of Christianity. While traversing the dreary wilds of the interior in the service of our Divine Master, we have often met with marked kindness from the simple aborigines; and when far from any human habitation likely to afford us shelter, after a weary day's journey, we have made our bed on the ground under a friendly bush, and retired to rest, after commending ourselves and attendants to God in prayer, with a sense of security which was owing in a large degree to the wide diffusion of Christian truth; for the well-fed camp-fire was generally sufficient to keep off any wild beasts which might haunt the neighbourhood. "Verily godliness is profitable unto all things, having the promise of the life that now is, and of that which is to come."

157. A Child Redeemed by a Missionary.—During the first visit of the Rev. R. Moffat to Moselekatse, the great chief of the Matabele in South Africa, an affecting incident occurred which he thus describes:— "There was a poor man, whose appearance, dress, and manner informed me that he was truly the child of poverty, and perhaps of sorrow. This led me to take more notice of him than of any other of the chief's attendants. I felt sympathy for the man, supposing he had been compelled to follow the train of the chief, and leave behind him a family ill-supported, or some beloved member sick. No; his downcast looks arose from other causes. He had two sons, about the ages of eight and ten. These had been absent in a neighbouring glen, when a party of Matabele warriors seized the boys, and carried them as spoils to headquarters. He and his partner in affliction had for more than a year mourned the loss of their children, and by taking a few trinkets and beads, his little stock of ornaments, the father hoped to obtain their release.

"After a journey of deep interest and a flattering reception, and days passed in festivities and displays of kindness to the strangers, the man sent in his humble petition by one who could approach the presence of the king, offering the little he had to redeem his boys. Some time afterwards the proprietor of his sons came and seated himself before my waggon, as I drew near to witness the transaction. The poor man spread his ragged mantle on the ground, and laid on it a few strings of beads and some native-made ornaments, valuable to him, but on which the haughty noble would scarcely deign to cast his eye. The father sighed to see his look of scorn. He then drew from his tattered skins which he had brought with him, and on which he reposed at night, a small dirty bag, containing a few more half-worn beads, and placed them beside the former: these were borrowed. The scornful look was again repeated. He then took from his arms two old copper rings, and rings of the same material from his ears. The chief answered the anxious eyes of the father with a frown and an indignant shake of the head. More beads and a half-worn knife were added, but to no purpose. At length the haughty chieftain said one of the boys had died of cold the preceding winter, and for the other he must have oxen.

"The poor disconsolate father had not a goat to give, much less oxen, and was turning away sad and sorrowful, and was about to commence his journey homeward, a distance of two hundred miles, when the missionary spoke to him words of comfort and encouragement, and promised to try what he could do for him on the morrow. The next day Mr Moffat offered beads of a more tempting character for the ransom of the poor captive boy, and succeeded in obtaining his freedom. The father returned home with his long-lost treasure, blessing the white man who had been to him such a kind benefactor. Some time afterwards, when travelling through the country, the mother of the boy visited the waggon of the missionary, and thanked him with streaming eyes for redeeming her son from bondage. This he felt to be an ample recompense.

158. The Gospel promotes Peace.—When the birth of Christ was announced to the shepherds watching their flocks by night on the plains of Bethlehem, the angelic host sung, "Glory to God in the highest, on earth peace and good-will toward men;" and there has no event ever occurred in this world so calculated to exercise a pacific influence on the unruly and warlike passion of sinful men. Wherever the gospel of the grace of God is faithfully preached in heathen lands, among other good effects which it produces in the minds of those who receive it, is a disposition to live in peace and amity, instead of indulging their former propensity to engage in war and bloodshed. Missionaries have, moreover, frequently been the honoured instruments in the hands of God, not only of sowing the seeds of concord and unity among the people of their charge, but of reconciling contending armies, and of preventing war and bloodshed when heathen tribes have been ready to pounce upon each other. This has often been the case in Southern Africa, where the Kaffirs, Hottentots, and other savage tribes, in former times, were seldom at peace among themselves long together. Numerous instances have come under our notice of missionaries successfully acting as mediators and peace-makers between factious native tribes.

Nor has the gospel been less influential as a harbinger of peace in Polynesia. The Rev. J. M. Orsmond, a missionary at Eimeo, on one occasion heard several chiefs conversing among themselves in reference to the change produced among them by the gospel, when he caught and noted down the following sentences:—"But for our teachers, our grass on the hill, our fences and houses, would have been ashes long ago." "But for the gospel we should now have been on the mountains, squeezing moss for a drop of water, and smothering the cries of our children by filling their mouths with grass, dirt, or cloth." "Under the reign of Messiah we stretch out our feet at ease, eat our food, keep our pig by the house." "We did not know more than our ancestors, our kings, and our parents, and were all blind, till the birds flew across the great expanse with good seeds in their mouths, and planted them among us. We now gather fruit, and have continual harvest. It was God who put it into the hearts of those strangers to come to us. We have nothing to give them. They are a people who seek our good;

but we are a people of thorny hands, of pointed tongues, and we have no thoughts." "If God were to take our teachers from us, we should soon be savages again." "Our hearts delight in war; but our teachers love peace, and we now have peace." May the word of prophecy soon be fulfilled, when the heathen shall "beat their swords into ploughshares, and their spears into pruning-hooks," and when "nation shall not lift up sword against nation, neither shall they learn war any more" (Isa. ii. 4).

159. **Change in Rarotonga.**—Adverting to the wonderful change effected by the introduction of Christianity into Rarotonga in the short space of ten years, the Rev. John Williams says:—" In 1823 I found the natives all heathens; in 1834 they were all professing Christians. At the former period I found them with idols and maraes, or heathen temples; these in 1834 were destroyed, and in their stead there were three spacious and substantial places of Christian worship, in which congregations amounting to six thousand persons assembled every Sabbath-day. I found them without a written language, and I left them reading in their own tongue the 'wonderful works of God.' I found them without a knowledge of the Sabbath, and when I left them no manner of work was done during that sacred day. When I found them in 1823, they were ignorant of the nature of Christian worship; and when I left them in 1834, I am not aware that there was a house in the island where family prayer was not observed every morning and every evening. I speak not this boastingly; for our satisfaction arises not from receiving such honours, but in casting them at the Saviour's feet; 'for His arm hath gotten Him the victory,' and 'He shall bear the glory.'" At the same time the missionaries express their belief, that a large proportion of the inhabitants of this highly-favoured isle had become the subjects of the saving grace of God, whilst upwards of three thousand children were receiving instruction in the mission-schools, many of whom owed their very lives to the advent of Christianity.

160. **Savage Island Christianised.**—In no part of the world has the gospel of Christ triumphed more gloriously than in Polynesia. Many pages might be filled with interesting facts illustrative of the wonderful changes which were brought about among a rude and barbarous people by the introduction of Christianity; but it may be better to cite one instance, that of Savage Island—so called by the great navigator Captain Cook, on account of the barbarity of the inhabitants above that of all the islands he had visited. Their unabated ferocity continued till visited by messengers of mercy several years afterwards. Then the providence of God brought to Samoa a native youth of Savage Island, whose ferocity was subdued, and whose confidence was won by the power of Christian love. He heard of Christ, and wondered; he learned to read His Word, and believed; and, impelled by love to his country and compassion to his kindred, he returned to his dark home, accompanied by teachers from Samoa, who made known to the people the grace of the Redeemer.

The Rev. W. G. Lawes, the European missionary who first settled in Savage Island, thus describes the wonderful change which had been effected there, principally by the instrumentality of native teachers from Samoa:—" Fifteen years ago the natives lived in the bush like brutes; now villages and neat plastered cottages evidence the progress of civilisation. Fifteen years ago anarchy, war, and bloodshed prevailed throughout the island; now law, order, and peace. Fifteen years ago the people were all dark and degraded, strangers to prayer and praise; now, clothed and in their right mind, they surround their family altars night and morning to bow down to the God of heaven, while the air is vocal with their songs of praise. Fifteen years ago they had no written language; now they have the gospels and other books, with two thousand readers. Fifteen years ago they were all, before God, dead in sin; now there are 360 in Church fellowship, living to His glory, besides many who, we have reason to hope, are 'new creatures in Christ Jesus.'"

161. Children Saved by the Gospel.—The changes effected by the introduction of Christianity into the various islands of Polynesia were numerous and remarkable; but nothing gave greater joy to parents and children than the abolition of infanticide. While the nation remained in their heathen state, thousands of infants were put to death as soon as they were born, especially if they were girls; but after the advent of the gospel the value of human life became better understood, and all the children were carefully preserved. Adverting to this pleasing circumstance, the Rev. John Williams says:— "Frequently have our feelings been most powerfully excited at the examination of our school-children, and scenes more affecting than some which have been witnessed on such occasions it is scarcely possible to conceive. One of these, which occurred at my own station of Raiatea, I will briefly describe. Upwards of six hundred children were present. A feast was prepared for them, and they walked through the settlement in procession, most of them dressed in European garments, with little hats and bonnets made by those very parents who would have destroyed them had not Christianity come to their rescue. The children added much to the interest of the day by preparing flags with such mottoes as the following— 'What a blessing is the gospel;' 'The Christians of England sent us the gospel;' 'Had it not been for the gospel, we should have been destroyed as soon as we were born.' On some of the banners were inscribed texts of Scripture, as—'Behold the Lamb of God which taketh away the sins of the world;' 'Suffer little children to come unto me,' and other similar passages. After proceeding through the settlement, they were conducted to the spacious chapel, and opened the service by singing the Jubilee Hymn in the native language. The venerable old king took the chair. He had formerly been worshipped as a god, and had led forth his fierce warriors to battle; but he evidently felt that he never occupied a station so delightful or honourable as that of presiding at the examination of the children of his people. These were placed in the centre of the chapel, and the parents occupied the outer seats. Each class was then called up and examined, and after this, children from the different classes were selected, and questioned by the missionary. Whilst this was proceeding the appearance of the parents was most affecting. The eyes of some were gleaming with delight, as the father said to the mother, or the mother to the father, 'What a mercy it is we spared our dear girl!' Others, with saddened countenances and faltering voices, lamented in bitterness that they had not saved theirs. One venerable chief was much excited, and exclaimed, 'Oh that I had known that the gospel was coming! —oh that I had known that these blessings were in reserve for us! then I should have saved my children, and they would have been among the happy group; but alas! I destroyed them all. I have not one left.'"

162. A Pleasing Surprise.—Having received pleasing intelligence from Papeitra and Vahapata, two native teachers left at Aitutaki a few months before, the Rev. Messrs Williams and Bourne, then labouring at Raiatea, hastened to visit the island. After about five days' pleasant sail they reached the place, when their small vessel was soon surrounded by canoes filled with natives from the shore. These they kept off for some time, being suspicious of foul play; but they received a grateful salutation from every canoe that approached. Some of the natives cried out, " Good is the Word of God : it is now well with Aitutaki! The good Word has taken root at Aitutaki." Finding, however, that the missionaries did not repose entire confidence in their assertions, some held up their hats, which being of the European shape was a sure sign of the wearers having renounced idolatry. Others exhibited their spelling-books in evidence of the truth of what they stated. As the missionaries approached the settlement they saw a flagstaff with a white flag flying, which satisfied them that the teachers were alive. At length the chief's canoe came alongside, when they learned from Tebati, one of the first who embraced the gospel, that the maraes, or heathen temples, were burned; that the idols which had escaped the general conflagration were in the possession of the teachers; that the profession of Christianity was general—so much so, indeed, that not a single idolater remained; that a large chapel was erected, nearly two hundred feet in length, plastered, and awaiting their arrival to open it.

Mr Williams says :—"This news was as delightful as it was unexpected. When the teachers came on board, they not only confirmed all that had been told us, but added that the Sabbath was regarded as a sacred day, no work of any kind being done on it; that all the people, men, women, and children, attended divine service; and that family prayer was very general throughout the island. At hearing this good news joy beamed in every countenance, and gratitude glowed in every heart. We hastened to the shore to be eye-witnesses of what had been effected. The natives crowded around the boat; and having to drag it a considerable distance, they amused and delighted us. Some tried to spell long words, others repeated portions of the Catechism or a prayer, whilst others again engaged in singing a verse of a hymn. Indeed every one seemed anxious to show what progress he had made in the new religion."

163. Friendly Islands Evangelised.—The Friendly Islands were so called by Captain Cook, who regarded the natives as more kind and friendly than those of some of the other groups that he discovered or visited. But when the aborigines became better known to Europeans, they were found to be not so *friendly* after all, for they were constantly at war with each other, and were guilty of the horrid crimes of infanticide and cannibalism, to say nothing of their gross idolatry and moral degradation. To show the extent of their ferocity, it only need be added, that of the first party of missionaries sent to instruct them, they murdered some, and drove the rest from the islands. When the mission was resumed nearly fifty years ago, the prospect of success was anything but promising; and, for many years, the work of the missionaries was most arduous and discouraging. At length a gracious influence descended upon the people, and they were induced to abolish idolatry and adopt the worship of the true and living God. The desire to learn to read became universal, and at the present day a larger proportion of the population in the Friendly Islands can read and write than in any country of Europe. Multitudes, moreover, became the subjects of the saving grace of God, and were united in Church fellowship. Many of the converts became preachers of the gospel, and teachers in the mission-schools, and the work is now largely carried on by their agency, with a few European missionaries to attend to its general oversight. The advancement of the people in matters relating to their civil and social condition is equally remarkable. Judges and magistrates have been appointed to act under the judicious and able superintendence of King George, who is a Christian and a gentleman every whit, and a code of laws have been framed and put in force which would do honour to any king and to any country. Never was a Scripture prophecy more literally fulfilled—"A nation shall be born in a day"—than in the case of the Friendly Islands. And this great and wonderful change may be directly traced to the benign influence of Christianity. The people may say in truth, "The day-spring from on high hath visited us, to give light to them that sit in darkness and in the shadow of death, to guide our feet into the way of peace."

164. **A Sabbath in Tonga.**—The introduction of Christianity to the Friendly Islands has produced an entire revolution in the moral and social condition of the natives; and every one who now visits them is struck with the evidences which he beholds of the wonderful power of the gospel. The inhabitants of the entire group are now nominally Christian, and it is believed that a large proportion of them are the true disciples of Christ, King George and his noble queen Charlotte being among the most zealous, devoted, and useful of the nine thousand native converts who are united in Church fellowship. The Rev. Robert Young, who visited the Friendly Islands in 1853, as a deputation from the British Wesleyan Conference, giving an account of a Sabbath he spent in Tonga, says:—

"At half-past five o'clock A.M. the bell of the chapel summoned the inhabitants to worship. It was a meeting for prayer, and attended by about 300 persons. The king and queen were present, and both engaged in prayer. The former took a review of God's mercies to them as a people, contrasting their present with their former condition, noticing the arrival of the missionaries, together with the Book of God in their own tongue, and describing in grateful language, and with much hallowed feeling, the happy results they had realised, &c. The queen in her prayer also gave thanks for the arrival of the Scriptures, and said the book was valuable not because of its paper and ink, but because it brought good tidings to sinners, and from Genesis to Revelation was full of the Saviour. The response from every part of the chapel to this part of her prayer told that she had touched a tender chord, and elicited the grateful feelings of many a heart. At eight o'clock the Sunday-school began, and the children were examined in the Conference Catechism. The result was highly satisfactory. At nine o'clock the bell was again heard, and in every part of the town the beating of the native drum announced that the hour had come for beginning the public worship of God. The people repaired with steady steps to their beloved Mount Zion; and as they went up to worship the Lord, the joy which sparkled in their eyes and beamed in their countenances seemed to say, 'Lord, we have loved the habitation of Thy house, and the place where Thine honour dwelleth.' The chapel, which is without benches, and will accommodate on its matted floor six or seven hundred persons, was much crowded; many, also, were on the outside, seated upon the grass. Mr Amos began the service. The singing was good, and when an abridgment of the Liturgy was read, the responses from every part of the sanctuary indicated deep and reverential feeling. I preached, Mr Amos acting as interpreter, and the people listened with great attention whilst I set before them the glorious Redeemer, and His claims upon their affections and services. Many a heart was moved, and many a sigh went up to heaven. Oh, what a service! May I never lose its holy savour! At two o'clock the Sunday-school reassembled in the chapel. I counted thirteen classes, all squatted on the floor, each one forming a ring around its teacher, one of whom was the queen, who takes a deep interest in the rising generation. At 3 o'clock the public worship commenced, and the tribes again appeared before the Lord. Mr Turner officiated; and whilst he referred to former times, describing the difficulties he had experienced in commencing the mission among them, and then contrasted the state of things which the present scene exhibited, very powerful emotion was excited, and both preacher and people seemed as if they would have departed in a chariot of fire. Thus ended the public services of my first Sabbath in the Friendly Islands,—a day of light and power and glory which can never be forgotten in time or in eternity."

165. **Christianity in Fiji.**—The Rev. John Nettleton, Wesleyan missionary just returned from Fiji, addressing a public meeting in connection with the Newcastle Conference of 1873, gave the following particulars of the present state of Christianity in those islands, which were a few years ago so completely involved in heathen darkness:—"The greatest part of his work in Fiji had been the training of a native agency. That work had been crowned with wonderful success. In the entire group there were only ten English missionaries; but every Sunday nearly a thousand pulpits were occupied by converted natives, who preached in their own tongue the gospel of Christ. More than fifty were ordained ministers; about five hundred were catechists, and the remainder formed a noble army of local preachers. The labours of these men had been greatly blessed in the conversion of souls; and yet some of them twenty years ago were not only heathens, but cannibals. The natives themselves acknowledged how great had been the change among them. Instead of the idol-temple they had now the sanctuary of God; instead of the heathen priest, the minister of Christ; and instead of intertribal war, peace and joy of the Holy Ghost. And these changes had been

brought about by God's blessing on the labours of two men—men who, as the natives said, had weaker voices and weaker arms than themselves. Next to the raising up of a native agency, the translation and circulation of the Bible had been most fruitful of good. The Bible had been the Armstrong gun against Popery, and had saved the people from being seduced by Jesuit teaching. Through the reading of the Bible in Fijian many had been converted. At present the mission in Fiji was in a most prosperous state; yet there were not a few difficulties arising from political circumstances." From recent returns we learn that there are connected with the Wesleyan Missionary Society in Fiji about ten European missionaries, fifty-two native missionaries, 26,000 Church members, and 55,000 scholars in the mission-schools. To these must be added 110,000 attendants on public worship. In fact the islands are rapidly being christianised.

166. The Gospel in Madagascar.

—In the large and fertile island of Madagascar mission-work has been carried on in a manner and with results which have few parallels in the history of the Church since the days of the apostles. The population is estimated at 5,000,000, and the people appear to be of the Malay type, and are supposed to have come originally from Asia, with a mixture of the negro element from the adjacent coast of Africa. The gospel was first carried to Madagascar in 1818, by missionaries of the London Society. The king, Radama I., protected and encouraged the strangers, from the secular advantages which he saw his country would derive from their instructions. Schools were therefore established, the Bible translated, and a few hopeful converts made, and a considerable amount of preparatory work was done when, in 1828, Radama I. died. He was succeeded by the eldest of his twelve wives, who usurped the throne, and, after a few years, madly determined to put a stop to the good work which was begun. The missionaries were consequently obliged to leave the island, and a dreadful persecution of the Christians began, which lasted till the death of the queen in 1861. But the work was of God, and He sustained His people amid the sufferings of banishment, cruel torture, and of martyrdom itself.

After the lapse of nearly a quarter of a century, in 1862, the mission to Madagascar was recommenced by the London Missionary Society, Radama II. having ascended the throne, who was favourable to Christianity. On resuming their evangelical labours among the Hovas, the missionaries were delighted to find that many of the early converts to the faith of the gospel had not only maintained their steadfastness during the long and gloomy night which had brooded over their unhappy country, but they had actually been instrumental in winning others to Christ, so that the Christians appeared to be more in number than when the missionaries left the island, notwithstanding the sufferings to which they had been exposed. From this time the work was prosperous beyond all precedent. Memorial churches were erected on the very spots where some of the martyrs suffered, large congregations were gathered, schools established, and converts made, with a rapidity, and on a scale seldom equalled and never surpassed in any part of the mission-field. On the 8th of September 1869, idolatry was formally abolished, and the royal idols publicly destroyed by order of the queen and government. The mission of the London Society was reinforced by the appointment of several additional missionaries, and their converts were soon numbered by tens of thousands.

Nor is this great and glorious work confined to the noble Society who was the chief instrument in its commencement. Mr Joseph Sewell, a Quaker evangelist, on returning from Madagascar, says :—" There are about fifteen or twenty churches under the care of the Church and Propagation Societies. There are upwards of one hundred other churches which are formed after the model of the churches of the capital, but over which the London Missionary Society can exert no influence. There is another matter which I think is not generally understood. In the central part of the island, during the days of persecution, there arose a Church which is not exactly in accordance with the character of the Independents, or Episcopalians, or Methodists, or the Society of Friends. The nation has a Church of its own. Its pastors and officers are chosen by the people ; but we see in some instances thirty or forty preachers taking their turns, and going out to visit a district by an arrangement similar to that which is made among the Methodists."

167. Progress in India.—A very remarkable statement in reference to the progress of Christian missions in India appears in a bluebook just published by the authority of Government. In the educational section of the official account very high value is placed on the labours of the missionaries, and facts are given which throw a flood of light on this oft-controverted subject. Statistics show that a great increase has taken place in the number of converts to Christianity during the last twenty years. In 1852 the entire number of Protestant native converts in India, Burmah, and Ceylon, amounted to 22,400 communicants, among a body of 128,000 of native Christians of all ages. In 1862 the converts were 213,182, and the native Christians were 213,182. In 1872 the communicants were 78,494, and the converts, young and old, numbered 318,363. There are at present 381 native ordained ministers in India, Burmah, and Ceylon, with nearly as many from Europe and America ; and the native contributions towards the support of the work are reported to amount to the sum of £16,000. The native clergy and ministers constitute an important body of men, having generally received a high education in English institutions. The passage which treats of the "general influence of missionary teaching," is very striking in the testimony which it bears. It closes by saying, "The Government in India cannot but acknowledge the great obligation under which it is laid by the benevolent exertions made by these six hundred missionaries, whose blameless example and self-denying labours are infusing new vigour into the stereotyped life of the great populations placed under English rule, and are preparing them to be in every way better citizens of the great empire in which they dwell."

These facts were generally known to the friends of missions before ; but we were scarcely prepared to see them thus frankly acknowledged in a Government bluebook, when the authorities had in many instances assumed such a different attitude towards the missionaries and their work in former times. We gratefully accept of this small instalment of justice, and thank God for the change which has taken place in the views and proceedings of the " powers that be " since the time that William Carey, and other devoted pioneer evangelists were scarcely tolerated in their zealous efforts to diffuse the knowledge of the truth among the teeming millions of our Indian Empire.

168. Success in Burmah.—Few missions have been more successful than that of the American Baptist Society to Burmah. The work was beset with numerous difficulties in its commencement, and for many years little progress was made. But Dr Judson and his devoted associates laboured and suffered, as seeing Him who is invisible, and they had their reward. After a long night of toil the morning dawned at last, and they lived to see the mission in a state of great prosperity. And since their day the work has extended to almost every part of the empire, and has produced remarkable results in the hilly regions inhabited by the Karens. In the last report of the work in Burmah we find the following statement:—"Of all the missions, that among the Karens has been the most prosperous, numbering 276 churches, with 14,403 members, and 335 preachers. The self-supporting plan is in successful operation. The people are poor; yet for the last two years not one of the fifty-eight pastors of the Toungoo Association has received any outside help, a comfortable support having come, for the most part, from the respective churches. The Bassein Karens have built their own chapels without any aid from the mission funds, and are doing nobly in the cause of education. The Sagu Karens have fifty-two students in the Karen Theological Seminary, twenty ordained pastors, thirty-eight unordained pastors, and fifty licensed preachers."

169. Missions in China.—Missionary work in China, as conducted by Protestant Missionary Societies of Europe and America, was very small and feeble in its commencement; but of late years it has assumed an attitude and proportions which bid fair to secure ultimate success. In 1807 good Dr Morrison went out, a lone missionary, to plant the standard of the Cross among a heathen population estimated at four hundred millions in number. For several years he laboured incessantly at the translation of the Sacred Scriptures, and the preparation of grammars and lexicons, which have been very serviceable to his successors in the noble enterprise. When the mission of the London Society was strengthened by the sending out of additional labourers, more extensive and aggressive work was entered upon in the way of preaching, teaching, and the circulation of the Scriptures, and a few converts were gathered into the fold of Christ.

But it was not till the opening of the country to missionaries and merchants of the West, in 1842, that the work of evangelising China was entered upon more extensively by different denominations. From this period the field was entered by the Wesleyans, the Presbyterians, and the Baptists from England, and by the missionaries of the Methodist Episcopal Church and others from America. The Societies whose agents are now labouring in China are twenty-two in number, and the ordained missionaries are estimated at about one hundred. These are assisted in their work by about two hundred native catechists and teachers, and the results of their united labours are such as to call forth the sincere gratitude of all who feel an interest in the mission cause, and to excite hopeful anticipations of still greater success in time to come.

Whilst some fruit has been reaped

on the respective mission-stations in China, there is reason to believe that instances of real conversion to the faith of the gospel have been more numerous and more distinctly marked among the Chinese emigrants to Australia, California, and other countries. At these great centres of population, missions have been organised with special reference to the spiritual benefit of the "Celestials," and a considerable amount of success has been realised. A prosperous little church of Chinese converts has been organised, as the result of the Wesleyan Mission to this class of emigrants in Australia. Writing under date of November 3, 1871, the Rev. Josiah Cox, who paid a visit to the Chinese converts at Melbourne at the request of the British Conference, says, "I have had the satisfaction of resuming my Chinese preaching. The Chinese class here numbers twenty members, and it has rejoiced me to hear from nearly all of them a clear testimony of the converting power of the gospel."

170. Commencement in Japan.—A correspondent, writing from Japan under date of April the 15th, 1872, gives the following graphic description of what he saw of heathenism, and of the early workings of the missionary enterprise in that mysterious land, so shut up in former times against all external influences, but now in the course of being thrown open to commerce, science, and the gospel:—"It was at the great temple of Sheba in Yedo, and but shortly after our arrival in Japan, that we first obtained a sight of heathenism in its reality. We were in company with kind friends, some of whom were missionaries from China, and others of whom were labourers in Japan. All of us were under the valued guidance of the Rev. Mr Ballagh, of Yokohama, whose missionary zeal is only equalled by his courtesy to strangers. We entered the temple, which stood at the base of a hill, and bore evident marks of great antiquity. In a spacious recess stood the great idol, elaborately carved and elegantly gilded, while in the front of him were placed vases of bronze and candlesticks, with other things of curious device. Before the image there knelt an assemblage of worshippers, mute and motionless, and with their faces bowed to the floor. A priest, with shaven head and long silk robe, sat upon a cushioned seat slightly elevated, and repeated his prayers before the people with an earnestness and rapidity which was as wonderful as it was distressing. Other priests kept time with the prayers, by regularly repeated strokes upon little bronze anvils. While we stood watching the scene, and listening to the peculiar tinkling sound of the numerous little hammers, a polite priest came along and invited us further into the temple. We thanked him, but remained where we were, and soon a little group of persons began to collect about us. One of the missionaries, Mr Ballagh, began to speak to them pleasantly, and gradually assumed a more serious and earnest manner, as he pointed out to them what was going on before the altar. Some of them began to ask him questions, and the group became larger, as the curious drew near to hear his answers. We could understand little of what was being said, though we noticed that the voice of the speaker, in his zeal to make known the truths of salvation, became louder and louder, until it penetrated into the recesses of the temple, and struck the ears of the worshippers. The priest within had now begun to read in a large ancient-looking book, and most of the prostrate faces were raised from the floor. But the voice of the missionary seemed to have more attraction than that of the priest, for one by one we saw men get up, and quietly draw nearer to the speaker. Even one of the priests stole stealthily up to the railing which separated us from those within, and listened, with eyes fixed upon the bold stranger who dared to bring such a message within the very pale of Buddha. The little audience gave an attentive and respectful hearing for some time, and perhaps we may hope that some of the seed sown may bear fruit unto eternal life."

With reference to the missionary work on his station, Mr Ballagh himself writes as follows:—

"The daily prayer-meeting continues well attended. The week-night prayer-meeting also, and the three services on the Sabbath overflow. Persons of all ages and grades attend, occasionally a prince or high officer. The converts are full of zeal, pray with great earnestness, and are beginning to take part in exposition of the Scriptures and in preaching. On the 10th of March it was my unspeakable pleasure to baptize nine of my pupils; and, in conjunction with Dr Brown, to ordain an elder over them. This man, who is an Apollos, 'mighty in the Scriptures,' was their choice, and they organised themselves into a Church of our Lord Jesus Christ, at the same time he was set apart to be their spiritual ruler. Thus the Church of Christ is founded in Japan, and I trust the Lord will add daily to it such as shall be saved."

171. The Retrospect.—It is impossible to take a retrospective view of what has been already accomplished by the faithful preaching of the gospel in different parts of the world, without feelings of sincere gratitude to God that His servants have not been permitted to labour in vain, or to spend their strength for nought. The general, collateral, and miscellaneous results of missions have been numerous and diversified, and such as might well attract the notice of the political economist as well as that of the Christian philanthropist. The diffusion of Christian truth, and the consequent civilisation of barbarous tribes in many distant lands, have created a demand for European manufactures, and given an impulse to trade and commerce to an extent which is truly remarkable. Wandering hordes of savages, constantly at war with each other when in their heathen state, have been collected into peaceful Christian villages; the rising generation are being trained up in a knowledge of God's Holy Word in the mission-schools, and a goodly number of genuine converts to the faith of the gospel have been united in Church fellowship, and gathered into the fold of the Redeemer. These, and many other blessed results of the missionary enterprise, are calculated to confirm the faith and encourage the zeal of all who take an interest in the work; nor are they less satisfactory when viewed as tangible proofs of the fact that the gospel of Christ, when faithfully preached, and applied to the heart by the Holy Spirit, is still what it was in former times, "the power of God unto salvation to every one that believeth." Let us then go forth and scatter abroad with unsparing hand the good seed of the kingdom, fervently praying, at the same time, that the showers of blessing may descend upon the heritage of the Lord, to render it abundantly fruitful.

"Oh, multiply the sower's seed!
And fruit we every hour shall bear;
Throughout the world Thy gospel spread,
Thy everlasting truth declare."

VII. REMARKABLE CONVERTS.

172. Prime Object of Missions.—However pleased we may be with the general results of Christian missions, as seen in the social and moral elevation of the barbarous tribes to whom the gospel is sent by the respective Societies engaged in the work, we must remember that there is a higher object which is constantly kept in view, and without the accomplishment of which the friends and patrons of the enterprise could not be satisfied. We mean the direct and true conversion of sinners to God. Every Christian minister, and especially every missionary to the heathen, is commissioned by the great Head of the Church, not merely to improve the condition of the people among whom he labours, but to win souls to Christ. When the Redeemer called Saul of Tarsus immediately after his conversion to labour in His vineyard, he defined his errand in language which could scarcely be mistaken. He said, "The Gentiles, to whom now I send thee, to open their eyes, and to turn them from darkness to light, and from the power of Satan unto God, that they may receive forgiveness of sins, and inheritance among them which are sanctified by faith that is in me" (Acts xxvi. 18). The apostle never lost sight of this the first and grand object of his calling. Nor will the modern missionary, amid the varied departments of Christian labour in which he has to engage, forget that his prime business is to bring sinners to Christ, if his heart be right with God.

It is a pleasing fact, that in almost every part of the world where mission-stations have been established, and where the good seed of the kingdom has been sown, fruit has been reaped of this highest and best kind. And some of the native converts have been remarkable for their piety, zeal, and devotedness to Christ, showing that "God is no respecter of persons; but in every nation he that feareth Him and worketh righteousness is accepted with Him" (Acts x. 34). Nor have there been wanting instances of superior intelligence and ability among the members of our native churches, qualifying men of different complexions and language for the service of the sanctuary, to which they were evidently called by the great Head of the Church. Nothing can be more encouraging than to contemplate examples of genuine piety and devotedness to God, in whatever position of life they may be found in the mission-field, especially if they prove, as is generally the case, helpers in the work of the Lord.

173. A Romish Convert.—The conversion of a bigoted Roman Catholic has generally been regarded by Christian missionaries as more difficult than that of a dark, benighted pagan; but the grace of God is sufficient even for this, and some pleasing instances have come under our notice in the course of our labours. At a Love-feast held at Bailey-Brough, in Ireland, on the 21st of April 1830, a man stood up and spoke as follows:—"Here I stand, who have been taught to say my prayers on beads, and go to mass, which I attended till I was upwards of twenty years of age, when I happened to hear a Wesleyan missionary preach, and I felt that I was a sinner. I then heard regularly, when I could, these men of God, and soon found peace in Jesus. At length my father told me that I must hear them no more, or else leave his house. I asked him why he said so. Was I not a better son than when I was cursing and swearing and drinking (which he knew I was guilty of before I heard the Methodists), and why should he now send me away? He said that the priest told him that nothing would do well with him if he allowed me to stay in his house and hear the '*swaddlers;*' that therefore I must swear that I would hear them no more, or else leave him for ever. I refused to swear this, and immediately packed up my clothes, and said, 'Father, the Lord is a rich provider; I will trust in Him.' I kneeled down and prayed for him and his, and bade him farewell with the tears rolling down my cheeks: and now I can say, to the glory of God, that He is indeed a rich provider. He has given me a wife that fears and loves Him; and though I had not one shilling when I left my father's house, I have now abundance of this world's goods, the privilege of lodging a missionary, and a large class at my house. But the best of all is, I have the power and presence of Christ in my heart. Oh, how thankful I ought to be that I have escaped out of darkness, superstition, and idolatry!"

174. Father Grassi.—One of the most remarkable conversions to the faith of Protestant Christianity in modern times which has come under our notice, was that of a Romish priest known as Father Grassi. This abbé was not an obscure priest, or one on whose name and prospects any cloud rested. He was a man of more than ordinary intelligence and respectability in Rome, and was regarded by many as a pillar of the so-called Catholic Church, in which he had been brought up from infancy, and of which he was a talented minister. From post to post, with growing distinction, had he advanced, till after thirty-six years spent in performing successively the duties of priest, confessor, and curate, he occupied an honourable place in the Chapter of the great Basilica of St Maria Maggiore. In the early part of 1873 Father Grassi became acquainted with Mr Van Meter, an American gentleman who was busily engaged in establishing Christian schools of the genuine Protestant type in the capital of Italy. About the same time he also came in contact with the Rev. Mr Wall of the Baptist Missionary Society. Through the instrumentality of these devoted servants of Christ, with the blessing of God, the deluded Romish priest was led to see the errors of the corrupt system in which he had been trained. And, what is better still, his eyes were opened to see himself as a sinner in the sight of God, and he was brought as a humble suppliant to the mercy-seat of Christ. Having sought and found redemption through the great Atonement, he could no longer remain in the priesthood of the Church of Rome, but nobly came forth, forsaking emoluments, honours, and expectations, to join the small Baptist Church under the care of Mr Wall. Of this little Christian community he became a zealous and devoted member, and in due time he will no doubt prove a successful evangelist to his deluded fellow-countrymen.

But the most remarkable circumstance in the history of this noted convert was the fact of his being summoned before the Inquisition, to recant his heresies or endure the penalty. Writing from Rome, under date of Oct. 22, 1873, in reference to this matter, Mr Van Meter says:—
"Grassi entered alone, and the door was shut. We could only beg God to keep him, and enable him to 'open his mouth boldly' and declare the truth. Soon loud and earnest talking was heard. Again and again admission was demanded and promised, but not granted. For nearly an hour we waited, then the door opened, and our brother was with us again. Taking my hand, and pressing it to his heart, he said, with deep emotion, '*E finito! E finito!*' 'It is finished! It is finished!' Grassi not only stood firm to the principles of Protestantism which he had espoused, but before he left the Inquisition he administered a scathing rebuke to the Popish authorities who arraigned him. Among other cutting things he said, 'O you inquisitors, pontiffs, cardinals, and prelates, God speaks to you. To what have you brought the true Church! She that was so pure, so beautiful, so glorious, ye have betrayed, violated, despoiled, wounded and crucified, by your doctrine, superstition, and immorality, and sealed her tomb by your blasphemous dogma of infallibility. Hear what God says to His suffering children—"The God of peace shall bruise Satan under your feet shortly." Do you not tremble at these words? Who but Satan instigated and inflicted the tortures in this place? Oh, could these walls, within which so many have been burned, speak—could this roof but echo back the cries of agony from your innocent victims, and the vaults beneath us reveal the corpses of those who have been buried alive—no other sentence of condemnation would be required. But the breath of God has for ever extinguished the fires of the Inquisition, and swept away your power. Therefore I stand before you to-day and declare these truths, while you dare not touch a hair of my head. Farewell, Church of my youth; farewell, companions of my ministry. Alas! alas! it has been a ministry of destruction. Oh, if my word has yet any weight with you, I beseech you to open your eyes to the light, to abandon the system of darkness in which you are groping, and accept the true light which Jesus offers you.'"

It is stated that six of Grassi's former associates followed him out of the Church of Rome to inquire "What is truth?"

175. **The Blind Colporteur of Beyrout.**—Among the missionary converts to the true faith of the gospel, from among the nominal Christians of the Greek Church in the Holy Land, there have been raised up many eminent disciples of the meek and lowly Jesus. One of these, the Blind Colporteur of Beyrout, is worthy of special mention. Soon after he was brought to a saving knowledge of the truth, his piety and zeal pointed him out as a suitable person for some department of Christian labour, notwithstanding his blindness, and he was employed in carrying about for sale copies of the Holy Scriptures under the direction of the missionaries. In this service he has been engaged for several years, and

has been made very useful, not only in circulating the Sacred Scriptures, but also in speaking to the people from the fulness of his heart of the contents of the blessed Book of which he has obtained a remarkable knowledge, and of his own experience of the things of God. The following specimen of his labours, from an account given by himself, may serve to convey some idea of this wonderful man :—

"I met a number of people one day, who demanded of me why I had left my former religion. I told them because of the sinful worship of images, the belief in the intercession of saints, &c., and I gave them a long address on the subject, quoting largely from the Scripture such passages as 'No man cometh to the Father but by me,' &c. As I left them, I asked one of them especially to come to church on Sunday, and to let me know that he was there, as I cannot see. And on Sunday, as I was entering the church, he took me by the hand, but said nothing. I wondered, and said, 'What do you want, brother?' He answered, 'I am he whom you invited to church,' and I was very pleased. I continue to go to the hospital on days when friends are allowed to visit the patients. There are generally many people there, and I go from man to man, repeating texts of Scripture for their comfort, and offering up prayers for them. The patients receive me gladly, and the doctors do not hinder me. I was passing a house one day, when some women invited me in. They were very kind and polite, and told me they wanted to buy a book of prayers. I asked them if they could read. They said they had learned to read many years ago in Mrs Thompson's school. They told me that they never let their husbands go out to work until they had had reading and prayer together, and, what is a very rare thing in this country, they make a practice of asking a blessing before every meal. I found that they had considerable religious knowledge. I repeated a chapter to them, and sold them a 'Golden Treasury.' They pressed me to visit them often. The quiet religion of this house, in the midst of all the idolatry and superstition of the city, made me think of the seven thousand in Elijah's time who were known only to God. Let us hope that it is even so in Syria."

176. The Power of Kindness.— The gospel of Christ was introduced into the town of Sheik Mohammed, in Syria, in a very remarkable manner, and it had to struggle with numerous difficulties before it became firmly established. About the year 1862, a man named *Ishoc el Kefroony*, by reading a Bible that he obtained from a colporteur, became a Protestant Christian almost before he knew it, and some time before he saw a missionary. Previously he had been a magician, and the most unlikely man in the place to be converted. When he heard of the missionaries at Tripoli, he went to see them, and after the interview declared his faith, went home, burned his books of magic, and gave up the Greek Church, of which he had been a nominal member. He was immediately put under the curse of the priest, and could only find friends among his Moslem neighbours whose sick he visited and doctored.

The head man of the town, Yusif el Khoory, kept up an organised persecution against Ishoc. He hired men to root up his crops, cut off his water-supply, turn his cattle out of the pasture; and this not succeeding in bringing Ishoc back, he hired a notorious assassin, who, with a company of the villagers, attacked him in the valley one night, and left him for dead. But Ishoe afterwards crawled home, bleeding and badly wounded, and did not recover from the murderous assault for some time. For years after that he never dared to go out of his house alone after dark. He lived just below the town, under the brow of the hill. Organised mobs repeatedly surrounded his dwelling, and were only driven off with the aid of a few friendly Moslem neighbours. Once these fellows were repulsed by seeing the gleam of Ishoe's rifle barrel, as he pushed it through a knothole in the door. Two or three times they threw down a part of his house. They destroyed crop after crop for him, and head after head of his cattle, until he was greatly distressed by his losses; yet he never lost an opportunity to speak for Christ and His gospel. When matters became a little more quiet, on one occasion, a few of the people applied to the missionaries for a Christian school, and Ishoe gave the use of a little house in the centre of the village for the purpose; but the old enemies soon stirred up the opponents, and they drove the school out of the village two or three times. Still they persevered.

At length Christian kindness and patient perseverance on the part of Ishoe, and two or three other converts who acted with him, triumphed over every foe. The ringleader of the persecution, Yusef el Khoory, had occasion for Ishoe's testimony as a witness in a lawsuit. He scarcely knew how to expect his compliance after the treatment he had received, but he nevertheless ventured to summon him. When Ishoe stood up in the court and testified to the truth, in favour of his avowed enemy, Yusef was fairly subdued, and from that moment he was converted into a friend. He not only discontinued his opposition, but began to aid the cause in various ways. The mission-school consequently prospered, converts were gathered in, a new school-house and place of worship were erected, Yusef el Khoory sending his masons to help to build it, and giving the stones for the window caps and sills. "There these stones now stand," says the missionary, "a testimony of the power of a gentle gospel life in softening the stoniest of hearts, and turning away the wrath of the bitterest of adversaries."

177. Peter Jones.—Several Indians were brought to a saving knowledge of the truth, through the instrumentality of the missionaries who were appointed to labour at the Credit and Grand rivers, Upper Canada, in 1823. Among these was a young chief named *Kahkewaquanaby*, which means "sacred waving feathers," referring to feathers plucked from the eagle. He was brought up in all the superstitions of his tribe, with whom he had wandered about for fourteen years, when his father, who had embraced Christianity, had him baptized as Peter Jones, and sent him to school for nine months to learn to read, write, and cipher. Having heard a good deal about the Christian religion, he began to think it true; but when he saw the whites get drunk, quarrel, fight, and cheat the poor Indians, his faith was staggered. On the 1st of June, he with his sister went to a camp-meeting which was held in the township of Ancaster, to "see how the Methodists worshipped the Great Spirit in the wilderness." On Saturday, after hearing faithful sermons, and witnessing the prayer-meetings, Peter began to feel "very sick in his heart." On Sunday, in all the services, he says, "I thought the black-coats knew all that was in my heart, and that I was the person addressed. In spite of my Indian heart, tears flowed down my cheeks at the remembrance of my sins." On Monday his distress of mind increased. In the evening he attended the prayer-meeting, from which he returned weary to his tent, and had fallen asleep, when he was aroused by the intelligence that his sister Mary was converted, and he returned to the meeting. He found his sister as happy as she could be; and she exhorted him to seek the Lord, telling him what great things He had done for her. Continuing in prayer until the dawn of day, he was enabled to believe in Christ to the salvation of his soul. He says:—"That very instant my burden was removed, joy unspeakable filled my heart, and I could say, 'Abba, Father.' The love of God being now shed abroad in my heart, I loved Him intensely, and praised Him in the midst of the people. Everything now appeared in a new light, and all the works of God seemed to unite with me in uttering the praises of the Lord. The people, the trees of the woods, the gentle winds, the warbling notes of the birds, and the approaching sun, all declared the power and goodness of the Great Spirit. And what was I, that I should not raise my voice in giving glory to God, who had done such great things for me?"

Soon after his conversion Peter Jones began to call sinners to repentance, and ultimately he became an able and successful native missionary. In this capacity he continued to labour for many years, and it is believed that he was instrumental in bringing many of his fellow-countrymen to a saving knowledge of the truth. On two occasions he visited England, and on the 14th of September he was presented to Her Majesty the Queen, at Windsor Castle, to whom he brought a petition from the people of his tribe, praying for a proper title to the lands which they occupied. Of this important event the young chief made a particular record in his journal. Towards the close of which he says:—"The Queen smiled, and then said to me, 'You were in this country before?' I said I was here eight years ago. Her next question was how long I had been here this time, and when I was going to return. I told her I had been here about ten months, and that I was going to sail next week. I moreover informed Her Majesty that I had travelled a good deal in England, and that I had been highly pleased with the kind reception I had met with. When I had finished my talk, she bowed to me in token of the interview being over, so I bowed and retired."

Peter Jones attended several missionary meetings while in England, and the people were much interested by his simple and earnest addresses. In London he delivered a very effective speech from which the following is an extract:—"My Christian brothers and sisters, I shake hands with you all this day in my heart. I feel, my Christian friends, that your God whom you have been worshipping and talking about this day, is my God also. I feel that the same religion that warms your hearts, and makes you glad, warms my heart, and makes me glad also. I am come a great way, my white brothers and sisters. I am come from over the great waters, from the wilderness of America. I am come at the request of my brothers and sisters in that land, who love the Great Spirit, to shake hands with you, and to see what God is doing among you. Suffer me to tell you that the Lord hath done great things for poor Indians in the wilds of Upper Canada. The poor Indians had been a long time sitting in darkness, and praying to the sun and moon, and many other things that are no gods, not seeing the good things that you see, and enjoying the good things that you enjoy. But through the labours of good men, good Methodist people, who came to us at Credit River, and pointed out to us the Lamb of God that takes away the sins of the world, these poor Indian people, who were the remnant of a once-powerful nation, were made to rejoice in God their Saviour. Before this time we knew nothing about the proper worship of the Great Spirit. We did not come to Him by Jesus Christ; but now many have learned to love and serve Him. You see before your eyes the effects of preaching the gospel to poor Indians. In my early days I was brought up a heathen, but about eight years ago I was led to attend a Methodist meeting. I was made to feel my sins, and to fall down and pray to God for mercy all night, and just as daylight came, God spake peace to my heart. Oh, what joy came into me then! Then I remembered my poor relations and my poor countrymen; and with tears in my eyes I went and told them what God had done for my soul. And then they began to weep also, and to call on the Great Spirit; and soon the whole tribe of my people fell down and worshipped the Great Spirit in the name of Jesus Christ. I thank you, Christian friends, that you have sent missionaries to Canada, and I shake hands with you all in my heart. This is all I have to say at present."

On his return to Canada, Peter Jones continued to labour for the benefit of his people to the utmost of his power, till a few years ago, when he finished his course with joy, and entered into rest. His widow, who still survives, wrote a beautiful memoir of her dear departed husband, to which we are indebted for some of the particulars given above.

178. **John Sunday.**—Among the converts to the faith of the gospel who were gathered into the fold of the Redeemer, in Upper Canada, through the instrumentality of Peter Jones, was a young Indian chief who was baptized by the name of John Sunday, his native name having been *Shawundais*, which signifies "thunder and lightning." He was soon afterwards employed as a class-leader and local preacher, and ultimately in the higher position of an assistant missionary. In this capacity he laboured for many years, and was the means of doing much among the people of his tribe.

In 1836 John Sunday paid a visit to England, and the friends of missions were delighted with his simple statements in the numerous meetings which he addressed. Having gone to school for some time, he had learned to read and write, and he spoke very fair English. There was, moreover, a spice of humour in his speeches which was calculated to amuse as well as to edify his audience. The following extract may serve as a specimen. Concluding his address by an appeal to the benevolence of the people, previous to the collection, he said, "There is a gentleman, I suppose, now in this house; he is a very fine gentleman, but he is very *modest*. He does not like to show himself. I do not know how long it is since I saw him, he comes out so little. I am very much afraid he sleeps a great deal of his time, when he ought to be going about doing good. His name is *Mr Gold*. Mr Gold, are you here to-night? or are you sleeping in your iron chest? Come out, Mr Gold; come out, and help us to do this great work, to send the gospel to every creature. Ah, Mr Gold, you ought to be ashamed of yourself, to sleep so much in your iron chest! Look at your white brother, *Mr Silver*, he does a great deal of good in the world, while you are sleeping. Come out, Mr Gold! Look, too, at your brown brother, *Mr Copper*, he is *everywhere!* See him running about doing all the good he can. Why don't you *come out*, Mr Gold? Well, if you *won't come out* and give us yourself, send us your shirt, that is a BANK NOTE, and we will excuse you this time."

179. Peter Jacobs. — Another Indian convert in Upper Canada was Peter Jacobs, whose early history may be gathered from his own statements at missionary meetings, which he attended on the occasion of his visit to England in 1843. He appeared on the platform at Exeter Hall, London, in the costume of the Chippewa nation, to which he belonged. He was introduced to the meeting by Dr Alder, and in the course of his address he made the following touching remarks:—"I am exceedingly happy to have the honour and pleasure of addressing such a great assembly as this,—the greatest assembly I ever met with in my life; and in looking at this great Christian assembly, I see that more than two-thirds of this great hall are occupied by ladies. What a different thing it is when we have an assembly among our countrymen in North America! But I can account for this very well. Yours is a Christian nation. About fourteen years ago I was myself a heathen, and used to worship the sun and the moon, and other gods, as I supposed. We were all in that state that we had a very indistinct idea of the Great Being. We thought He was so far away that He would just let men do as they pleased. My friends Peter Jones and John Sunday have told you of the great work that has been done in the Canada mission; all these things you know of, and I shall not speak of them now; but I will speak of my own conversion. When I was in my heathen state, I heard a missionary speak of a beautiful heaven where nothing but joy was to be experienced, and of the awful flames of hell into which the wicked shall be cast if they do not believe on the Lord Jesus Christ. I made inquiry if there was any possibility of a Chippewa Indian getting to heaven. I was told that heaven was open to all believers in Christ Jesus. I was very glad when I understood this; I began to pray. I said, 'O Christ, have mercy upon me, poor sinner, poor Indian!' This was the beginning of my prayer and the end of my prayer. I could not pray any more, because I did not know any more English. I thought if I prayed in Chippewa Christ would not understand me. Christ affected my heart very much. I felt just like the wounded deer. When we shoot a deer in the heart with bow and arrow, he runs away as if he was not hurt; but when he gets to the hill, he feels the pain, and lays down on that side where the pain is most severe. Then he feels the pain on the other side, and turns over, and so he wanders about till he dies. I felt pained in this way; I felt pain in my heart, but could not get better. I went with Peter Jones to dine with a gentleman, and before dinner Peter Jones said grace in English. I thought God would understand that. But he said grace after meat in Chippewa; and I thought, If God understands your Chippewa, He will understand mine. I then went up into a stable where hay was kept, and there I prayed, 'O my heavenly Father, now have mercy upon me, for the sake of Thy Son Jesus Christ.' Then I prayed again, 'O Jesus, the Saviour of the world, I did not know that Thou didst die for me personally. Now, O Jesus, the Saviour of the world, apply now Thy precious blood to my heart, that all my sins may depart;' I wanted rest and sleep, but I could not rest. Like the wounded deer, I turned from side to side and could not rest. At last I got up at midnight and walked about my room: I made another effort to pray, and said, 'O Jesus, I will not let Thee go until Thou bless me;' and before break of day I found that my heavy heart was taken away, and I felt happy— I felt the joy which is unspeakable and full of glory. Then I found Jesus was sweet indeed to my soul. Then after that I had a desire that all my people should know the Saviour, and in my feeble way I have been endeavouring to do good ever since to the present time. And I have met with many encouragements.

"Now after that time the revival of religion commenced among my people, and hundreds and thousands have been converted since, and they are now a happy people. The people have thrown away the scalping-knife and the tomahawk, and have taken the Bible and the hymn-book instead, and many of them have become preachers of the gospel. I thank you for the kindness I have met with in England. Pray for me, and when you give to the cause of missions, pray that God may sanctify it to the end you give it. Let us do all the good we can during the few remaining days we have to live. I am sure you will do so, and I trust I shall endeavour to do the same, until the happy hour shall arrive when our Lord and Saviour Jesus Christ shall say unto you and to me, 'Well done, good and faithful servant, enter thou into the joy of thy Lord.'"

"I was a stricken deer, that left the herd
Long since; with many an arrow deep
    infixed,
My panting sides were charged, when
    I withdrew
To seek a tranquil death in distant
    shades.
There I was found by One who had
    Himself
Been hurt by the archers. In His side
    He bore,
And in His hands and feet, the cruel
    scars.
With gentle force soliciting the darts,
He drew them forth, and healed, and
    made me live."

180. **Catherine Brown.**—We have a remarkable instance of the power of the gospel and the benign influence of Christian instruction in the case of Catherine Brown, a Cherokee Indian girl, whose history is truly interesting. Catherine was born in 1800 near Willston, fifty miles south-west of the town of Brainerd, of heathen parents; the nation to which she belonged being entirely ignorant of the character of the true God, and of Jesus Christ the Saviour of men. All they knew of the Divine Being was comprehended in a few fantastic notions of the Great Spirit, whom they regarded as the author of the visible creation. Early in the spring of 1817, the missionaries of the American Board arrived in the Cherokee country, and soon after opened a school at Brainerd. Catherine Brown joined the school on the 9th of July in the same year. She was comely in appearance, easy in her manners, and modest and prepossessing in her demeanour. From the very first she attracted the attention of her

teacher as a girl of more than ordinary promise. Nor did she disappoint the anticipations which were raised concerning her. Her rapid advancement in the acquisition of knowledge was surprising. From reading words of one syllable she was able in sixty days to read intelligibly in the Bible, and in ninety days she could read as well as most persons of common education. After writing over four sheets of paper, she could use the pen with accuracy and neatness without a copy.

Catherine had been in the school but a few months before divine truth began to exert an influence upon her mind. This was manifest in an increased desire to know the Christian religion, and in a greater sobriety of general deportment. Whilst she was in this state of mind the Rev. E. Cornelius, a missionary of the American Board, made his first visit to Brainerd. His conversation and preaching had much effect upon the Cherokees, and on the white people in the neighbourhood of the station. On the first Sabbath in November 1817, four persons were much affected during the service, among whom was Catherine Brown. Her chief object of solicitude now was that she might know the will of God and do it. She sought the kingdom of heaven with great earnestness, and in December she obtained the pardon of her sins, and a conscious sense of her acceptance with God, through the merits of Christ. She soon afterwards began to pray with her associates, and to assist in teaching the Lord's Prayer to the younger girls in the school. She wept and prayed for her people in secret places, as well as in the company of her female friends at their weekly prayer-meetings, and was made instrumental in the conversion of her brother David, who ultimately became an assistant missionary, and in conjunction with his sister was the means of bringing his parents and many others to a saving knowledge of the truth.

At length Catherine Brown became the teacher of a mission-school, and laboured in every possible way to promote the temporal and spiritual welfare of her people. The Lord greatly blessed her efforts, and she was a burning and a shining light in a dark, benighted world. In the mysterious providence of God this remarkable Indian convert was cut down in the bloom of life, and in the midst of her labours. She was attacked with that insidious disease, pulmonary consumption, and her health gradually declined, till she sunk into the arms of death. But her end was in beautiful harmony with her holy and useful career. To a female friend who called to see her during her illness, she said, "I have been wishing to see you for several days. I think I shall not live long. You have done much for me. I thank you, and hope the Lord will reward you. I am willing to die if it be the will of God. I know that I have experienced His love. I have no desire to live in this world but to do good. But God can carry on His work without me." As death advanced, and the powers of nature gave way, she frequently offered her hand to the friends around her bed. Her mother and sister weeping over her, she looked steadfastly at the former for a short time, filial love beaming from her eyes, and then closed them in the sleep of death. She departed this life on the 18th July 1823, in the twenty-fourth year of her age.

181. **Cornelius, the Negro Preacher.**—Among the early converts to the faith of the gospel, as the result of the Moravian Mission to the Island of St Thomas, in the

West Indies, was a poor negro named Cornelius. Notwithstanding his humble condition in life, he was a man of considerable talents, and by dint of incessant study and application, he learned to read and write the Creole, Dutch, Danish, German, and English languages. He was, moreover, an acceptable and useful preacher of the gospel. Till 1767 Cornelius was a slave; but having purchased the freedom of his wife, he obtained his own, and subsequently that of their six children. He had learned the business of a mason, and he laid the foundation of six mission-chapels. He laboured indefatigably for the spiritual welfare of the poor negroes, and for that of whites also, till 1801, when his health and strength entirely failed.

Feeling that his life was drawing to a close, Cornelius sent for his children and grand-children, who soon surrounded his bed. He then summoned up all his strength, and thus addressed them:—"I rejoice exceedingly, my dearly beloved children, to see you once more together before my departure; for I believe that my Lord and Saviour will soon come and take your father home to Himself. You know, my dear children, what my chief concern has been respecting you, as long as I was with you; how frequently I have exhorted you with tears not to neglect the day of grace, but to surrender yourselves, soul and body, to your God and Redeemer, to follow Him faithfully. . . . Now attend to my last wish and dying request. Love one another; do not suffer any quarrels and disputes to rise among you after my decease. No, my children, love one another truly; let each strive to show proofs of love to his brother or sister. Do not suffer yourselves to be tempted by anything to become proud, for by that you may even miss of your souls' salvation; but pray your Saviour to grant you lowly minds and humble hearts. If you follow this advice of your father, my joy will be complete, when I shall once more see you again in eternal bliss, and be able to say to my Saviour, 'Here, Lord, is poor Cornelius, and the children Thou hast given me.' I am sure our Saviour will not forsake you; but I beseech you not to forsake Him."

The venerable patriarch soon afterwards died in peace in the eighty-fourth year of his age, leaving behind him six children, twelve grand-children, and five great grand-children.

182. Poor Moreau.—Among the poor slaves who were dragged away from their native land in Africa by thousands, at the commencement of the present century, and sold to the planters of America and the West Indies, was a negro youth named Moreau, whose brief history is one of mournful interest. He appeared to have received an unusual education from some Mohammedan priest before he was stolen away from his African home, as he was able to speak and read Arabic with ease and fluency. He had, moreover, the manners, principles, and feelings of a well-bred gentleman. But these high qualities did not exempt him from a life of bondage. He was taken to North Carolina, where he was purchased by a person who treated him with more kindness than fell to the lot of many of his companions in tribulation. Poor Moreau was supplied with an Arabic Bible, which he studied with great care. His mind was powerfully affected while perusing it, and he was ultimately led to profess his faith in Christ and to unite himself with the people of God. From that time he disliked to be questioned in reference to his early history. A blank book was therefore given him, and he was requested to write an account of his life. He kept it for some time, and at length returned it filled with Arabic writing. It was sent to an Arabic scholar, and was found to contain, not the history of poor Morean, but the pith of the scheme of Redemption, in a series of Scripture passages from the Old and New Testaments. On the last two pages was the following appeal to his kindred, all of whose names he gives in pure Arabic :—" Salaams to all who believe on the Lord Jesus Christ. I have given my soul to Jesus, the Son of God. O my countrymen, Bundah and Phootoor and Phootdalik, give salaams to Mohammed Said, and Makr Said, and all the rest. Come, come, come, come to Jesus the Son of God, and ye shall find rest to your souls in the Day of Judgment. Come, come, come, come, come, come to Jesus the Son of the living God. Ye shall enter Paradise for ever, amen." This remarkable man soon after died in the faith and hope of the gospel, a specimen of a vast multitude who have found the Saviour in the land of their bondage.

183. Peregrine, the Mohammedan Convert.—Mrs Gilbert, the devoted wife of Nathaniel Gilbert, Esq., who introduced Methodism to the West Indies, gives, in a letter to the Missionary Committee in London, an interesting account of a negro slave of more than ordinary intelligence, who was brought under the influence of the gospel in the island of Antigua, and converted from the principles of Mohammedanism, in which he had been trained, to the faith of Christ.

Peregrine, as he was called in his heathen state, was born at Senegal in Western Africa, and was captured when quite a boy, and stolen away from his native land. He was the son of a chief, and had been educated from his infancy in the doctrines of the false Prophet. When brought as a slave to Antigua, his superior intelligence, and the fact that he could read and write Arabic, caused him to be singled out as one qualified for a position above that of a field-labourer or an ordinary domestic servant, and he was employed as office messenger to the Colonial Government. In this capacity he was often brought into contact with Mrs Gilbert, who embraced every opportunity of conversing with him on the subject of religion. At first Peregrine was very inaccessible, and raised all manner of objections to " white man's religion," declaring his disgust and horror at the glaring immorality which abounded in the colony among a people professing Christianity. But Mrs G. asked him if there were not bad as well as good people in his own country among those who were strict Mohammedans, and showed him that there were many good Christians to be found in Antigua, if he would only go where they were in the habit of meeting together. At length she induced him to attend the Wesleyan Chapel, and at the same time made him a present of an Arabic Bible, which he read and studied with devout attention. The blessing of God attended the means thus employed to enlighten the mind of the poor benighted African, and he gradually emerged into the glorious light of the gospel.

In concluding her interesting narrative, Mrs G. says :—" His misery of mind at last brought him to pray, which he had never done before, that God would show him what was right ; his prayers were heard, and he called Jesus his Lord and his God. He was publicly baptized by the Rev. Mr Whitehouse, denouncing all the delusions of the false Prophet. It was an affecting scene, and peculiarly so to me. He chose the name of Peter himself. At the Love-feast he spoke in a manner which affected the whole house. He said, 'I came to Antigua, I no know the true God; I say Mohammed my God. I go to chapel, I go away, I laugh at it. Such-and-such people (mentioning their names) talk about Jesus. I say, No, Jesus no God; Mohammed my God. My heart then hard; but now I know Jesus God, Jesus my God. I have Him in my heart,' and he clasped his arms across his breast. This is indeed one among many instances which show that Jesus is hastening His kingdom, and bringing along with Him millennial grace and glory in the West, as well as the East."

184. Cato Madan.—One of those who received the gospel soon after it was first preached at Cayon, in the West Indies, was a negro named Cato Madan; but it was not till after the chapel was built at that place that he gave evidence of any particular work of grace in his heart. He then became very attentive to the missionaries, and as they generally lodged in the chapel on the occasion of their visits, he would stay with them after the preaching till eleven or twelve o'clock, asking them questions, and conversing on the subject of religion. He now appeared to be convinced of sin; clear views of divine truth opened upon his mind, and he was enabled to believe in Jesus Christ, to love Him sincerely, and to walk in His commandments with holy joy and delight. He began to assist in meeting the classes, learned to read and write, watched over the people, took care of the children, and was acceptable to all. A long course of usefulness was anticipated for this remarkable native convert; but it pleased God to cut him off in the prime of life, soon after he had begun to exert himself with good effect for the benefit of his fellow-bondsmen. When taken ill, his manager, Dr D., was at a loss to find out his disorder, and laboured much to save so useful a slave; but Cato said, "The physic will do me no good, I am going home." One of the Class-Leaders visiting him, found him so happy, that he stood amazed, having never conceived that God imparted such a degree of love and peace and joy on this side death, and he returned greatly instructed and refreshed. He was very anxious that all should come to a knowledge of the truth; and calling for one whom he had often exhorted in vain, he said, "I have often warned you to forsake sin, and you would not: kneel down, and say after me, 'Father, I have sinned against heaven, and before Thee, and am no more worthy to be called Thy son.'" The overseer of the estate to which Cato belonged, came in and asked him if he knew him. Cato replied, "Yes, you are my master. God bless you!" The overseer desired to know if he had any request to make before he died. He replied, "Only one; and that is, that I may be buried at the chapel." Having made this request, the pious negro blessed them, and died. On the following day he was buried in the chapel-yard according to his request, and a large concourse, including two white overseers, attended his funeral, and marched in a regular procession for nearly a mile. Soon afterwards, the Rev. John Brownell preached a funeral sermon for poor Cato, and such was the influence which attended it, that many were induced to turn to the Lord, and a revival of the work of God commenced which continued

K

for a long time, and multitudes were gathered in to the field of the Redeemer.

185. The Power of Gospel Truth.—An aged man in the neighbourhood of Port-au-Prince, Hayti, having been invited by a friend to visit that city to hear the missionaries, came in from the country one Sunday for that purpose. He sat for some time, as he afterwards told the missionary who had officiated on the occasion, without being particularly struck with what he heard, until the minister said, "He that liveth in sin is the slave of the devil." "Ah!" said the old man to himself, "it is I: I live in sin, I am the slave of the devil. Oh!" said he, "it gives me such a pain in my heart, that I cannot rest. I thought I was free. Once I was the slave of men: now I am free from men, but I am the slave of the devil. Ever since," he said, "that word has followed me everywhere: when I rise up, and when I lie down, I think of it; and when I go out to my work, and when I sit down to my meals, I think of it. I feel like a man that wants something which he cannot find. O minister, we are poor ignorant creatures, we know nothing; but you have the Word of God, and you can tell us out of the Word of God what we must do. I am willing to forsake what the Word of God says I must forsake, and I am willing to do what the Word of God says I must do. I beseech you, minister, to tell me what I must do to be saved." The missionary pointed him to the Lamb of God which taketh away the sin of the world; and he was subsequently made a happy partaker of that liberty with which Christ makes His believing people free, and became a consistent and useful member of the Church of Christ.

186. Henry Wharton.—Among a considerable number of converted natives who have been raised up on our respective stations as the fruit of missionary labour, and called to preach the gospel to their fellow-countrymen, perhaps none has been more eminent or more useful than the Rev. Henry Wharton, who finished his course a short time ago in the island of Madeira. Mr Wharton was born in Granada, West Indies, about the year 1820, and at an early period was sent to the Wesleyan Sabbath-school, where he was brought under religious influences while yet a boy. We have often heard him refer with much feeling to the occasion of his first prayer, offered from the heart. It was the result of a lesson given in the Sunday-school from the words of Jesus, "When thou prayest, enter into thy closet, and when thou hast shut thy door, pray to thy Father which is in secret; and thy Father which seeth in secret shall reward thee openly" (Matt. v. 6). With his youthful mind deeply impressed with the necessity and importance of secret prayer, little Henry returned home fully determined to obey the command of Christ. There was in his mother's house a certain little store-room where the family provisions were kept, called "the closet;" and, with childlike simplicity, attaching the idea of sanctity to this place, in connection with the teacher's lesson and the Saviour's injunction, he watched his opportunity, and stole unobserved into it, thinking that there his offering would be most acceptable, and having "shut the door," he offered his first prayer to God from a sincere and penitent heart. Retiring from the hallowed spot unobserved by any member of the household, the young disciple felt a secret pleasure in having endeavoured to do his duty, and was soon given to understand that prayer offered in any secret place, with a sincere heart, answered to the conditions of the Saviour's injunction about entering into the closet. After his return from Scotland, where he was sent for a few years to a boarding-school, young Wharton was led to seek the Lord, and soon became a personal partaker of the salvation of the gospel.

On being appointed to labour in the island of Granada in 1841, the writer first became personally acquainted with Henry Wharton. He was then a teacher in the Sabbath-school, and his intelligent, bronzed, happy-looking countenance, struck me as that of a youth who was possessed of more than ordinary native talent, and well adapted for usefulness in the Church of Christ. I consequently took notice of him, lent him books to read, put him through a regular course of study and mental improvement; and with a view to his welfare, and to have him entirely under my own direction, I ultimately engaged him as a mission-school teacher, the duties of which he discharged with credit to himself and advantage to the station. Although this arrangement involved the giving up of a comparatively lucrative mercantile situation, he entered into it with alacrity and delight, and made satisfactory progress in his studies. Having officiated as a local preacher for about two years, Mr Wharton, believing that he was called of God to the work, offered himself as a candidate for the ministry, and was duly accepted by the District Meeting and Conference of 1840. The first two years of his ministerial life were spent as the colleague of the writer in the Biabou Circuit, in the island of St Vincent. We lived under the same roof, and, being brought into the closest and most happy bonds of Christian fellowship, mutual attachments were formed as lasting as life itself. Towards the close of this period the young missionary felt it upon his heart to offer himself as an ambassador of Christ to Africa, the land of his maternal ancestors, believing that he could endure the trying climate better than any European.

This noble offer was gladly accepted by the Committee, and on the 10th of January 1845, he embarked for England on his way to the scene of his future labours. On his arrival in London, he preached with great acceptance both in Jewin Street and City Road Chapels; and the directors of the Society were well pleased to have such an agent to send forth to Western Africa. From various causes, Mr Wharton was detained longer in London than was at first expected. At length, however, everything being ready, he embarked for Africa, and arrived in safety at Cape Coast on Monday the 22d of June, where he was received in the most kind and cordial manner, both by the missionaries and their people.

It soon fell to Mr Wharton's lot to proceed to Kumasi, the blood-stained capital of Ashanti. From this stronghold of pagan darkness and cruelty, under date of the 1st of August 1847, he wrote a long and interesting letter, a brief extract from which will show by what kind of scenes he was surrounded. Among other things, he says:—" It is with no ordinary degree of pleasure that I take up my pen to address you from this barbarous field of missionary labour. I was honoured with a grand public reception on my arrival. At a moderate calculation there could not have been an assemblage of less than ten thousand souls, all immersed in the grossest ignorance and superstition,—literally 'without hope and without God in the world.' One incident I must not omit to mention; and, being the first of the kind I had been called to witness, I shall never forget it. Whilst waiting to receive the respects of the king and his counsellors, two men about to be sacrificed were marched along near where I sat. They were in a state of complete nudity, and their arms were closely tied behind their backs. Long spear-knives were thrust through their cheeks, from which the blood flowed copiously, and curdled on their breasts. The moans of one of the victims in particular was heart-rending. Never till then did I really feel myself to be in *miserable, degraded, pitiless Africa.*"

After describing other thrilling scenes which he witnessed in Kumasi, Mr Wharton gives an interesting account of his missionary labours, which were not in vain in the Lord. On returning from the interior, he was stationed for several years at Akrah, where he was instrumental in winning many souls for Christ. In 1872 he was appointed General Superintendent of the Gold Coast district. Early in the following year several of the stations were destroyed by the savage Ashantis, who invaded the Protectorate. The horrors of this war made such an impression upon Mr Wharton, whose health was in a very delicate state, after twenty-seven years' labour on the coast, that a change became absolutely necessary. He therefore embarked for Madeira, where he arrived on the 10th of October 1873, in a very feeble state. On the following day he sank into the arms of death, expressing a confident hope that he was going to that place where there is "rest for the weary."

187. **Old Tanta Mariann.**—Old Tanta Mariann, or Aunt Mary, was a truly pious negress at the River Gambia, Western Africa, the first mission-station occupied by the writer in 1831. When I first became acquainted with this venerable native Christian, I was much struck with her simple piety, love for God's House, and ardent attachment to the missionaries and their families. The secret of this was clearly revealed when she related her Christian experience, which she often did with streaming eyes, and told how the Word preached came with convincing power to her heart, and made it "sore" on account of sin, and how she found peace and comfort through believing on the Lord Jesus Christ. Although at the time alluded to the head of old Tanta was white as wool, she regularly attended the Sunday-school for adults, and made a laudable attempt, with the aid of spectacles, to learn to read the Word of God for herself. Her success was very partial, however, and she often complained that by reason of her age her mouth had become so "hard," that it could not pronounce the difficult words to be learned from the book. When she succeeded at length in making out the word "Jesus," she rejoiced exceedingly, as one who had found great spoil.

But although old Tanta was a poor reader, she was mighty in prayer, especially in Jolloff, her native language, and her voice was often heard in the social prayer-meetings. She was, moreover, regular in her attendance at the public worship of God; and such was her love for the class-meeting, that she met in *three* classes every week, and declaring that she received a blessing at each of them, she requested permission to contribute her class

Crossing the River Prah between Cape Coast and Kumasi.

pence, the same as the other members, at every meeting. But the most touching recollections I have of this dear old African convert, relate to her unwearied attention and sincere sympathy in seasons of affliction. When we were down with fever, she would remain at the mission-house day and night and do everything in her power to soothe and comfort us. The same kind attention she paid to the mission families generally, and it is not too much to say that, on some occasions, it is believed that she was the means of preserving the lives of the dear servants of God when the fever was at its crisis.

Old Tanta was still living when we left the Gambia station; but she has since passed away to the "better country," and we have no doubt but in the last great day she will be one of that vast multitude, who will "come from the east and from the west, and from the north and from the south, and sit down in the kingdom of God."

188. **Africaner.**—One of the first converts to the faith of the gospel in Great Namaqualand, after the Rev. R. Moffat had laboured for nearly nine years with very little visible fruit, was Africaner, the notorious Hottentot chief and freebooter. This savage and warlike chieftain had for many years been the terror and scourge of the whole country; but when he came under the influence of the gospel, he was convinced of sin, wept like a child, and sought and found the pardoning mercy of God, through faith in the precious blood of Christ. So thorough was the change which passed upon this remarkable heathen convert, that the lion became a lamb. "During the whole period that I lived there," says Mr Moffat, "I do not remember having occasion to be grieved with him, or to complain of any part of his conduct. His very faults seemed to 'lean to virtue's side.'"

The attachment of Africaner to his teacher was great, and when Mr Moffat went to Cape Town, he requested permission to accompany him. The missionary consented, although he knew that the experiment would involve some risk, as several parts of the country through which they would have to pass had been frequently laid waste by the robber chieftain and his retainers before he was converted. The distance to be travelled was about six hundred miles, and at various stages of their progress the greatest surprise was expressed by the Dutch boors at seeing Mr Moffat once more, as they had long since heard that he had been murdered by Africaner. At one place the missionary ventured to mention the fact of Africaner's conversion, when a Dutch farmer answered, "I can believe almost anything you say, but that I cannot credit. There are seven wonders in the world, that would be the eighth." Mr Moffat assured the farmer that the desperado had become a changed man. "Well," said he, "if what you say is true, I have only one wish, and that is to see Africaner before I die; and when you return, as sure as the sun is over our heads, I will go with you to see him, though he killed my own uncle." At this announcement the missionary was somewhat embarrassed; but at length he resolved to reveal the secret, and conducting the farmer to the waggon, pointed to the chief, and said, "This is Africaner." The farmer was astounded. Starting back, he said, "Are you Africaner?" The chief doffed his old hat, made a respectful bow, and said "I am;" at the same time testifying to the truth of the missionary's statement respecting his conversion. Then exclaimed the farmer, "O God, what a miracle of Thy power. What cannot Thy grace accomplish?" and he invited the whole party to partake of his hospitality.

The conversion of Africaner was accelerated by a remarkable dream which is worthy of a passing notice. Mr Moffat says:—"I heard Africaner relate this dream only once, and it seemed to have been revived in his mind by looking at a mountain opposite to which we sat, and along the steep side of which ran a narrow path to the top. He supposed in his dream that he was at the base of a steep and rugged mountain, over which he must pass by a path, leading along an almost perpendicular precipice to the summit on the left of the path; the fearful declivity presented to the view a furnace of fire and smoke mingled with lightning. As he looked round to flee from a sight which made his whole frame tremble, one appeared out of those murky regions, whose voice, like thunder, said there was no escape but by the narrow path. He attempted to ascend thereby, but felt the reflected heat from the precipice (to which he was obliged to cling) more intense than that from the burning pit beneath. When ready to sink with mental and physical agony, he cast his eyes upwards beyond the burning gulf, and saw a person standing on a green mount, on which the sun appeared to shine with peculiar brilliancy. This individual drew near to the ridge of the precipice, and beckoned him to advance. Shielding the side of his face with his hands, he ascended through heat and smoke such as he would have thought no human frame could endure. He at last reached the long-desired spot, which became increasingly bright, and when about to address the stranger, he awoke. On being asked what was his interpretation of the dream, Africaner replied that he thought the path was the narrow road leading from destruction to safety, from hell to heaven. 'The stranger,' he said, 'I supposed to be that Saviour of whom I had heard, and long were my thoughts occupied in trying to discover when and how I was to pass along the burning path;' then with tears in his eyes, he added, 'Thank God I have passed!'"

After his conversion, Africaner continued steadfast in the faith, and was a great comfort and help to the missionaries. The Rev. J. Archbell gives the following account of the closing scene in the life of this remarkable man:—"When he found his end approaching, he called all the people together, after the example of Joshua, and gave them directions as to their future conduct. 'We are not now,' said he, 'what we once were, *savages*, but men professing to be taught according to the gospel. Let us then do accordingly. Live peaceably with all men, if possible, and if impossible, consult those who are placed over you before you engage in anything. Remain together as you have done since I knew you; then when the directors think fit to send you a missionary, you will be ready to receive him. Behave to any teacher you may have sent as to one sent of God, as I have great hope that God will bless you in this respect when I am gone to heaven. I feel that I love God, and that He has done much for me, of which I am totally unworthy. My former life is stained with blood; but Jesus Christ has pardoned me, and I am going to heaven. Oh, beware of falling into the same evils into which I have led you, frequently led you; but seek God, and He will be found of you, to direct you!' Soon afterwards he passed away to his eternal rest, a remarkable instance of the saving power of the gospel."

189. Two Early African Converts.

—Conversions to the faith of the gospel have sometimes resulted from very feeble instrumentality and under circumstances which clearly proved the work to be of God. The first Christian missionary to South Africa was the Rev. George Schmidt, who proceeded to that country in 1736, and commenced the Moravian settlement of Genadendal (the Vale of Grace) among the poor Hottentots of the Cape Colony. After labouring for about six years with a measure of success, he found it necessary to visit Europe. But when he wished to return to his station, he was prevented from doing so by the jealousy of the Dutch Government. The mission was consequently relinquished till 1792, when it was resumed by the Revs. Messrs Marsveldt, Schwinn, and Küchnel, sent out by the Moravian Missionary Society. After the lapse of fifty years they found part of the walls of Mr Schmidt's humble dwelling still standing, and some fruit-trees which he had planted with his own hand, growing in the wilderness which had once been the missionary's garden. But what was most remarkable, they also found one of the early converts of the devoted pioneer still adhering to the truth of the gospel. She was a poor Hottentot woman named Magdalena, who had been taught and baptized by Mr Schmidt at an early period of his labours. She was now about seventy years of age, and had a tolerable recollection of her former teacher, who had given her a New Testament on his leaving the station, which she preserved as a precious relic. She brought the Sacred Book to the missionaries, and assured them that it had been the means of keeping alive the spark of grace in her heart during the long night of half a century that she had been deprived of a gospel ministry. How true is the declaration of Jehovah, "The word that goeth forth out of my mouth shall not return unto me void; but it shall accomplish that which I please, and it shall prosper in the thing whereto I sent it."

A similar instance occurred in connection with the early missionary labours of the devoted Dr Vanderkemp. The doctor entered Kaffirland in 1799, but after toiling for a short time he was obliged to return to the colony, and confine his attention to the Hottentots. His brief sojourn among the warlike Kaffirs was not in vain, however, for the Rev. S. Kay, who followed in his track many years afterwards, says:—"Within the last few days several have been added to our number, amongst whom is one whose case is worthy of particular notice. She is an aged Hottentot, who was baptized by the late Dr Vanderkemp, about thirty years ago. During the short time that the devoted missionary spent among the Kaffir tribes, he taught her and two other females the alphabet. This knowledge she afterwards improved by assiduous application, so that she was at length enabled to read the Sacred Scriptures, a copy of which, presented by her venerable tutor, she still retains to this very day. Although from that time to this she had never enjoyed the privilege of a Christian ministry, she has retained a sense of religion, and a very strong attachment to her Bible."

190. Unexpected Fruit.

—Writing on the 16th of October 1823, the Rev. Barnabas Shaw records the following incident, which occurred on one of his journeys to Namaqualand, in South Africa, at a place called Rim-hoogte, on the northern bank of the Elephant River:— "During the day an old Mozambique slave came up to our waggon, and asked for a Dutch hymn-book. On asking if he could read, he took a small school-book out of his leathern sack, and read, 'For God so loved the world, that He gave His only-begotten Son, that whosoever believeth in Him should not perish, but have everlasting life.' This circumstance being very surprising to me, I inquired by whom he had been taught to read? He said, 'My master, some time ago, hired one of your Namaquas to take care of the sheep. When he came amongst us we knew nothing of God or prayer, but he commenced singing hymns and praying with us every evening. He then read out of the Book and told us of Jesus Christ. The words which he preached were so good for me that I longed to read them for myself. He was willing to teach me, and gave me his books; but the hymn-book is old and shattered, so that I can scarcely read it. I long for another. Our teacher has gone away from us to the station, yet we still sing and pray together with our fellow-slaves every evening; and, whilst I am watching the sheep in the day, I try to improve myself. Others of the slaves have begun to pray, and long to be taught.' How various are the instruments employed in spreading the savour of divine truth! The poor Namaqua leaves Lily Fountain: he commences a journey of at least one hundred and sixty miles, in order to become the shepherd of a farmer on the Elephant River. Surrounded in his new situation by a number of slaves, almost as ignorant of God as the beasts which perish, he commences praying with them, and for them. Seeing them far from God, he begins to 'prophesy' according to his ability; and, from the fruits of his labour it is evident that he spoke to 'edification and exhortation and comfort.'"

191. Mothibi, Chief of the Batlapis.—For many years after the gospel had been introduced among the Bechuanas, Mothibi, the paramount chief of the Batlapis tribe, held out against its influence, and continued in his heathen state. At length, however, when most of his people had learned to read, and when many of them had been savingly converted to God, the aged chieftain was constrained to submit to the power of divine truth. Adverting to this event, so encouraging to the missionaries, the Rev. Mr Edwards says:— "Mothibi, our old king, feeble with age, stood forward with others to make a public profession of his faith, by being baptized. He has for some time been reckoned among the dead, his people viewing him as one of the past generation. I had heard a few months before his last visit to us, that he was becoming much concerned about the state of his soul, and could no longer conceal his fears, which only increased the longer he kept silent. Being quite overwhelmed, he made known his alarm to the believers, and requested their counsel and sympathy. Morisanyane, the native reader at his residence, was made useful to him. Mothibi at length entreated his sons to take him to Kuruman, to see his own missionaries. Immediately on his arrival at the station he bent his feeble steps to the mission-house. Never before, I believe, did he visit a missionary with so much anxiety and diffidence. I found him not inclined to speak much, but rather disposed to hear what might be said to him. He said, however, that 'he had come to speak about his soul—that he was an old man, great from age, but without understanding. There is nothing left,' he exclaimed, 'but my old bones and withered skin. I heard the Word from the beginning (twenty-five years ago), but never understood, and now have no rest night nor day; my soul is sorrowful, and burning with anguish; my heart is sick, and rises into my throat; my mind is dark, and my memory cannot retain the good Word; but though it forsakes me it does me good, and leaves something behind in my soul which I cannot explain, but which causes me to hope. I wish to cast myself at the feet of Jesus, the Son of God, in hope and expectation that He will have mercy on me.' Those who lived near to Mothibi, testified that he had often been seen to weep for his sins, and his lost state as a sinner, and as he professed to trust in Christ only for salvation, I felt free to admit him to Church fellowship by baptism. Although the rightful chief of 20,000 Bechuanas, he stood with as much humility as the poorest of his servants, and I regard him as a monument of what grace can do, even in the eleventh hour."

192. Paternal Affection.—The concern manifested by native converts for the salvation of their heathen relatives and friends is often very striking. A remarkable instance of this appears in the case of Mamonyantsi, a Matabele captive, who, becoming a servant in the mission family at Kuruman, soon learned to read, and was subsequently brought to a saving knowledge of the truth. From the time of her conversion and baptism to the day of her death she was a living epistle of the power of the gospel. "Once," says the missionary, "when visiting the sick, as I entered her dwelling I found her sitting with a part of the Word of God in her hand, bathed in tears. Addressing her, I said, ' My child, what is the cause of your sorrow ? Is the baby still unwell ?' ' No,' she replied, ' my baby is well.' ' Your mother-in-law ?' I inquired, ' No, no,' she replied, ' it is my own dear mother.' Here she again gave vent to her grief; and, holding out the gospel of Luke in a hand wet with tears, she exclaimed, ' My mother will never see this Word, she will never hear this good news.' She wept again and again, and said, ' O my mother and my friends, they live in heathen darkness; and shall they die without seeing the light which has shone on me, and without tasting that love which I have tasted ?' Raising her eyes to heaven she sighed a prayer, and I heard the words again, ' My mother, my mother !'

"This," continues the missionary, "was the expression of affection of one of Africa's sable daughters, whose heart had been taught to mourn over the ignorance of a far-distant heathen mother. Shortly after this evidence of divine love in her soul, I was called upon to watch over her dying pillow, and descended with her to Jordan's bank. She feared no rolling billow. She looked on the babe to which she had lately given birth, and commended it to the care of her God and Saviour. The last words I heard from her faltering lips were, ' My mother !'"

193. The Mantatee Convert.—When the first mission-station was commenced in 1834, for the benefit of the warlike Mantatoos at Umperane, in Southern Africa, strange scenes presented themselves to the missionary and his wife on every hand. They could scarcely move without seeing the skulls of those who had been slain in battle, it being the custom of the tribe never to bury the remains of the fallen. They also witnessed every day the most appalling proofs of the cruelty and degradation of the people among whom their lot was cast. They nevertheless commenced their work in the true missionary spirit, and their labour was not in vain in the Lord. One of the first converts to the faith of the gospel was the oldest son of the chief Sikonyela, who had been placed at the mission-house by his father for instruction. Although only eleven years of age he was addicted to the drinking of Kaffir beer, and was often found in a state of disgraceful intoxication. The missionary told his royal pupil plainly, at the beginning, that he had an immortal soul, and that all impenitent drunkards would spend an eternity of misery in hell. Next morning his mother brought him a basket of strong beer; but he refused to drink it. He immediately took it to the door and poured it out on the ground, requesting his mother never to bring him any more; and from that day he never again tasted a single drop. In 1838 a gracious revival of religion commenced on the station. Many of the young people in the school were convinced of sin, and found pardoning mercy. The young chief, who for two years had been a serious inquirer, was in deep distress of mind. He wept aloud while his teachers spoke to him of the love of God in Christ Jesus, and began to cry for mercy. At the end of two days the Lord spoke peace to his soul. The missionary was delighted beyond measure to hear the young convert earnestly praying for the nation at large, and for his father in particular.

When the news of the young chief's conversion reached the ears of Sikonyela, he came to see his son, and examined him most closely as to the change which he professed to have experienced. In answer to the questions, How do you know that you are pardoned? What is it like? the young convert replied, "For a long time I have felt myself a sinner; but last Saturday my heart became full of grief. I saw I should go to hell if I died. I felt God was angry with me, and I could not rest. I wished to serve God, and to love Him; so I went behind a large rock in the mountain, and there I prayed that the Lord would pardon me; but my heart became more sore. I wept and prayed that the Lord Jesus would wash me in His blood. While I was praying I felt all my sins taken away, and my heart was filled with joy. I now love God very much, I feel very happy, and have no sorrow at all." This noble confession satisfied Sikonyela. He said, "I believe all my son says is true. I wish I felt the same." The youth was baptized by the name of David, and henceforth walked consistently as a disciple of Christ, and became useful to his fellow-countrymen.

194. Perseverance Rewarded. —Writing from Cape Town, Cape of Good Hope, on the 31st of July 1847, the Rev. Richard Ridgill says: —"At our English prayer-meeting, on Monday evening last, a soldier found peace with God, and three or four persons have this week begun to meet in class. I held a Lovefeast for the Dutch members last night, in Sydney Street Chapel. It was a deeply-interesting occasion; and as one and another rose to testify of the grace of God, I felt much encouraged to persevere in preaching repentance and remission of sins in the name of Jesus. One man present at the Love-feast for the first time, said he must tell of the Lord's goodness. He had been brought up in the Lutheran doctrine, baptized and confirmed in that Church; but for thirty-eight years after his confirmation continued to be a slave of Satan. About two years ago, during an attack of illness, induced by indulgence in intoxicating liquors, he was brought to see the wickedness and danger of his conduct; he repented of his sins, and determined to serve the Lord. By the grace of God he has been faithful to his vow, and bore an honourable testimony to the renewing power of divine grace."

In the history of this man's search for happiness there were some striking and admonitory features. He had resided for many years in the neighbourhood of the Moravian Missionary Institution at Groene-Kloof, when it was his constant practice, though enslaved by sin, to read his Bible through twice a year. When he became convinced of sin, he retired daily to pray amid the rocks and bushes. His anguish of mind only seemed to increase, and he was ready to despair, when it occurred to him that he had heard the missionaries say that those who seek the Lord must never cease to pray. The hour of his deliverance drew near: the pains of hell got hold upon him, and he hastened to his accustomed place of prayer upon the mountain-side. He knelt him down and called upon God; there was no voice, nor any that regarded. Hour after hour passed, and still he prayed. The heavens became dark with gathering clouds; but he minded not the coming storm. Heedless of the rain which began to pour down, he pleaded and wrestled with the Lord: conscious only of his spiritual danger, he felt no bodily discomfort. He did not pray in vain. He found, in the midst of the storm, the peace of God which passeth all understanding, and he went down to his house justified."

195. An Aged Convert.—Christian missions have often been made a blessing to our countrymen in distant lands, as well as to the dark, benighted heathen. At a meeting for Christian fellowship held by the Rev. Richard Ridgill in Sidney Street Chapel, Cape Town, Cape of Good Hope, on the 30th of July 1847, there was a striking instance exhibited in proof of this. Towards the close of the meeting there stood up an elderly Scotchman, who, after forty years residence in the country, spoke Dutch with the fluency of a native. He said, "When I look around me, I see that I am the eldest in years, and I have no doubt but I am the eldest in sin. I have been a wicked sinner, the chief of sinners; but in my seventieth year I found salvation. Is not this mercy unspeakably great? Yes, my friends, God receives sinners in the eleventh hour; nay, He saves after the eleventh hour. Bless the Lord, O my soul! My friends, help me, help me to praise the Lord!" The old man's eyes filled with tears of grateful joy, and he sat down weeping. "Yes, my brother," said the missionary, "we will help you to give thanks unto God;" and, with united hearts and voices, the whole congregation rose and sang, "Praise ye the Lord; Hallelujah!" The missionary adds:—"The conduct of this aged sinner since his conversion has been most exemplary. His regular attendance at the means of grace would put many to shame. It is now eighteen months since he joined the society, and though residing at a distance of four miles, he has only been absent from class once. Whether the fierce south-east or the boisterous north-west wind blow, in summer or in winter, John Smith is always present."

196. Hadara, the Abyssinian Convert.—The story of Hadara, a youthful convert in the far-distant East, is full of interest, and affords a remarkable illustration of the providence and grace of God. Hadara was born in Abyssinia about the year 1815. The people in that country are not all heathen strictly speaking; large numbers are Christians in name, though they are very ignorant, and addicted to many pagan customs.

When Hadara was very young, he was taught to pray to saints, and to fast often. As it was proposed to bring him up to be a priest, he was careful to mind these things, and to attend to many vain and sinful rites. He was told, that if he went as a pilgrim to Jerusalem, he would become holy and happy, and all his sins would be forgiven. From this time all his thoughts were engaged in contriving how he should get there. He had no money, so he hired himself as a servant to a person named Gergis, who said he was going to that city. But Gergis was a base man; and after he had got the lad away from his home, he sold him for a slave. Hadara, however, managed to run away from the country where he was in slavery, and got back to his own land.

He now engaged himself as a servant to a missionary. Among the first truths his new master taught him were that every prayer made to saints was a proof of unbelief towards God, and therefore sinful; and that all true prayer is offered to the Almighty in the name of our Lord Jesus Christ. He began to think seriously about the right way to pray. After this he met with some missionary papers which gave an account of the conversion of several heathens. Reading these little papers made him anxious to have a New Testament. He now for the first time saw his state as a sinner, and cried to God for mercy. He found that neither a pilgrimage to Jerusalem, nor the merits of saints, could secure for him the favour of God: it was only the blood of Christ that could cleanse him from his sin.

His kind friend the missionary was at length taken ill, and had to leave the station to return to Europe. Hadara loved his own country, yet he was willing to leave it, that he might attend to his master's family on the long and weary journey homeward. This he did with sincere affection. He drove the camels over the desert, cooked the food at their encampments, kept watch at night, carried his master's sick child by day, or helped to bear his afflicted mistress, and did everything in his power to promote their comfort.

Hadara grew in piety, and it was proposed that he should be educated in Europe, and then return to his own land to preach the gospel to his countrymen. But God was pleased to order it otherwise. The youth took cold, and became very ill. At length it was seen that he could not live long: he knew it, and now he thought more than before of the death of Christ as an offering for sin, and quoted many passages of Scripture in reference to the Atonement. He wished to return to Abyssinia, to tell his friends what the Lord had done for his soul; yet he was willing to die. "I shall be gone in a short time," he said. When asked where he was going, he replied, "First to the grave; then I shall rise again with a clear understanding—not so dark as it is now. I shall see the Lord himself, and know all truths clearly, clearly." His last words were, "I am going to heaven."

197. Rasalama, the Madagascar Martyr.—

Among the Christian martyrs of Madagascar who suffered during the reign of the late queen, after the missionaries had been expelled from the island in 1836, none was more eminent for piety and devotedness to God than a native female convert named Rasalama. When she was taken prisoner, she "rejoiced that she was counted worthy to suffer affliction for believing in Jesus." This saying of hers was no sooner reported to the judges than she was put into heavy irons and severely beaten. So long as she had strength, she sought comfort in singing her favourite hymns. The day before her execution, the ordinary chains she wore were exchanged for other rings and bars. These were fastened round her hands, feet, knees, and neck, which were then drawn together, thus forcing the body into a position of great agony; but she bore the insult and the pain with remarkable meekness and resignation. At length the day was fixed for her execution, the intelligence of which she received with demonstrations of joy and gratitude to God, for she regarded it as the day of her redemption and release from suffering, and from the cruelty of the tyrant's power.

As Rasalama was led away to the fatal spot where she was to seal the truth and sincerity of her Christian profession with the testimony of her blood, she exhibited no signs of fear or dismay; but continued to sing hymns of praise to God, and thus set an example to be followed by many others, who afterwards were called to tread the same pathway to death and heaven. When passing the sanctuary in which she had been accustomed to worship, she exclaimed, "There I heard the words of the Saviour." When she was reviled by her cruel persecutors and murderers, she reviled not again. The only request she made of her executioners was for a brief interval, that she might offer a few words of prayer to God before she passed out of time into eternity. This was granted, and she kneeled down upon the rocky ground. Some said in derision, "Where is the God she prays to, that He does not save her now." Others looked on with pity; but she, regardless of all around, held communion with the Divine Saviour, and while thus commending her spirit into His hands, the executioners from behind buried their spears in her body. So calm, so firm was this noble sufferer, that even the hard men who took her life were constrained to say, "There is some charm in the religion of the white people which takes away the fear of death;" while a courageous young man, who had accompanied her to the last, exclaimed, as he turned from a spectacle at once so sorrowful and so sublime, "If I might die so tranquil and so happy a death, I would not be unwilling to die for the Saviour too."

198. The Australian Settler.—

John Lees, a British colonist in New South Wales, and one of the earliest converts to the faith of Christ after the commencement of the Wesleyan Mission to that country, was a very remarkable man, and his entire history was a striking illustration of the providence and grace of God. For many years previous to his acquaintance with the missionaries he was a daring transgressor of God's law, and lived in open sin and rebellion against the Almighty. Nor did he readily yield to the claims of truth on hearing the gospel faithfully preached. It was not till he was reduced to the greatest straits, and it became evident that the Lord had a controversy with him, that the daring transgressor was constrained to submit to the authority of heaven. He was notoriously addicted to intemperance, and by his dissipated habits, and the consequent neglect of his farm, his family was reduced to a state of utter destitution. At length nothing of his little property remained but one pig; and this he was about to take from the sty to pay a score which he had contracted with one of his neighbours who sold intoxicating drinks. At this period of his life, and in this crisis of his affairs, God made use of singular means to convert his soul, and turn him from the error of his ways. Living in the midst of the woods of New Holland, and of course making use of wood for fuel, he stepped one night out of his miserable hut to bring in a log to lay on the fire. Stooping down for the purpose, he grasped in the dark, with the log of wood, a large venomous snake. The horrid reptile opened its poisonous jaws, and inflicted on his hand a most painful bite. Knowing how certainly and how soon death proceeds from the bite of some kinds of snakes in that country, and fearing he had been bitten by one of the worst, he saw himself on the brink of eternity, and felt he was awfully unprepared. He fainted; and recovering his senses, he began to cry to God for mercy, and never rested till he found peace in believing, the true "balm of Gilead," the precious blood of Christ, being applied to his guilty conscience at the same time that a suitable remedy was found for the bite of the snake on his hand, which, by the blessing of God, proved effectual in promoting his recovery.

The life of John Lees was thus mercifully spared; and having become a new creature in Christ Jesus, for upwards of twenty years he adorned the doctrine of God his Saviour by a holy walk and conversation. The temperance, charity, zeal, and Christian benevolence of the Australian convert became very conspicuous; and having built at his own expense, and presented to the Connection, a new Wesleyan Chapel, and for a length of time supported the cause of Christian missions with a princely liberality, considering his means, he was called to his heavenly inheritance in a good old age, leaving an example worthy of being imitated.

199. **An Earnest Inquirer.**—"A young South Sea Islander," says a missionary, "came loitering about my house one day in an unusual manner. Knowing him to be one of the baser sort, I said, 'Friend, have you any business with me?' Tears gushed into his eyes, and he could hardly speak at first. At length he replied, 'You know I am a wicked man. Shame covers my face, and holds me back. To-day I have broke through all fear. I want to know,—is there room for *me*? Can *I* expect mercy?' When asked how such thoughts came into his mind, he replied, 'I was at work putting up my garden fence. Greatly wearied, I sat down on a little bank to rest, and said within myself, All this garden, and death for my soul; all this great property, and death for ever! Oh, what shall I do?'" This reflection, which was no doubt prompted by the influence of the Holy Spirit, made the poor heathen unhappy, and he resolved to go to the missionary to inquire what he must do to find the way of peace. Then and there he received suitable counsel; and from that time he availed himself of every opportunity of hearing the gospel, and ultimately became a pious and devoted Christian.

200. **Buteve, the Spiritual Beggar.**—The Rev. John Williams gives

the following interesting account of Buteve, a remarkable native convert in the island of Rarotonga :—"In passing one evening from one station to the other, my attention was arrested by seeing a person get off a stone seat by the wayside, and walk upon his knees into the centre of the path, when he shouted, 'Welcome, servant of God, who brought light into this dark island; to you we are indebted for the Word of salvation.' The appearance of his person first attracted my attention, his hands and feet being eaten off by a disease which the natives call *kokovi*, and which obliged him to walk upon his knees; but notwithstanding this, I found that he was exceedingly industrious, and not only kept his ground in beautiful order, but raised food enough to support his wife and three children, having learned to manage his hoe with the stumps of his arms. In reply to his salutation, I asked him what he knew of the Word of salvation. He answered, 'I know about Jesus Christ, who came into the world to save sinners.' On inquiring what he knew about Jesus Christ, he replied, 'I know that He is the Son of God, and that He died painfully upon the cross to pay for the sins of men, in order that their souls might be saved, and go to happiness in the skies.' I inquired of him if all the people went to heaven after death? 'Certainly not,' he replied, 'only those who believe in the Lord Jesus, who cast away sin, and who pray to God.' 'You pray to God, of course?' I continued. 'Oh yes,' he said, 'I very frequently pray as I weed my ground, and plant my food; but always three times a day, besides praying with my family every morning and evening.' 'Well,' I replied, 'that is excellent; but where did you obtain your knowledge?' 'From you, to be sure; who brought us the news of salvation but yourself?' 'True,' I replied; 'but I do not ever recollect to have seen you at either of our settlements to hear me speak of these things, and how do you obtain your knowledge of them?' 'Why,' he said, 'as the people return from the service I take my seat by the wayside, and beg a bit of the Word from them as they pass by. One gives me one piece, another another piece, and I collect them together in my heart, and, by thinking over what I thus obtain, and praying to God to make me know, I understand a little about His Word.' This was to me altogether an interesting incident, as I had never seen the poor cripple before, and I could not learn that he had ever been in a place of worship. His knowledge, however, was such as to afford me both astonishment and delight, and I seldom passed his house, after this interview, without holding an interesting conversation with him."

201. The Parting Prayer.— The piety, pathos, power, and genuine eloquence frequently displayed by the native converts on some of our mission-stations are truly remarkable. When the Rev. John Williams was about to leave his people at Riatea, in the South Seas, for a time, on a visit to England, the parting scene was very affecting. He preached to a large congregation, and administered the sacrament of the Lord's Supper to a large number of devout communicants. Being much exhausted, he called upon one of the members to engage in prayer. This he did in a manner which was so striking, that the missionary noted down the substance of it afterwards, from which the following is an extract in a free translation :—"O God, the high and blessed Jehovah, we praise Thee for all the goodness Thou hast wrought towards us. While we see the bread broken in our presence, may the eye of our heart be looking at the body of our Lord Jesus, as broken upon the cross for us; and when we see the wine poured into the cup, may the ear of the heart be listening to the voice of the Lord Jesus, saying, 'This cup is the new covenant in my blood, which was shed for the remission of sins.' Let not what the apostle says be applicable to us; never may we eat and drink condemnation to ourselves. Forbid that we should take nails, and fasten the Lord Jesus again to the cross. Once He has been put to pain for us; may that suffice: may we never take the spear of sin, and pierce again His side, thus crucifying Him afresh, and putting Him to an open shame. In partaking of this sacred feast, may our hearts be warmed, may our love to the Saviour be made greater, and may our faith be made stronger." Then referring to the departure of his beloved pastor and his family, he said, " O God, tell the winds about them, that they may not blow fiercely upon them; command the ocean concerning them, that it may not swallow them up; conduct them in safety to their far-distant country, and give them a happy meeting with their relatives; and then conduct them back again to us. But should we never meet again around the table of the Lord below, may we all meet around the throne of glory above."

202. Brave Christian Youth.—In a recent letter, the Rev. Mr Murray, of the London Missionary Society, relates the following instance of bravery and moral heroism, under trying circumstances, exhibited by a lad belonging to the Loyalty Islands who had received his training from the missionaries in that group:—" A large fishing-boat left Cape York, on the 18th of August, for some place in the Straits. She had proceeded but a short distance, however, when she was capsized. The party in the boat consisted of four persons, namely, two white men, a native boy, and a lad from Mare, Loyalty Islands, called by the white men Billy. His native name was Waeania. It was impossible to get the boat righted, so the white men and the boys could only cling to the keel, and be drifted hither and thither as the winds and tide might carry them. Everything that was in the boat was lost, so they had neither water nor provisions. Billy could have swam to the shore where the boat was capsized without any difficulty; but he chose rather to abide by his companions and share whatever dangers and privations might await them. After being drifted about for sixteen hours they were cast ashore on Woody Island; but as there is neither water nor provisions to be found on that island, their condition was nearly as trying as when they were clinging to the bottom of the boat, and unless something could be done speedily, one at least of the party must soon have died. Help might be obtained at an island three and a half miles distant; but how was it to be reached? Brave Billy was equal to the occasion; and after a consultation between him and Mr Jardine, he determined to attempt to swim to the island—a formidable undertaking for a youth who had already been sixteen hours in the water without nourishment of any kind. And so Billy felt it; but after committing himself to God in prayer, and getting ready to start, he said to Mr Jardine, 'Charlie, suppose me catch the land, me see you again; suppose me die, good-bye.' And so he set out in dependence on God, and God enabled him to 'catch the land.' The needful help was obtained, and the party was soon rescued from their perilous position. Of course their gratitude to Billy knew no bounds. Billy checked their expressions of it, however. 'Don't thank me,' said he, 'thank God; it is God who has done it.' It is pleasing to add that his noble conduct has been highly appreciated and suitably rewarded."

203. Poor Lolohia.—The first genuine convert to Christianity in the Friendly Islands, was a native youth named Lolohia, whose brief history is one of mournful interest. From his childhood he was afflicted with a scrofulous disease common in the islands, and its ravages had made him an object of pity; but his countenance was fine, and his disposition was mild and cheerful. Before the Rev. John Thomas came to Tonga, Lolohia had been staying with an elder brother at Vavau, where both their minds were much impressed by a few words spoken about Jehovah by an English sailor who lived on the island. When they heard the same words advanced with still greater earnestness by the missionary, their hearts yielded; they gave up their idols, and determined that the Lord should be their God. They were the first scholars in the mission-school at Hihifo, and being youths of rank and importance, from their mother having become the wife of the chief Ata, their coming influenced others, and a considerable number were soon brought under instruction.

Lolohia showed strong attachment to God's house and ministers, and when he was unable to walk to the school and chapel, on account of his affliction, he got the other boys to carry him as best they could, and which they did sometimes in a kind of wheelbarrow constructed for the purpose. In all the trials through which the missionaries had to pass at an early period of their labours, in consequence of the strange conduct of the chief Ata, and other adverse circumstances, poor Lolohia was their fast and sympathising friend; and he often declared that if they were obliged to leave the island, he would go with them wherever they went. As his views of Christ and His atoning work became clearer, his faith increased, and he was sweetly assured of his personal interest in the Saviour, and he could rejoice in hope of the glory of God. He was then at his own request baptized into the faith of the gospel, his mother and Ata offering no objections.

For some time before his death, Lolohia was the head and guardian of a company of praying youths who lived near him, and who often united in prayer and praise in the room of the invalid. He bore his long affliction with perfect patience and resignation to the will of God; and when the end drew near, and preparations were made for removing him to a small house near the burying-ground, after the manner of the natives, he said to his friends, "Yes, let us go." And when Mr Thomas called to see him, he received him with a smile, and said, "My love to you. Let us pray," and with language of prayer on his lips, his redeemed spirit passed away to be "for ever with the Lord," the first-fruit of a glorious harvest, thenceforth to be gathered from the Friendly Islands.

204. Mary and her Bible.—The Rev. G. M'Dougall, a Wesleyan missionary in Manatoba, relates the following touching incident which came

L

under his notice whilst labouring among the native Indians of that country:—"To a young girl we gave the Christian name of Mary. When she first entered our school, she was nearly as wild as the beautiful antelope that sports on our plains; but she soon became interested in her books, and what was better still, she earnestly sought and found the Saviour. When about fourteen years of age, she was taken very ill, and for weeks was confined to her poor couch; but in those hours of languishing Mary's great comfort was her Indian Bible. Many a time when I have entered her humble abode, I have seen the dying girl with the precious Book lying on her lap, with her eyes resting upon its sweet promises. There appeared to be only one thing that gave her anxiety—her father was a drunkard. On the day of her death I was sent for at her request. When I arrived I found her in a sitting position, her hand resting upon her Bible. After praying with her, I asked her if she had any request to make, or anything in particular that she wanted to state. She answered, 'I have, I want to tell you that I am very happy. But I know I shall soon be with Jesus, and there is only one thing that troubles my heart; I fear I shall never see my father again.' The dying girl then lifted her Bible, and calling to her wretched parents, said, 'Father, take this Book of God, and promise me that you will never touch the fire-water again.' The poor man came and knelt by her side, and accepted the dying gift, and promised that he would never touch the accursed fire-water again."

205. King George Tubou.— When the gospel was introduced into Polynesia, after a long and gloomy night of watching and waiting and working, many remarkable conversions were witnessed; but none was more important in its results than that of George Tubou, the chief of Haabi, and heir-apparent to the whole of the Friendly Islands. In early life he was fierce, savage, and warlike, and entirely devoted to the superstitious practices of his country. Soon after the commencement of the mission, he became deeply impressed with what he saw and heard on the occasion of his visits to Tonga, where the first station was established, and he was at length thoroughly convinced of the truth of Christianity. He consequently put away his idols, erected a sanctuary for the worship of the true and living God, and earnestly requested a missionary to instruct him and his people in the knowledge of divine things. When his request could not be granted, on account of the lack of labourers, such was his anxiety to have a teacher, that he actually engaged an English sailor to read prayers in his chapel at Lifuka till a missionary should arrive. In these strange services he joined as best he could; but there is no wonder, considering the circumstances, that he made little progress in religious knowledge. It was when on a visit to Vavau that George Tubou experienced a saving change of heart, and became a new man in Christ Jesus. The circumstances attending this important event were most affecting and interesting. A genuine religious revival was in progress; hundreds of natives were crowding the penitent prayer-meetings, crying for mercy, believing in Christ, and stepping into the glorious liberty of the children of God. Among the rest of the inquirers came George the chief of Haabi, and his noble wife Charlotte. They attended several meetings, prayed earnestly, and wept bitterly, but failed to find peace.

One night, after returning home from the meeting, while meditating upon the simple plan of salvation as set forth by the missionary, George was enabled to appropriate to himself the merits of Christ, and became the subject of peace and joy in the Holy Ghost. As soon as the fact of the chief's spiritual conversion became known to the people of the *lotu*, it was the cause of great and sincere rejoicing. His devoted wife found peace soon afterwards, and they both of them became henceforth unreservedly consecrated to the service of the true and living God. George now made rapid progress in the acquisition of knowledge, and soon became an acceptable and useful local preacher and class-leader; and Charlotte also took charge of a class of females, which she led on in religious knowledge and experience in a most delightful manner.

When by the death of Finau, in 1833, George became king of Vavau as well as Haabi, and when shortly afterwards, by the addition of Tonga to his dominions, he became supreme ruler of all the Friendly Islands, he retained the simplicity of his Christian character, and governed his kingdom with true dignity, according to the laws of God. He, moreover, displayed superior mental ability in his new and responsible position, as well as unquenchable zeal in the cause of God, which was ever dear to his heart. Nor did he fail to regulate his conduct, both in public and in private, according to the requirements of the Sacred Scriptures, so far as he understood them. One of his first public acts after his conversion was to liberate all his slaves, whilst he required his subordinate chiefs to do the same. He also framed and promulgated a code of laws based upon the Word of God, appointed magistrates and judges to aid him in the government, and by firmness, kindness, and magnanimity, won the heathen portion of his subjects to the side of Christianity; so that in the course of a few years, with the co-operation of the missionary, a change was brought about in the social and moral condition of the Friendly Islands, which excited the admiration and gratitude of all who were favoured to witness it.

King George of the Friendly Islands, and his subjects, rapidly improved in their temporal circumstances after their conversion to Christianity. As trade and commerce increased, to facilitate communication between the islands, the king purchased a beautiful little schooner, the fate of which developed a fine trait in his character. He was very fond of his new vessel; but she had not made many voyages when she was unfortunately wrecked on a coral reef. The men in charge of her were almost afraid of communicating the sad news to their royal master, thinking it would distress him beyond measure. On reaching Nukalofa they met the king, with his New Testament under his arm, on his way to the chapel to meet his Bible-class. On hearing of the wreck, instead of yielding to a fit of immoderate grief, as they expected, George calmly said he was sorry to lose the schooner; "but," said he, as he held up his Testament in his hand, and looked upon the messengers with a smile, "that is only a temporal loss, and may be repaired; so long as we have the Word of God we are rich indeed, and have cause to be thankful." He then gave instructions to the men what to do, and proceeded to meet his class as if nothing had happened.

In 1853 King George sailed in the missionary-ship *John Wesley*, on a visit to Australia, in company with the Rev. Robert Young, who had been sent out as a deputation to inspect the missions in the Southern World by the British Conference. On taking leave of his royal companion in travel, Mr Young thus expresses himself:— "I had now spent several weeks in the company of the king, and, during that period, I had not observed an act contrary to the strictest Christian propriety, nor had I heard a foolish word from his lips. In all my intercourse with him I was deeply impressed with his mental power and his genuine piety, and I felt persuaded that, had he possessed European advantages, he would have been one of the greatest men of the age."

206. Joel Bulu.—Among the host of converts to the faith of the gospel, who have been called to proclaim the glad tidings of salvation to their fellow-countrymen in the South Sea Islands, none has been more useful, or attained to greater eminence, than Joel Bulu, a native of Tonga, who both there and in Fiji, did good service in the cause of Christian missions. His interesting history will be best stated in his own language, in an extract from his autobiography, as translated by one of the missionaries:—

I was born at Vavau in the heathen days; nor was it till I was a big lad that the *lotu* came to our land. When I heard the report of it, I was full of anger, and my soul burned with hatred against it. "And shall our gods be forsaken?" I cried in wrath. "As for me, I will never forsake them." One day I heard a man talking of the *lotu*, who said it promised a land of the dead, different from *bulotu*, of which our fathers spoke—even a home in the sky for the good, while evil men were cast into a dreadful place, wherein there burned a fire which none could quench. On that very night I went forth with the lads of the town. It was a fine night; and looking up to the heavens, where the stars were shining, this thought suddenly smote me—"O the beautiful land! If the words be true which were told us to-day, then are those *lotu* people happy indeed;" and my soul longed with a great longing to reach that beautiful land. I could not rest, so I went to another town where dwelt a Christian chief, to tell him I wished to *lotu*. "Good is your coming," said the chief, for great was his joy. "But why do you want to *lotu?*" "I have heard," was my reply, "of the good land whither you go after death; therefore do I wish to *lotu*, that I also may be a dweller in the sky." So they prayed over me, and thus it was that I turned to Christianity; but of its meaning I knew nothing. Then came Mr Thomas to Vavau; and, standing under a tree in the public square, he preached to us from the parable of the tares among the wheat. It was this sermon that pierced my soul; for I had thought that I was one of the wheat, but now I found I was among the tares. As I heard I wept and trembled, for I thought, "I shall never see the good land." When the sermon was over, and the people rose to go, I sat in my place quaking for fear, and weeping in great anguish, for all the strength had gone out of my body. "What is the matter with you?" they asked. I said, "Pray for me, pray for me, I beseech you." So they all knelt down and prayed for me, first one and then another, till they were tired, but I found no comfort; so I arose, and going into an empty outhouse, I knelt down, and there by myself wept and prayed before the Lord, for now I felt that I was a sinner; the wrath of God lay heavy upon my soul, and I hated myself because of my evil ways. "Oh, what is that repentance whereof the preacher told us?" I cried. "Lord, let me find it, that I may live;" for so dark was my mind, that I did not know that this sorrow and fear of mine were marks of repentance. Thus I continued for a long while seeking the Lord in prayer with many tears.

At last there came a day in 1834, whereon the missionaries (of whom Mr Turner was one) assembled us together to hold a Love-feast; and when we had sung a hymn and prayed, then Mr Turner stood up to declare the work of God in his soul. My heart burned within me while I listened to his words; for in speaking of himself he told all I had felt, and I said to myself, "We are like two canoes, sailing bow and bow, neither being swifter nor slower than the other." Thus it was with me when he told of his repentance; but when he went on to speak of his faith in Christ, the forgiveness of his sins, and the peace and joy which he found in believing, then said I, "My mast is broken, my sail is blown away; he is gone clean out of my sight, and I am left here drifting helplessly over the waves." But while I listened eagerly to his words, telling of the love of Christ to him, my eyes were opened. I saw the way, and I, even I, also believed and lived. I was like a man fleeing for his life from an enemy behind him, and groping along the wall of a house in the dark to find the door, that he may enter in and escape, when lo! a door is suddenly opened before his face, and straightway, with one bound he leaps within. Thus it was with me as I listened to the words of Mr Turner: my heart was full of joy and love, and the tears streamed down my cheeks. Often had I wept before, but not like former weeping were the tears which I now shed. Then I wept out of sorrow and fear, but now for joy and gladness, and because my heart was full of love to Him who had loved me and given Himself for me; and Mr Turner, seeing the tears raining heavily down from my eyes, called upon me to speak. "Stand up, Joel," said he, "stand up, and tell us how it is with you." So I stood up; but it seemed to me as if my soul was parted from my body, and I remember nothing more until I found myself lying on the mat, and the missionaries weeping over me, and saying, "What is this?" "I live!" said I, "I live! Let us rise, that I may declare the mercies of God." And even while I spoke there arose a great cry in our midst, and a burst of weeping, for the hearts of all were strangely moved. Oh, what a day was that! Never can I forget it—the prayers and praises and the tears of joy. There were many, who, like myself, had long been seeking the Lord, and who now found Him to the joy of their souls.

Soon after his conversion, Joel Bulu was called to be a teacher of others, and for nearly forty years he has been a faithful labourer in the Lord's vineyard, first in the Friendly Islands, and then in Fiji. For simple piety, ardent zeal, and usefulness in winning souls to Christ, he is a fine specimen of a large and rapidly increasing class of native missionaries, who have been raised up in the South Sea Islands to proclaim to their fellow-countrymen the unsearchable riches of Christ.

207. Varani, a Chief in Fiji.—Never was the regenerating power of divine grace more gloriously magnified than in the case of Varani, the chief of Viwa, and a noted warrior and cannibal, who was converted to the faith of the gospel some time after the *lotu* reached the island to which he belonged. Adverting to this notable event, the Rev. John Hunt says—"He had long been convinced of the truth of Christianity, but was prevented from making a public profession of it by his connection with Seru, the chief of Bau. He had long acted as the human butcher of this young chief, who was the Napoleon of Fiji. Varani learned to read during the early part of the year; and, what is still more important, he began to pray. Often would he retire into the woods to entreat God to have mercy on his soul. He was, in fact, so fully convinced of his need of a Saviour, that the name of Jesus became very precious to him. If he found, in the course of his reading, a passage which referred to the love of Christ to sinners, he would kiss the book for joy and thankfulness. Varani would talk about nothing but religion, either to heathens or Christians. He was obliged to go to war, but it was exceedingly against his will. The Lord protected him in a remarkable manner. On one occasion he was ordered to attempt to set fire to a town, and had to approach very near to effect his purpose. He was perceived by the enemy, and a musket-ball passed close to his head. He immediately fell on his knees to thank God for his deliverance, not merely from death, but from hell, which he feared much more than death, and which he fully believed would be his portion if he died without making a public profession of Christianity. He felt that praying while he still remained a heathen would not do, but that he must take up his cross and follow Christ, as His professed disciple, before he could hope for salvation. This conviction induced him at length to inform the chief of Bau that he must become a Christian. The chief, as might be expected, endeavoured to dissuade him from taking such a step, at any rate at present. This, however, only led Varani to exhort the chief to join him. Seru, the chief, knowing the firmness of the man, said no more, and thus gave an unwilling assent to what he evidently disapproved.

"All that remained was to take the important step, which is always done, if the person is able, by bowing the knee in the house of God at a public service. Providence, even as to the time of taking the step, evidently interposed. I had published, on the Sunday before Good Friday, that we should observe that day as a 'sacred day,' in honour of the death of our Saviour. Varani heard of this, and determined that this should be the day of his decision. He came early in the morning to inquire when this day would return. I informed him, of course, not till another year. 'Then,' said he, 'I'll become a Christian to-day.' A short time after, the bell rang for the prayer-meeting, which Varani attended, and at which he publicly, to the joy of many, bowed before Jehovah's awful throne. As soon as he returned from the chapel, his first trial came. A messenger arrived from Bau to inform him that a chief had been shot dead in the night; and, according to heathen custom, he was expected to take up arms and commence a fearful slaughter in retaliation; but he stood firm, and acted the part of a Christian.

"When Thakombau, the king, heard of Varani's conversion, he was very angry, and resolved not to lose his greatest warrior without a struggle. When first informed of the event, the king said in an angry tone,

'Have you seen him pray?' 'Yes,' was the reply. 'Tell him, then, to go to his God for his food: he shall have none from my lands. He has not hearkened to my speech: I told him to wait a little, and then we would become Christians together. Tell him to remain at Viwa. He is not to come to Bau any more, or receive riches from me.' When the message was delivered to Varani, he replied, 'I do not want riches. I want to go to heaven more than to receive riches and go to hell. The lands are the Lord's. If He sees fit, I shall not want food. If I am hungry, it will be but for a little time before I die and go to heaven, and I shall never be hungry there.' The next day the king sent to demand the riches which Varani had obtained by his conversion! 'They belong to us. Why have you become a Christian? What have we done, that you have become angry with us, and left us?' Varani sent back the following answer:—'You well know that I receive no riches by becoming a Christian. You ask, Why have I become a Christian? My reply is, To save my soul. It is not because I am angry with you; but I was afraid to wait longer, lest I should die and lose my soul!'

"This important event occurred in 1845, and from that time forward Varani gave evidence of a real change of heart, and witnessed a good confession in the presence of many adversaries. His fellow-chiefs were awed into acquiescence to his new course of life, and they also ultimately embraced Christianity. Varani, moreover, became a great help to the missionaries in the arduous work in which they were engaged in the earlier stages of that wonderful reformation which has taken place in Fiji. He was remarkable for his simple piety, earnest zeal, and Christian consistency. He was, moreover, mighty in prayer; and there is reason to believe that by his influence and counsel he was instrumental in winning many souls for Christ, whilst at the same time he made steady progress in the knowledge and love of God.

"Varani had pursued his course with credit to himself and satisfaction to the missionaries for about eight years from the time of his conversion, when towards the close of 1853 his valuable life was brought to an end in a manner truly appalling to contemplate. He exercised the prerogatives of a subordinate chief with Christian dignity, and was ever ready to obey the reasonable commands of his superiors in rank. An insurrection had broken out in Levuka, and Varani, with a party of men, was despatched to bring a small heathen tribe to terms of reconciliation. The most mild and pacific overtures were tendered, which at first promised to be successful; but in a spirit of treachery the heathens watched their opportunity, surrounded Varani and four of his companions, and put them to death without a moment's warning. The remains received Christian burial at the hands of the missionaries; and when the intelligence reached Viwa, many houses were filled with lamentation. The survivors testified that their devoted Christian chief, Varani, engaged with them in prayer repeatedly on board the vessel in which they sailed on their ill-fated mission, and that in the last struggle he displayed a spirit worthy of his profession."

208. **A Hindu Female.** — On Sunday, July 16th, 1854, the Rev. Murray Mitchell, Free Church of Scotland missionary to Poonah, in India, baptized a middle-aged female convert whose character and course

were somewhat remarkable. Her name was Jijibai, and she is described as belonging to a respectable caste, and as truly pious, although not so intelligent as some others who were about the same time gathered into the fold of Christ. On her baptism being delayed for a while, till she obtained a clearer knowledge of Scripture history and the plan of salvation, she pleaded earnestly that she might be admitted, by the sealing right, into the heavenly family. At the same time she confessed her ignorance, saying, "I know nothing, I am as dull as a clod; but I clasp the feet of Jesus, I clasp them to my breast." Her husband was already a Christian, having been baptized in 1851, and he did all in his power to instruct and encourage her. When thoroughly grounded in the faith of the gospel, the new convert was wont to sing while at her work, after the manner of her country-women; but she no longer sung the idolatrous and obscene ditties which are too frequently heard from the lips of the heathen. Her extemporaneous songs were always of Jesus and the great salvation. Hearing Jijibai thus engaged on one occasion, the missionary got her husband to write down the words of her song, which are truly illustrative of her simple piety; they were as follows:—

"To my poor house a stranger has come,
  Even King Jesus, the darling of heaven,
  I run to bid Him welcome.

"With gods of stone what more have I to do?
  I clasp my Saviour's feet;
  My soul clings to Jesus.

"The Lord of all is my Father now,
  Jesus is my Brother now,
  I shall not want.

"Since I clasped Thy feet to my bosom,
  Rich, rich am I, O Jesus!
  Oh, leave me never!"

209. A New Disciple.—Writing from a mission-station in India, in 1872, Mrs Scott says :—"I have good and cheering news of the happy conversion and baptism of a poor heathen. About six months ago this poor Hindu heard for the first time the words of life from our brother Kandura. The first time he heard of Christ's atonement for sin, he seemed deeply interested, and as Kandura could only remain in that village a few days, he begged that the Bible might be left with him, that he might read the wonderful news for himself. These six months he has been reading and praying; and now he comes and tells us how he has found in the Holy Book a commandment that those who have accepted Christ's atonement shall be baptized, and that he wishes to obey all the Saviour's commandments. In order to test his sincerity, I said to him, 'You know full well that if you become a Christian your brothers and your wife will cast you off; you will lose your land, your cows, and your buffaloes, and your village-people will point the finger of scorn at you; what will you do then?' He replied, 'God will be with me. I can give up wife and house and lands, if necessary, *but I cannot give up my Saviour.*' I sent him home to tell his wife and his brothers that he was to be baptized as soon as Mr Comfort returned from Shillong. Promptly at the end of the week he returned, saying his brother had called him a crazy fool, and had told him not to come near him again. But his wife inclines to the new religion, and we hope she will soon accept of Christ as her Saviour.

"Mr Comfort returned on Thursday last, and on Saturday this man was received into the fellowship of the Church, being baptized on the Sabbath following. I called him a

Hindu in the former part of my letter. He is not, properly speaking, a Hindu, but a Rabha Cosaree, of whom there are many near Gowahati. I trust many more of them will be brought into the kingdom of Christ."

210. The Cleansing Blood of Christ.—It is recorded of a certain Hindu on the Malabar coast in India, that he had inquired of various devotees and priests how he might make atonement for his sins, and find peace for his soul. At last he was directed to drive iron spikes, sufficiently blunt, through his sandals; and on these spikes he was to walk on pilgrimage to a celebrated heathen shrine, a distance of 250 coss, that is, about 480 miles. If through loss of blood or weakness of body he was obliged to halt, he might wait for healing and strength. He undertook the journey, and proceeded for some distance, in much pain and distress of both body and mind. While halting under a shady tree where the gospel was sometimes preached, a missionary came and delivered an impressive sermon, in the native language of the people, from that important text, "The blood of Jesus Christ His Son cleanseth from all sin." The Word came with power to the man's heart; he believed the good news; and before the missionary had finished his discourse, he rose up, threw off his torturing sandals, and cried aloud, "That is what I want;" and he became a living witness that the blood of Christ does indeed cleanse from all sin. By his subsequent walk and conversation, and by his humble but earnest efforts to benefit others, he proved himself to be a sincere convert to the faith of the gospel.

211. Two Hospital Converts.—It was a happy idea to send forth missionaries who had studied medicine, and who would be able to heal the body, as well as to point the sinner to the Good Physician for the healing of his soul. Medical missions have been greatly blessed in China, India, and some other countries. Two conversions occurred not long ago, in connection with the South Travancore medical mission, of more than ordinary interest.

A poor man named Esakie, from Cottikodoo, was taken into the hospital with a fracture; his leg had been broken while in the jungle, and his friends and relations had ascribed the accident to the malignity of *Mallankarunkali*, the deity of the jungle. They had frightened him by saying, if he would not propitiate this deity with offerings, more harm would befall him. Having no means to make offerings, he uttered this prayer to the heathen god. "God, I am now unable to make any offerings to thee; but if thou healest my leg, I will offer thee a fowl and some eggs. Have pity, and do not kill me!" Of course there was no good result. A Christian in the neighbourhood advised him to go to the mission-hospital at Neyoor, assuring him that he would be kindly treated there. On his arrival the fracture was set right, and he had valuable opportunities of hearing about Christ, who was bruised for our iniquities. The native missionary often prayed with him; and ere long Esakie himself was heard praying with great earnestness, "O Lord, I confess I am a sinner. Forgive my sins, for the sake of Jesus Christ. Show me Thy light; guide me in the right path, through Jesus, Amen." When leaving the hospital cured, he earnestly asked for a book, which he promised to get some one to read to him, as he could not read himself. "I have no fear," said he, "now of the jungle deity."

The case of Yesudian, from Muladnoodoo, is also interesting. He was a mason, who had his thigh fractured by the falling of an arch in the Roman Catholic church. One of the workman was crushed to death, but Yesudian was taken to the mission-hospital and cured. During his stay there he learnt several of the Psalms, and read a book entitled "The Christian Husbandman." The priest visited him in the hospital five times, and was greatly astonished at the rapidity with which he got well. He was fond of reading the religious books supplied by the missionary, and soon learnt to speak to the heathen patients about the miserable condition of sinners, and the way of salvation opened by Jesus Christ. He often expressed his gratitude to God for sparing him, when other workmen had been crushed to death. Early in the present year he became a member of the Church of Christ, and sat down at His table, saying that God's mercy had constrained him to give his heart to Jesus, and to commemorate His dying love. His case is the more encouraging, because the priest, who had partially supported him while in the hospital, had used all his power to induce him to join them. It is to be hoped that both these converts will hold on their way, and be made a blessing to their dark, benighted fellow-countrymen.

212. James Ah Ling.—A few eminent converts have been won to Christ from among the Chinese, as the results of Christian missions in their own country, and still more from among the emigrants who have found their way to different countries. One of the most remarkable of those who have come under our notice was a young man named Ah Ling, who arrived in Australia about the year 1856, as an emigrant seeking employment. There he came under the sound of the gospel, which, through mercy, was made the power of God unto his salvation. On being admitted into the Christian Church, he was baptized by the name of James, and became a faithful disciple of the Lord Jesus Christ.

The account which James Ah Ling gives of his conversion is as follows:—"In a prayer-meeting held in Daylesford Chapel, after a sermon preached by the Rev. John Mewton, I wept for my sins. Again and again they prayed for me. At last, while kneeling at the communion rail, I received power to believe, and my heart changed. Before I could only cry for grief; now my heart was filled with peace and joy. So I passed out of darkness to light, and, like the pilgrim, I lost my heavy burden."

Being a young man of more than ordinary intelligence, the Chinese convert was soon employed as an evangelist to his fellow-countrymen, first at the gold-diggings, and afterwards in Melbourne, in connection with a Wesleyan mission which was inaugurated for the benefit of the Chinese emigrants. This enterprise was commenced, and has been carried on at the expense of a few friends of missions, who felt a deep interest in the spiritual welfare of the strangers from the "Flowery Land;" and on the death of Mr Hill, who had taken the lead in the work, S. G. King, Esq., generously undertook the maintenance of James Ah Ling, that he might devote himself entirely to the mission. In visiting from house to house, and looking after newly-arrived Chinese emigrants, as well as in preaching to them the glorious gospel of the blessed God, the young evangelist was made instrumental in winning many souls to Christ. By the liberality of friends in Melbourne, a commodious Chinese chapel has been erected, called "*The House of the sound of peace.*" It was opened for divine worship on the 10th of January 1872, under the most favourable circumstances, and James Ah Ling still labours among his fellow-countrymen, with a zeal and diligence which give good promise of still greater results. Others, also, are being raised up, as the fruit of missionary labour, to take their part in diffusing abroad the knowledge of Christ, and every true friend of missions will earnestly pray for the blessing of God on their united labours.

" Give the pure gospel word,
    The word of general grace,
Then let them preach the common Lord,
    The Saviour of our race.

" Oh, let them spread Thy name,
    Their mission fully prove;
Thy universal grace proclaim,
    Thy all-redeeming love!"

VIII. HAPPY DEATHS.

213. The Closing Scene.—It is related of the Rev. John Newton, that on calling at a certain house, in the course of his pastoral visitations, he mentioned the death of a gentleman who was well known to those present, when a lady exclaimed, "Indeed! and how did he die?" "Madam," replied the venerable minister, "there is a far more important question than that, namely, How did he live?" He then proceeded to descant, with his wonted pathos and power, on the necessity and importance of a *holy life*, if we would make sure of a *safe* and *happy death*. Whilst we freely admit the correctness of this view, it is, nevertheless, a fact that the happy and triumphant deaths of Christian believers have always been a source of consolation and comfort to surviving friends, and are not to be lightly esteemed. The closing scene, however, of many a true Christian's life has been darkened by mental weakness or severe bodily pain, and no opportunity has been afforded of expressing any sentiment in the article of death. But when it pleases God in His wise and gracious providence to make the departure of His saints calm and peaceful and happy, and to permit them to testify to His grace and mercy in prospect of eternity, it is matter of sincere gratitude and joy.

Such scenes of calm resignation to the will of God in prospect of death, and of holy triumph over the last enemy, have often been witnessed in the mission-field; and, considering the brief and limited experience of many of the native converts, the attendant circumstances have sometimes been truly remarkable. Without attaching undue importance to missionary incidents of this class, we think happy deaths may fairly be regarded as collateral proofs of the genuineness of the work, especially when they have been preceded by holy lives. The Word of God is often verified in our day, as in ancient times. "The wicked is driven away in his wickedness; but the righteous hath hope in his death."

214. A Happy Indian Boy.—The Rev. Mr Bernau, of the Church Missionary Society, in the "Narrative of his Labours in British Guiana," gives an interesting account of the happy death of a little Indian boy, the only surviving son of a chief named Aramoosy. This chief was a savage, warlike Indian of South America, who lived near to Mr Bernau's station on the Essequibo River. For a long time he kept aloof from the missionary and his work. At length he was visited by affliction and bereavement, and when four of his children had been removed by death, the heart of the savage heathen was so far softened that he gave up his only surviving son, a bright little boy of eight or nine years of age, to be brought up at the mission-school. At length the boy fell sick; and his father fearing he would die, came and carried him off secretly into the woods, for the purpose of conjuring the evil spirits on his behalf. The little invalid took with him his Testament, Prayer-book, and Hymn-book; but no one knew where he had been carried. When Mr Bernau heard that he had been carried off, he says:—

I gave my scholars a holiday, in order that they might seek in all directions for their companion. When they succeeded in finding him, I immediately went to him, "I am wretched, I am miserable," said the poor child; "oh, take me back with you!" "I cannot," I replied, "without your father's consent." Seeing the boy's misery, Aramoosy at length consented to bring him back the following day. When I visited him, I said to him, "My child, where is your hope? for I think you will not be much longer in this lower world." He replied, "You have often told us in the school that Jesus Christ shed His blood for sinners; you also said He invites children to come to Him; I have come to Him." "Do you believe that your sins are forgiven?" "I do believe," he replied, "that He has forgiven my sins." Some days after, he said, "I believe that this will be my last day." He was prayed with and comforted.

His father came to see him, and he said to him, "Father, God gave you five children, and He has taken them away, one after another; I am the last. I fear if I had grown up, you would not have given me up to God. You do not care what the missionary says; and when he begs you to come and settle near him, and learn about Jesus, you say, 'Wait a little.' I fear the time will never come." The boy was right, the "more convenient season" never came. Aramoosy died soon after in the woods. The savage heathen was, however, greatly moved by his child's address; and although an Indian in his native state never weeps, when I met him, as he left his son, tears were on his face. This being the only instance which has come to my knowledge where an Indian in his unconverted state has been seen to shed tears, I inquired what was the matter. Aramoosy made no reply, and passed on. When I called again to see the child, he repeated what he had said to his father; and when I asked whether he had spoken with the affection due to a parent, he replied that he thought he had, and added, that he hoped he had not sinned in speaking to him. About midnight he begged that the boys, who were sleeping in the adjoining room, would procure a light. This being done, he requested that they would sing the hymn—

"How sweet the name of Jesus sounds
In a believer's ear!
It soothes his sorrows, heals his wounds,
And drives away his fear."

When that was ended, he said, "I should like much to see the missionary once more;" but when he was told the hour, he said, "No, he is tired, do not call him." He then requested the bystanders to pray; and as they were praying around his hammock, his happy spirit departed into the regions of bliss and glory.

215. **Franzen.**—Franzen was a South American Indian who was brought to a saving knowledge of the

truth through the instrumentality of the Rev. Mr Bernau, a Church missionary in British Guiana. From the time of his conversion the poor Indian, having learned to read, cheerfully devoted himself to the work of teaching others, and became very helpful to his missionary. It was his only grief that he could not serve the Lord as he wished to do, because of his ignorance and weakness. Often have I heard him speak (says the missionary), with a glowing heart, of the love of Jesus, earnestly inviting, and entreating with tears, the people of his tribe to turn to the living God.

Being one night out fishing, Franzen caught a severe cold; and from that time his health began rapidly to decline. I saw him almost daily; and when telling him one day that this trial was likely to be his last, his eyes brightened, and taking me by the hand, he said, "Then you think I am so near heaven? Now, then, I will begin to settle my affairs, and only think on Jesus; for since I have known aright what He has done for me, I have ever wished to be with Him." On my reading some verses of Romans viii., he remarked, "This is a lovely Word, blessed Lord! and I thank Thee that I feel persuaded, that nothing in heaven or earth shall ever separate me from Thee." The day previous to his departure he sent for the missionary, saying, "I have called you to settle all about my children. I feel persuaded that you will be their father." Then, calling his three children, he said, "My dear children, you have no father; but the missionary will be all to you; follow him, love him, learn well, and soon we shall see each other again. I am going to your mother" (she having died some time before). "O my dear children! love your Saviour; for you know that He died for us. Will you not love Him?" He then gave each a blessing; and joining their hands with mine, said, "Go now with your father, why do you weep? I know he will care for you." After a little pause, he said, "Pray, oh! pray." He was asked, "Do you feel happy?" "Very happy; but sometimes I seem to be alone, as if walking in the bush; at other times it is dark about me. But here," laying his hand upon his heart, "here is light, here is rest! I am very happy." On leaving, I observed, "Franzen, look to Jesus, He will guide you till"——"Yes, farewell; soon we shall meet again." I called on him the following morning; but he seemed not to notice anything about him; his lips were moving, as if he were engaged in prayer. We all knelt at his bed-side, commending his soul to the Good Shepherd; and after a few hours he entered into rest. "Mark the perfect man, and behold the upright; for the end of that man is peace."

216. Little Amelia.—Little Amelia was the younger daughter of Franzen, the converted Indian in South America, who on his death-bed commended her and her sister to the care of the missionary, and who for some time afterwards lived at the mission-house. The death of her father made a deep impression upon Amelia's mind, and having herself become sick, although only seven years of age, she turned her thoughts entirely to God and heaven. When she became so weak as to be unable to leave her hammock, she desired to be taken to her late father's cottage, where the missionary visited her very often during her last illness.

One day (says Mr Bernau), when I was praying with the dear child, she pressed my hand, saying, "Thank you, sir! thank you!" At another time, having read to her of the New Jerusalem, she sat up in her hammock, and cheerfully discoursed upon the subject. "Oh yes," she said, "soon I shall be there." On being asked what made her believe that she should go there, she said, "Did not Jesus die for me also?" "But you are a child: do you think you are so great a sinner as many others?" "Yes, sir, I am a child; but you have often told us that even children need to pray for pardon, and for grace to change their hearts. I have thought on these words, and prayed, and oh!" (here she sighed deeply and wept) "I have felt my heart to be very sinful; but I know that Jesus has forgiven me; Jesus has adopted me as one of His." "But you are yet young; would you not like to live a little longer." "Yes, I might wish it; but I am afraid I should be unthankful to my Saviour. I remember you told us in the school that in heaven there will be no more sin, nor grief, nor death; there I wish to go, and soon I shall be there." She was hastening to her rest faster than I anticipated; and not having paid her a visit for several days, she sent to inform me that she was going away, and wished to see me. I went and conversed with her on the joys of heaven; but being very weak, she appeared to take little notice of what was said. Having read and prayed that the Lord in mercy might shorten her trial, and receive her into the joys of heaven, she raised herself, and uttered a loud and hearty Amen. Being asked, "Are you in great pain?" she replied, "Yes, sir, it is very great; but" —— "Do you wish for anything I can do for you?" "No, sir; but"— with a faltering voice she said—"will you please send a little coffee and sugar and some candles? for I should like my brother and sister to watch over me." "Well, do you wish for anything else." "No, sir, I shall want nothing at all; for my friends I ask it, to-night I shall be in heaven." She then called, "John! where are you, my brother?" John drawing near to the side of her hammock, she said, "Please watch over me this night; also my sister Leonora. And mind you love Jesus—see, I am very happy; I die." Her feelings overpowering her, she reclined in her hammock, and in a few hours breathed her last.

217. Leonora.—The elder daughter of Franzen, the converted Indian, sickened and died not long after her little sister Amelia. Having lived for some time in the family of the missionary, she had made considerable progress both in learning to read and in a knowledge of domestic concerns; and, what is better still, she was led to give her heart to God, and to love and to fear Him in the morning of life.

When she was taken ill (says the missionary), I often visited her, but found her, although twelve years of age, more reserved than her little sister had been. She seemed perfectly resigned, however, to God's holy will and pleasure, and I never heard her utter a complaint, though she must have been a great sufferer. When opening to her the condition she was in, she replied, "I thank the blessed Jesus for His mercy bestowed on me." I asked, "Do you, can you trust your soul to Him?" "Yes, of this I never doubted!" "Are you persuaded," I continued, "that your sins are forgiven you?" "I hope they will be forgiven me." "What makes you hope so?" "Why, sir, I often read the verse, 'The blood of Jesus Christ, His Son, cleanseth us from all sin.' Then I thought, How can this be? till one

Sabbath some time back, you made me understand it." "And how do you think your soul is made clean?" She then related the illustration I had made use of, and added, "It is also said, 'Purifying your hearts by faith.'" "And do you believe on the Son of God, Leonora?" "Yes, from that very day I felt something working in me, I knew not what; but I think it was the Holy Spirit which you say all must pray for— He it is. I am ready. O blessed Jesus, receive me, for Thou hast died for me!" "Is the Word of God sweet to your soul?" "Yes, indeed; but I beg you to give me a Bible with larger print; for my eyes, I don't know why, are getting dark." This being done she used to read for hours together, and it was truly edifying to see and converse with this dear child.

Being told one morning that Leonora had spent a very restless night, I called on her in the course of the day, saying, "Well, Leonora, how are you to-day?" "This day I am to be quite well, for I am sure it will be my happiest day." "Do you feel great pain?" "None whatever, but my feet are stiff and cold." "Are you at peace in your heart, and are you persuaded you will go to heaven?" "Yes, and please tell my brother John that I wish to see him before I die. Oh, sir, do take care of him; Jesus will bless you." John being called, and standing near her, she said, "John, my brother, you are left alone of our family. Oh, do come to Jesus, for He is good. I am going"—here her voice failed. She continued after a considerable pause—"I am going to the angels in heaven, and this evening I shall be there." John seemed very much affected, and began to weep; but she looked in his face, and said, "Brother, weep not, I shall soon be very happy. You, learn love." Fatigued with her exertion, she sank into her hammock. Some of her friends being present, we commended her in prayer to the Almighty Saviour; and when we rose she beckoned with her hand, but could not speak. At four P.M. she entered into her eternal rest, sensible and happy to her last moment.

218. **John Barry.**—One of the most remarkable negro slaves, whose history and character have come under our notice, was John Barry, who belonged to an estate called Sea-cow Bay, in the Island of Tortola. Before his conversion he was passionate and violent in his temper; but after he had been brought to an experimental and saving knowledge of the truth, through the preaching of the missionaries, he was mild and humble as a little child. He was, moreover, zealous for the Lord of Hosts. His leader was heard to say that John Barry had been the means of bringing nine persons to his class in a short space of time, all of whom proved to be sincere seekers of salvation. His attachment to God's house and worship was, moreover, strong and unwavering. He had the misfortune in early life to lose a leg, and was glad of the assistance of one made of wood. But notwithstanding this great disadvantage, he was in the habit of travelling ten miles on the Sabbath, going to and returning from the chapel at Road-town. He was not able to read, but the number of texts of Scripture and verses of hymns which he treasured up in his memory was astonishing. Nor did he neglect social and domestic worship. His thatched hut was frequently turned into a house of prayer for the benefit of himself and others when they could get no further. John's conduct and proceedings in regard to temporal matters

was in perfect harmony with his religious profession. The gentleman in charge of the estate to which he was attached related to the missionary how, on a certain day after his first arrival, he called John into his presence, and handed to him the keys to bring some articles from the store, charging him not to pilfer anything. At such a charge the honest negro was grieved, and said in a very civil way, "Sir, if you cannot trust me, you had better not give the keys into my hand." "I then perceived," continued the gentleman, "that I had brought myself under an obligation to soothe John's mind; so I told him to consider my charge as mere pleasantry, and to proceed with the keys. Afterwards I was so assured of his integrity, that I made him my overseer, which office he held as long as he lived."

It is not surprising that a life of uniform uprightness and consistent piety should be crowned with a happy and triumphant death. During John Barry's last illness he was graciously supported, and was frequently enabled to rejoice in hope of the glory of God. He was much employed in repeating hymns and passages of Scripture which he had treasured up in his memory. On the last day of his life, and shortly before his departure, he remarked, "God says, 'They that seek shall find; to those that knock it shall be opened; and they that ask shall receive.' Now the chains are broken; the fetters are knocked off; the prisoner is loosed; mercy flows free!" He then repeated—

"Away with our fears, the glad morning appears,
When an heir of salvation is born!
From Jehovah I came, for His glory I am,
And to Him I with singing return."

This was sung by his sister, and others around him. She then prayed. He said he heard but did not see. "Yea," said he, "I hear a sweet voice whispering in my ear, but do not see who it is." His sister answered, "It is the voice that is music in the sinner's ear." Lifting up his hands, he cried out, "Now I go," and his happy spirit returned to God who gave it. Thus died John Barry, on the 17th of July 1833, shortly before the great emancipation. But although a slave in body, he was free in spirit, for "whom the truth makes free, they are free indeed." His wooden leg was reverently buried in the same grave with him, and many tears were shed during the funeral service.

219. **Robert Keane.**—A remarkable instance of the consoling and sustaining power of the gospel, and of patient endurance of affliction, occurred in the case of Robert Keane, a converted negro, in the Island of St Vincent, at an early period of the mission. Robert was brought to a saving knowledge of the truth soon after the arrival of the first missionary in the country, and for several years he had exemplified the religion of Christ, when he was overtaken by the affliction which terminated in death. Robert was a sugar-boiler; and one day, while at work, a drop of boiling sugar fell on his arm. The place soon fretted to a serious sore, which extended day by day till the whole arm and hand became inflamed and mortified, and at length his fingers actually fell off. The disorder then ascended to his head, which became affected so much that his eyes dropped out, and this was soon followed by several pieces of his skull. His feet also were attacked by the same mysterious gangrene, and both came off. Yet he still survived, and bore all this with remarkable patience and resignation,

and at times rejoiced in hope of being received into that place where neither sorrow nor affliction nor death can enter. He hailed the visits of the missionary and his Christian brethren with gratitude and joy, and earnestly joined with them in their devotions, till at length death put a period to his sufferings.

"The last time I visited him," said the Rev. Mr Taylor in a letter to Dr Coke, "I could not bear to look upon him; but talked to him and prayed with him at his chamber door. When I asked him how he did, he replied that he was just waiting the Lord's time, when He should be pleased to call him. 'Massa,' he said, 'two eyes gone; two hands gone; two feet gone; no more dis carcase here. O massa, de pain sometimes too strong for me; I am obliged to cry out, and pray to de Lord for assistance.' When he came to the close of life, he exhorted all about him to be sure to live to God, and especially his wife, who had continued with him all the time of his affliction, and attended to him with marked fidelity and affection." At length Robert Keane died happy in God, assuring all around him that he was going to be for ever with the Lord.

"O what are all my sufferings here,
  If, Lord, Thou count me mete
With the enraptured host to appear,
  And worship at Thy feet?"

220. Berbice Kendal.—Berbice Kendal was a negro convert of more than ordinary piety and devotedness to God. Having been brought to a saving knowledge of the truth soon after the missionaries commenced their labours in British Guiana, he held on his way without wavering, amid all the difficulties of slavery and heathen darkness by which he was surrounded. He was for upwards of thirty-five years a living witness of the saving power of divine grace, and an example of all that was holy and of good report in the Christian life. He was a man of humble abilities, but such were his piety, holy consistency of character, and general uprightness of conduct, that his influence for good in the Church and neighbourhood was most extensively felt. By his care and industry while in health and strength, he had succeeded in making some provision for the supply of his wants in his declining years; so that he wanted for nothing in his last illness, and his devoted wife was unwearied in her attention to his comfort. But the happy state of his mind was the most remarkable circumstance in his case. He had learned to read the Scriptures for himself, and he made the New Testament his constant companion, dwelling with delight upon its precious promises. The missionary who regularly visited him says, "Perhaps never in any individual of his class were the closing scenes of life more happily illustrative of the power of Christian piety." Having expressed his full trust and confidence in the atonement of Christ, and exhorted all around him to give their hearts to God, and prepare to meet Him in heaven, he quietly passed away to be for ever with the Lord.

221. "I shall see Jesus, and that is enough."—After speaking of the blessings resulting from the generous gift of the British and Foreign Bible Society of a copy of the New Testament with the Book of Psalms to every emancipated slave in the West Indies who was able to read, the Rev. James Scott of Berbice, says:—
"In May last year, I went to see an aged man, a member of the Church, who had long been confined to his bed by an accumulation of diseases.

I found him lying on a miserable pallet in a dark and dingy room. He was all alone, without a relative, and, I fear, with but few friends to minister to his wants. By his right shoulder I saw his large New Testament, bearing evidence of being often read, but still in good preservation. After making the usual inquiries as to his health, I inquired into the state of his mind in relation to God and the other world. 'My hope,' said he, 'is in Jesus;' and taking his Testament, he opened it and read to me the third chapter of John. Reaching the sixteenth verse, he said, 'I can go no farther than this; this is my hope—here I drop my anchor—God is love. Jesus died for me; here I find peace to my mind. I have this to think about in my loneliness—I shall see Jesus, and that is enough.' Three months after, this weary pilgrim reached his happy and long-looked-for home."

"He by Himself hath sworn,
I on His oath depend;
I shall on eagles' wings upborne
To heaven ascend:
I shall behold His face,
I shall His power adore,
And sing the wonders of His grace,
For evermore."

222. A Happy Negro Girl.—A little slave-girl named Betsy Cameron, aged ten years, died very happy in Antigua, West Indies. When only six years old she learned to read the Scriptures, and soon afterwards she was afflicted in such a way as to be unable to walk. In this decrepit state she continued for some years, till it pleased the Lord to take her to Himself. During her long affliction she evinced remarkable patience and resignation, considering her tender years. Having no hope of recovery, the poor sufferer was intent on preparing for her final change, and, through the mercy of God in Christ Jesus, she was brought into a very happy state of mind. She was often visited by her Christian friends, who were constrained to rejoice with her in her glorious prospect of eternal bliss.

A few days previous to her departure, Betsy Cameron sent for her teacher, a pious young woman who had been brought up in the mission-school. When she came, the dear girl said to her, "Good-bye." She answered, "Where are you going, Betsy?" "I am going home." "What home do you mean?" "Heaven." "But don't you feel unworthy to go to such a place?" "Yes; I know I am a sinner, but Jesus has pardoned my sins." "Betsy, shall I sing and pray for you?" "Yes." "What shall I sing?" "Behold the Saviour of mankind!" They then sung and prayed, in which she joined. Mr Thwaites, the missionary, also visited her, to whom she spoke in the same pleasing manner, repeatedly saying she was not afraid to die. He said, "Betsy, do you not murmur nor repine when you see other children running about, and you confined so long?" She said, "No, sir, except when I see all the children going to the Sunday-school. I look after them till they are gone, and then I sit down and cry." The night she died it was proposed to anoint her chest. She said, "It is of no use—I am going home—to get some rest." She prevailed upon the friends in attendance to desist for a time; and during this repose her happy spirit passed away to God her Saviour.

223. Happy Death of a Negro Boy.—The late Rev. William Fox, who succeeded the writer as a missionary at St Mary's on the River Gambia, Western Africa, communicated the following account of the last illness and death of a little negro boy:—"John Cupidon, one of our excellent assistants, had charge of two of these friendless children, rescued from slave-ships, and on his removal to St Mary's he took them with him. In the latter part of the year 1841, Robert Clarke, the elder of the two, died: I had myself frequently seen him during his illness. The circumstances of his death were as follows:—Feeling that he could not live much longer, he inquired for Cupidon, who was immediately by his side; when this poor African slave, aged about thirteen years, said in broken accents, 'Massa, me bin call you, for tell you me now 'bout for die, but me no 'fraid for die. Jesus Christ pardon all my sins, and my soul is happy in de Lord.' This was pleasing, especially to John Cupidon, under whose roof he had lived, and who had often prayed with and for him. But this was not all; the dying lad went on to say, 'And me bin call you, also, massa, for tank you, for all de goodness you bin to me. You bin teach me berry well in de house, and berry well in de school; and now me going to Jesus.' And then, lifting up his withered hand, he shook hands with his faithful friend and master, saying, 'Tank you, massa, tank you; good-bye, good-bye.' And in a few minutes after this he breathed his last. Thus died Robert Clarke, one of our schoolboys in Western Africa."

mical disease of a painful character. Among these was a married woman who had been a very diligent inquirer after divine truth. Before the disease began to assume a fatal appearance, she spoke very clearly on the immense value of the instructions to which she had lately paid so much attention, at the same time professing the most lively hope of eternal life through the atonement of Jesus. A few days subsequent to this declaration, feeling that the harbingers of death had arrived, she called her husband and friends, and addressed them in language affecting and arousing, exhorting them to believe in the words of Jehovah, and to flee for refuge to Jesus as the only Saviour. 'I am going to die.' This was startling language from the lips of a Mochuana. Some listened with amazement, and others wept. 'Weep not,' she said, 'because I am going to leave you; but weep for your sins, and weep for your souls. With me all is well; for do not suppose that I die like a beast, or that I shall sleep for ever in the grave. No! Jesus has died for my sins; He has said He will save me; I am going to be with Him.' Shortly after bearing this testimony, she, who a few months before, according to her own language, was as ignorant as the cattle in the fold, now left the world with a full assurance of eternal life beyond the grave."

224. First-fruits.—Speaking of the first-fruits of his labours among the Bechuanas in South Africa, and the gathering in of a few sheaves into the heavenly garner, the Rev. R. Moffat says:—"About this time the following circumstance occurred, which was of the Lord, to encourage us, and strengthen the faith of those who had put their hands to the gospel plough. Several females had been carried off by the *kuatse*, an epide-

225. Blind Mamotlobogi.—One of the early Bechuana converts at the mission-station at Kuruman, in South Africa, was an aged female named Mamotlobogi. She was afflicted with blindness, but she was led to the house of God by her grandchildren; and whilst sitting under the sound of the gospel, it pleased the Lord to open the eyes of her understanding to see herself as a sinner, and Christ as an all-sufficient

Saviour. From that time till her death, a period of several years, she continued to adorn her profession by a consistent walk and conversation. At length the infirmities of age prevented her attending public worship as she desired, and for two or three months prior to her decease she was confined to her house altogether. During this time she was much engaged in holy meditation and prayer, and in speaking of the goodness and loving-kindness of the Lord to her. The Rev. Mr Edwards, the missionary, says:—"On one occasion when I visited her, I had positively to restrain her, that she might not exhaust her strength. Knowing that she could not survive, she admonished all who visited her to think and live for eternity. A few days before her death she wished her children to be gathered together in her presence, desiring to speak with them before her departure. They accordingly surrounded her bed; and when informed that all were present, she addressed them in substance as follows:—'My children, I wish you to know that I am to be separated from you; but you must not on that account be sorrowful. Do not murmur at the thought of my decease. The Lord has spared me not a few days: He has taken care of me many years, and has ever been merciful to me; I have wanted no good thing. I know Him to whom I have trusted the salvation of my soul. My hope is fixed on Jesus Christ, who has died for my sins, and who lives to intercede. I shall soon die and be at rest; but my wish is that you will attend to these my words. My children, hold fast your faith in Christ. Trust in Him, love Him, and let not the world turn you away from Him; and however you may be reviled and troubled in the world, hold very fast the Word of God, and faint not in persevering prayer. My last word is, strive to live together in peace. Avoid disputes. Follow peace with all, and especially among yourselves. Love each other; comfort each other; assist and take care of each other in the Lord.' After this charge to her children, she said but little. Her last words were spoken a few hours before her death, when a Church member called upon her. She heard his voice, and said, 'Yes, I know thee, Mogami, my brother in the Lord. I am going, but thou wilt remain. Hold fast the Word of God. Turn not from His ways, and take a message to thy wife, my sister in the Lord, that she must use all diligence to ensure eternal life.' Soon after this she entered into that rest which remaineth for the people of God."

226. Joseph Qualaka.—The mission-stations in South Africa have often proved asylums for the oppressed and afflicted. Among those who came to Butterworth in Kaffirland to seek medical aid was a native named Qualaka, who, through the means of grace, accompanied by divine influence, became a Christian, was baptized as Joseph, and for three years, till the time of his death, maintained a character of holy consistency.

Joseph Qualaka, on several occasions, exhibited remarkable firmness and decision of character. When the Kaffirs threatened to take all that he had if he went to live at the station, he said, "You may take all I have, and kill my body; for I have heard the Word of God, and that will save my soul." About two years after his baptism, a person came to Butterworth for the purpose of alluring Joseph, by great promises, to leave the station, when he replied to the man by saying, "Before the Word of God came into the land my father was murdered, and my mother died before the Word of God was brought to our ears: I have got the Word, I will not leave it." His zeal led him to watch over the interests of the station with quite a fatherly care; and from his extensive acquaintance with the customs and usages of the Kaffirs, he was always sought in cases of a temporal nature when difficulties arose. But his piety to God shone through all his proceedings; his attendance on the means of grace was unremitting; his attention to those who were seeking the Lord was very great; and his faithfulness in exhorting and reproving was manifest till the last.

During his last illness Qualaka was constantly speaking to those about him concerning their souls. Two days before he died he said to a young woman who was in the house, "O Bongo! God is great; why will you not serve Him?" To one of his fellow-worshippers he said, "William, a man cannot say that he is converted because he is baptized. God is very great." When in great bodily pain, he said to the missionary who visited him, "I have great pain, but I leave myself in the Lord's hands. I have peace. I have a good hope. I am glad I have served the Lord." A short time before he died he was heard to say in prayer, "Lord, Thou comest to fetch me; oh, stop close to me!" Then he called for his only son. When the lad came before him, he was unable to speak; but he fixed his eyes upon him with much parental affection, and soon after expired.

227. Little Mie David.—Mie David was a little African boy, who died very happy at the early age of seven years, at a station of the Moravian Missionary Society at the Cape of Good Hope. The missionary who furnished the account says:—

He had long been suffering, and during his illness had frequently sent for me, with the request that I would come and pray with him. I had visited him the evening previous to his departure; and no sooner had I entered the hut, than he immediately expressed his joy at my visit, and said to those who were standing around him, "Now my dear teacher is with me." He then asked me to sit down by his side and exclaimed, while his eyes beamed with joy, "I shall soon be going to my Saviour." On my asking him if he really thought his end was so near at hand, he cheerfully replied, "Yes, dear teacher, my Saviour will soon be coming." On this he folded his little hands, lifted up his eyes, and said, "O my Saviour, come, come soon!" After lying silent for a few moments, he again turned towards me, and said, "Dear teacher, please sing a verse for little Mie." We were all deeply affected, and joined in singing the hymn beginning—

"Jesus makes my heart rejoice.
I'm His sheep, and know His voice."

For a time he joined with us in a clear voice, folding his hands over his breast; but in the middle of the second verse his breath stood still; his ransomed soul had taken its flight to glory. This scene was rendered doubly impressive by the striking contrast between the riches of divine grace, of which this little child was a monument, and the poverty and meanness of the hut in which he had breathed his last. "Blessed are the dead that die in the Lord."

228. Esther Jones.—Writing from Butterworth Station in Kaffirland, South Africa, December 1830, the Rev. John Ayliff says:—

On September the 30th, Esther Jones, one of our members, was called from this suffering state to the rest which remaineth for the people of God. Since her baptism her conduct had been such as to adorn the doctrine of God her Saviour. She was particularly marked for tenderness of soul; and generally, when attending the means of grace, the bench and the ground where she was kneeling would be literally watered with her tears. Her illness was short, and her end was peace. A short time before her death, as Mr Jenkins, the assistant, went into her hut, she said, "O sir, pray for me; I have need of your prayers." On the day of her death, being asked if she was afraid to die, she replied, "I am not afraid! I am not afraid! Jesus is my friend! Jesus is my friend!" About three minutes before her departure, she said, "O sir, I feel happy! I feel happy!" and, bringing her hand over her breast, she exclaimed, "My heart is very happy! I have a friend—Jesus is my friend! Jesus died for me! I am not worthy! I am not worthy!" She then fell back into the arms of her daughter, and departed to her friend Jesus, whom her soul loved.

"Jesus, lover of my soul,
Let me to Thy bosom fly,
While the nearer waters roll,
While the tempest still is high."

"Hide me, O my Saviour, hide,
Till the storm of life be past;
Safe into the haven guide,
Oh, receive my soul at last!"

229. The Dying Namaqua.—One of the men who accompanied the chief of the Little Namaquas, when he went in search of a missionary in 1815, and providentially met with the Rev. Barnabas Shaw near the Elephant River, was Girt Links, who soon afterwards became a genuine convert to the faith of the gospel. By his upright conduct and general excellency of character, he endeared himself to all who knew him, and he enjoyed the confidence of the Rev. Messrs Shaw, Edwards, Jackson, and Bailie, the devoted missionaries who in succession laboured at Khamiesberg. The writer first became acquainted with Girt Links in 1853, and he will never forget the fervour of his prayers, and the earnestness of his testimony as to the great change which had passed upon himself and his brethren of the Hottentot race since the missionaries came among them.

In 1860 the old disciple began to sink beneath the weight of years and his numerous infirmities. He was confined to his hut for a length of time, during which he was frequently visited by the Rev. J. A. Bailie, the missionary then in charge of the station. Mr Bailie always found the aged pilgrim trusting in the merits of the Redeemer, and calmly waiting his final change. When Girt Links found that his end was approaching, he sent for the missionary, stating that he had something particular to say to him before he died. Mr Bailie hastened to the hut of the dying Namaqua, which was about four miles from the mission-house. On reaching the place, poor old Girt was very glad to see his beloved pastor once more; but he was almost too late, as the speech of the aged invalid had nearly left him. His friends raised him up in a sitting posture, and he proceeded to relate, in a faint but distinct tone of voice, his views and feelings with regard to the gospel and a future state of being. In his own native language he expressed himself substantially as follows:—"I have at this moment *a particular impression of the immortality of the soul*, for my body is already half dead. I have lost the use of both legs and one arm, and if my soul were not immortal, it would be half dead also; but instead of that, I am constantly thinking of God and heaven, and I can think with great ease and freedom. I have also *a special conviction that the Bible is God's Book*, and its blessed truths are constantly running through my mind, and afford me great comfort in my affliction. I wish to say further that *I now see more clearly than ever that the missionaries are not common men*, but the servants of God sent to declare unto us His Holy Word." The dying saint now looked round upon the friends who had assembled to hear his last words, and addressing them particularly, he said with all the earnestness which his failing strength would permit, " Pay great attention to the word of your teachers, and remember that they speak to you in the name of the Lord." Being faint, he said, " I have done." He was then laid down again, and about an hour afterwards his redeemed spirit departed in the full assurance of faith to a brighter and better world above.

230. Light in the Valley.—The last deathbed scene witnessed by the writer, in Southern Africa, made an impression upon his mind never to be effaced. It was that of Sophia Lutgens, the wife of a native teacher, who resided at Rondebosch, about four miles from Cape Town. Her little infant had died a few months before, and being delicate, she never seemed fully to recover from the shock of her bereavement. She was for some time confined to her bed, during which I visited her frequently, and always found her calmly trusting in the merits of Christ, and fully resigned to the will of God. As the end drew near, her confidence and joy, in prospect of heaven, seemed to increase. On one occasion, when I had been commending her to God in prayer, and, after rising from my knees, had spoken to her a few words of encouragement and comfort, she looked up, and with heavenly radiance beaming in her emaciated bronze countenance, she replied in her own sweet language, " *Ja Mynheer, gy spreekt de waarheid; ik ben nu in het dal der schaduwe des doods; maar Gode zy dank het is niet donker. Aan het ende daarvan, schynt, hamelsche licht; en binnen kort zal ik met den Heer voor eevwig zyn*," which may be thus rendered, " Yes, sir, you speak the truth; I am now in the valley of the shadow of death; but thank God, it is not dark. I see heavenly light shining in at the other end, and I shall soon be for ever with the Lord." Shortly afterwards she passed away to her eternal rest,—one of a large number of natives of South Africa who have been gathered into the fold of Christ through the instrumentality of Christian missions.

" Oh, may I triumph so,
 When all my warfare's past;
 And, dying, find my latest foe
  Under my feet at last."

231. A Christian Baboo.—The *Bengal Christian Herald* says :—" We are exceedingly sorry at the loss of our excellent friend, Baboo W. C. Mookerjea; but this is no small consolation to us, and to all our Christian readers, that he died 'the death of the righteous.' A month before that occurrence, when a friend, with the view of awakening him to his duties, asked him, ' Woomesh Baboo, the doctors say your case is a very difficult one, but what do you think of yourself?' He replied, ' Brother, I had some hope of recovery before, but now I have none.' The friend asked, ' Do you pray for your recovery?' He answered, ' I pray, saying, Lord, let Thy will be done.' Then the friend asked him, ' Are you prepared for death?' He replied, 'What do you mean by preparation? Jesus Christ is my only preparation.' During the last illness of this devoted native Christian, Jeremy Taylor's 'Holy Living and Dying,' and the Word of God, were his constant companions; and he felt great delight in singing hymns, and in hearing them sung by others. He seldom talked of anything but things eternal, and never doubted for a moment the love of Christ to his soul. He firmly believed that His infinite mercy would not cut him off. His love to the cause of Christ was strong to the last. 'If I recover this time,' he often said, 'I shall devote myself more thoroughly to the work of the Lord.' While apparently unconscious, and not very far from death, he cried out, 'Victory to Jesus! victory to Jesus! Let it be said everywhere in the world, Victory to Jesus!'"

232. The Dying Hindu.—A missionary labouring in Calcutta communicates the following account of the happy death of a Hindu convert to Christianity, whose name is not given:—

He was ill for several weeks, during which there was a perceptible preparation for his approaching change. His conscience was tender, so that he wept over his sinfulness and hardness of heart; he became more indifferent to the world, and more anxious about eternal realities; manifested much desire for prayer and religious conversation, and exhibited more gratitude to God for His mercy in calling him to a knowledge of His gospel, and a more entire reliance on Christ as his Saviour.

For some days before his death he lay in a kind of stupor, and seemed conscious only for a short time when roused. But on the night of his departure, he appeared to awake as from sleep, and very wonderfully to revive. He sat up, and conversed with the greatest self-possession with his wife and child, and a native preacher who visited him. The wife of the dying man, who was herself a Christian, and had been the means of his conversion, said to him, "Well, do you put your faith in Christ as your Saviour?" He replied very emphatically, "Undoubtedly, undoubtedly; yes, undoubtedly, I believe in Him entirely for salvation." At one time he said repeatedly, "Come, Lord Jesus, why dost Thou delay? I am ready: open unto me the door of life." His wife said to him, "Alas! you are dying; what will become of me?" He replied, "I have committed you into the hands of God our Father." She said, "But what will become of the boy?"—an interesting youth of nine years of age. He said, "Christ our Saviour will take care of him." He then called the little boy to him, and embraced him; when his wife said, "Ah! what right have we to treasures that are only lent?" Soon after this he called her to him, laid hold of her hand affectionately, and said, "We are yet united in affection." She replied, "Yes; not in life only, but for ever." Then taking her hand again, he prayed for her and the child, and said to his wife, "Then can you let me depart to-day?" She replied, "Yes, I can; why should I prevent you from going to the Saviour? I will not hinder your entering the gate of life everlasting." At his desire his attendants then began to sing the Evening Hymn in Bengalee; and when that was concluded, they commenced, at his request, another on death, of which the chorus is, "Everything on earth is vanity, O brother; but the love of Christ, that alone is substance.' While they were singing this hymn' the dying Hindu fell back on his bed, breathed a gentle sigh, and expired.

233. Christ Precious.—A returned missionary from India relates an interesting incident in reference to a female convert from Hinduism. Being brought near to the gates of death by a lingering illness, the poor woman was visited by the missionary frequently, and he always found her simply looking to Jesus, and hoping for salvation only through Him. On one occasion, when her pastor inquired as to the state of her mind, she replied, "Happy! happy! I have Christ *here*," laying her hand on the Bengalee Bible; "and *here*," pressing it to her heart; "and Christ *there*," pointing towards heaven. Happy Christian! to whatever part of the universe she might be removed, the Lord of the universe was with her, and she was sure of His favour. "Whom have I in heaven but Thee? and there is none upon earth that I desire beside Thee. My heart and my flesh faileth; but God is the strength of my heart, and my portion for ever." The happy convert soon afterwards gently passed away from earth, to be for ever with the Lord.

"Whom have I on earth below?
Thee, and only Thee, I know:
Whom have I in heaven but Thee?
Thou art all in all to me."

234. The Little Burman Girl.—A little girl in Burmah, who had been trained in the mission-school, and on whose youthful mind a gracious impression had been made by the instruction she had received, gave a noble testimony to the power of religion in her last moments. When very ill, and brought near to the gates of death, she looked up to the kind lady who called to see her, and who had been her teacher, and said, "I am dying, but am not afraid to die; for Christ will call me up to heaven. He has taken away all my sins, and I wish to die now, that I may go and see Him. I love Jesus more than anything else." So she passed away, to be for ever with the Lord.

"Jesus shall reign where'er the sun
Doth his successive journeys run;
His kingdom stretch from shore to shore,
Till suns shall rise and set no more.

"People and realms of every tongue
Dwell on His love with sweetest song,
And infant voices shall proclaim
Their young Hosannas to His name."

IX. CHRISTIAN BENEVOLENCE.

235. Human Instrumentality. —If He had thought proper to do so, the Almighty could no doubt have converted the world to Himself without employing human instrumentality. He might have given to mankind, by the inspiration of His Spirit, a written revelation of His mind and will, as He has done, and left the matter there. Or He might have commissioned, from the courts of heaven, holy angels to wing their way to different parts of the world, as messengers of His mercy to the fallen and the lost, to tell them of His redeeming love, and to beseech the rebellious sons of men to be reconciled to Him. But it is evident, from the manner in which the Bible has been treated, that if it had been left to itself, its silent testimony would have been in many instances disregarded. And if the proclamation of the gospel had been committed to heavenly angels, winging their way through the air from place to place, feelings of alarm might have been excited by their sudden and unexpected appearance, which would probably have thwarted the object of their benevolent visits, and neutralised the effects of their message of mercy. Nor could celestial angels who have never sinned preach the gospel from *experience*, as penitent believers in Christ.

But it is in vain to speculate on what God might have done. We have to do with the fact of the plan which He has actually adopted to make known the good news of salvation to our lost and fallen race. That is to commission men of like passions with ourselves to preach His blessed gospel, declaring from their own experience the doctrines relating to the plan of salvation by faith in our Lord Jesus Christ. Before His ascension, the Redeemer said to His disciples, and the same He says in effect to every one who bears His name, "Go ye into all the world, and preach the gospel to every creature." By adopting this system of human instrumentality for the promulgation of His truth, the great Head of the Church gives an opportunity for every one to take a part in the glorious work. As the men sent forth must be sustained in their labours, there is a loud call upon the members of the Church to aid them, not only by their sympathy and prayer, but also by the contribution of their benevolent offerings towards the expenses inevitably involved in the missionary enterprise. To facilitate the arrangements connected with the financial department of the work, as well as to superintend it in all its details, Missionary Societies have been organised, and Christian people may confide to them their contributions with the assurance that they will be carefully and conscientiously applied to the purpose for which they are given.

236. Benevolence enjoined in Scripture.—There is no duty more clearly taught in the Sacred Scriptures than that of Christian benevolence, or giving of our substance, as the Lord has prospered us, to relieve the poor, to support the gospel, and to extend the interests of the Redeemer's kingdom in the world. Under both the former and the latter dispensations the moral obligation of God's people to open their hearts and their hands to the claims of genuine charity is clearly set forth, and the blessedness of conscientiously attending to it is explicitly stated. "Honour the Lord with thy substance, and with the first-fruits of all thine increase. So shall thy barns be filled with plenty, and thy presses shall burst out with new wine" (Prov. iii. 9, 10). "Give unto the Lord the glory due to His name: bring an offering, and come before Him: worship the Lord in the beauty of holiness" (1 Chron. xvi. 29). "They shall not appear before the Lord empty. Every man shall give as he is able, according to the blessing of the Lord thy God, which He hath given thee" (Deut. xvi. 16, 17). "Who goeth a warfare at any time at his own cost? who planteth a vineyard, and eateth not of the fruit thereof? or who feedeth a flock, and eateth not of the milk of the flock?" (1 Cor. ix. 7.) "If we have sown unto you spiritual things, is it a great matter if we shall reap your carnal things?" (1 Cor. ix. 11). "Do ye not know that they who minister about holy things live of the sacrifices, and they that wait at the altar are partakers with the altar? Even so hath the Lord also ordained that they who preach the gospel should live of the gospel" (1 Cor. ix. 13, 14). "Let him that is taught in the Word minister unto him that teacheth in all good things. Be not deceived, God is not mocked; for whatsoever a man soweth, that shall he reap" (Gal. vi. 6, 7). "He which soweth sparingly shall reap also sparingly; and he that soweth bountifully shall reap also bountifully" (1 Cor. ix. 6). "Charge them that are rich in this world that they be ready to give and glad to distribute, laying up in store for themselves a good foundation against the time to come, that they may attain eternal life" (1 Tim. vi. 17-19). "To do good and to distribute forget not; for with such sacrifice God is well pleased" (Heb. xiii. 16). "Whoso hath this world's good, and seeth his brother have need, and shutteth up his compassion from him, how dwelleth the love of God in him" (1 John iii. 17). "Remember the words of the Lord Jesus, how He said, It is more blessed to give than to receive" (Acts xx. 35). "Every man according as he purposeth in his heart, so let him give; not grudgingly or of necessity: for God loveth a cheerful giver" (2 Cor. ix. 7).

237. Liberality of the Israelites.—It is doubtful whether ever the world witnessed a more magnificent display of large-hearted munificence for a religious object than that which was exhibited by the children of Israel, on the occasion of the erection of the tabernacle in the wilderness. Having received explicit instructions from the Almighty with reference to the formation of the sacred edifice, Moses spake unto all the congregation of the children of Israel, saying, "This is the thing which the Lord commanded, saying, Take ye from among you an offering unto the Lord: whoever is of a willing heart, let him bring it, an offering unto the Lord; gold, and silver, and brass, and blue, and purple, and scarlet, and fine linen," &c. (Exod. xxxv. 4-6). And those who were skilled in the arts of spinning, weaving, and embroidery, were called upon to give of their labour to prepare the necessary furniture and appendages of the sanctuary. The people went forth from the presence of their leader and lawgiver animated by one spirit in reference to the holy enterprise; and right nobly did they perform their duty in this matter.

It is said that "they came, both men and women, as many as were willing-hearted, and brought bracelets and ear-rings, and rings, and tablets, all jewels of gold; and every man that offered, offered an offering of gold unto the Lord. And every man with whom was found blue, and purple, and scarlet, and fine linen, and goats' hair, and red skins of rams, and badgers' skins, brought them. Every one that did offer an offering of silver and brass, brought the Lord's offering; and every man with whom was found shittim-wood, for any work of the service, brought it. And all the women that were wise-hearted did spin with their hands, and brought that which they had spun, both of blue and purple and of scarlet, and of fine linen. And all the women whose hearts stirred them up in wisdom spun goats' hair. And the rulers brought onyx-stones, and stones to be set for the ephod, and for the breastplate; and spice, and oil for the light, and for the anointing oil, and for the sweet incense. The children of Israel brought a willing offering unto the Lord, every man and every woman whose heart made them willing to bring all manner of work, which the Lord had commanded to be made by the hand of Moses" (Exod. xxxv. 22-29).

So abundant was this offering that the artisans "spake unto Moses, saying, The people bring much more than enough for the service of the work which the Lord hath commanded to make. And Moses gave commandment; and they caused it to be proclaimed throughout the camp, saying, Let neither man nor woman make any more work for the offering of the sanctuary. So the people were restrained from bringing. For the stuff they had was sufficient for all the work to make it, and too much" (Exod. xxxvi. 5-7). The value of these offerings which were thus brought in the course of a few weeks, has been estimated at £200,000 of our money.

238. **Macedonian Liberality.**—It was a noble testimony which the Apostle Paul bore to the Christian liberality of the Macedonian converts to the faith of the gospel, when writing to the Corinthians. "Moreover, brethren, we do you to wit of the grace of God bestowed on the churches of Macedonia; how that in a great fight of affliction the abundance of their joy and their deep poverty abounded unto the riches of their liberality. For to their power, I bear them record, yea, and beyond their power, they are willing of themselves; praying us with much entreaty that we would receive their gift, and take upon us the fellowship of the ministering to the saints. And this they did, not as we hoped, but first gave their ownselves to the Lord, and unto us by the will of God" (2 Cor. viii. 1-5).

When the Church of Christ everywhere reaches an elevation thus fervent and holy and pure, and when all who bear the Christian name are, like the Macedonians, "willing of themselves" to contribute to the various objects of charity which come before them, and that to the utmost of their power, yea, and "beyond their power," and "entreat" the collectors to receive their gifts, it will be a happy day for the cause of God in all its departments. Professing Christians, acting upon the instructions of the apostle in another place, and "laying by in store as the Lord has prospered them," will hold themselves in readiness as often as it is necessary, to replenish the treasury of the Church without pressure, or excitement, or a resort to those extraordinary and sensational methods of raising money which we have sometimes feared is scarcely consistent with the dignity, sanctity, and legitimate claims of the noble enterprise.

239. The Widow's Mites.—One of the most beautiful and touching examples of self-denial and entire devotedness to God which we find left upon record, is that of the poor but pious widow who came up to the temple, and presented her offering in a manner and with a motive which elicited the hearty commendation of Christ himself, who witnessed it with joy, and called the attention of His disciples to it. The sacred narrative is full of instruction. "And Jesus sat over against the treasury, and beheld how the people cast money into the treasury; and many that were rich cast in much. And there came a certain poor widow, and she threw in two mites, which make a farthing. And He called unto His disciples, and said unto them, Verily I say unto you, that this poor widow hath cast more in than all they that have cast into the treasury: for all they did cast in of their abundance; but she of her want did cast in all that she had, even all her living" (Mark xii. 41-44).

The same watchful eye is still upon the Lord's treasury, and Jesus still takes notice of the offerings which are presented there. He is, moreover, acquainted with the motives and circumstances of all who contribute towards the support and extension of His cause. He regards not so much the amount which is presented as the motive of the giver, and the amount still left in his possession of that which a kind Providence has entrusted to his care. Whether rich or poor, those who contribute of their substance to the cause of God on a scale like that of the poor widow, viewed in connection with the means at her command, will have their reward in the approving smile and the perpetual blessing of their Lord and Master.

240. Two Mites.—It has become somewhat common for Christian people to speak of their contributions to the cause of God, or to charitable objects generally, as their "*mite*," in allusion to the offering of the poor widow in the gospel; and it is to be feared that this is often done without carefully considering and laying to heart that noble example of self-denying benevolence. So thought a devoted minister of Christ, when a wealthy widow lady, a member of his congregation, came to him in the vestry, to say that, not being present when the collection was made on the previous Sabbath for Foreign Missions, she wished to add a trifle as the "widow's mite," at the same time putting down a sovereign on the table. The minister thanked her with a smile, remarking that if every member of the congregation who happened to be absent on the collection-day would thus kindly think of it afterwards, it would be well. But knowing the circumstances of the lady, and her generous disposition also, he ventured to add, "Your contribution is very acceptable, madam; but you will excuse me if I remind you that the widow in the gospel, to whom you have alluded, gave *two mites*." This gentle and timely hint had its desired effect, and the lady immediately added another sovereign to her contribution, good-naturedly confessing that she had more left than the poor widow had, for which she was thankful.

241. Missionary Contributions Abroad.

Whenever a congregation is gathered, and a Christian Church is organised in distant lands, the people are taught the scriptural duty of giving for the support and extension of the work of God as the Lord has prospered them. Hence Missionary Associations are formed, and public meetings are held in a manner similar to that which is adopted at home. It is true that in some countries the people have little or no money; but they are not the less liberal on that account. They give what they have, and it is turned into money, and passed on to the missionary treasury for the support of the work. From this kind of training, and the prevalence of Christian principles, many mission-stations have become entirely self-supporting already; and in addition to the efforts made to sustain the work among themselves, the people in some places contribute considerable sums to send the gospel to the "regions beyond." The native converts in the Friendly Islands, who are far from wealthy, in 1872 contributed to the Mission Fund the noble sum of £4401, 10s. 11d.; and we have witnessed instances of Christian liberality in the mission-field, such as we have never seen surpassed in any country. The amount received by the Wesleyan Missionary Society from Foreign Auxiliaries last year was £41,623, 9s. 1d. To produce these results, missionary-meetings are held on every station, and the proceedings are frequently of a most enthusiastic and interesting character.

242. Missionary-Meeting in Fiji.

The Rev. John Leggoe, writing from Lakimba, one of the Fiji Islands, gives an interesting account of a missionary-meeting held there in the month of March 1871. Each tribe came, led by their respective chiefs, to the chapel, singing as they came, and passed in, still singing, up to the table, on which they laid their gifts. In reference to one little incident, he says:—"A very affecting scene occurred during the collection, the particulars of which I will briefly give. An old chief was leading his tribe to the chapel, and as soon as he reached the door he was deeply moved and greatly excited, and with tears streaming from his eyes, he cried out, 'What shall I give unto the Lord? Oh that I had something to give Him in return for all that He has given me! Oh that I were rich, that I had gold or land to give! I have only this mite (holding up a sovereign). No! this is not all, I will give *myself*—my body, my soul, my all!' Who can doubt that the Lord accepted the offering."

243. First Missionary-Meeting in Namaqualand.

When the late Rev. T. L. Hodgson paid a visit of inspection to the Wesleyan mission-stations in Great Namaqualand, South Africa, in the year 1841, it was thought a favourable time to hold the first missionary-meeting at Nisbett Bath, and thus to initiate the native converts into the habit of contributing as the Lord had prospered them for the support and spread of the gospel. Several of the head men and native teachers spoke very effectively, and the people listened to their statements, as well as to the appeals of the missionaries, with marked attention. Indeed, an interest was excited on behalf of the perishing heathen such as had never been felt before, and the people, from the chief downwards, were so affected that they were disposed to do their utmost to help forward the good work. Money was almost unknown in the country at that time, but they gave what they had. The contributions were noted down at the close of the meeting, as they were announced, and the list read as follows:—

 3 Cows valued at 36 rix-dollars.
 10 Oxen ,, 200 ,,
 2 Heifers ,, 14 ,,
 4 Calves ,, 28 ,,
 147 Sheep ,, 441 ,,
 59 Goats ,, 177 ,,
 1 Bull ,, 7 ,,

These 226 head of cattle, with a few skins and ostrich feathers brought by the little children, when sold, brought to the funds of the Society the sum of £67, 14s. 6d., as the amount of the missionary contributions for the Nisbett Bath Station for that year.

244. Missionary-Meetings in the West Indies.—Some of the most animated and enthusiastic missionary-meetings we ever attended were in the West Indies, among the newly-emancipated slaves. When converted negroes were occasionally induced to speak a few words, we had a rich treat. Nor were the results, in the aggregate, small or insignificant. If there were no very large or princely contributions, the comparatively small offerings of the people were so numerous that when added together they frequently amounted to a considerable sum. In the little island of St Vincent, with a population of about 28,000, the proceeds of the meeting, and the contributions of the people in the year 1843, amounted to the noble sum of £410, 2s. 10d. This amount was remitted to England, to help to send the gospel to Africa and other heathen lands, and no part of it was spent in the island, the mission being at that time entirely self-supporting. A fact like this is encouraging, inasmuch as what has been done on one station may be accomplished in others, and it is hoped that the same principle of self-support and of genuine missionary zeal will ultimately become as extensive as the work itself in various parts of the world.

245. A Negro Missionary-Meeting.—At a missionary-meeting held among the negroes of the West Indies many years ago, these three resolutions were agreed upon:—" 1. We will all give something. 2. We will all give as the Lord has prospered us. 3. We will all give willingly." As soon as the meeting was over, a leading negro took his seat at the table, with pen and ink, as secretary and treasurer, to note down what each came to give. Many came forward and gave, some more and some less. Among those who came was a comparatively rich old man, almost as wealthy as all the others put together, and threw down upon the table a small silver coin. "Take dat back," said the secretary; "dat may be according to de first resolution, but it not according to de second." The rich old man accordingly took it up, and hobbled back again to his seat, in a great rage. One after another came forward; and as almost all gave more than him, he was fairly ashamed of himself, and he again went up and threw a larger contribution on the table, saying, "Dar, take dat." It was a valuable piece of gold; but it was given so ill-temperedly, that the sable secretary answered again, "No; dat won't do yet. It may be according to de first and second resolutions, but it is not

Street scene in Demerara after the arrival of Chinese and Indian Coolies.

according to de last;" and he was obliged to take up his coin again. Still angry at himself and all the rest, he sat a long time till nearly all the people were gone, and then came up to the table with a smile on his face, and very pleasantly handed a large subscription to the treasurer. "Very well," said the courteous but dignified official; "dat according to all de resolutions."

246. Scott Chinn's Speech.—

In 1869 a series of missionary-meetings was projected among the coloured Methodist Episcopal Churches of New Orleans. At one of these it was arranged that an eccentric veteran named Scott Chinn should make the collection speech. The brother who preceded him greatly tried the old man's patience by the length of his address. "He will spoil the meeting," whispered Scott to the chairman. "He's too long in the wind." At length the speaker closed by an eloquent reference to the apocalyptic angel flying through the midst of heaven. As soon as the way was open, Scott Chinn was on his feet in a moment, and with an earnestness of voice and action characteristic of the negro race, he made an animated speech in broken English, which may be fairly rendered as follows:—

"I have been afraid some of these brethren would talk too long, and that the angel flying through the heavens would get clear out of sight before they finished. That angel, brethren, is the missionary angel. He takes the everlasting gospel with him wherever he goes—to every nation and kindred, and tongue and people." ("Mighty angel!" shouted some in the congregation.) Inspired with his conception, and animated by the enthusiasm of his audience, the sable patriarch stretched himself to his full height, and reaching out his hand toward the angel whom he seemed to see before him, he exclaimed, "O thou angel of mighty wing, tarry with us a little while in this missionary-meeting. We are the people your Lord sent you to find. Fold your wings, and rest a while here. You have been flying so long, and you have many a long weary flight before you. Blessed angel, are you not very tired? Then rest, for this is the Lord's day, the Lord's house, and the Lord's people." Turning to the congregation, now up to the white heat of excitement, he continued, "Children, you may thank your stars, and the good Lord, that the flying angel came this way to-night, and he is going to stay a while with us. He is folding his wings, and looking right at you now. He wants to see what we are going to give to send the everlasting gospel round the world. I will tell you what we will do, children. The angel's wings are broken a little with the big wind from the four corners of the world. See! he needs some more feathers in his wings, that he may fly better with the everlasting gospel through the midst of heaven. Up now, and bring on the feathers for the angel's wings." In an instant the people were on their feet, filing into the aisles, and marching in time to the swell of song, as is their manner when they make the collections, to the table in the altar, on which they placed their offerings of pennies and postage-stamps. Suddenly the patriarch called out, "Stop there, stop that singing." The order was promptly obeyed, and all waited to see what was wrong. "What is on the table?" he demanded, pointing to the pennies and stamps. "What you call these? Feathers for the angel's wings? He cannot fly round the world with these. These are nothing but pin-feathers. Bring on your long quills for the angel's wings." The song and the marching were resumed, the offerings greatly enlarged, and the series of meetings held among the coloured people realised that year nearly the sum of £200.

247. Liberality of an Emancipated Slave.—A female slave, in Kingstown, St Vincent's, who was a member of the Wesleyan Methodist Society, was desirous of purchasing her freedom. She laboured hard, and, by dint of industry and carefulness, saved three doubloons (about ten guineas sterling). Her mistress, who, though not a member of society, yet was a regular attendant at chapel, was led to think that she ought, in consideration of the long and faithful services of her slave, to give her her freedom, and she accordingly did so. The slave, full of joy at such a boon as this, came to the missionary, and presented him with the whole of the three doubloons which she had saved from her hard earnings. This she did as an offering of gratitude to God, who had put it into the heart of her mistress freely to emancipate her; at the same time expressing a wish that the money might be devoted to sending missionaries to Africa, that they might preach to her countrymen that gospel which had been the means of effecting for her a twofold freedom—one from the bondage of sin, and the other from a state of civil slavery.

248. Prudence Necessary in Collecting.—A zealous and intelligent youth, a juvenile collector for Home and Foreign Missions, set out one fine Monday morning with his book and his bag, to try what he could do for a cause he dearly loved. At the first house where he called he found the woman busily engaged in washing, and on asking her if she would kindly give him something for the missions, she said, "No, I sha'n't; go away." At another house the servant came to the door, and then called her master, to whom the boy said, "If you please, sir, will you give me something for the missions?" "No," was the answer, "I don't believe in Foreign Missions; if you had been collecting for Home Missions, I might have given you something." "I am collecting for Home Missions as well," answered the boy. But after all, the final reply was, "I've nothing for you." After a while the courageous little collector came to a large house where he heard the sound of music. He ventured to knock at the door: the servant came and went to tell her master. "What do you want?" asked the gentleman. The boy told his errand. "Come inside," said the master of the house, "it is my little girl's birthday to-day, and she has a party of young friends; we'll see what they say about it." He then took the boy into the room where the party was assembled, told the company what he had come for, and proposed that they should make a collection. They did so, and it realised six shillings and sixpence.

When the boy got home, he began to moralise, and asked himself what lessons he had learned from his morning's experience. The conclusion to which he came is worthy of being recorded for the guidance of others. He had learned, first, never to call at a house to collect on the washing-day; secondly, that those who won't give to Foreign Missions, won't give to Home Missions; thirdly, never to despair. These lessons of wisdom and prudence are worthy of the consideration of all whom they concern.

249. Try Again.—On all our foreign mission-stations, especially in the British Colonies, the system of juvenile collecting for the missions has been introduced the same as at home, and we have witnessed some interesting scenes in connection with this department of the work. When the collectors brought in their respective amounts obtained for the Christmas offering at Rondebosh, Cape of Good Hope, on one occasion I observed a little coloured boy with his card mutilated, and evidently repaired by being stitched with needle and thread. I said to him, "Well, Johnny, you must have been in the war; what is the matter with your card?" He replied, "Please, sir, I went first to a Roman Catholic lady, and asked her for a penny for my Christmas offering. She looked at the card, and on seeing it was for missions, she tore it in pieces, and threw them on the floor, telling me to "begone, as she had nothing to give for missions." I said, "Well, my little boy, that was a poor beginning, I am afraid you would be discouraged." He replied, "No, sir, I picked up the pieces, and my sister sewed them together, and told me I must try again. I then went to people that were not Roman Catholics, and they gave me, and I have got four shillings and sixpence." I said, "You are a brave little fellow, I hope you will one day be a missionary." And he did actually become a mission-school teacher, and was made very useful. The lesson to be learnt from this little incident is happily expressed in the chorus to one of the infant-school melodies.

"If you don't at first succeed;
Try, try, try again."

250. The Way to Succeed.—A pious young lady was persuaded by her minister to become a missionary collector. She was, however, so unsuccessful in canvassing her district, as to fail in twenty-three cases out of twenty-four applications which she made for subscriptions. She felt so deeply discouraged, that she at once resolved to relinquish the work she had undertaken. She accordingly informed her minister of her want of success, and her consequent resolution. He seriously inquired whether she had first gone into her closet, and asked God to crown her efforts with success. She candidly acknowledged she had not done so. She was then affectionately urged to adopt this plan, and afterwards to canvass her district once more. This appeared perfectly reasonable, and she engaged to act on the recommendation of her pastor. From her private devotions, in which she received a personal blessing, she went forth to canvass her district a second time, trusting in a higher Power for the success of her efforts. The result was remarkable. She returned with a joyful heart, having to her agreeable surprise failed in one application only, and happily succeeded in the remaining twenty-three.

251. Unexpected Liberality.—A rich old gentleman was, several years ago, called upon by two female collectors for a society which had for its object the spread of the gospel throughout the world, and was respectfully asked to subscribe to it. He replied that he had been thinking about it, but wished first to become better acquainted with the plan of the institution, and he desired them to call again. The collectors left with the gentleman a report and some papers, which he read with much interest. When the young ladies called again, the gentleman told them he had made up his mind to subscribe *a guinea a year*, and immediately began to count out upon the table a number of guineas. When he had got to twenty-one, the young ladies stopped him, saying that their time was rather precious, they would feel obliged if he would kindly give them his subscription, that they might go. The old gentleman still continued to count the guineas out on the table. They interrupted him a second time, when he simply remarked that he hoped they would suffer him to go on; and on he went, till he had counted down eighty guineas. "There, ladies," cried the old gentleman, "I promised you a subscription of a guinea a year; I am eighty years old, and there are eighty guineas."

It is best to begin in early life to work and give for the Lord; but when this has been neglected, the next best thing to do is to imitate the liberal old gentleman, who made good his subscription for every year that he had lived, and thus redeem the time to the utmost of our power, knowing that the opportunity will soon be gone for ever. The Saviour set forth the subject in its true light, when He said, "I must work the works of Him that sent me while it is day, for the night cometh when no man can work."

252. Intelligent Giving.—When Christian benevolence is the result of intelligent inquiry, reading, and study, it is more likely to be large-hearted, systematic, and commensurate with the object contemplated, so far as circumstances will permit. We have a striking instance of intelligent giving, in humble life, in the case of Mr J. Whitehead, an account of whom was published in the *Wesleyan Magazine*. It is there said of this devoted Christian, that "he took a deep interest in the cause of missions: he purchased the notices monthly, and read them with tears and many prayers, and always contributed according to his means." About a year before he died he called upon the superintendent minister, and, with a flood of tears, said, "I and my wife sat up most of the night reading the Missionary Notices, and we are distressed to find that the Committee cannot do all the good they wish for want of funds. The missionaries in the West Indies are dying with excessive labour, and the people are left in some places as sheep without a shepherd. What can be done? My wife and I have resolved to give half a sovereign extra." Laying down the money, he begged it might be sent to the Committee, saying, "The missionaries must not die for want of help." This was at a time when Mr W. and his wife were subsisting on an annuity of ten shillings per week. "Thus, in their great trial of affliction, and the abundance of their joy, and their deep poverty, abounded to the riches of their liberality."

253. The Orphan Girl's Offering.—Great interest was excited in the cause of missions at Lynn, in Norfolk, by the visit to that town of the converted Indian chief Peter Jones, in the year 1846. The seed then sown bore fruit after many days, a striking instance of which is given in a communication from the Rev. James B. Holroyd, as follows:—

The morning after the next Missionary Anniversary, I answered a gentle knock at the door, when a little girl presented me with a small brown-paper package, modestly saying, "Please, sir, I have brought this for the missions." On opening it, I found that it contained four shillings. I then asked her, "Have your parents sent you with this money?" She replied, "I have no parents. My father was a pilot, and was lost in Yarmouth Roads; and my mother is dead." I then asked her, "With whom do you live?" She answered, "With my uncle and aunt." "Have they sent you with this money?" "No, sir," she said, "it is my own: I have *a penny a week*, sir." I asked, "Do your uncle and aunt know that you have brought this money?" "Yes, sir; I have *a penny a week*, and I began to save it last missionary-meeting."

The idea that this little orphan girl had given 4s. out of 4s. 4d., her whole year's income, was to me one of the noblest acts of benevolence on behalf of the heathen world I had ever known. But my surprise and admiration were greatly increased when I learned how she got her *penny a week*. For one halfpenny a week she carried all the water an aged female used; and for the other halfpenny she took breakfast every morning for a young man at the shop where he worked. Verily, the cause of missions will never languish if the children and young people of our churches at home and abroad imbibe the spirit of the noble enterprise as did the little orphan girl of Norfolk.

254. Charles Raven's Last Contribution.—A young man named Charles Raven, in humble circumstances, showed a remarkable attachment to the mission cause from his childhood, and all that he could give or collect for the purpose was cheerfully consecrated to the noble enterprise. His last contribution of £5, the result of many year's careful saving, was presented to the Society under circumstances peculiarly affecting. Charles was then about eighteen years of age, and had been unwell for some time, though not quite laid aside. On returning from chapel one night in 1844, he could not lie down from difficulty of breathing, and his grandmother sat up with him. Early next morning there was an evident change; and while his father went out to call for a religious friend, the grandmother perceived that something rested on his mind, though he could not speak a whole sentence, and she proceeded to ascertain what it was by questions. Did he wish to say something to his father? "No." Did he wish to say anything about money? "Yes." Did he wish to give something to the missions? "Yes." What? "Five"—he could say no more. "Five pounds?" rejoined his grandmother. "Yes: there," he exclaimed, and indicated by his countenance and manner that he had done with the world. Just then a friend came in who was present three years before when he found peace with God, and asked him, "How do you feel, Charles?" He replied, "Very comfortable," and with emphasis repeated, "*very comfortable*." "You feel Christ precious?" "Yes." The friend adds, "Just then he seemed in the midst of the river, where the water runs strongest; he said aloud, 'He is with me; He is with me; He does support me.' And while he was praying, the agony of death was over, and in a few moments he fell asleep in Jesus."

255. Rain Contribution.—Once a little girl, who loved her Saviour very much for having so loved her, came to her minister with eighteen shillings for the Missionary Society. "How did you collect so much? Is it all your own?" asked the minister. "Yes, sir, I earned it." "But how, Mary—you are so young and so poor?" "Please, sir, when I thought how Jesus had died for me, I wanted to do something for Him, and I heard how money was wanted to send the gospel to the heathen: and as I had no money of my own, I earned this by collect'ng rain-water, and selling it to washerwomen for a penny a bucket. That is how I got the money, sir." "My dear child," said the minister, "I am very glad to hear that your love to your Saviour has led you to work so long and so patiently for Him; now I shall gladly put down your name as a missionary subscriber." "Oh no, sir, please; not my name." "Why not, Mary?" "Please, sir, I would rather no one knew but Him; I should like it to be put down as 'Rain from heaven.'"

256. Missionary Beans.—A most ingenious method of aiding the mission-fund was adopted some time ago by a humble villager in Norfolk. He felt that he ought to do something more than he had hitherto done for the spread of the gospel in heathen lands; but his means were limited, and he scarcely knew what plan to adopt to accomplish the desired object. At length the thought struck him that he might take half a pint of beans, which cost only about a halfpenny, to the approaching missionary-meeting, and challenge some one to plant them and give the proceeds to the Society. He did so, and before the meeting commenced, he placed the beans on the platform, without any other person knowing about it. He attached a note to them addressed to the chairman, requesting that some friend or friends would take them and grow them for three years, and give the proceeds to the mission cause. The chairman that year happened to be a farmer; he read the note, and asked the question, who would grow the beans? The villager himself rose, and offered to take half of them if the chairman would take the other half, which he at once agreed to do. At subsequent missionary-meetings the produce of the pint of beans was reported as follows:—The first year, 11 pints; the second year, 9 bushels; and the third year, 276 bushels, which, when sold, realised for the mission-fund the sum of £81, 14s. 9d., which was handed to the treasurer.

"I was so satisfied with the result," writes the Norfolk villager, "that I resolved to grow a quarter of a pint of beans for the missions for three years more, which promised a far greater yield than the former three years—so much so, that I was obliged to make an appeal for land to grow them on, in which I have had great success. Not only are my neighbours assisting me, but a gentleman near Peterborough, and another gentleman near Warrington, in Cheshire, hearing of the scheme, kindly offered to assist me in growing them in this and the last year, so that instead of £81, I hope before Christmas next to be able to send to the treasurer of the mission-fund on behalf of Africa at least £120. Can you not do something similar? Because the Bible says, 'He that soweth sparingly shall reap sparingly; but he that soweth bountifully shall reap bountifully.'"

257. Missionary Pigs.—When the Rev. John Williams returned to his own station in Riatea from the Hervey Islands, in 1828, he brought with him £66 as the contributions of the native Christians at Rurutu to the mission-fund; and a still larger sum was raised on another island for the same object in a very novel manner. He had taken to Aitutaki the first pigs the natives had ever seen, and a few years afterwards he observes:—"I was explaining to the people one evening the manner in which English Christians raised money to send the gospel to heathen countries. On hearing this, they expressed their regret at not having money, that they also might enjoy the privilege of helping in the good work of causing the Word of

God to grow. I replied, 'If you have no money, you have something to buy money with.' This idea was quite new to them, and they wished to know at once what they possessed which would buy money. I said to them, 'The pigs I brought to your shores on my first visit here, multiplied so greatly that all of you have now an abundance; and if every family in the island were to set apart a pig for causing the Word of God to grow, and when the ships come, to sell them for money, instead of cloth and axes, a valuable contribution might be raised.' The idea delighted them exceedingly; and early the next morning the squeaking of the pigs, which were receiving a particular mark in the ear for this purpose, was heard from one end of the settlement to the other. In the interval a ship had been there, the captain of which had purchased the pigs, and paid for them most honourably; and now, to my utter astonishment, the native treasurer put into my hands £103, partly in bills and partly in cash. This was the first money they had ever possessed, and every farthing of it was dedicated to the cause of Christ. They had previously contributed two hundred and seventy pigs as their offering to the mission-fund."

258. Missionary Hens.—The practice of setting apart one or more hens, with a view to give the proceeds to the mission-fund, has been adopted by humble cottagers in various parts of Europe; but it may not be generally known that it has begun to prevail also in Africa and other distant lands. A missionary, recently arrived from England, attended a missionary-meeting at a place called Diep River, about ten miles from Cape Town, Cape of Good Hope, in the year 1859, and observing that the people were very poor, he ventured to suggest two or three ways in which they might furnish themselves with something to give to the cause of missions, in which they evidently felt a deep interest. Among other things, he mentioned that in his last circuit at home there was a poor woman whose means were very limited, and who, in order to make a trifle to give to the missionary collectors, set apart a hen for the purpose, which, proving to be a good layer, the proceeds of the eggs when sold amounted to several shillings a year. The idea of each family having a missionary hen was so novel and so amusing, that the people were greatly interested, and many at once resolved to adopt the plan. For several weeks afterwards the principal topic of conversation was the missionary hens, which had been solemnly tabooed, and were pointed out with great pleasure to their friends and visitors. At the next missionary-meeting at Diep River the proceeds of the missionary hens were a prominent item in the subscription list, and they have ever since been a considerable source of income to the Society, as will appear from the following statement based on the local report:—

	£	s.	d.
1860. Proceeds of missionary hens,	5	5	0
1861. ,, ,,	2	0	0
1862. ,, ,,	3	4	0
1863. ,, ,,	6	4	0
1864. ,, ,,	3	6	0
1865. ,, ,,	3	7	0
1866. ,, ,,	2	0	0
1867. ,, ,,	2	4	0
1868. ,, ,,	5	10	0
1869. ,, ,,	3	6	0
Total in ten years,	£36	10	0

259. Missionary Ducks.—The Rev. Mr Holroyd says:—

I was once at a missionary meeting in Scarborough, Yorkshire, when two poor boys of about ten years of age came on the platform, and one of them gave me a parcel containing 12s. 8d., which they had raised in the following manner:—One morning, when on their way to school, one of the boys, who had a hen, told his companion that she wanted to sit, but that he had neither eggs nor money to buy any. The other boy replied, "I have as much money as will purchase twelve duck-eggs; and if you will let your hen sit on them, we will join to buy food for the young ducks; and whatever they may be sold for, more than we have paid for food, shall be given to the missions." To this the boy agreed, and from the twelve eggs eleven young ducks were reared and sold, and the above sum was what they had gained by them, which they brought and gave in aid of the mission cause, according to the agreement.

260. Missionary Bees.

The idea of the "little busy bee" winging its way over hill and dale in quest of the sweetest flowers, and working day after day to provide the means of sending the gospel to the perishing heathen, is a very beautiful one, and we have known it literally carried out on a scale and with results worthy of a passing notice. The largest amount realised from this source, and which came under our personal observation, in any one year, was in 1850, when eight hives set apart for the mission cause produced honey which was sold for the sum of £8, 14s. If this plan were more generally adopted, many a humble cottager would have the satisfaction of taking a part in the noble enterprise, who, without the exercise of a little care and ingenuity, will necessarily remain without the means of doing so.

261. Missionary Fish-pots.

It may be necessary to explain, for the information of English readers, that a "fish-pot," in the West Indies and in some other countries, is a vessel made of wicker-work, or net stretched on hoops, which, when sunk to the bottom of the sea, acts as a trap, into which the fish are decoyed by a bait, and from which, when once in, it is next to impossible to escape. It has of late years become a common practice for fishermen connected with our mission-stations to set apart a fish-pot for the benefit of the mission-fund, and to present the proceeds of the fish caught in it at the next anniversary. At a meeting recently held at Morley, in Jamaica, a black man regretted that his missionary "fish-pot" had only made four shillings last year, and was ashamed to present so small a sum. "However," said he, "I will try to do better next year, if spared."

262. Missionary Cats.

The idea of "missionary cats" may excite a smile. But Madam Pussy is an important personage in the West Indies, and in some other countries where rats and mice are so troublesome and destructive, in the boiling-house, and among the sugar-canes and coffee-plants. We knew an instance in which a native Church-member set apart the proceeds of his cat, which he called "Molly," to the mission-fund. "Molly" was a prolific pussy, and frequently had a number of kittens, each of which was sold for a shilling or eighteen-pence, and the money sacredly devoted to the cause of God. Many were amused at the missionary-meeting to hear the name of "Molly" read out in the list, with the number of shillings she had brought to the treasury during the year, and a few resolved to adopt the same, or some similar plan, to raise a little to contribute to so good a cause.

263. Missionary Cocoa-nut Trees.

— At a missionary-meeting held a short time ago in Jamaica, a paper was sent up to the platform by a negro woman, with a request that it might be read to the audience, with a view to show how the writer contrived to have something to give to the cause of missions. It was headed, "*History of a Cocoa-nut Tree*," and the tenor of it was as follows:—"In 1851 I attended a missionary-meeting. Among other things, one of the speakers told us that one reason why people complained that they had no money to give when they were asked to subscribe to the Missionary Society, was because they made no provision beforehand, and that if they would only do something—for example, plant a tree, and set it apart for missions—they would never have cause to complain. When I went home, I planted five cocoa-nut trees, one of which I set apart for the cause, and had it marked '*Mission Tree*,' so that in time to come any one might know that the tree was separated from the others. The mission tree grew faster than the other trees; so much so, that if you saw it now, you would think it had been planted long before the rest. In 1856 it began to bear. It is now the most fruitful tree of all, and every year I get twelve shillings for the cocoa-nuts, which I give to the cause; and now I have no trouble, when the time comes round, to find money for my contribution to the Missionary Society." The reading of this document, and the announcement of the contribution by which it was accompanied, were received with applause, and the good woman found many imitators in her industry and foresight to provide something to present to the Lord at the Missionary Anniversary.

264. Missionary Cherry-Trees.

—At the annual missionary-meeting held in City Road Chapel, London, on the 1st of May 1820, the Rev. John Angell James, of Birmingham, related the following interesting anecdote:—" I knew a good man in Berkshire who had a cherry orchard. He bethought himself what he could do for the mission cause, and at length selected two cherry-trees, the fruit of which he would devote most sacredly to the cause of missions. Nor did it appear that those missionary cherry-trees suffered more from blight than any others. When his friends occasionally visited him, he allowed them the full range of his orchard. 'Of every tree of the garden you may freely eat,' said he; 'but of these two trees you shall not eat—they belong to God.' The fruit was carefully kept separate, was brought to market, and the proceeds remitted to the Missionary Society. No part of the price was kept back, and last year nearly thirty shillings, the proceeds of these two trees, was sacredly appropriated to the cause of missions." "Every man," continued Mr James, "has not his cherry orchard, but every man may render unto God a tithe-offering of the little he possesses for the spread of the gospel throughout the world."

265. Various Ways and Means.

—In looking over the report of the Wesleyan Missionary Society for one year, we find among the contributions the following suggestive items:—Eight "missionary hens" had produced the sum of £9, 12s. 8d. Two "missionary pigs" were sold for £2, 1s. Three "missionary geese" brought £3, 8s. Ten "missionary sheep" brought to the treasury the sum of £17, 6s. Fourteen "missionary lambs" yielded £22. Credit is given for a "piece of orchard ground "to the amount of £3, 19s. 3d.; whilst "first-fruits" are put down at £6, 12s. 6d. Nor should the sale of "missionary flowers" at Dover and Taunton be overlooked, as in each case £1 was realised for the Society. Five "teetotalers" forwarded the sum of £7, 2s. Six "boarding-schools" contributed £55, 10s. 2d. to the mission-fund; whilst the "missionary baskets" and "bazaars," supplied chiefly by the nimble fingers of Christian ladies, realised the handsome sum of £172, 8s. 2d. A returned missionary had contributed more than £50 as "profits on books" which he had published in the interests of the Society. At Dover £1, 1s. was given by a gentleman "in grateful remembrance of kindness shown to his sailor-boy by the missionaries in a foreign land." In the Portsmouth Circuit "birth-day offerings" amounted to £1, 12s. 6d. In Jersey a "missionary jug" is forwarded containing £2, 3s. 4d. At Plymouth a remarkable combination occurs. One is a contribution of a "teapot" containing £4, and the other that of a "powder-barrel," with the sum of £13, 0s. 3d. From Gwennap we have an exemplification of Christian principle in a "thank-offering" from "workmen in a powder-mill," for the preservation of life and property, £4, 13s. From Teignmouth we have an illustration of the voluntary taxing principle, in a sum of £8, 17s. 7d., as a "toll on cattle killed" by a party during the year; no mean number, amounting as it does to £2, 2s. 11d. From the South Circuit some good friend contributed "one pound of butter weekly," the amount realised during the year being £2, 3s. 4d. In the Thirsk list there is the "sale of matches by two lads." And there is scarcely any end of "marriage-offerings," "thank-offerings," &c., to the mission-fund.

Verily, "where there is a will there is a way."

266. Seasonable Legacy.—A touching incident is related in connection with the financial affairs of the American Board of Foreign Missions, which may well encourage the hearts of anxious friends of the enterprise. The foreign secretary of this excellent institution left his office one Monday afternoon with a weary step, and a wearier look, after spending weeks in plodding through the various estimates sent in by the different missions in Turkey, India, China, Japan, Micronesia, &c., of the probable expenses of 1874. In all these missions *success* called for enlargement; yet the state of the funds rendered retrenchment needful. How could he counsel retrenchment? where could he begin to cut down the estimates? Again and again he had been over them; he could not find *one* case in which he had the heart to suggest it. His spirit and his mind were both burdened. He walked slowly along; he was to dine with a fellow-labourer. Suddenly he meets a friend, who accosts him with, "You have heard, I suppose, of the legacy left you by a member of my church?" "No! what?" with a half-hopeless smile of inquiry. "Why, twenty thousand dollars" (£4000). How little the quiet, modest man who had left this as his last contribution to the funds of the Mission Board knew how appropriately it would come in, or what a timely relief it was to afford to an overburdened spirit! He who sees the end from the beginning knows how and when to help His feeble children in their endeavours to carry on His work in the world. Why *do* we ever doubt?

267. A Child's Self-denial for the Mission Cause.—The Swedish

Missionary Society was formed in Stockholm in the month of January 1825, when many persons of slender means enrolled themselves among its supporters, an annual subscription of the small sum of 3s. 4d. being the principal condition of membership in an auxiliary, which was ultimately instituted for their special accommodation. After a public meeting held in the Wesleyan chapel, a little girl, named Lina, about six years of age, thus addressed her parent, "Please, mother, do let me be a member of this little Society: we could not afford to join the big one, but this little one will just do for me." "You know not what you ask," replied the mother; "our support is so uncertain, that frequently I cannot tell where to-morrow's meal is to come from; and though I conscientiously and gratefully put into the plate at the missionary-meetings as much as possible, I dare not bind myself to pay even the small sum required for membership." "O mother!" responded Lina, "I can be a member without taking any money from you." "How so?" asked the interested parent. "You give me every morning to my coffee a rusk; now I can manage to do without this, and the price of it, I suppose, will be enough to make me a member of this little Missionary Society. Do, mother, let me be a member." "My darling child," said the mother, with a full heart and streaming eyes, "if you are willing to give up your rusk for the sake of Christ, I shall gladly follow your example, and we shall both be members." They went up to the secretary at the next meeting, entered their names, and the Rev. George Scott, who relates the interesting incident, assures us, that so long as he continued a missionary in Sweden, this devoted mother and daughter continued to contribute towards the support of the mission cause. This noble instance of self-denial and disinterestedness for the propagation of the gospel in heathen lands may well cause those to blush for shame who indulge in useless luxuries, whilst they neglect the claims of genuine charity and Christian benevolence.

268. A Good Reason for Giving.—A pious negro in the West Indies came, on one occasion, to a missionary, to present a contribution to the funds of the Society. The missionary thought the negro offered a larger sum than was consistent with his circumstances, and took occasion to tell him so, when the poor but liberal man insisted on giving it, at the same time saying, "Massa, the work of the Lord *must* be done, and I shall soon be dead."

If all professing Christians looked at personal work for God in the light of eternity, they would probably act with greater promptitude, zeal, and earnestness than they are in the habit of doing.

269. Paying Rent to the Lord.—Writing on the 21st of January 1844, the Rev. Samuel Allen says:— "An aged female in the Blackburn Circuit being very ill, promised that if the Lord would spare her, she would give £20 to the Wesleyan Missionary Society. Her health was restored, and she redeemed the pledge by subscribing £5 annually for four successive years." As she was not in affluent circumstances, the writer, when conversing with her some weeks ago, said, "I suppose we must lose your subscription now." Her reply was worthy of the cause which she had espoused. She observed, "The Lord has given me a house to live in; and while He thus favours me, I am resolved to *pay Him the rent*, by giving £5 a year to our missions."

270. By Little and Little.—There is great advantage in missionary collectors calling upon their subscribers, by mutual arrangement, at short intervals and at stated periods, say *weekly* or *monthly*. This was strikingly exemplified in the case of a collector who called upon a person in moderate circumstances, and asked for a contribution. This person being inexperienced in such matters, inquired what amount was expected. The collector said some persons gave a guinea a year. "Oh!" said the person, "I cannot afford to give that, but I will give you a shilling a week."

271. My First Penny.—Early one morning a little boy, about five years old, on awaking from sleep, looked up, and on seeing his father, said, "Papa, I am going to put my penny in the missionary-box." Papa said to his little son, "Who told you to put your penny in the missionary-box?" "Nobody but myself," was the ready reply of the juvenile subscriber to the mission-fund. But what penny was this that he called his *own* penny? I will tell you. It was the *first penny* that this little boy ever gained by his industry. But you would like to know what he worked at to get a penny for his wages? Well, here is a copy of a bill given him by his teacher—"Master E. has *merited* the sum of one penny. Payment on demand." He had worked hard at his lessons, and so kept at the top of his class for a certain time, for which he obtained a penny; and this penny he gave to God, to help to make Him known to the poor heathens, who know Him not, and are dying in their sins. It was but a small sum; but, like the widow's two mites, it was ALL he had in the world that he could call his *own*, and he gave it of his own free will, and with evident pleasure, and you know "the Lord loveth a cheerful giver." You may be sure that his papa and mamma were delighted with what their little boy did. And so will every thoughtful little boy make his parents' hearts glad who is disposed to give his pence to the cause of Christ, instead of spending them in sin and folly.

272. That's my Penny.—An interesting and intelligent lad, who had nothing to give at a country missionary-meeting to which he was going, except a solitary penny, was somewhat disconcerted, the more so because he was much teased by his sister on account of the smallness of his contribution. She repeatedly remarked, "What is a penny? What good can it do? And besides, it will never be noticed among all the money that will be given by others." The boy was encouraged, however, by his pious mother, who advised him not to mind the taunts of his sister, who happened to have a larger sum to give, but to take his penny and give it from a pure motive; and if it were not noticed by man, it would be known to God, who was well pleased with the poor widow's mites. Away they went to the meeting at the appointed time. All were interested with the addresses, and the little fellow frequently wished he had more to give. At length the collection was made, and the boy with a heavy heart dropped in his penny. According to custom, the money was counted in the vestry, that the amount might be announced to the meeting. By and by the secretary stepped forward on the platform, and stated that he had pleasure in announcing to the meeting that the collection amounted to the sum of "six pounds, five shillings, and A PENNY." When the little boy heard mention made of *a penny*, he was so moved that he could scarcely restrain himself, and whispered, somewhat loudly, to his sister, "Hear that, *that's my penny;* you said it was so little it would never be noticed, and the gentleman has told the whole congregation." His mother said "Hush!" and the matter dropped; but the little boy had the better of his sister for once, and he was disposed ever afterwards to triumph on account of the public notice that was taken of his *penny* contribution.

273. Take care of Pence.—The following is a pleasing instance of the good resulting from attention to this adage. Some years since there was collected in a certain small village in Lincolnshire about twenty-five shillings a year, in small sums, previous to the missionary-meeting; but this sum, in process of time, had gradually dwindled down to 8s. 6d. Last year a few friends of the cause resolved to divide the village into districts, with a person appointed to each, to canvass every house for small subscriptions of a penny or half-penny per month, which are now regularly received without any difficulty. These small contributions will this year amount in the aggregate to about £2, 10s., showing an increase of nearly 600 per cent. Is not the neglect of the pence of the poor in many instances a cause of the diminution of the interest in the cause of Christian missions?

274. Farthing Movement.—In some places where the people are generally poor, and with a view to "gather up the fragments, that nothing may be lost," a plan has been adopted for collecting the smallest of the Queen's coins in aid of the mission cause, and a "farthing movement" has been inaugurated which promises, like every-thing good, to be a success. As an illustration, we give the following fact from the *Primitive Methodist Missionary Magazine*:—"The annual missionary or 'farthing meeting' was recently held in the schoolroom at Newport, Isle of Wight. The bags and boxes brought in by the twenty-three collectors, representing fifteen families, contained 8624 farthings, being an increase on last year of 1624. Other amounts brought up the total to £10, 14s. 4d., being an increase of £1, 16s. 8d. for the year. "Whilst the wealthy give of their abundance princely contributions to help to spread the gospel throughout the world, let the Lord's poor, and the little children, give and collect for the mission-fund as best they can, and the glorious enterprise will triumph. The smallest service done for Christ, with a single eye to His glory and a pure motive, will have the approbation and smile of Him who will "not despise the day of small things."

275. The Importance of Littles. —The following simple but beautiful lines are well calculated to show the importance of *littles* in various aspects, and especially in reference to the glorious missionary enterprise:—

" Though trifling in your eyes
 The little mites appear;
Yet to my charming words
 A moment lend your ear.

" Look on the mighty deep,
 And contemplate the sea:
If 'twere not for the DROPS,
 Where would its *vastness* be?

" Behold the emerald field,
 Where sheep and oxen feed:
If 'twere not for the BLADES,
 Say, where would be the *mead?*

" The oak its shelter gives,
 When flocks from tempests flee:
But if the LEAVES were gone,
 Where would the *shelter* be?

"The smooth extended strand,
   That checks the roaring deep:
Say, if the GRAINS were gone,
   Where would the billows sweep?

"Were LITTLE WORDS despised,
   How would *a book* appear?
How could the preacher speak,
   Or how his hearers hear?

"Despise not then THE PENCE,
   They help to make the pound;
And each may help to SPREAD ABROAD
   The GOSPEL'S JOYFUL SOUND."

276. Entire Self-consecration.

—The genius of Christianity being so thoroughly missionary in its character, the holy religion which we profess in this highly-favoured land demands of its adherents entire consecration of body, soul, talents, property, time, influence, and all they have and are for the promotion of the honour and glory of God, and the salvation of our perishing fellow-men. "We are not our own, we are bought with a price;" and it is our duty as it is our privilege to "glorify in our bodies and in our spirits which are His." Let us then address ourselves afresh to the great and noble work which is before us, of doing our part, according to our circumstances and ability, towards the subjugation of the world to Christ. Let every man, woman, and child who professes to be a disciple of Jesus "come up to the help of the Lord, to the help of the Lord against the mighty." There is a part for every one to act in this glorious enterprise, and all may help by their prayers, their sympathy, or their contributions. Or, to use another figure frequently employed in Scripture, let us listen to the voice of the Master, and promptly do His bidding, when He says, "Go work to-day in my vineyard;" and verily, our labour will "not be in vain in the Lord."

"Disciples of Jesus, why stand ye here idle?
   Go work in His vineyard, He calls you to-day;
The night is approaching, when no man can labour;
   Our Master commands, and shall we delay?

"Our field is the world, our work is before us,
   To each is appointed a message to bear;
At home or abroad, in the cottage or palace,
   Wherever directed, our mission is there.

"O'er islands that sleep in the wave-crested ocean,
   We'll scatter the truth, and its fruit it will bear;
O'er ice-covered regions, and rock-girded mountains,
   The Lord will protect us, His children are there.

"Instead of the thorn shall the myrtle be planted;
   The desert shall blossom and bloom as the rose;
The palm-trees rejoicing shall spread forth their branches,
   The lamb and the lion together repose."

X. MISCELLANEOUS INCIDENTS.

277. Value of Missionary Intelligence.—The value and importance of information in matters relating to art, science, and general literature, are universally acknowledged; and it is no less necessary on questions of a moral, social, and religious character. With reference to the missionary enterprise, if we would maintain our interest in it, understand its claims, and prosecute it with vigour, we must make ourselves acquainted with its history, working, and results in all their departments. After considerable experience and observation, both at home and abroad, we feel confident that, as professing Christians in general, and the rising generation in particular, become more thoroughly acquainted with the character of different countries, the manners, habits, and superstitions of the natives, and the wonderful power of the gospel in raising them to the position of men and brethren, the more active will they be in their efforts to provide the means for sending the good news of salvation to the ends of the earth.

We would therefore earnestly recommend to our youthful readers the careful perusal of missionary narratives, and other books relating to the geography and history of the different countries of the globe, and to the social and moral condition of the different tribes of men. There are works of this description which, for real interest and attractiveness, surpass any books of romance or fiction that were ever written. And they possess properties to which such publications can lay no claim, insomuch as they set before their readers matters of sober truth, relating to the glory of God, the welfare of man, and the promotion of the Redeemer's cause and kingdom upon earth. Verily, nothing can have a stronger claim upon our attention than matters of such weighty importance.

278. Financial Progress.—In 1808, thirty-nine years after the first missionaries were sent out by the Wesleyan Conference, and seven years before the formal organisation of the Missionary Society, Dr Coke, as general superintendent, published a report setting forth the financial state of the missions. From this, it appears that the receipts for the previous year had amounted to the "great sum" of £4761, 13s. 4½d. But it was also stated that "the disbursements had far exceeded the income, and that there was a balance due the treasurer of £4, 3s. 1d." The report goes on to say that they were not disheartened on account of their present circumstances, and that they appealed confidently to their friends to enable them to meet their expenditure and to clear off the debt!

How different is the condition of the Wesleyan Missionary Society now! and what wonderful progress has been made in its financial resources in the course of sixty-five years! The report for 1873 states the income of last year amounted to £156,910, 12s. 5d., and that a debt of several thousand pounds had been entirely liquidated. But large as the annual income of the Society may appear, it is scarcely sufficient to enable the Committee to maintain existing missions in a state of efficiency, and to enter upon the new spheres of labour that are opening up and presenting themselves to view in every direction. They also appeal with confidence to the friends of the enterprise for increased contributions, to enable them to support and extend the work in a manner worthy of its claims.

279. Female Agency.—Christian missions are largely indebted to the zealous agency of pious, devoted females; not only as collectors at home, to raise the means to send the gospel to dark, benighted heathen nations, but also as actual labourers in the field, in departments of the work for which they are specially adapted. By no society is this kind of agency more highly appreciated or more carefully utilised than the American Board of Foreign Missions. It is stated in a recent report, that "with a single exception, one or more unmarried ladies, in most cases two, are to be found at each mission-station of the Board throughout the Turkish Empire. They constitute an integral part of the mission force; and the value of their work, the necessity of their co-operation in order to the true success of the missionary enterprise in reaching the homes of the people, is now conceded on every hand. What to the more conservative in the mission-field as well as at home was regarded as an experiment, has been proved a success. Homes that the customs of society forbid men to approach are open to the visits of missionary ladies, and crowded often with eager listeners. The possible elevation of woman is no longer a question even in the minds of the Turks, to say nothing of the efforts now in progress to secure it everywhere among the Armenians. Common schools follow quickly upon the visits of the missionary, even in the most secluded villages; and high schools for girls in the great centres, and normal schools for the education of teachers, are already begun or in contemplation. As this new movement for the education of women was mainly begun by the example and efforts of missionary ladies, married as well as single; so it now falls naturally very largely under their guidance and supervision, and they are in constant communication with their sisters at home, through the 'Woman's Board,' organised for their assistance. Who can estimate the influence in the establishment of Christian homes throughout this great empire of thirty devoted Christian women from the homes of our own favoured land?"

280. Affection and Kindness of Africans.—Notwithstanding the abject condition to which the African race has been sunk by long years of bondage and oppression, we have met with many touching instances of genuine affection and kindness among the negroes, both male and female, with whom we have come in contact. Indeed, those who are brought under the influence of religion are proverbial for their attachment to their ministers and teachers.

A striking illustration of this occurred to the Rev. Mr Chapman, the Wesleyan missionary at Kumasi, the capital of Ashanti, in Western Africa. His health had entirely failed, and he was consequently obliged to leave for the coast in a state of great weakness and prostration. Describing his journey, the missionary says:—"In leaving Kumasi, I found myself entirely at the mercy of the Africans. I was two hundred miles from the nearest European, without a horse to ride upon; and having to make my way through a dense forest, where the roads were, in many places, not more than eight or ten inches in width; now entangled in brushwood, then in deep gulleys; again in a more open space, exposed to the vertical rays of the sun, and with hardly the hope of reaching the coast alive.

"I commenced my journey with eight hammock-men; these were to take me down to Cape Coast Castle. The difficulty of carrying a man in these hot climates, where only two bearers can be employed at the same time, is very great. I had, therefore, on all my former journeys, walked as much as possible. On this occasion I rode out of Kumasi; but, upon reaching the forest, in consideration of the distance to be performed, and the necessary fatigue the men must undergo, I determined to try my strength in walking, and getting down from my travelling-chair, commenced my journey on foot.

"I walked with difficulty to myself for a few yards, and was beginning to wonder how we should reach the coast if I could not succeed better, when one of the men came up to me, requesting me not to walk, saying they could carry me very well. I thanked him for his kindness, but told him I would walk a little longer. 'No, master,' he said, 'you must not walk, you are not strong to-day; we have watched you, and you go from side to side, and your knees are not strong, and you do not walk straight as you did.' I said, 'Well, never mind that; you have a long journey before you, and will have quite enough to do before we reach the coast; I must walk.' 'No, master,' he said again, 'you must not walk, we will carry you.' I again thanked him, and was proceeding, when another of the men planted himself before me, and said, 'Master, you must not walk to-day; if you do, you will die on the path, and then what shall we do?' Then he drew himself up to his full height, and stretching out his arms as far as possible, to indicate his strength and vigour, he said, with a look of kindness which expressed more than words, 'Master, we are plenty strong to-day, plenty strong; we can carry you well, get up at once and ride.' To please them I did so, thankful for the relief, but fearing that they would soon become weary. But I was mistaken; for four days they carried me from morning till sunset, scolding if I attempted to tax my strength by walking, and saying they had plenty of strength to carry me. We journeyed thus till we reached the little town of Prasu, where we rested a couple of days, and then set out again. During the whole of the distance they watched me as though each was personally responsible for my safety, each one seeming to vie with his fellow in acts of kindness and care. When we reached Cape Coast Castle, which we did at the end of the tenth day, I could not but feel that for the preservation of my life I was, under God, indebted to the voluntary kindness of these men, two or three of whom had, but a short time before, embraced the Christian religion."

281. **An Indian's Idea of Christ.**—While the Rev. Mr Kirkland was

a missionary to the Oneidas, being unwell, he was unable to preach on the afternoon of a certain Sabbath, and told good Peter, one of the head men of the Oneidas, that he must address the congregation in his stead. Peter modestly and reluctantly consented. After a few words of introduction, he began a discourse on the character of our Saviour. "What, my brethren," said he, "are the views which you form of the character of Jesus? You will answer, perhaps, that He was a man of singular benevolence. You will tell me that He proved this to be His character by the nature of the miracles which He wrought. All these, you will say, were kind in the extreme. He created bread to feed thousands who were ready to perish. He raised to life the son of a poor woman who was a widow, and to whom his labours were necessary for her support in old age. Are these then your only views of Christ? I tell you they are lame and defective. When Jesus came into our world, He threw His blanket around Him, but *the God was within*." And so the Indian preacher proceeded to descant, with great power and pathos, on the true and proper divinity of Jesus Christ, the Son of God and the Saviour of men, as Mr Kirkland himself assured President Dwight some time afterwards.

282. The Pleasing Surprise.—It is a wonderful thing to a Kaffir that a book should talk, or that one person should express his meaning to another by written signs. "Your child can read," said a missionary one day to a Kaffir who had sent his son to the mission-school. "No," said he; "I cannot believe that. You white people may be able to read, you are so clever; but you cannot teach us to read; it is impossible." "Come here," said the missionary to the child. The boy stepped forward. "Let your father hear you read this," continued the missionary. He read; the father listened; he was astonished, and, clasping his child to his breast, he wept over him for joy.

283. The Faithful Negro.—In the records of the early African coast-trade, we find a remarkable instance of the honourable principles and fidelity of a negro, which has seldom been surpassed by any one, even in civilised countries. A New England sloop, trading to Guinea in 1759, left there the second mate, William Murray, sick on shore. Murray was at the house of a black man named Cudjoe, with whom he had contracted an acquaintance. He recovered, and continued with his black friend till some opportunity should offer for his return home. In the meantime a Dutch ship came into the roads, and some of the blacks going on board her were treacherously seized and carried off as slaves. The relations and friends, transported with sudden rage, ran to the house of Cudjoe, to take revenge by killing Murray. Cudjoe stopped them at the door, and demanded what they wanted. "The white men," said they, "have carried away our brothers and sons, and we will kill all white men. Give us the white man you have in your house, for we will kill him." "Nay," said Cudjoe, "the white men that carried away your relations are bad men, kill them when you can take them; but this white man is a good man, and you must not kill him." "But he is a white man," they cried, "and the white men are all bad men, and we will kill them all." "Nay," said he, "you must not kill a man that has done no harm, only for being white. This man is my friend, my house is his fort, I am his soldier, and I must fight for him! You must kill me before you kill him. What good man will ever come again under my roof, if I let my floor be stained with a good man's blood?"

The negroes, seeing Cudjoe's resolution, and being convinced by his discourse that they were wrong, went away ashamed. In a few days Murray ventured abroad with his friend, when several of the natives took him by the hand, and said they were glad they had not killed him; for he was a good (meaning innocent) man, and their god would have been very angry, and would have spoiled their fishing!

284. The African Shepherd-Boy.

—Far away in the interior of Africa there lived a little shepherd-boy whose history is one of pleasing interest. While tending the sheep among the hills, he met another shepherd-boy who had learned to read at a mission-school, and who had a Testament of his own. This boy read some of it to his little friend, and that which interested him most was the sweet story of the Babe of Bethlehem. How much astonished was the other boy to see a book, and to hear his companion read out of it! He listened with great attention, and believed every word he heard, although he could not, as yet, comprehend its meaning. He longed to *see* the Babe of Bethlehem—that Babe that was wrapped in swaddling-clothes, and laid in a manger.

"Can I see Him?" eagerly inquired the Bechuana shepherd-boy of his more intelligent young friend; "tell me where He is." "He is at the mission-station," replied the young reader. "Did you ever see Him?" "No, I never saw Him; but I know He is there, for the people talk to Him, and sing to Him. I have heard them." The astonished child made up his mind to go to the station to see this Babe with his own eyes. It was a long journey; but he joined a party that was going to the "school place," as they called the station. He walked part of the way, and was glad, when an opportunity offered, to get a ride in a farmer's waggon drawn by oxen, over hill and valley, through rough forest-paths and through rushing streams.

At length the party arrived at the mission-station, on a Saturday evening, and the little shepherd-boy was kindly received by a converted Bechuana woman. He partook of supper, and slept in her hut. Next morning he heard the chapel bell. He knew not why it sounded, but he followed his kind hostess to the chapel. He listened with delight to the sweet singing; he looked earnestly at the missionary when he opened the Bible and began to read. And what was the chapter that was read that morning? It was the second of Luke, the very chapter that tells about the Babe in Bethlehem. And now the shepherd-boy looked round, hoping to see the glorious Babe. At length he saw a little child such as he had never seen before. It was of fair complexion, with blue eyes and light hair. "It is the Babe of Bethlehem," thought the shepherd-boy; "the Babe I longed to see I have found at last."

When the service was over, the delighted boy told his Christian friend that he had seen the Babe of Bethlehem. At first she could not understand what he meant, but she soon found out his mistake. The blue-eyed babe was the missionary's own child. But then the good woman told him *who* the Babe of Bethlehem really was, *what* He did, and *where* He is. She told him of His love in dying upon the cross, and of His glory at His Father's right hand. The boy believed her words, and he soon loved Jesus, though he could not see Him. He did not wish to leave the mission-station; and having obtained permission to live there, he attended the school, learned to read his Bible, grew up to be a Christian man, and ever afterwards delighted to tell his fellow-countrymen of the love of Him who was once a Babe in Bethlehem.

235. His Promise cannot Fail.
—For several years after most of the West India Islands were open to receive the gospel, St Eustatius, which belonged to the Dutch, continued closed against the establishment of a permanent mission, by reason of the opposition of the authorities to the religious instruction of the slaves. A few of the negroes and free persons of colour had, however, been brought to a saving knowledge of the truth by the occasional visits of the missionaries, and by their intercourse with the negro converts from the neighbouring islands. These were incessant in their prayers that by the interposition of Divine Providence the way might be opened for the residence of missionaries among them. Writing to Dr Coke from St Kitts, on the 17th of April 1794, the Rev. Mr Harper says:—"The hope you express of St Eustatius being opened for the gospel affords me much satisfaction. The seed sown in that island has not perished. There are almost forty who still meet in class, and some of them appear to be much in earnest. They go some distance into the country, that they may have an opportunity of meeting together in quietness; and as often as their circumstances will permit, they visit us in St Kitts. Twelve or fourteen of them are now here. I was this morning speaking with one of them, who said, 'In our prayers God assures us that His gospel will be preached among us. We have prayed for it. He promises to grant us what we pray for, and His promise cannot fail.'"

Truly the promise of God did not fail. A missionary was soon afterwards permitted to commence his labours in St Eustatius, and it has been a prosperous station for more than half a century. During this period, it is believed that thousands of precious souls have been won for Christ, and landed safely in heaven through its instrumentality; and there are now upwards of three hundred native converts united in Church fellowship.

286. Ludicrous Mistake.
—The natives of Africa, in common with those of other heathen countries, are remarkably fond of iron when they once become acquainted with its value, and they will work up old nails, and other articles of that metal, into spears, knives, and ornaments of various kinds, with considerable skill. They are generally ignorant, however, as to the difference between cast iron and that which is malleable. A ludicrous illustration of this occurred on one occasion, which confirms the truth of the proverb that "honesty is the best policy." Two men had succeeded in stealing from the missionary an iron cooking-pot. Having just taken it from the fire, it was rather too warm for handing conveniently over a fence, and the savage attempting to do so, it fell on a stone, and was cracked. "It is iron," said they, and off they went with their booty, resolving to make the best of it; that is, if it would not do for cooking, they would transform it into knives and spears. After some time had elapsed, and the hue and cry about the missing pot had nearly died away, it was brought forth to a native smith, who had laid

in a stock of charcoal for the occasion. The pot was farther broken, to make it more convenient to lay hold of with the tongs, which are generally made of the bark of a tree. The native Vulcan, unacquainted with the brittle nature of cast iron, having with his small bellows of goat skins produced a good heat, drew a piece from the fire. To his utter amazement it flew into shivers at the first stroke of his little hammer. Another and another piece was brought under the action of the fire, and then under the hammer, with no better success. Both the thief and the smith gazed with eyes and mouth dilated on the fragments of iron scattered round the stone anvil, declaring their belief that the pot had been bewitched, and concluded that iron cooking-pot stealing was a bad speculation.

287. Curious Incident.—Adverting to his travels in the interior of Africa, the Rev. R. Moffat relates the following curious incident:—" Reclining on a rock one day, waiting till my shirt, which I had washed, was dry, I noticed a crow rise from the earth, carrying something dangling in its talons. On directing my companions to the sight, they said, ' It is only a crow with a tortoise; you will see it fall presently;' and down it fell. The crow descended, and up went the tortoise again to a still greater height, from which it dropped, and the crow instantly followed. I hastened with one of the men to the spot, and scared away the crow from the mangled tortoise, on which it was enjoying a feast. On looking around on the flat rock, there were many wrecks of former years; and on my remarking I did not think the crow was so cunning, my companion replied, ' The kites do the same thing,' which I have since frequently observed."

288. Witty Retort.—When China became open to the preaching of the gospel and the circulation of the Scriptures, the friends and supporters of the British and Foreign Bible Society, of whom the Rev. John Angel James of Birmingham was one of the most active, devised a plan for sending one million copies of the New Testament into the country. A special fund was accordingly raised for this purpose, and the scheme was effectually worked out, the missionaries exerting themselves nobly to circulate the precious boon, which was no doubt the means of shedding spiritual light on many a gloomy district. But this act of Christian benevolence did not pass unchallenged by the Romish priesthood, Cardinal Wiseman declaring, in one of his sermons, that " no apprehension need be felt about the circulation of this million of Testaments, as the Chinese bootmakers and shoemakers were using them up as waste paper in their respective manufactures." When Dr Beaumont heard of this strange utterance, he wittily remarked, " Then are the feet of the people shod with the preparation of the gospel of peace!"

289. Exposed by an Elephant.—The Rev. Mr Pettit in his recent work on the Tinnevelly Mission, gives a very remarkable and well-authenticated anecdote of the sagacity of an elephant, which is both amusing and instructive. While the large new chapel at Nagercoil was in course of erection, the missionaries obtained the loan of a trained elephant for the purpose of drawing the timber used in the building. The late Mrs Mault, who took a deep interest in the undertaking, kindly saw the animal regularly fed, lest the food should be stolen by the attendant. One day the allowance of rice seemed very deficient in quantity, and the animal gave unmistakable indications of an unsatisfied appetite. The good lady, having her suspicions, spoke out, and earnestly expostulated on the subject with the keeper. Raising his hands to heaven, the man loudly, and with great apparent earnestness and sincerity, repudiated the idea of his having taken any of the rice from the elephant. "Do you think, madam, that I would be capable of doing such a thing? No, never! no more than I would deprive my own children of their daily food!" Whilst the keeper was thus speaking and gesticulating to confirm his declaration of innocence, the sagacious elephant slily extended his trunk, unfastened the man's waist-cloth, thereby spilling out the missing rice, which the pilferer had secreted in his bosom. Thus was the dishonesty of the cunning Hindu servant exposed, and himself covered with shame and confusion, by the dumb but intelligent creature he was employed to attend.

290. Petty Annoyances.—The petty annoyances and discomforts to which missionaries are exposed in some countries are numerous and distressing. A few instances may be given as illustrations. The Rev. R. Moffat says:—"My situation was not very well suited for study among a noisy rabble and a constant influx of beggars. Writing was a work of great difficulty, owing to the flies crowding into the inkhorn, or clustering round the point of the pen, and pursuing it on the paper, drinking the ink as fast as it flowed. The night brought little relief; for as soon as the candle was lighted, innumerable insects swarmed around so as to put it out. When I had occasion to hunt, in order to supply the wants of myself and people, a troop of men would follow; and as soon as a rhinoceros or any other animal was shot, a fire was made, and some would be roasting, while the others would be cutting and tearing away at the ponderous carcase, which is soon dissected. During these operations they would exhibit all the gestures of heathenish joy, making an uproar as if a town were on fire."

At an early period of the Bechuana Mission the Rev. Mr Hamilton was often placed in peculiarly trying circumstances. In addition to great manual labour in digging a long watercourse, preparing ground, and building, he had been compelled, from his scanty allowance, to toil with his own hands, to preserve himself and his family from beggary, while exposed to heavy taxes to keep nobles in good humour, enduring unremitting liberties, taken by those who seemed to think they had a lawful right to obtain by any and all means what they could lay hands upon of the missionary's property. One day, having no mills at that time to grind corn, he sat down, according to ancient custom, and with two hand-stones, as they were called, the upper being turned with a handle fixed in the top, he laboured and perspired for several hours, in order to obtain as much meal as would make a loaf sufficient to serve him for about eight days. Having kneaded and baked his gigantic loaf, such a one as had not graced his shelf for many a month, he went to chapel, and returned to his hut in the evening with a keen appetite, promising himself a treat of his coarse home-made bread, when, alas! on opening the door of his hut, and very naturally casting his eye to the shelf, he perceived the loaf was gone. Some one had forced open the only little window, which appeared too small for a human being to enter, but had served as a place of egress for thief and loaf too; and thus vanished all his hopes of bread for supper, and many succeeding meals.

291. Instant in Season and out of Season.—
An interesting and amusing picture of missionary life in the interior of Africa is given by the Rev. R. Moffat, when describing a visit which he paid to Moshesh, in the Bechuana country, South Africa. "On reaching the place," he says, "after having travelled the whole day over a rough and bushy country, and walked much, I was fit only to throw myself down to sleep. The moment I entered the village the hue and cry was raised, and old and young, mother and children, came running together as if it were to see some great prodigy. I received an affectionate welcome, and many a squeeze, while about five hundred human beings were thrusting themselves forward, all exerting themselves to the utmost of their power to get a shake of the hand. Some, who scarcely touched it, trembled as if it had been the paw of a lion. It was nearly midnight before they would disperse; but their departure was a great relief to a wearied man; for their exclamations of surprise, and their bawling out to one another in two languages, were anything but melodious.

"The next morning was the Sabbath. On awaking from a short sleep, and emerging from my canopy, before my eyes were thoroughly open, I was astonished to find a congregation waiting before the waggon. At the same moment some individuals started off to different parts of the village to announce my arrival. All hastened to the spot. I confess I was more inclined to take a cup of coffee than to preach a sermon, for I still felt the fatigues of the preceding day. I took my Testament and hymn-book, however, and with such singing as I had, gave out a hymn, read a chapter, and prayed; then taking the text, 'God so loved the world,' &c., discoursed to them for about an hour. Great order and profound interest were maintained. A few strangers drew near with their spears and shields, who, on being beckoned to, instantly laid them down. Two milkmaids, who had tied their cows to posts, stood the whole time with their milking-vessels in their hands, as if afraid of losing a single sentence. The earnest attention manifested exceeded anything I had ever before witnessed, and the countenances of some indicated strong excitement.

"After the service, I walked to a neighbouring pool in the bed of the river, to refresh myself with a wash, hoping on my return to get something like a breakfast, but found that by some mistake the kettle was not boiling. The people were again assembled, and again requested me to preach. On begging half an hour for refreshment, the chief's wife hobbled off to her house, and immediately returned with a large wooden vessel full of sour milk, saying, with a smile on her countenance, 'There, drink away, drink much, and you will be able to speak long.' Having cheerfully accepted this hasty African breakfast, I resumed my station, and preached a second time to, if possible, a still more attentive congregation. In the evening, after the cows were milked, a congregation for the third time stood before my waggon, to whom I again preached till a late hour, after which I was thankful to retire to rest."

292. Repeating the Sermon.—
After preaching with more than ordinary freedom and pleasure to a large congregation of Bechuanas, in South Africa, the Rev. R. Moffat

was much struck with the pains which the people took to treasure up what they had heard. Describing what he witnessed on the occasion close to his travelling-waggon, he says:—"When I had concluded, my hearers divided into companies, to talk the subject over; but others, more inquisitive, plied me with questions. While thus engaged, my attention was arrested by a simple looking young man at a short distance, rather oddly attired. He wore what was once a pair of trousers, with part of one leg still remaining. For a hat he had part of the skin of a zebra's head, with the ears attached, and something not less fantastical about his neck. I had noticed this grotesque figure before, but such sights are by no means uncommon in Africa, where the natives are not particular what they hang about their bodies for dress or ornament. The person referred to was holding forth with great animation to a number of people who were all attention. On approaching, I found, to my surprise, that he was preaching my sermon over again, with uncommon precision, and with great solemnity, imitating, as nearly as he could, the gesture of the original. A greater contrast could scarcely be conceived than the fantastic figure I have described and the solemnity of his language, his subject being eternity, while he evidently felt what he spoke. Not wishing to disturb him, I allowed him to finish his recital; and seeing him soon after, I told him he could do what I was sure I could not—that was, preach again the same sermon verbatim. He did not appear vain of his superior memory, but simply remarked, pointing to his forehead, 'When I hear anything great, it remains here.' This young man died in the faith shortly afterwards, before an opportunity was afforded him of making a public profession."

293. Address of an African Chief.—When Mosheshe, the king or paramount chief of the Basutos, a powerful tribe in South Africa, had obtained missionaries to instruct his people, he delivered a very remarkable speech, from which the following is an extract, in a free translation:—"Rejoice, you Makare and Mokatchani! you rulers of cities, rejoice! There are many sayings among men, some are true and some are false; but the false have remained with us and multiplied; therefore we ought to pick up carefully the truths we hear, lest they should be lost in the rubbish of lies. We are told we have all been created by one Being, and that we all sprang from one man. Sin entered man's heart when he ate the forbidden fruit, and we have got sin from him. These men say that they have sinned; and what is sin in them is sin in us, because we came from one stock, and their hearts and ours are one thing. Ye Makare have heard these words, and you say they are lies. If these words do not conquer, the fault will lie with you. You say you will not believe what you do not understand. Look at an egg: if a man break it, there comes only a watery and yellow substance out of it; but if it be placed under the wings of a fowl, there comes a living thing from it. Who can understand this? Who ever knew how the heat of the hen produced the chicken in the egg? This is incomprehensible to us, yet we do not deny the fact. Let us do like the hen. Let us place these truths in our hearts, as the hen does the eggs under her wings; let us sit upon them, and take the same pains, and something new will come of them."

294. Source of Light and Comfort.—When travelling on the banks of the Orange River, between Namaqualand and the Griqua country in South Africa, the Rev. R. Moffat came to a heathen village, where an incident occurred of which he gives the following description:—"We had travelled far, and were hungry, thirsty, and fatigued. From the fear of being exposed to lions, we preferred remaining at the village to proceeding during the night. The people of the village rather roughly directed us to halt at a distance. We asked water, but they would not supply it. I offered the three or four buttons which still remained on my jacket for a little milk; this also was refused. We had the prospect of another hungry night at a distance from water, though within sight of the river. We found it difficult to reconcile ourselves to our lot, for in addition to repeated rebuffs, the manner of the villagers excited suspicion.

"When twilight drew on, a woman approached. She bore on her head a bundle of wood, and had a vessel of milk in her hand. The latter, without opening her lips, she handed to us, laid down the wood, and returned to the village. A second time she approached with a cooking-vessel on her head, and a leg of mutton in one hand, and water in the other. She sat down without saying a word, prepared the fire, and put on the meat. We asked her again and again who she was. She remained silent, till affectionately entreated to give us a reason for such unlooked-for kindness to strangers. The solitary tear stole down her sable cheek when she replied, 'I love Him whose servants you are, and surely it is my duty to give you a cup of cold water in His name. My heart is full, therefore I cannot speak the joy I feel to see you in this out-of-the-world place.' On learning a little of her history, and that she was a solitary light burning in a dark place, I asked her how she kept up the life of God in her soul, in the entire absence of the communion of saints. She drew from her bosom a copy of the Dutch Testament which she had received from Mr Helm, when in his school some years previous, before she had been compelled by her connections to retire to her present seclusion. 'This,' she said, 'is the fountain whence I drink; this is the oil which makes my lamp burn!' I looked upon the precious relic printed by the British and Foreign Bible Society, and the reader may conceive how I felt, and my believing companions with me, when we met with this disciple, and mingled our sympathies and prayers together, at the throne of our heavenly Father."

295. Native Reasoning.—When there was such a general disposition in the South Sea Islands to abandon the ancient superstitions and embrace Christianity, the natives were, no doubt, actuated by various motives, which were overruled by Divine Providence for the advancement of His cause and kingdom. Some thought that by their receiving the gospel, vessels would be induced to visit them, and they would thus become possessed of various useful articles, of which they had heard wonderful accounts. Others seemed to think that by adopting the new religion, their cruel wars might come to an end, and their lives be prolonged. A striking illustration of native reasoning on the subject was given at a large meeting, held for the purpose of consultation as to the course that should be pursued. A venerable chief stood up and said, "It is my wish that the Christian religion should become universal among us. I look," continued he, "at the wisdom of these worshippers of Jehovah, and see how superior they are to us in every respect. Their ships are like floating houses, so that they can traverse the tempest-driven ocean for months with perfect safety; whereas, if a breeze blow upon our frail canoes, they are upset in an instant, and we are sprawling in the sea. Their persons, also, are covered from head to foot in beautiful clothes, while we wear nothing but a girdle of leaves. Their axes are so hard and sharp, that with them we can easily fell our trees and do our work; but with our stone axes we must dub, dub, dub, day after day, before we can cut down a single tree. Their knives, too, what valuable things they are! how quickly they cut up our pigs, compared with our bamboo knives! Now, I conclude that the God who has given to His white worshippers these valuable things must be wiser than our gods, for they have not given the like to us. We all want these articles, and my proposition is, that the God who gave them should be our God." This speech produced a powerful effect; and, although a heathen priest attempted to weaken it by various adverse suggestions, the people generally expressed an opinion in favour of the *lotu*, and acted accordingly. If their motives in many instances were of a secular character, when they came fully under religious instruction, they were led to embrace the truth as it is in Jesus.

296. Division of Labour Extraordinary.—A most ingenious method of securing and treasuring up the truth of God is adopted by the new converts to Christianity in some of the South Sea Islands, a method which might be adopted with advantage in other countries. Before the commencement of the public service on the Sunday morning, the natives meet together in classes of ten or twelve families each, and distribute among themselves the respective portions of the sermon each individual should bring away; one saying, "Mine shall be the text, and all that is said in immediate connection with it;" another, "I will take care of the first division;" and a third, "I will bring home the particulars under that head;" thus the sermon is appropriated before it is delivered. In some of the more advanced stations, where the New Testament is in the hands of the people, the missionaries are in the habit of naming passages of Scripture which are illustrative of the particulars under discussion. For instance, if the missionary is preaching upon the love of Christ, his first division may be to describe the nature and properties of that love, and under this head, if he refer to its greatness, after having illustrated his point, he will desire his hearers, without specifying the verse or verses, to read with attention the third chapter of St Paul's Epistle to the Ephesians, where they will find some sentiments applicable to that part of the subject. Opening their Testaments, the converted natives will find the chapter referred to, and make a mark against it. A second division may be the unchangeable nature of the Saviour's love; and the preacher having concluded his observations on this, he will desire the congregation to read carefully the eighth chapter of St Paul's Epistle to the Romans, where they will find some passages illustrative of that particular. Again opening their Testaments, the chapter is sought and marked as before. Thus they proceed through the entire discourse. At a convenient time, the respective classes meet, and after commencing their social service with singing and prayer, one of the most intelligent of the members, as leader, begins to inquire, "With whom is the text?" and proposes a variety of questions upon it. After this he asks for the divisions of the discourse; and when one has been given, he will say, "To what portion of Scripture were we referred?" The chapter having been named, they proceed to read it carefully over, and the verses thought to be most applicable are selected for observation. This is found to be a most excellent method of proceeding, as it not only induces the people to pay great attention to the sermon; but to search the Scriptures with interest, and also to exercise their minds on the meaning and application of what they hear and read.

297. The Talking Chip.—Whilst engaged in the erection of the new chapel at Rarotonga, a little incident occurred to the Rev. John Williams, which he relates as follows:—"As I had come to the work one morning without my square, I took up a chip, and with a piece of charcoal wrote upon it a request that Mrs Williams would send me that article. I called a chief who was superintending his portion of the work, and said to him, 'Friend, take this; go to our house, and give it to Mrs Williams.' He was a singular-looking man, remarkably quick in his movements, and had been a great warrior: but in one of the numerous battles he had fought he had lost an eye. Giving me an inexpressible look with the other, he said, 'Take that! she will call me a fool and scold me, if I carry a chip to her.' 'No,' I replied, 'she will not; take it, and go immediately; I am in haste.' Perceiving me to be in earnest, he took it, and asked, 'What must I say?' I replied, 'You have nothing to say; the chip will say all I wish.' With a look of astonishment and contempt, he held up the piece of wood, and said, 'How can this speak? has this a mouth?' I desired him to take it immediately, and not spend so much time in talking about it. On arriving at the house, he gave the chip to Mrs Williams, who read it, threw it away, and went to the tool-chest, whither the chief, resolved to see the result of this mysterious proceeding, followed her closely. On receiving the square from her, he said, 'Stay, daughter, how do you know that this is what Mr Williams wants?' 'Why,' she replied, 'did you not bring me a chip just now?' 'Yes,' said the astonished warrior, 'but I did not hear it say anything.' 'If you did not, I did,' was the reply, 'for it made me to know what he wanted, and all you have to do is to return with it as quickly as possible.' With this the chief leaped out of the house; and catching up the mysterious piece of wood, he ran through the settlement with the chip in one hand and the square in the other, holding them up as high as his arms would reach, and shouting as he went, 'See the wisdom of these English people; they can make chips talk!' On giving me the square, he wished to know how it was possible thus to converse with persons at a distance. I gave him all the explanation in my power; but it was a circumstance involved in so much mystery, that he actually tied a string to the chip, hung it round his neck, and wore it for some time. During several days following, we frequently saw him surrounded by a crowd, who were listening with intense interest while he narrated the wonders which this chip had performed."

298. Roasting Stones.—When the framework of the first chapel erected at Aitutaki, under the direction of the native teachers, was finished, they resolved to wattle and plaster it with lime, having learned the art of making lime from coral from the European missionaries at Riatea. They therefore desired the chiefs to send their people to cut a large portion of firewood; and when this was done, they requested them to send to the sea for a quantity of coral rock, which was brought to the shore and piled upon the wood. The natives did as they were desired, but could not imagine what all this singular process of preparation was to effect. At length the teachers requested them to set light to the firewood; and as soon as it began to blaze, they could contain themselves no longer, but commenced shouting, "O these foreigners, they are roasting stones! they are roasting stones! Come, hurricane, and blow down our bananas and our breadfruit; we shall never suffer from famine again, these foreigners are teaching us to roast stones." The missionaries told them to wait patiently, and they would see the result. At daylight the following morning they hastened to the spot, and to their utter astonishment, the burnt coral was reduced to a beautiful powder, and they were so surprised at its softness and its whiteness, that they actually whitewashed their hats and native garments, and strutted about the settlement admiring each other exceedingly. A part of the chapel being wattled, the teachers mixed up a portion of the "roasted stone" with some sand, and plastered it on the space that had been prepared, taking care to cover it up with mats, and to send the people away, lest, prompted by curiosity, they should snatch it down before it became hard. Early next morning they all hastened to see the wonderful sight; and when the covering was removed, a beautiful sheet of white plaster was presented to their astonished view. They examined it minutely, retired exclaiming, "Wonderful! the very stones in the sea and the sand on the shore become good property in the hands of those who worship the true God and regard His good Word."

299. Rejected Idols.—On landing at the island of Aitutaki in 1822, the Rev. John Williams was much struck with the change which had been effected in the course of a few months through the instrumentality of two devoted native teachers. Idolatry had been generally abolished, a large Christian sanctuary had been erected, and the people were learning to read and write with a rapidity truly astonishing. "While walking through the settlement," says Mr Williams, "we saw two grim-looking gods in a more dishonourable situation than they had been wont to occupy, for they were sustaining upon their heads the whole weight of the roof of a cooking-house. Wishing to make them more useful, we offered to purchase them from their former worshipper. He instantly propped up the house with other pieces of wood, took out the idols, and threw them down; and while they were prostrate on the ground, he gave them a kick, saying, 'There—your reign is at an end.' On receiving two fish-hooks for them he was highly delighted." The devoted missionary, with grateful heart, adds, "What a revolution of sentiment and feeling! A few months before this man was a deluded worshipper of these senseless stocks."

300. Agreeable Surprise.—On the 22d of May 1850, a beautiful vessel, which had left San Francisco on the 7th of April, was wrecked on the weather reef of Ongea, one of the Fiji Islands. Knowing the savage, cannibal character of the natives, the shipwrecked mariners looked at each other in mute despair. A momentary silence reigned unbroken, save by the roar of the breakers and the dismal sighing of the wind. The sea making continual breaches over the vessel, and threatening to sweep the decks fore and aft, the crew, after a brief consultation, destroyed all the spirits on board, and then took to the boats. They were aware of their danger from the cruel natives, but there was no choice; so they pulled towards the shore, from which they were distant about seven miles. After crossing other reefs, they approached so near the shore as to see the natives standing on the beach.

"They approached," says Mr Plunkett, "and made signs; but we could not understand them. For a while we lay upon our oars, for the purpose of discussing how we should act: some were for seeking a passage out to sea, and shaping their course for the Isle of Pines, nine hundred miles distant; others were for urging our way through the reefs towards the shore. I was of this number, for I preferred the *natives* to the *billows;* and in this, at last, all concurred. We hoisted our ensign, and gave it a cheer; upon which the natives launched a canoe and came off, giving us a hearty *shake hands*. We were astonished, and having landed, the moon shone forth and the bay was tranquil. We once more trod the green sward, and my heart beat quick. Being met by several natives, they conducted us to a hut, where an ample supper of yams and cocoa-nuts was provided. Before retiring they had prayers in their native language; and as they sang their evening hymn, I felt a calm devotion, to which, I regret to say, I had long been a stranger. I need not say I was agreeably surprised to find that, instead of being among cannibals, I was in the midst of devout Wesleyans. Oh, what gratitude I felt towards the missionaries, these brave soldiers of the Cross, who came into these distant lands to teach the will of God to these benighted people! Well and faithfully have they laboured, and we derive the benefit of those labours. No longer were the diabolical orgies of the heathen priest tolerated. The wail of victims no longer fell upon the ear; the solitude was undisturbed by sounds of midnight massacre. All here was peace, piety, and religion."

301. Testimony to the Value of Missions.—In the year 1864 one of the most affecting narratives was published in Australia of shipwreck, suffering, death, and rescue, which we ever read, and we observed with gratitude how much the survivors were indebted to the benign influence of Christianity when they landed upon an island, once the abode of savage cannibals, but now transformed, by the renewing power of the gospel, into a civilised country. The leading particulars of the touching story were as follows:—

"The ship *All Serene* was capsized in a heavy gale in the South Seas. In the emergency of the moment, with a view to save life, a few boards were hastily nailed together, to make a kind of punt; and in this frail vessel thirty-one persons were crowded, nineteen of whom were saved after having been twenty days on board. At the end of this period, after passing through indescribable sufferings and privations, the survivors reached the island of Kandavu, one of the Fiji group. When the natives beheld this strange-looking vessel approaching their shores, with a party of white men on board, they were afraid, and hid themselves, supposing they were slavers. The poor shipwrecked mariners were no less alarmed, being aware of the savage and cruel character of the Fijians; but being in great distress, they ventured to land.

"At length," says the writer of the narrative, "we succeeded in attracting the attention of one of the natives, as he was leaving the house by the back-door. He saw our helpless condition at a glance, and in a few minutes many more came from their places of concealment, and gathered around us. None of us could speak a word of their language, neither could we understand anything they said, with the exception of one word—it was the word *missionary*; but this word made us feel perfectly safe. They conducted us to a small village, leading and supporting us all the way, and seeming to vie with each other in their unremitting attention to us. The kindness of these natives was remarkable. They took us into their houses, and they seemed to anticipate our every wish, and evinced the greatest delight in being allowed to minister to our wants, holding the reviving cup to our lips, and supplying us with plenty of food. We succeeded in making them understand that there were more of our comrades on the beach, and many of them went with torches (as the moon had now gone down), and brought them to the village.

"On the following morning some of them went to inform the Rev. Mr Nettleton, of the Wesleyan Mission, who resided twelve miles from the village. He came to see us on the next day. This was a happy meeting; he prayed with us, and we cried like children. We learned from him that we were on the island of Kandavu, one of the Fiji group, and that we must have come four or five hundred miles in the punt. He also told us, that if we had not made for this island, we must have perished, as this is the outer island of the group, and we had struck on the most southern point of it. The natives showed great reluctance to part with us; but Mr Nettleton took us all away in boats to the mission-station, and afterwards sent them presents in return for their kindness to us. He left half our number with his brother missionary, the Rev. W. Fletcher, about eight miles from where we had landed, and took the other to his own place.

"We remained nearly two months under the care of these gentlemen. Would that I could speak in terms of praise equal to the merits of these two missionaries and their most amiable ladies. All I can say is this—they administered solace to our wearied spirits; they supplied us with many temporal comforts; they clothed our nakedness, and healed our wounds. It is but justice to the other few white inhabitants of the island, to say that they also treated us with uniform kindness. May God bless them all!"

302. **Negro Shrewdness.**—One Sunday morning a missionary was preaching at a village called Balley's Bay, about four miles from St George's, Bermuda. After the service had commenced, a negro stranger entered the chapel, and listened to the sermon with marked attention. As soon as the service was over, he went into the house of one of the members, and when asked what he thought of the sermon, he made the following shrewd remarks, "Minister be very good man, or very bad man: if bad man, den he know something of witchcraft; for," said he, "minister, when preaching at Balley's Bay told me all dat be in my heart. If he be good man, den God must have told de preacher all about me."

On one occasion a negro servant

went to the market to purchase fish for his master's dinner. On seeing several kinds of fish laid out on the stall, he examined them minutely, and put his face very near to them, as if he was smelling whether they were fresh or not. When she observed the prying conduct of the negro, the fish-woman began to scold, and asked him what he was doing. "Me no do nothing, ma'am," he replied; "me only just ask de fish what is de news from de sea." "Well," responded the woman, "and what do they say?" "Dem say," replied Sambo, "dem know nothing aboud de sea, coss dem no been dare for two weeks!" This broad hint as to the staleness of the fish set the woman in a rage, and there occurred one of those scolding scenes which are not at all uncommon in a West India fish-market.

When travelling in the interior of Africa, and hearing what was supposed to be the roar of lions among the mountains, the writer once asked an intelligent young native if he could obtain for him a young lion, that he might try to bring it up as a tame domestic animal. The negro replied, with an arch smile, substantially as follows—"Massa, suppose you walk with me up de mountain-side, to de ravine where de lions live, I will show you plenty young ones; den massa can catch one for himself, coss big lion will be angry if black man catch him pickaniny!" These are only specimens of shrewdness and wit which we witness every day in Africa and the West Indies, among a people who are generally all alive with humour and fun.

303. Discomforts and Privations.—The Rev. John Brownell, a Wesleyan missionary in St Kitts, speaking of Good Friday 1803, says:—"This has been a day of great weariness. The congregations have been large, and I trust that good has been done. But I am become so weak with excessive labour and riding in the sun, that I am afraid my time in the West Indies will be short, unless I obtain assistance by the speedy arrival of missionaries from England." And writing in his journal on the following Sabbath, he observes:—"Last night I came to Old Road, and found a class-meeting in the chapel. I slept in the pulpit; and on raising my head between three and four o'clock in the morning, I found the people assembled for public worship. We continued singing, praying, and preaching till daylight. We had a delightful love-feast at Palmeto Point; and at four o'clock I preached at Basseterre. The chapel, which is now greatly enlarged, was exceedingly crowded, and numbers who could not obtain admission stood on the outside. How inadequate are my abilities for the instruction of this vast congregation! Send help, O Lord, send help, that these souls may not perish for lack of knowledge!" Thus was the zealous servant of the Lord jubilant in the midst of his labours and privations; for although he had no better bed than the old pulpit, and his fare was hard indeed, the readiness with which the people received the gospel message filled his heart with gratitude and joy.

When labouring in the island of Trinidad, the writer on one occasion left Port of Spain for Carenage on horseback, to preach to a people who had never till then been favoured with a gospel ministry. Not knowing where I should find a lodging for the night, I fixed my hammock to the saddle behind me, with the intention of slinging it under a tree, or in the open shed where I expected to hold the service. We had a blessed meeting, and I had reason to hope that some good was done; but when I was about to sling my hammock and turn in for the night, the poor negroes came round me, and entreated me not to do so, declaring that if I did, the vampire bats would draw my life's blood, and that I should be dead in the morning. As they kindly offered me a lodging in one of their huts, where I should be more safe, if not more comfortable, I accepted their offer, and they provided me a bed as best they could, and also supplied me with a homely supper, for which I was thankful. On rising in the morning, I found that the kindly warning of the poor negroes was not without cause, for my horse was dreadfully bitten by the bats, and the blood had flowed copiously from several wounds. On all my subsequent visits the people invariably provided me a lodging in one of their huts, and I defended my horse as best I could.

When travelling in Africa, after a weary day's journey, I have often had to make my bed upon the ground, and to wrap myself in a skin-blanket, as a trifling shelter from the weather. But even this is not much of a privation compared with the want of food or water, which is often experienced when traversing the wilderness. Nor are discomforts and privations new items of ministerial experience. The Apostle Paul speaks of being "in weariness and painfulness, in watchings often, in hunger and thirst, in fastings oft, in cold and nakedness." Every missionary must learn to "endure hardness as a good soldier of Jesus Christ." Still the missionaries and their families have strong claims on the sympathy and prayers of Christian people in more highly-favoured lands.

· 304. **Little Trials.**—In addition to the real dangers and privations to which Christian missionaries and their families are frequently exposed whilst engaged in the dissemination of the gospel in distant lands, they are subject to numerous petty annoyances which are worthy of a passing notice. The mention of some of these may be amusing to dwellers at home, but the experience of them is far otherwise to those most immediately concerned.

If the missionary proceeds to a cold climate, he has often to envelope himself in furs, and finds it difficult to defend himself against the intense frost and snow, and the piercing winter blast of the bleak north to which he is often exposed. He is, moreover, frequently surrounded by his Esquimaux attendants and their hungry dogs, by which he is drawn in his little sledge when he travels, and his circumstances are anything rather than comfortable and cleanly when he lights a fire in the evening, cooks his food, and bivouacs for the night in a friendly snow-drift. When his lot is cast within the tropics, if he escapes fever for a time, he soon feels the effects of the *prickly-heat*, the annoyance of which is only known to those who have suffered from it. Then perhaps his feet are attacked with *chiggoes*, which penetrate beneath the skin, and produce a strange sensation till carefully extracted by a skilful negro servant, to say nothing of the danger and suffering involved if they are allowed to remain in their living nests till they propagate their species. In some parts of the West Indies the *beatrooch*, a little red insect of similar habits to the chiggoe, is apt to attack the person, especially the feet and legs, and often prove very troublesome: while the mosquitoes, in low and swampy localities, are a perpetual torment. On the coast of Demerara, it is necessary for the traveller to wear a gauze veil, to protect himself from the noxious insects, myriads of which darken the air, whilst at the same time he has his face covered with a linen mask to screen him from the influence of the saline particles which float in the air, and which, in combination with the intense heat, completely blister the skin if exposed for any length of time.

In most tropical climates various other kinds of insects and reptiles are met with in great abundance, and become uncomfortably familiar. This is the case, especially, with sundry kinds of *flies*, *ants*, *cockroaches*, *centipedes*, *scorpions*, *serpents*, &c. Some of these will enter the larder, attack the provisions, and, without great care, destroy or pollute that on which the family depends for subsistence. Small and insignificant as is the ant, it will sometimes enter and take possession of a dwelling-house, causing the inhabitants to retire, and emptying it of everything which can be destroyed. These are specimens of the little annoyances of everyday life with which we soon become familiar in the mission-field.

305. The Little Missionary.—There was once a little girl, only three years old, who was the means of bringing a dark, benighted heathen to the knowledge and worship of the true and living God. Perhaps you would like to know where she lived, and by what means she accomplished such a great and good work. Well, I will tell you. The story is a very simple one, but suggestive of useful lessons.

Little Mary lived in India, and had been early taught to think and speak of God, and to love the Lord Jesus Christ, who came into the world to save sinners. Her constant attendant was a young Hindu, named Saamy, who was quite proud of his precious little charge. As they were walking out one day in a beautiful shady grove, they passed a little heathen temple, when the Indian servant approached the door, with little Mary in his arms, and bowed to the idol, which was a hideous-looking image made of stone. The lisping little child was much affected, and exclaimed, "O Saamy, what for you do that." "My dear Missy," said the servant, "that is my god." "Your god!" exclaimed the child—"your god, Saamy! Why, your god can no see, no hear, no walk. Your god a stone god. Saamy. My God make you, make me, make everything." Yet Saamy, whenever he passed the temple, bowed to the idol, and the child still reproved him. Although the Hindu servant did not seem to care for what was said, he still loved his baby teacher. Some time afterwards, when he heard that his little friend would soon be sent to England, he said, "What will poor Saamy do when Missy go to England? Saamy no have father, no have mother." "O Saamy!" said little Mary, "if you love God, He will be your Father and your Mother too."

On hearing this the poor heathen promised that he would try to love God. "Then," said little Mary, "you must learn my prayers," and she began to teach him "Our Father," &c. Soon afterwards Mary's father was surprised and delighted to see Saamy enter the room at the time of family worship, and still more so to see him take off his turban, kneel down, and say the Lord's prayer after his master. The fact was, the lispings of the little child had brought the Hindu to a knowledge of the true God, for Saamy did not merely bow the knee, he worshipped God in spirit and in truth, and henceforth became an earnest and devoted Christian.

P

306. In Helping Others we Help Ourselves.—In 1864 the West India and Pacific Steamship Company's steamer *Askalon*, bound from Liverpool to Port-au-Prince, was lost under circumstances peculiarly remarkable. She left the Mersey early in November, about a week before the *Columbia*, which was wrecked on the French coast, and experienced bad weather from the commencement of the voyage. On the 14th a fearful hurricane was encountered. The sea broke over the ship with fearful violence, sweeping away the boats, and other movables on deck. She continued in this condition for two days, rolling and straining fearfully. At length the sea broke in the skylight, and the water rushing down into the engine-room, put out the fires and stopped the engines. The crew exerted themselves to the utmost, with the hope of keeping the vessel afloat; but on the 15th it was found that she had ten feet of water in her hold. At this juncture the Dutch barque *Almonde* hove in sight; and seeing the critical state of the *Askalon*, she at once bore towards the sinking steamer, and after extraordinary exertions, succeeded in taking on board the crew, thirty-seven in number, and one passenger, and the *Askalon* was accordingly abandoned just before she went down. Singular to relate, soon after the Dutch barque had rescued the crew of the British steamer from the danger to which they were exposed, it was discovered that she herself had sprung a leak, having encountered the full force of the gale; and, but for the help afforded in working the pumps by the additional sailors thus received on board, would probably have been also lost. By the assistance thus afforded, however, in the order of Divine Providence, the *Almonde* was kept afloat, and reached England in safety. On arriving at Folkstone, Captain Hoare and the passengers were landed, but the English crew remained on board the barque that had saved them, and gladly assisted in working her over to Bremenhaven, where, through their instrumentality, she arrived in safety. Thus the captain and crew of the *Almonde*, by humanely endeavouring to save the men on board the sinking *Askalon*, did in fact unwittingly save themselves.

This touching incident affords a striking illustration of the reflex influence of Christian effort for the benefit of others. In His wisdom and goodness the Almighty has so arranged the working of Christian ethics, as to establish an immediate and inseparable connection between the faithful discharge of individual duty with the enjoyment of personal blessing. It is our imperative duty to flee to the rescue of those who are perishing for lack of knowledge; but in doing so, we are sure to receive more than we give in personal blessing: for in breaking the bread of life to others we shall be abundantly blessed in our own souls.

307. Perishing in the Snow.—It is recorded of a certain traveller, that when crossing the Alps in the winter season, he was overtaken by one of those dreadful snowstorms which are so common and sometimes so fatal in those elevated regions. He bravely toiled up the steep ascent, despite the driving sleet and the piercing cold, till, entirely exhausted and benumbed, he sank down on the snow, under the painful apprehension that he might rise no more. Just at this appalling crisis he was overtaken by another traveller, who was also much exhausted and benumbed with the cold, and who felt as if he too must perish in the storm, as many had done before.'

But, moved with compassion, the man who was the least affected of the two, commenced to rub the stiffening limbs of his companion in tribulation, and by persevering efforts succeeded in restoring animation, so that he was at length enabled to rise to his feet and pursue his journey. The man who had thus rendered such timely help to the perishing traveller now discovered that the effort had quickened the circulation in his own limbs, and that he was better able to walk than before. The deliverer and the rescued now moved forward together; and as the storm abated, they were favoured in the good providence of God to reach a place of refuge in safety.

So has many a weak and trembling Christian been strengthened and invigorated in his own spirit by earnest, persevering efforts to benefit and save others who were in a perishing condition. In every point of view genuine Christian benevolence is wise and good and blessed, yea, "it is more blessed to give than to receive."

308. The Missionary's Farewell.—The following lines, written by a missionary on board a ship, just after having taken the last look at his dear native land, are so natural, and so expressive of what many have felt in similar circumstances, and so well calculated to excite sympathy in every feeling heart, that they may with propriety be placed on record here :—

" England, farewell! a happier land than
  thee
I have not seen, nor e'er expect to see;
So fair thy beauties, and thy faults so
  few,
So sweet thy comforts, and thy sons so
  true.

" Here mighty rivers roll their ample
  tide ;
There fruitful rills adorn the green
  vale-side :

Majestic rocks for ornament and shield,
And graceful furrows, which full plenty
  yield.

" Thou fairest land of my nativity!
I bless the Hand that cast my lot in
  thee ;
I love thy temples and thy God adore,
Who made my cup of bliss in thee
  run o'er.

" I love thy happy myriads who embrace
The joyful tidings of a Saviour's grace,
And thou hast those who twine around
  my heart,
From whom 'tis only less than death
  to part.

" But God has called, and I must speed
  away
In other lands to point the *living way*,
By which poor heathens all may be forgiven,
And rise at last to all the joys of
  heaven."

309. Affection and Gratitude.—Among the fruits of missionary labour which the writer was favoured to reap on some of the stations which he occupied in foreign lands were several young men, who were ultimately called to preach the gospel of Christ to their fellow-countrymen. One of these, a native of the West Indies, was a remarkable instance of the special providence and grace of God, and in token of his love and gratitude, he wrote the following lines in the scrapbook of his friend and minister, when about to leave the station. They will speak for themselves, and need no comment, showing as they do that Christian missionaries are not permitted to labour in vain, or spend their strength for nought :—

" Unfolding here salvation's healing
  plan,
My steps you pointed to the realms of
  light ;
You brought and taught me in the
  Christian fold,
To serve my God, and in His laws
  delight.

"Here many a heart has felt thy sooth-
    ing power
When bowed beneath a sense of guilt
    and care,
And oft in misery's pining, cheerless
    hour
You dried the widow's and the orphan's
    tear.

"Here many a toilsome, solitary hour,
    You've travelled to declare your
        Saviour's name;
Opened a wide and an effectual door,
And gladly here His saving power
    proclaim.

"But now called hence a distant flock to
    feed,
No more your active virtue here shall
    glow;
But love unquenchable and zeal
Shall add fresh laurels wheresoe'er you
    go.

"Long may you live to aid your fellow-
    men,
To point the tender youth in wisdom's
    way,
Unfold the beauties of salvation's plan,
And train immortals for eternal day.

"And when from earth's vain fleeting
    view you pass,
Follow'd by works in endless peace to
    rest,
Your bright example, oh! may I pursue,
For ever blessing, till I'm ever blessed."

310. Success of the Gospel.—It is demonstrable that the success of the gospel in the last hundred years is greater than that which it has achieved in any preceding hundred years. We look back on the first ages of Christianity, and sigh for the gift of tongues, and for Pentecostal blessing; and yet in the last century more has been done to give the Bible to the world, than was done in the first ten centuries of our era. Twenty versions at most were made in the first one thousand years; in the last one hundred years a hundred and twenty have been made—in languages spoken by more than half the globe. There are more conversions in heathen countries in the present day, in proportion to the number of preachers employed, than there are at home. Even when Constantine proclaimed Christianity as the religion of the Roman Empire, the nominal Christians did not exceed one-hundredth part of the population of the entire globe. Nominal Christians now form one-fifth. Each new generation of the modern world consists of 30,000,000 of children, and they have to be Christianised one by one. Of these 30,000,000, 6,000,000 (one-fifth) become nominally Christians, and a considerable portion of them really Christians.

311. Missionary Bullocks.—In the Banbury Circuit there is a small village named Little Bourton, the inhabitants of which number about one hundred and fifty. A few years ago the missionary income of this place, from all sources, did not exceed £5. The chapel is small and the members few. Mr John Archer, the society steward there, is a farmer, a respected local-preacher, and an enthusiastic supporter of the mission cause. In 1870 he conceived the plan of buying a bullock about the month of May, keeping it on his farm till it was fit for the butcher, and then selling it, and giving the profits realised to the Missionary Society. Mr Archer not only did this himself, but he induced many of his friends in the Circuit to go and do likewise, and the result has been a great success. Many "missionary bullocks" are yearly fed by many friends of the good cause in the Banbury Circuit, and many pounds thus find their way into the missionary exchequer. The farmer does not miss the little that the young bullock costs; and the animal being constantly under his care, as constantly reminds him of its purpose, and keeps alive his interest in the work.

From the above and other causes, Little Bourton in 1873 raised over £50 for the mission-fund, and there is reason to believe that in future this amount will be still farther increased.

There are thousands of Methodists scattered over England who have grazing-farms, and who could well afford to make an experiment similar to that which has been so successfully tried in the Banbury Circuit. May we ask them to do so during the coming year? If so, we venture to predict that the result will surprise and delight all those who take an interest in missions.

312. Difficulties of Translation.

—None but those who have experienced them can fully appreciate the difficulties connected with reducing to a written and grammatical form the barbarous languages spoken by different tribes in heathen lands, and of translating the Scriptures into them. We have an illustration of this in the following little incident :—The Rev. T. S. Grimshawe once stated at a public meeting that he had met with Mr Colemeister, who had laboured as a missionary among the Esquimaux for thirty-four years, and had translated the four Gospels into the Esquimaux language. Among a variety of interesting questions which Mr Grimshawe put to him, he inquired as to a point of some curiosity and difficulty respecting his translations. Knowing how imperfect barbarous languages generally are, and how inadequate to express any abstract idea, Mr Grimshawe requested him to say how he translated the word "Saviour." Mr Colemeister said, "Your question is remarkable, and perhaps the answer may be so too. It is true the Esquimaux have no word in their language to represent the Saviour, and I could never find out that they had any direct notion of such a Friend. But I said to them, 'Does it not happen sometimes when you are out fishing, that a storm arises, and some of you are lost and some saved?' They said, 'Oh yes, very often.' 'But it also happens that you are in the water, and owe your safety to some brother or friend, who stretches out his hand to help you.' 'Very frequently.' 'Then what do you call that friend?' They gave me in answer a word in their language, and I immediately wrote it against the word Saviour in Holy Writ, and ever afterwards it was clear and intelligible to all of them." Thus the missionary has to feel his way as best he can, amid many difficulties, and in this department of his work as well as in others he has a special claim upon the sympathy and prayers of the friends of the enterprise.

313. Heartfelt Testimony.

—A celebrated minister, travelling in America, lodged one night at the house of a planter, who informed him that one of his negro slaves, a man upwards of seventy years of age, who could neither read nor write, was yet eminently distinguished for his piety and knowledge of the Scriptures. Having some curiosity to learn what evidence such a man could have of the divine origin of the sacred records, he went out in the morning alone, and, without making himself known as a clergyman, entered into conversation with him on the subject. After starting some of the common objections of infidels against the authenticity and divine inspiration of the Scriptures, in a way calculated to confound an ignorant man, he said to him, "When you cannot even read the Bible, nor examine the evidence for or against its truth, how can you know that it is the Word of

God?" The negro replied, after reflecting for a moment, with becoming modesty, but with unhesitating confidence, "You ask me, sir, how I know that the Bible is the Word of God? I know it by its effects upon my own heart."

Happy are they who, like the poor negro slave brought under the saving influence of the gospel, can "set to their seal that God is true," and bear their heartfelt testimony to the divine authority of the sacred records from the simple fact of their effect on their own hearts.

314. Poor Old Moses.—The correspondent of an American periodical gives the following pleasing account of a pious Christian negro,—a specimen of a large class who by the blessing of God upon a preached gospel have been gathered into the fold of the Redeemer :—

In the month of May I left the residence of a friend in the great valley of Virginia, and took a ride for the benefit of my health. I followed the course of a small stream for some miles, without seeing the habitation of man. At length I espied, near the end of the valley, and at the foot of a mountain, an aged negro at work on a small farm. His woolly head was whitened with age, and the deep wrinkles in his face, and a stoop in his shoulders, indicated that he had seen many years and suffered many hardships. Glad to see and converse with a human being after my solitary ramble, I alighted from my horse, and addressed him as follows : —"You seem to be enduring the curse pronounced upon fallen man—getting your bread by the sweat of your brow." "Ah! massa," said he, wiping the perspiration from his sable face, "I have no reason to complain, however hard my work may be. I have a great many blessings left yet : I have Jesus Christ and His gospel, and that is enough for poor old Moses." "As you seem to be quite shut out from the world here, I suppose you have but few temptations," I observed. "Ah! massa," said he, "wherever I go I carry this bad heart with me," putting his hand to his breast, "and that is it which lets in the world. I have to pray against the world at night and in the morning, and then I have to fight against it all day. And that is no light or easy matter. The devil can get up here in these mountains as well as anywhere else, for you know he tempted our Saviour on a mountain." "My good old friend," I said, "you seem to have been long a pilgrim to the heavenly country." "For forty years," said he, "I have found that the Lord has been good to me, and he that trusts in the Saviour shall never be moved." "But are you never tempted to forsake the Saviour?" I inquired. "I know that my heart is very deceitful," he replied, "and Satan keeps trying to get old Moses ; but my Master in heaven says, 'By grace are ye saved through faith ; and that not of yourselves, it is the gift of God.' This is my hope, that He who has begun a good work will finish it. When you plant corn, massa, ye don't go away and leave it, and let the birds pull it up, or the grass or the weeds kill it ; so when God plants the good seed in the sinner's heart, He does not go away and leave it to die."

Delighted with the old negro's conversation, I further remarked, "You say you are tempted sometimes ; how?" "Yes, massa," he replied ; "the devil will come and whisper in my ear, 'Moses, you serve a bad Master ; He sends sickness and poverty and trouble ; He sends the fly to kill all your wheat.' But I say, Devil, liar; Jesus no bad Master. He knocked at the door of my heart, and I would not let Him in; and then He knocked again and again, until I was obliged to open the door, and ever since I have found Him to be good. He has bound up my heart when it was broken; He has come to my bed when I was sick; He has borne with my sins; He has not cast me off because I was poor and old, and did not love Him as much as I ought; and then He died for poor Moses' soul. Oh no! He is not a bad Master. He may take away my wife and children; He may burn my house and lay me on a sick-bed, and smite me with His own dear hand; still I would love Him, and say it was all for my good." As the old negro said this a tear stole down his furrowed cheek. Shortly afterwards I bade the old man farewell, with a confident hope of meeting him in heaven. Later on I learned that he was remarkably punctual in attending divine worship, and was considered by the congregation to which he belonged to be a very pious man.

We have met with hundreds of converted negroes in Africa and the West Indies, as intelligent, sensible, and pious as good old Moses of Virginia; and when we have conversed with them on the deep things of God, or heard their testimony to the renewing power of divine grace in their hearts, in Christian fellowship, we have often wished that the friends of missions at home could see and hear for themselves what God has done by the power of His gospel for the sable sons and daughters of Ham.

315. **Sokappa Reddy.**—The Christian Vernacular Education Society, for the printing, publication, and circulation of religious tracts and books in the various languages of India, is doing a great and good work, as the auxiliary of the direct preaching of the gospel. The following account of a remarkable convert is one among many which might be adduced as illustrations of the usefulness of this valuable institution:—

In the year 1859 a Hindu named Sokappa Reddy, in his zeal for the religion in which he had been trained from his childhood, devoted himself to a life of an ascetic, making a vow to Siva that he would wear an iron cage round his head until the completion of a certain tank, for which about £600 was required. This iron cage was about a foot and a half wide, and two feet high, weighing about three pounds. For seven years this cage was not removed, and for that length of time he could not recline at full length, but had to sleep upon the floor, resting against the wall, with the lower portion of the cage padded with a cotton cloth, to prevent the abrasion of his neck and shoulders by friction. During the whole of this time he had to abandon his wife and family, and live as a Sivite ascetic in a monastery. With the above exceptions, his life was free from privations. His bread was given him, and his water was sure. Money for all his requirements, and subscriptions for the tank, were provided by many of his own caste, who rejoiced that one of their class had devoted himself to what they considered a religious life. While he had a general superintendence over the work on the tank, he also had charge of the plantain-gardens of his younger brothers, and thus found some relief from the monotonous round of his daily life. He was a bigoted heathen, ignorant of the claims of all other religions, and had a blind, engrossing hate for the Christian families which were springing up around him, which was manifested whenever a Christian approached him. One day a son-in-law of Gnanamutthu entering his garden, he inquired who he was. Learning he was a Christian, he beat him severely, and drove him from the garden. The Christians, aware of his hatred of them, feared to go near him.

Yet, strange to say, the deluded, fanatical, and persecuting Sokappa Reddy was brought under the influence of divine truth, and is now a devoted servant of the Lord Jesus Christ, the friend and associate of those he was wont to afflict, and an earnest Christian, full of faith and zeal for the cause of the Redeemer. A monthly magazine of the Christian Vernacular Society is said to have been the means of first awakening him to a sense of his sin and folly. Other Christian books further enlightened his mind, and he was at last converted by reading the Scriptures, which he studied long and diligently. He is now, like the Apostle Paul, earnestly labouring to propagate the faith which he once laboured to destroy, and striving to bring others to a saving knowledge of the truth.

316. Twentyfold.—At a missionary-meeting held in the Wesleyan preaching-room, on one occasion at the village of Shallfleet, in the Isle of Wight, there was a good influence, and the people seemed interested with the addresses that were delivered; but the weather being unfavourable, the collection proved to be a few shillings below that of former years. On hearing this, the minister said, "I am very sorry; I don't like to see you decline. What must be done?" Mr Fiander, the leader of the society class, a man of quiet zeal and perseverance, said, "Let us make another collection, sir; I will give another shilling." George Leal, a humble farm-labourer, but an ardent lover of the mission cause, responded. "And so would I, if I had one with me." "I'll lend you a shilling, George," said the leader, and suiting the action to the word, handed him one to drop into the plate. "Well done, George Leal!" exclaimed the minister, "the Lord will reward you tenfold." This little episode stimulated others; the plate went round a second time, and the deficiency was more than made up. When the meeting was over, and the minister was taking leave of the people, he greeted George Leal with unusual warmth, remarking, "Remember what I said, George, the Lord will reward you tenfold."

The next day, when George Leal went into the field to his ploughing, he had not gone many yards when the ploughshare turned up a beautiful bright sovereign. George called to his master, and asked if he knew who had lost a sovereign, quite willing to give it up. "Nay, George," said the farmer, "it must have been in the ground many years; it is thy own good luck, keep it." On the next preaching night, George Leal hastened to Shallfleet, and seeing the minister coming along, he went to meet him, and said, "Please, sir, you made a mistake about the shilling." Thinking the poor man was impatient for the promised return, the minister said, "You must not be in too great a hurry, George, the reward is sure to come in some way."

"I have got it," said George; "but it was not tenfold, it was *twentyfold*." From that day to this George Leal has been a very liberal supporter of the mission cause, according to his means.

317. Rice Lake Indian Mission. —In the month of September 1874, an interesting visit was paid to the

Wesleyan mission-stations at Rice Lake and Alderville, in Upper Canada, by the Rev. Gervase Smith, M.A., the deputation from the British Conference, of which, after describing his journey thither, he gives the following graphic account:—"Nine o'clock found us on the lake under the guidance of the strong arm of Mr Brooking. The boat carried us some distance from the shore; the scene was inspiring. The whole village was bathing in the morning sunlight, while the white mission-house and the shining spire of the mission-church occupied the central position. As we crossed the lake the water was beautifully calm, and the air exquisitely balmy. The lake is 21 miles long, and in several places it is 10 miles wide. It owes its name to the fact that several thousands of acres of rice-plants grow upon it. The crops were ready about a fortnight before our visit, when nearly all the Indians of Hiawatha went in their canoes to the scene of action. They paddle among the rice-beds, and expertly crush the grain out of the ear over the side of the canoe, leaving the plant itself, which is from 10 to 14 feet high, in the water for the next year's growth.

"After three hours' hard rowing, Mr Brooking brought us to the landing-place on the other side of the lake. We beached the boat and hid the oars in the brushwood, and proceeded on foot. We found ourselves five miles from Alderville; and the sun being excessively hot, we called at a Methodist farmhouse, from which we were kindly conveyed to our destination. On nearing the settlement we came upon the Indian graveyard, in the centre of which lie, well guarded, the remains of Father Case, a celebrated missionary in Canada. We were received at the mission-house with affectionate attention. A message was sent over to good John Sunday, and in a few minutes we entered the house of the grand old Ojibeway chief. We should not in England regard his dwelling exactly as a palace, but it is looked upon as such here because of the grand old ruler who lives in it. As might have been expected, he looks much older than when we last saw him in an English missionary meeting. His fine figure is now bending beneath the weight of years, and his sight has become dim, but his heart seems as young and as fresh as ever. He received us with great affection because of the country and the Conference from which we came. By a process which I must not stay to explain he made out his age to be seventy-eight. He introduced us to his aged wife and grandchildren; and after prayer, in which he heartily joined, we said 'Good-bye' to this worthy man, whom we do not expect again to see till the morning of the resurrection.

"After several inquiries concerning the mission-work at Alderville, we proceeded to Hiawatha in time for the evening service. About one hundred persons assembled in the church, most of whom were Indians. Mr Cornforth gave to them an earnest address on the subject of personal religion, and I spoke for a little while on Acts x. 34, 'Of a truth I perceive that God is no respecter of persons, but in every nation he that feareth God and worketh righteousness is accepted of Him.' They were very attentive throughout the service. The singing was measured, shrill, and weird. They seem to prefer the melancholy airs, the effect of which on my own mind was very touching. After the public service Mr and Mrs Brooking invited the converted Indians to a love-feast in the mission-house.

About twenty-five attended, of whom eight or ten briefly and modestly related their experience. They were chiefly old men and women who spoke, and they all expressed their thankfulness that the gospel had been sent amongst them. I should say that before the public service the children of the school gathered in the mission-garden, and sang, while we were at tea, several hymns and songs. Both of us went out to them. One gave them a brief address, and the other, who was far more popular, distributed as many sweets among them as made their dark faces glisten for the whole of the evening. We left the place and the people on the following morning, deeply impressed with the reality and even grandeur of the work which God has wrought in these latter days amongst this degraded race."

The native Indians flock to hear the gospel, and are apparently deeply affected with a concern for the salvation of their souls. Numbers have been added to the Church in that neighbourhood."

Many pages might be filled with interesting records of the same kind, gathered from the narratives of missionaries who have been labouring with success among the different tribes of North American Indians, ever since the early period referred to above, and there is good reason to believe that, whilst the gospel has been the means of elevating them in the scale of being, and promoting their temporal comfort, it has also been the means of preparing thousands for a brighter and better world above, for "Godliness is profitable unto all things, having the promise of the life that now is, and of that which is to come."

318. Converted Indian's Testimony.—At the close of a sermon preached many years ago to the aborigines in the woods of America, an Indian stood up with tears in his eyes, and thus addressed the audience:—"I desire to bless God that ever white people came to this country. White people brought the Bible and the religion of Jesus Christ with them. White people prayed and laboured for the conversion of the heathen, and I stand up this day as a living witness of the power of God's converting grace in answer to their prayers. Continue to pray for the conversion of more heathens, that they also may be brought to the knowledge of Jesus." In the magazine from which this incident is taken, we read as follows:—"It is with singular pleasure we add that information has been received from the border of the Indian nations, 200 miles from Hartford, that the Lord is pouring out His Spirit abundantly.

319. How the Gospel came to Rurutu.—The island of Rurutu is about 350 miles from Raiatea, in the South Seas. To the place last named, Christianity was introduced at an early period; but the inhabitants of Rurutu were ignorant of the fact till it was brought to their notice in a manner which clearly shows the wonder-working hand of Divine Providence. The island having been visited with a severe epidemic, attributed to the anger of their gods, Aunra, the chief, and a party of his men, resolved to put to sea in two large canoes, to see if they could find a country more healthy than their own, and one where the gods were more propitious. They arrived at the island of Tubuai; and, after having recruited their strength and spirits, they determined on returning to their native isle, hoping that the plague was stayed. They had no sooner launched their vessels, and committed themselves once more to the mighty deep, than they encountered a tremendous storm from which, during three weeks, they were exposed to the most imminent peril. Of the crew of one of the canoes, the greater part perished at sea. The chief Anura, to whom the other belonged, and his party, were driven about they knew not whither, suffering much from want of food and water. At length He "whom winds and seas obey" guided them to the Society Islands. They were driven on the coral-reef which surrounds the island of Maurua, the inhabitants of which showed them no small kindness. To their newly-found friends they related the evils which had befallen them in their own country and at sea, as they believed, through the anger of their gods. The Mauruans told the strangers that they once worshipped the same deities; but that, having discovered them to be lying spirits, they had now become worshippers of Jehovah, the one true and living God; at the same time giving them an account of the manner in which Christianity had been introduced among themselves, pointing to the demolished temples and mutilated idols in confirmation of their statement.

The astonished strangers, on hearing that white men, who had come in ships from a distant country to bring the good tidings of salvation, were living on islands, the summits of whose mountains were in sight, determined to proceed thither immediately. A westerly wind setting in, Anura and his friends again launched on the deep, not now to fly from their heathen gods, but to search for those who could explain to them more fully the nature of the astonishing news they had heard. Not being acquainted with the coast of Porapora, they missed the entrance to the harbour, and were driven to Raiatea. On landing, their astonishment was great to see the missionaries, their wives and families, and the converted natives in European dresses, with hats and bonnets; and their neat white cottages, together with the various useful arts which had been introduced among the people. When they were conducted to the public worship on the Sabbath, they beheld with wonder the assembled multitude, listened with delight to the singing, and heard with solemn awe the message of God's mercy to sinful men. At once they were convinced of the superiority of the Christian religion, and concluded that God had graciously conducted them there for the purpose of making them acquainted with its inestimable blessings. Having placed themselves under the instruction of the missionaries, Anura and his companions made rapid progress in learning. They soon mastered the spelling-book, committed to memory the principal part of the Catechism, and read fluently in the gospel narrative; and, better still, they were brought under the gracious influence of divine truth, so as to love the worship and people of God.

When they had been about three months at Raiatea, Anura expressed a strong desire to return to his native isle, that he might carry to his relatives and fellow-countrymen the knowledge he had obtained of the true God and His Son Jesus Christ; manifesting at the same time, in the most affectionate manner, his fears that he should find very few of his friends alive, as, when he left, "the evil spirit was devouring them so rapidly." An opportunity at length presented itself; the kind-hearted captain of an English ship having generously offered to land the party at Rurutu on his homeward voyage. But when the time came Anura was unwilling to return to the "land of darkness without a light in his hand," by which he meant some person to instruct him and his people in the truths of the gospel. The members of the native Church of Raiatea were consequently assembled to consider Anura's desire, and to inquire who among them would go as teachers to the heathen of Rurutu. Two of the deacons who were among the best men on the station came forward and volunteered their service. They were therefore set apart for the work in an interesting meeting convened for the purpose. Most of the night previous to their departure was spent in prayer and praise, and in providing them with some necessary and useful articles. Every member of the church brought something as a token of love and of personal interest in the enterprise. One presented a razor, another a knife, a third a roll of native cloth, a fourth a pair of scissors, and others various useful tools. They were also supplied with elementary books, and a few copies of the Gospels in the Tahitian language, from which their own does not materially differ.

The missionaries at Raiatea being anxious to know what reception would be given to the teachers and to the chief Anura and his companions on their return to Rurutu, sent a boat of their own with a native crew to accompany them, and to bring back the intelligence. After an absence of little more than a month they returned to tell of the surprise and joy with which the people hailed the arrival of their long-lost friends, and of Christian teachers to instruct them in the nature of the new religion which was everywhere beginning to prevail in the South Sea Islands. The boat was, moreover, laden with rejected idols—trophies of victory won by the Prince of Peace, the people having turned to the worship of Jehovah.

On reading the letters which accompanied them, and on beholding with their own eyes these evidences of the triumphs of the gospel, the missionaries declared that they felt a measure of that sacred joy which they supposed the angels of God will experience when they will ultimately shout, "The kingdoms of this world are become the kingdoms of our God and of His Christ."

320. Shipwreck and Death of the Rev. Émile Cook.—The Rev Emile Cook was the son of the Rev. Dr Charles Cook, one of the early Wesleyan missionaries to France; and, up to the time of his lamented death, he had himself laboured as a zealous and devoted minister of the French Conference. During the siege of Paris in 1871, Mr Cook suffered much, and was unwearied in his attentions to the wounded and the dying. At the close of the war his brethren elevated him to the position of President of the French Conference, and soon afterwards, in 1873, he was deputed to attend the great gathering of the Evangelical Alliance in New York, as the representative of the Protestant Churches in France. It was on his return voyage in the *Ville du Havre* that he suffered shipwreck, that vessel coming into violent and sudden collision with the *Loch Earn*, when many perished. His health received a shock from which he never fully recovered. The Rev. William Arthur gives the following account of this mysterious dispensation of Divine Providence :—

"We must now add to the names of the victims of the disaster by which the *Ville du Havre* perished, that of the Rev. Emile Cook. On the fatal night of the collision, he suffered a lengthened period of immersion in the sea. On board the *Loch Earn*, of course, he had only such clothes as the sailors could give, and his share when many wanted. When the shipwrecked crowd was taken on board another vessel, he would not leave M. Weiss, a brother in the ministry, who was wounded and unable to be removed; and so he stayed on the damaged ship. She soon gave signs of sinking. For days it was a slow battle with death in the form of a gaining leak. He prayed and cheered his companions with hope of deliverance. At last the moment came. The *British Queen* neared the *Loch Earn* just in time to receive the sufferers on board before she sank. Mr Cook was landed at Plymouth, and without any pause hastened to his family in Paris. Serious disease soon set in, but recovery was hoped for. The physicians sent him to the Isle of Hyères, in hope that so mild a climate would restore him. But inflammation of the lungs set in, and imminent danger was acknowledged by the doctors. On the 29th of January 1874 he passed away. In all his illness he was filled with peace. He had passed through the twofold siege of Paris, having made his escape in an ambulance. The twofold shipwreck followed, and has proved to be the means of calling away this true and faithful servant of Christ. A widow and seven children are left to feel the full weight of a sorrow to which all who knew Mr Cook will be sensible."

321. Prayer Answered.—Several years ago a few Moravian missionaries sailed from London for the Island of St Thomas, in the West Indies, where they were going to preach to the poor negro slaves. The vessel in which they sailed was the *Britannia*. The first part of their voyage was pleasant and prosperous, and in their hearts, as well as with their voices, the missionaries often thanked God for His goodness to them. But before they reached their destination one day a serious danger threatened them. In the distance they saw a pirate-ship. What could the captain, the sailors, and the passengers do, far away on the wide ocean? Each did what he thought wisest and best, under the circumstances. The captain thought it best to put the ship in a state of defence; so he mustered and armed his men as best he could and exhorted them to "sell their lives as dearly as possible." The sailors were of course obliged to obey their captain. But the missionaries thought it best to pray. They accordingly went down into the cabin; and there they prayed very earnestly to God for protection. They remembered God's promises, and they thought, "If God be for us, who can be against us?" (Rom. viii. 31.) When the pirate-ship came within gunshot of the *Britannia*, it began to pour out a heavy fire from the cannon ranged along its deck. At the same time it tried to get nearer in order to throw its grappling-irons on board the *Britannia*, that the crew might jump from one vessel to the other, to do their work of destruction. It seemed at first as if there was little chance of escape from such an enemy. The captain had no cannon and very few sailors, and these not trained as fighting men. His heart was sinking in the fearful prospect before him. He had powerful helpers on board, however, although he did not know it. These powerful helpers were the missionaries, on their knees in the cabin praying. Their prayers were a better defence for the ship than a hundred guns and a thousand armed men.

The power of the missionaries' prayers was seen in the result. The moment the pirates tried to throw their grappling-irons, their ship was tossed violently by the waves, so that not only did the irons fail to catch hold, but the men that held them were thrown into the sea. The pirate-captain was vexed at this disaster, but he told more men to come and throw the grappling-irons again. They shared the same fate. Seeing that he could not succeed in this way, he ordered his men to keep on firing at the *Britannia* till she should sink. But this plan also strangely failed. The balls missed their aim and fell into the sea. But as they kept on firing, the smoke became very thick and hung about the vessels for some minutes, hiding them from each other's view. The pirates hoped that they were doing great mischief, and that the ship would soon sink. But what was the astonishment of the pirate-captain, when a sudden gust of wind cleared the smoke away, and he saw the *Britannia* at a considerable distance, with all her sails set, and speeding away! Thus wonderfully did God answer the prayers of the missionaries, and save the vessel in which they sailed, and all on board in their time of peril. The pirate-captain confessed, many years afterwards, that, in connection with his signal failure to seize his prize, there was a mysterious influence at work which he could not understand.

322. Way to be Reconciled.—The Rev. W. Johnson, who laboured for many years with great success as an agent of the Church Missionary Society in Sierra Leone, Western Africa, among several other interesting particulars, gives the following incident as illustrative of the simplicity and sincerity of the liberated Africans when brought to a saving knowledge of the truth :—" In visiting a sick communicant, his wife, who was formerly in the mission-school, was present. I asked several questions, namely, if they read the Scriptures and prayed together (the woman being able to read); if they constantly attended public worship, and lived in peace with their neighbours. All these questions were answered in the affirmative. I then asked if they lived in peace and harmony with each other. The man answered, 'Sometimes I say a word my wife no like, or my wife talk or do what I no like ; but when we want to quarrel we shake hands together, shut the door, and go to prayer, and so we get peace again.'"

The missionary says that this method of keeping peace quite delighted him, and we respectfully submit that if the same means of reconciliation which were practised in this humble African home for the removal or prevention of "family jars," were more generally adopted in other lands, it would be to the advantage of all concerned, and tend to promote the peace and happiness of many a professedly Christian household.

323. Mysterious Music.—When the Rev. Christian Albrecht and his devoted wife were appointed to labour in Great Namaqualand, South Africa, they took with them from London a pianoforte, that Mrs A—— might be able to interest the natives with music occasionally, as well as cheer the loneliness of their residence among the heathen. This was the first instrument of the kind that had ever crossed the great Orange River. It answered the purpose well enough for awhile, but they had not been in the country long before they had to flee for their lives in consequence of the unsettled state of the surrounding tribes and the incessant wars and rumours of wars. In their haste the missionary and his wife took with them as many of their effects as possible, but the piano, as well as some other articles, was too cumbersome to be removed, and they made a deep hole in the sandy soil of the graveyard near the Warm Bath, and buried them, hoping to recover them again on their return to the station when the war had passed over.

Soon after the departure of the mission-family, the notorious chief Africaner and his people arrived at the station expecting to find considerable booty. In this they were disappointed, however, for the missionary's humble dwelling was empty. One of the chief's attendants strayed into the burying-ground, where already a few mounds distinguished it from the surrounding waste as the place of the dead. Stepping over what he supposed a newly-closed grave, he heard to his surprise soft notes of music vibrate beneath. He stood motionless, gazing over his shoulder, with mouth and eyes dilated, hesitating whether to stand still and see the dead arise, which he had heard the missionaries preach about, or take to his heels. After no little palpitation of heart, in order to assure himself of the reality of what he had witnessed, he mustered courage to make another trial, for the tones he had heard had died away. His second leap again aroused the sepulchral harp, which now fell with soft but awful cadence on his ear. Without casting an eye behind, he darted off to the camp, and with breathless amazement announced to Africaner the startling discovery he had made of life and music in the grave. The appearance of the man convinced the chief that he was in earnest, for reason seldom reels in that country. Africaner, fearless of the living or the dead, was not to be scared by the supposed spectre of the tomb. He instantly arose, and ordered his men to follow him to the spot. One jumped, and another jumped, and at each succeeding leap notes of softest music vibrated on the ear from beneath. Recourse was now had to exhumation, and the mysterious musician was soon brought to light. Mrs Albrecht's piano was forthwith dissected that each warrior might take a portion to wear as an ornament on his person. For many years afterwards remnants of the instrument might be seen among the natives.

The mysterious music played no more. Nor was it required, for Mrs Albrecht never saw the station again. After a visit to Cape Town, and when on the return journey, she sickened and died at Silver Fountain, on the 13th of April 1812; and many years afterwards the writer looked upon her lonely grave in the desert with peculiar feelings. Her bereaved husband did not long survive her. He also found a grave in African soil. But while God "buried His workmen He carried on His work." Africaner himself was soon afterwards converted, and a goodly number of his people, as well as himself, were gathered into the fold of the Redeemer.

324. Negro Boy and his Bible.— The Rev. Dr Philip, who laboured successfully for many years as a missionary in South Africa, gives the following pleasing incident in reference to a negro boy's anxiety to possess a copy of the Holy Scriptures:—"On one occasion, after having given a Bible to a negro girl whose mother had been left a widow with three children, a boy about ten years of age, her brother, pleaded very hard for one for himself. Agreeably to a rule I had laid down, to give but one Bible gratis to a family, I refused to give him one without money. After retiring a little, he returned with a skilling (threepence).

Informing him that I could not give him a Bible for that sum, he went away, and returned with another skilling. Finding this was not sufficient, he again tried to obtain more money, but in this he failed; making a fourth attempt, he succeeded, and obtained another skilling. He could do no more, his resources were exhausted; and he knew if he did not now succeed, he must be without a Bible. Under this impression you would have been affected to have seen this interesting boy in an imploring posture, with his arms extended, holding his skilling in his open hands, and the tears in his eyes, while he pleaded for a Bible. I could no longer resist his importunity. On inquiring how he procured the money, I was told that he got one skilling from his mother, and one from his brother, and that he pledged some playthings for the other. I gave him a Bible, and returned his skillings; and he could not have appeared more happy than he showed himself on this occasion if a crown had been put upon his head."

325. Alarm produced by a Cat.—In his interesting account of the introduction of Christianity into the Island of Rarotonga, the Rev. John Williams says:—"At this time a ludicrous circumstance occurred, which will illustrate the ignorance and superstition of this people. A favourite cat had been taken on shore by one of the teachers' wives on our first visit, and not liking his new companions, Tom fled to the mountains. The house of the priest Tiaki, who had just destroyed his idols, was situated at a distance from the settlement; and at night, while he was lying asleep on his mat, his wife, who was sitting awake by his side, musing upon the strange events of the day, beheld with consternation two fires glistening in the doorway, and heard with surprise a mysterious voice. Almost petrified with fear, she awoke her husband, and began to upbraid him with his folly in burning his god, who, she declared, was now come to be avenged of them. "Get up and pray, get up and pray!" she cried. The husband arose, and, on opening his eyes, beheld the same glaring lights, and heard the same ominous sound. Impelled by the extreme urgency of the case, he commenced with all possible vehemence vociferating the alphabet, as a prayer to God to deliver them from the vengeance of Satan. On hearing this, the cat, as much alarmed as the priest and his wife, of whose nocturnal peace he had been the unconscious disturber, ran away, leaving the poor people congratulating themselves on the efficacy of their prayers.

On a subsequent occasion, puss, in his perambulations, went to the district of the *Satanees;* and as the marae or temple stood in a retired spot, and was shaded by the rich foliage of trees of ancient growth, Tom, pleased with the situation, and wishing to be found in good company, took up his abode with the gods, and not meeting with any opposition from those within the house, he little expected any from those without. Some few days after, however, the priest came, accompanied by a number of worshippers, to present some offering to the god, and on opening the door, Tom very respectfully greeted him with a mew. Unaccustomed to such salutations, instead of returning it, he rushed back with terror, shouting to his companions, "Here's a monster from the deep! here's a monster from the deep!" Upon this the whole party hastened home, collected several hundreds of their companions, put on their war-caps, brought their spears, clubs, and slings, blackened themselves with charcoal, and, being thus equipped, came shouting to attack "poor puss." Affrighted at this formidable array of war, Tom immediately sprung towards the open door, and darted through the crowd of terror-stricken warriors, who fled with the greatest precipitation in all directions.

In the evening, these brave conspirators against the life of a cat were entertaining themselves and a numerous company of spectators with a dance, when Tom, wishing to see the sport, and bearing no malice, came to take a peep. No sooner did he present himself, than the terrified company fled in consternation; and the heroic warriors of the district again armed themselves and gave chase to this unfortunate cat. He escaped once more; but on the following night he ventured to creep under the coverlet of a family of natives when asleep, and whom he awoke with his purring. He was now pursued with clubs and spears, and put to death as "a monster of the deep."

326. Aitutaki evangelised.—When Christianity was introduced into some of the principal islands of the South Pacific Ocean, about half a century ago, the rapidity with which the work spread was perfectly astonishing. A mighty, unseen but Divine influence, appears to have been at work on the minds of the people to prepare them for the approaching change. No sooner was it known in one island what was taking place in another, than the people were ready to abandon their idols and bow down in worship to Jehovah. In some instances this occurred before a missionary arrived to instruct the people, and in others as the result of the humble efforts of native teachers to bring them to a knowledge of the truth. The narratives of some of the incidents which occurred read more like fairy tales than sober histories, and yet we know that they are true. Describing his visit to one of these islands to which native teachers had been sent, the Rev. John Williams gives the following account of what he witnessed, and of the manner in which the Gospel was introduced among the heathen natives:—

"After about five days' pleasant sailing we reached Aitutaki. A number of canoes crowded around us, filled with men, every one of whom was anxious to get on board our ship. We had, however, determined not to allow any canoe alongside, until we had seen either the chief or one of the teachers; for had the natives been hostile, they could easily have captured our small vessel. We received a grateful salutation from every canoe that approached us. Some of the natives cried out 'Good is the word of God: it is now well with Aitutaki! The good word has taken root at Aitutaki!' Finding, however, that we did not repose entire confidence in their assertions, some held up their hats, others their spelling-books to convince us of the truth of what they stated. As we approached the settlement we beheld a flagstaff with a white flag flying, which satisfied us that the teachers were alive. At length the chief's canoe came alongside, when we learned from Tebati, one of the first who embraced the Gospel, that the maras, or idol temples, were burned; that the idols which had escaped the general conflagration were in possession of the teachers; that the profession of Christianity was general: so much so, indeed, that not a single idolater remained; and that a large chapel was erected, nearly 200 feet in length, plastered and awaiting my arrival to open it. This news was as delightful as it was unexpected. When the teachers came on board, they not only confirmed all that had been told us, but added, that the Sabbath was regarded as a sacred day, no work of any kind being done on it; that all the people, men, women, and children, attended Divine service; and that family prayer was very general throughout the island.

"On hearing this good news, joy beamed in every countenance, and gratitude glowed in every heart. We hastened on shore to be eye-witnesses of what had been effected. The natives crowded around the boat, and, having to drag it a considerable distance, they amused and delighted us; for, instead of the unsightly gesticulations and lascivious songs in which they were formerly wont to indulge, some were now spelling long words, and others were repeating portions of the catechism or a prayer; another asking a blessing on his food; and others singing a verse of a hymn; indeed every one appeared anxious to show what progress he had made in the new religion.

"Shortly after landing we convened a meeting of the chiefs and people, at which we expressed our joy at hearing and seeing that they had demolished their maras, embraced the Gospel of Christ, and erected so fine and large a house for the worship of the one living and true God. We also informed them that we had brought two more teachers who, with their wives, would reside with them and to whom they must show kindness. After this interview we went to see the chapel which we found to be a spacious building, on which I gazed with delight. We next went to the teachers' house, and found it to be a neat, well-built cottage, plastered, and divided into five rooms. We commended them sincerely for their diligence, and for setting so good an example before the people. Posts for houses on a similar plan were collected in every part of the settlement; many dwellings were erected and others were in progress. Bedsteads had been made and hung with white native cloth, in imitation of those of their teachers. Little did I expect to see so much accomplished in so short a time. Eighteen months ago they were completely savage, wild and heathenish: now they had become mild, docile, diligent, and kind.

"Next day, while in the midst of an interesting conversation, our attention was arrested by a ringing sound. This was produced by striking an axe with a stone, which contrivance was their substitute for a bell. The ringer, or rather the striker, was followed through the settlement by a number of men and women, decently dressed in white cloth, and, when the congregation was assembled, we entered the spacious chapel. The six teachers with their wives, together with Papeiha and Vahapata, took their seats in front of the pulpit. As they were all clothed in European dresses, their appearance excited much surprise and interest; indeed, it was to the Aitutakians an ocular demonstration of the beneficial effects of Christianity. My esteemed colleague commenced the service with reading, singing, and prayer. I then preached my first service to them from one of the most delightful texts in the Bible, 'God so loved the world,' &c. It was indeed a delightful sight to behold from 1500 to 2000 people, just emerging from heathenism, of the most uncultivated appearance; some with long beards, others decorated with gaudy ornaments, but all behaving with the greatest decorum, and attending with glistening eyes and open mouth to the wonderful story of the love of God as displayed in the history of redemption. Many of them, however, were dressed very neatly; and I could not help contrasting their appearance with that which they presented when we first became acquainted with them. At that time also they were constantly killing and even eating each other, for they were cannibals; but now they were all, with one accord, bending their knees together in the worship of the God of peace and love."

In perusing such accounts as this and others which frequently occur in the early history of the South Sea Mission, we may remember for our encouragement in the prosecution of the missionary enterprise, that what the Gospel did for those poor, miserable, degraded outcasts it can do for others. We must exert ourselves in the good work with untiring vigilance, knowing that "in due season we shall reap if we faint not."

327. Rev. William Tranter.—

Among the early home missionaries of Wesleyan Methodism none was more laborious, persevering, or successful than the Rev. William Tranter, who entered the ministry in the year 1803, and who is now the oldest minister in the Connexion. He commenced his itinerant labours at a time when the work was in its infancy in many parts of Great Britain, and when those who engaged in it were subject to many privations. The scene of his earliest efforts to make known the good news of salvation, after he left his comfortable home at Madley, was first in Northamptonshire, then in Rutlandshire, and afterwards in the cold and bleak regions of Westmoreland, Cumberland, and Scotland, where he "endured hardness as a good soldier of Jesus Christ," and where he experienced many remarkable interpositions of Divine Providence in times of imminent peril. On the 29th of October 1874, Mr Tranter paid the writer a welcome visit, and we spent the day together very happily in conversation, prayer and praise. Although in the *seventy-first* year of his ministry, and verging upon one hundred years of age, the veteran servant of God became quite animated when speaking of former toils and triumphs, and while tracing all the way in which the Lord had led him these many years in the wilderness. Two remarkable instances of danger and deliverance by the good providence of God he related on this occasion, which are worthy of a brief record here:—

1. When travelling over the bleak and dreary mountains of the north in the depth of winter, when the ground was thickly covered with snow, and every trace of the usual road was completely obliterated, Mr Tranter having missed his way found himself, on one occasion, on the brink of a tremendous precipice. He was mounted on a small hardy Scotch pony, which had hitherto bravely waded through the driven snow up the mountain-side, but he felt convinced, from the appearance of the place, that if he proceeded, another step might plunge him into the yawning gulf beneath. He halted for a moment to consider what was best to be done, and to lift up his heart in prayer to God for direction. He resolved, if possible, to retrace his steps down the mountain gorge, following carefully the track marked in the snow, and he was at length providentially brought into the right path, which he discovered by the snow having been partly cleared away by the wind, and he ultimately reached his destination in safety.

2. On another occasion, Mr Tranter was journeying on horseback from Kendal to Arnside Tower, the residence of our mutual friend the late Mr Robert Gibson, where he was appointed to preach in the evening. On his way he had to cross a small

creek or arm of the sea near Milnthorp, which was safe enough at low water, but somewhat dangerous when the tide was up. Not being well acquainted with the locality, the preacher fearlessly plunged into the stream, but soon found to his sorrow that it was too deep to be forded at that place, and that the sloping sides were little better than quicksands which entangled the horse's feet in the most threatening manner. When in the most imminent peril, he was seen by a farmer who kindly came to his help, and succeeded in rescuing him from his dangerous position. Having been conducted higher up the stream, he crossed the water, and reached his destination without any harm beyond a thorough wetting. In giving this account Mr Tranter added that, from the commencement of this journey, a text of Scripture (Psalm xlii. 8) in which the phrase occurs,—"*the God of my life*," had been constantly running through his mind, and from which he was led to preach, on reaching his appointment, under a feeling and gracious influence never to be forgotten.

328. Singular Deputation.— When the Rev. John Williams arrived at Amoa, one of the Navigator Islands in the South Seas, he witnessed many strange scenes, one of which he describes as follows, to show the anxiety which was generally manifested for instruction in a knowledge of the Gospel :—" Just as the conversation terminated, our attention was arrested by the approach of about seventy females bringing gifts, and following each other in goose-like procession. These were preceded by four men, each of whom was bearing upon his shoulders a baked pig. On entering the house the men approached Makea and myself, and deposited their burdens at our feet. Each of the women also then laid down her present, and these were so numerous that, gigantic as my friend Makea was, he and myself were speedily concealed by the cocoanuts, bread-fruit, and yams, which were heaped up before us. On removing a portion from the top of the pile that we might catch a glimpse of our friends on the other side, we perceived that the principal woman and her daughter seated themselves by the two chiefs, one of whom she requested to be her spokesman. Through him she stated that they had heard of my intention to come to Amoa ; but, as the Christians of her settlement were only females, they could not expect to receive a visit from so great a chief as myself, and had therefore come to pay their respects to one from whom they had received the word of Jehovah. She then expressed her regret that their offering was so small, and accounted for it by saying that none of their husbands had yet become 'sons of the word ;' but still she hoped that I would accept it, as an expression of gratitude for having brought to them the knowledge of salvation.

" This was a novel and interesting event, and before replying to her address, I asked the teachers what they knew about this female chief and her friends. 'Oh,' said they, 'we know her well, her settlement is five miles away, and some time ago she came and resided with us for a month, during which she was exceedingly diligent in her attendance on our instructions. She then returned, collected all the women of her district, and so interested them by her statements, that very many have been induced to follow her example, and renounce their heathen worship. From that time to the present (they added), she has been constant in her periodical visits ; for as soon as her little stock of knowledge is expended, she returns and stays a few days with us to obtain more, which she treasures up and carefully carries back to her waiting companions.' The teachers also told us that she had built a place of worship, in which, when neither of them could attend, she herself conducted divine worship.

"After listening to this intelligence with surprise and delight, I expressed to my distinguished visitor the gratification I had derived from the interview, and exhorted her and her companions to be particularly circumspect in their conduct, that by their 'chaste conversation' they might 'win their husbands' to Christ. Having returned as handsome a present as I could make, our interview closed. The whole of the party presented a singular appearance; for although they had decorated themselves in their best style, and looked exceedingly handsome in the estimation of themselves and their countrymen, we hoped that their ideas upon this subject would soon be improved. The principal personage was tall and well-proportioned. Her dress consisted of a shaggy mat, dyed red, bound round her loins, which did not reach below the knees. The upper part of her person was uncovered, and anointed rather freely with sweet-scented oil, slightly tinged with turmeric rouge. Rows of large blue beads decorated her neck, and formed bracelets for her arms. Her head was shorn very bare, with the exception of a single tuft, about the size of a crown-piece over the left temple. From this hung a long lock of hair, which dangled carelessly about her neck. Several of the party were the unmarried daughters of chiefs. The costume of these differed from that of the married women; but they all presented a strange appearance, and were as proud of their strings of blue beads as any English lady of her most costly jewels. Their whole deportment, however, was consistent with modesty and propriety, and a further acquaintance with the Gospel would no doubt promote their improvement."

329. Badge of Christianity.—Describing a strange scene which presented itself to his view on arriving at Leone Bay, in the island of Tutuila, one of the Navigator group, the Rev. John Williams says:—"When about twenty yards from the beach, as the heathen presented rather a formidable appearance, I desired the native crew to cease rowing, and unite with me in prayer, which was our usual practice when exposed to danger. The chief who stood in the centre of the assembled multitude, supposing that we were afraid to land, made the people sit down under the grove of breadfruit, cocoa-nut, and other trees which girt the shore. He then waded into the water nearly up to the neck, and took hold of the boat, when addressing me in his native tongue, he said, 'Son, will you not come on shore? will you not land among us?' To this I replied, 'I do not know that I shall trust myself; I have heard a sad account of you in this bay, that you have taken two boats, and that you are exceedingly savage: and, perhaps, when you get me into your possession you will either injure my person or demand a ransom for my release.' 'Oh!' he shouted, 'we are not savage now, we are Christians.' 'You are *Christians?*' I said, 'where did you hear of Christianity?' 'Oh,' said he, 'a great chief from the white man's country, named Williams, came to Savaii, about twenty moons ago, and placed some *tama-fai-lotu*, "workers in religion" there, and several of our people who were there, began, on their return, to instruct their friends, many of whom have become "sons of the word." There they are; don't you see them?' Looking in the direction to which he pointed, I saw a group of about fifty persons seated under the wide-spreading branches of some large trees, apart from those whom he had ordered to sit down along the beach. Every one of this group had a piece of white native cloth tied round his arm. I inquired of the chief what this meant, when he replied, 'They are the Christians, and that cloth is to distinguish them from their heathen countrymen.' 'Why,' I immediately exclaimed, 'I am the person you allude to; my name is Williams; I took the workers in religion to Savaii twenty moons ago.' The moment he heard this he made a sign to the multitude, who sprang upon their feet, rushed to the sea, seized the boat and carried both it and us to the shore. Upon landing, Amoamo, the chief, took me by the hand, and conducted me to the Christians who wore the badge of their profession already mentioned; and after the usual salutations, I inquired where they had heard of Christianity. Upon this, one of their number, rather more forward than his brethren, replied that he had been down to the 'workers in religion,' had brought back some knowledge, and was now engaged in imparting it to his countrymen. 'And there is our chapel,' said he. 'don't you see it?' Turning to the direction in which he pointed, I saw a small rustic place of worship, which would hold about eighty or a hundred people, peeping through the foliage of bananas and breadfruit trees, in which it was embowered. Accompanied by my loquacious friend and two or three others, I asked him, on reaching the house, who performed service there on Sabbath-day? To this he instantly replied, 'I do.' 'And who,' inquired I, 'has taught you?' 'Why,' said he, 'did you not see the little canoe by the side of your boat when we carried you on shore just now? That is my canoe, in which I go down to the teachers, get some religion, which I bring carefully home and give it to the people; and when that is gone, I take my canoe again and fetch some more. And now you are come, for whom we have been so long waiting; where's our teacher? Give me a man full of religion, that I may not expose my life to danger by going so long a distance to fetch it.' I was truly grieved at being compelled to tell him that I had no missionary. On hearing this he was affected almost to tears, and would scarcely believe me; for he imagined that the vessel was full of missionaries, and that I could easily supply the demand." It is pleasing to be able to add that Tutuila was afterwards supplied with teachers, and soon became a prosperous mission-station.

330. Domestic Worship in Fiji.—The Rev. Joseph Dare from Australia, addressing the Wesleyan Conference assembled at Camborne in 1874, gave the following incident as illustrative of the prevalence of family prayer among the converts in Fiji:—I was taking tea with your missionary and his wife in the lone island of Kandavu, in the midst of 10,000 Fijians. As we were at tea the bell rang: the missionary said, "That is the signal for family worship. Now listen. You will hear the drums beat." And immediately they began to echo to each other around the shores of that southern sea. The missionary said, "There are 10,000 people on these islands, and I do not know of a single house in which there will not be family worship in the course of half-an-hour from this time." What a lesson this teaches to professing Christians everywhere!

331. King George's Speech.— The change produced in the Friendly Islands by the introduction of the Gospel, about half a century ago, is perfectly marvellous. Nor is the progress the people are making under the benign rule of King George Tabou less remarkable. A very respectable seminary called "Tabou College," in honour of the king, has existed for several years past, under the able management of the Rev. E. J. Moulton; the annual examination of which was held on the 29th of May 1874, when an interesting scene was presented to the view. In the presence of the King and Queen of the Friendly Islands, and of several governors, judges, and magistrates, the native students acquitted themselves well in reading, writing, arithmetic, geography, mensuration, algebra, Euclid, English, natural philosophy, divinity and singing. King George presided as usual, and the occasion was rendered memorable by the able and sensible speech which he delivered at the close of the exercises. After some of the governors and missionaries had expressed their sentiments, the king said:—"We will give God the glory of all the good we see. It is right we should praise the collegians who have done well; and so we do. We say, 'Well done.' Let me ask you to look around you—at Fiji. It is lost to the people. At Samoa, it is being lost. But Tonga, here, between the two places, has not yet been touched by a foreign power. Why and how is this? Is Tonga wise? No—it is foolish. Is Tonga strong? No, it is weak. Is Tonga rich? No, it is poor. Is Tonga numerously populated? No, we are few in number. We are a people and a kingdom to-day, because 'God is with us.' Look at what we are, at the good we have; it is the Lord's doing. It is true we are a people and a kingdom to-day, but unless we attend to instruction and seek to become wise, we shall waste away. You have heard to-day in the explanations by the collegians about the human body, that you must be careful what you eat and drink, and you must build better houses to live in, if you would continue to exist as a people. Look at the great nations of the earth; at Britain, France, Germany and America. They live because they are wise, and if we would continue a people and a nation, we must seek to become wise—wise about food, raiment and dwellings. In my youthful days there was no college, and I cannot do the things you students can; but this I can do: I can encourage *you*. Mr Moulton has told us that he is going on a visit to Australia, because of continued ill health. Well, this is right. We can never get him back from the grave if he die, but we may get him back from Sydney. Let him go and return to us again, and while he is away, you collegians must attend well to your work. And this is the end of my speech."

332. Punishment of Sin.—The Rev. John Thomas, of the Baptist Mission at Serampore, was an eccentric but shrewd and able man. A striking instance of his tact and presence of mind is recorded in connection with his labours among the Hindus. He was one day, after addressing a crowd of natives on the banks of the Ganges, accosted by a Brahmin as follows:—"Sir, don't you say that the devil tempts men to sin?" "Yes," answered the missionary. "Then," said the Brahmin, "certainly the fault is the devil's;

the devil, therefore, and not man, ought to suffer the punishment." While the countenances of many of the natives discovered their approbation of the Brahmin's inference, Mr Thomas, observing a boat with several men on board descending the river, with that facility for instructive retort for which he was distinguished, replied, "Brahmin, do you see yonder boat?" "Yes." "Suppose I were to send some of my friends to destroy every person on board, and bring me all that is valuable in the boat, who ought to suffer punishment—I for instructing them, or they for doing this wicked act?" "Why," answered the Brahmin with alacrity, "you ought all to be put to death together." "Ay, Brahmin," replied Mr T——, "and if you and the devil sin together, the devil and you will be punished together."

333. Faithful unto Death.— Many pleasing instances of Christian fidelity occurred among the native Christians in India during the sepoy rebellion of 1857, one of which may be given as a specimen. Through the instrumentality of Colonel Wheeler, who used to preach sometimes in the bazaar of the great city of Delhi, a Mohammedan named Wilayat Ali, was persuaded to give up his trust in the false prophet, and to believe in Jesus Christ as his Saviour. He was baptized, and, notwithstanding the persecution which he endured, he became a preacher in the bazaars. At length he became very popular, and thousands flocked to hear him. It is said that a great prince, Mirza Hajee, used to creep, like Nicodemus, to Wilayat's house to hear more about Jesus.

One Monday morning a friend rushed into the house, crying, "The sepoys! the sepoys! they are murdering the Christians!" Wilayat called Fatima his wife, and his seven children around him, and prayed :— "O Lord, we have fallen into the fiery trial! Oh help us to confess our dear Lord, that if we die we may obtain a crown of glory!" He then kissed his wife and children, and said, "Whatever comes, don't deny Christ. If you confess Him you will have a crown of glory." His wife cried bitterly, he said all he could to comfort her. "Oh, remember, dear wife, if you die you will go to Jesus, and if you live, Jesus will be with you. If any of the missionaries are alive, they will take care of you after my death; but if the missionaries should be killed, Christ lives for ever. Even if the children should be killed before your eyes, do not deny Christ." While Wilayat was yet speaking, a number of sepoys on horseback rode up to the house, and knowing him to be a Christian, said, "Repeat the Mohammedan creed, or we will shoot you." But he would not deny his Lord. "Tell us what you are," said one. "I am a Christian, and a Christian I will live and die," he replied. They dragged him along the ground, beating him about the head and face with their shoes. Not being soldiers they had no swords. "Now preach Christ to us," said some in tones of mockery. Others said, "Turn to Mohammed and we will let you go." "No, I never, never will," the faithful martyr cried; "my Saviour took up His cross and went to God, and I will lay down my life and go to Him." The scorching rays of the sun were beating upon the poor sufferer's head. With a laugh one of the wretches exclaimed, "I suppose you would like some water." "I do not want water," replied the martyr; "when my Saviour was dying, He had nothing but vinegar mingled with gall. But do not keep me in this pain. If you mean to kill me, do so at once." Another sepoy coming who was armed, uplifted his sword; the martyr called aloud, "Lord Jesus, receive my spirit!" and with one stroke his head was nearly cut off.

Fatima, his wife, who was standing under a tree, beheld the stroke, and, shrieking with agony, ran back to her house. But she found it on fire, and surrounded by people who were plundering it. Then she fled to Prince Mirza Hajee's house, where she discovered her fatherless children. At the end of three days, Mirza Hajee came to Fatima and said, "I dare not keep you any longer, but if you will become a Mohammedan, you will be safe, and I will give you a house, and three pounds a month for your support." But Fatima would not give up her Saviour. No one attempted to kill her, for very few knew that she was a Christian. After ten days, she escaped with her children out of the city of Delhi, and went to a village forty miles off. After three months, hearing that the English had taken Delhi, she returned there. But soon her little baby died, and she wept much. She knew, however, that it was gone to be with Jesus, and that gave her comfort. She now began to inquire about the missionaries; but found they had all been killed. But remembering the missionaries at Agra, her native town, she sent to one of them. Her joy was great, when an answer arrived, inviting her to go to Agra. She thanked God, and went to her native place, with all her surviving children.

334. What one Tract did.—A missionary in India was giving away tracts, when a little boy about eight years of age asked for one. At first he was refused, for he was so young that the missionary thought it would be better, as the tracts were scarce, to keep them for the older people. But the child begged so hard that he gave him one called "The Way to Heavenly Bliss." A few days afterwards the little fellow came again and asked for another tract. "But have you read the one I gave you before?" asked the missionary. "Yes," said he; and, standing up before all present, he repeated it from beginning to end. Having committed it to memory he had given it to another youth for the same purpose, and now applied for a second copy to be employed in the same way. On beholding such a proof of the good use that was made of the tracts, the missionary gladly complied with the request.

A copy of this same tract was the means of leading four persons to Jesus on another occasion. It was given in a public market in one of the largest cities in India by a missionary to a young man who read it, then came to know more about the way of salvation. He soon became a Christian. A young girl, who afterwards married this young man, also learned from this tract to love Jesus. Then his little brother was persuaded to go to the mission church and school. After he had gone some time, he said he had given himself to Jesus and asked to be baptized. He was only eleven years of age, and the missionary wanted to be sure that he understood what it was to be a Christian, so he delayed his baptism for a short time. Meanwhile the child was attacked with cholera, and his mother, seeing his danger, told him she wished to go to the temple and make offerings to one of the idols in order that he might recover; but he begged of her not to go. "I do not worship idols," said he; "I worship Christ my Saviour. If He is pleased to spare me a little longer in the world, it will be well; if not I shall go to Him." The last words he uttered were, "I am going to Christ the

Lord," and then he died. So he joined the Church in heaven first. Then to the young man's great joy, his old father was led to give up his idols to which he had prayed for more than fifty years, and was induced to come to Jesus for the pardon of his sins, and was saved and made happy. All this resulted from the influence of one tract with the blessing of God upon the truth which it contained, followed up by the instructions of the missionary.

335. **Self-denial for Christ.**— The Rev. A. Judson, missionary to Burmah, gives the following touching instance of self-denial for Christ. "A Karen woman offered herself for baptism. After the usual examination, I inquired whether she could give up her ornaments for Christ. It was an unexpected blow. I explained the spirit of the Gospel, and appealed to her own consciousness of vanity. I then read to her the apostle's prohibition, 1 Tim. ii. 9. She looked again and again at her handsome necklace, and then, with an air of modest decision, took it off, saying, 'I love Christ more than this.' Would to God that this spirit of self-denial and true sacrifice prevailed more extensively in the Church of Christ at home and abroad."

336. **Dr Morrison and the Little Girl.**—It is related of the great and good Dr Morrison, the first Protestant missionary to China, that when at New York, on his way to his distant field of labour, he was placed in an apartment where a little child had already gone to sleep. Awaking in the morning, she turned in her little crib as usual, to talk to her mother; but, seeing a stranger where she expected to find her parents, she raised herself with a look of alarm, and fixing her eyes steadily on his face, she said, "Man, do you pray to God?" "Oh yes, my dear," said the missionary, "every day. God is my best friend." The little girl then laid her head back on the pillow and fell asleep, as if she felt there could be no danger, even when in a room alone with a stranger who lived in the habit of prayer.

337. **Useful Lesson.**—A Christian minister had a wayward and indolent son, who, after having tried the patience of his parents to the very utmost, absconded from his home, went on board a ship as a common sailor, and left his native land. His sorrowful parents could only pray for him and send him good advice, from time to time, when made acquainted with his course and destination. While the vessel in which the boy had embarked was anchored in a foreign port, waiting to take in a fresh cargo, a party of sailors went on shore one day and brought back with them an intelligent native youth who could play some curious kind of music. He amused them for a long time, but at length he said, "You must now take me on shore." The sailors told him he must not go yet. "Oh, indeed, I cannot stay any longer," said the black boy, beginning to cry, "and I will tell you why. A kind Christian missionary has come to the village where I live. From him I have learned all I know about Jesus Christ, in whom I now believe and whom I desire to serve. This is about the hour when he meets us under the shade of a tree to tell us more about the Gospel, and I want to go and hear him." The sailors were quite overcome with the cries of the native youth, and at once rowed him on shore.

But no one was more impressed with this instance of love for the Word of God than the minister's prodigal son. It made a deep impression upon his mind, and taught him a lesson never to be forgotten. He felt condemned for his own sin and folly, remembering the privileges he had enjoyed in his highly favoured home. "Here am I," he said to himself, "the son of a minister in England, knowing far more about Jesus Christ than that poor heathen boy, and yet caring far less about Him! That little fellow is now listening to the Word of Life, while I am living in carelessness and sin." In great distress of mind he retired that night to his hammock; but the prayers and admonitions of his pious father came back to his thoughts, and reminded him not only of his sin and folly, but also of the way of salvation, concerning which he had been wont to hear from his childhood. The result was he sought and found mercy. How great must have been the joy of his parents, when their long-lost son returned home a true Christian, converted to God chiefly by the influence of the lesson taught by a native youth connected with a mission-station.

338. Good Missionary Meeting.—Complaints have sometimes been heard that public missionary meetings have declined in interest and popularity of late years. And there may be some truth in this, seeing that the novelty of the thing has passed away, and that such gatherings are much more numerous among all denominations now than at any early period of the enterprise. We believe, however, that by the adoption of proper means a good missionary meeting may still be realised. For the attainment of this object let ministers and people be *much in prayer* for the special blessing of God on speakers and hearers; let the preparatory sermons have a *direct bearing on the subject* of Christian missions, and not on mere, commonplace subjects, however excellent, as we have sometimes known them; and let the meeting be *well announced* both from the pulpit and in social intercourse, that it may be everywhere known and remembered. Most of these, and some other suggestions, are embodied in a striking article on the subject in the *Methodist Recorder* of the 16th October 1874, from which we make the following brief extract:—

"If we want a good missionary meeting we must *make a stir about it.* If it is coldly announced from the pulpit on the Sunday, together with half a dozen unimportant notices for the week, no wonder that nobody thinks of it. If a foolish regard to expenditure grudges a good bill announcing the meeting, no wonder that nobody outside knows anything of it. Advertise it well. In short, put steam into the thing and it will go. Don't and it won't. No missionary meeting need be a failure when there is anything like a congregation at the Sunday services. Then there is one thing more, as important as any, and perhaps more important. If we are to increase the interest of our missionary meeting, or even to sustain it, we must *look after the children.* For their own sakes we should interest them in this matter. They will be our adult audience in ten or twelve years. How much of the attachment to missions, of the ardour and self-sacrifice that we find in some of our oldest and best members, sprang from the imperishable memories of their childhood? Feelings were stirred forty or fifty years ago; and the chord is vibrating with sweet music still. For their own sakes interest the children. And interest the children, too, because of the life and enthusiasm that they can bring into a meeting. The best advertiser of the work is a little girl. Get her interested in it and she will tell everybody what is going to be. The next best—but a long way behind—is a little boy. He will tell his mother and all the boys of his acquaintance. Get the children interested, and the missionary meeting will be a success. Give them two or three hymns to sing at the meeting. Have these hymns printed and freely distributed among the people, and have a short hymn between the speeches. Let the children have a prominent and comfortable place in front of the gallery, directly opposite the platform, that they may both see and hear. Then there is one thing more: let it be distinctly understood that one of the speakers will *say something to the children*, and let care be taken to get somebody who will interest them, and you need not fear but others will be interested also. There are children everywhere, never so many as to-day, and where there are children no missionary meeting need fail. Even where juvenile missionary meetings are held, be sure to let the children have a share in the annual meeting."

339. An Ingenious Missionary. —Mr Boerressen, a Danish missionary, who laboured in one of the famine districts of India in 1874, is said to have made that calamity the means of greatly extending his Church. Being requested by the government to undertake the responsibility of distributing grain to the famishing natives in the neighbourhood of his station, he offered to do so without payment, but on condition that he might insist on preaching to the people before dispensing the food. This was agreed to, and the starving multitudes received the rice on the condition that they first listened to the missionary's sermon, which only lasted some twenty minutes. A great revival, it is stated, took place, and six hundred persons were baptized in the course of a few weeks. This is certainly a novel way of conducting missionary operations, and of compelling people to come in and to hear the gospel; but it seems to have succeeded to a considerable extent, and it remains to be seen how many of the six hundred converts will continue in the right path, when the distribution of rice has ceased, and things return to their usual course. Mr Boerressen appears to be a very shrewd, not to say a cunning missionary. Some curious things are related with reference to his proceedings at an earlier period of his career in India. It is said that he procured the land for his station at an almost nominal rent, and built his first church at a cost of six shillings. He is now erecting a more pretentious structure, which he estimates will cost at least fourteen shillings, and will seat 1000 persons—the materials and labour being gratuitously supplied. He depends upon no Society for funds to carry on his work, having undertaken it on his own personal responsibility; but at the same time he distinctly states that he would be glad of assistance from a charitable English public. However eccentric the plans adopted for the propagation of the gospel in heathen lands, the true friends of the cause will wish them success, so far as they are consistent with truth and righteousness.

340. Practical Gratitude.—The ship which carried the first Baptist missionaries to India more than fifty years ago, also carried a sailor boy named James Christie, who was converted during the voyage. The sailor boy rose in time to be a Christian captain, and after a long and honourable career, he died in peace in Albion, New York, in 1874. Nor did he forget his obligation to that branch of Christ's Church through the instrumentality of which he was brought to a saving knowledge of the truth. In addition to many acts of Christian benevolence during his life, he bequeathed at his death 10,000 dollars to the Baptist Missionary Union.

It would be well if all who have received benefit from Christian missions, directly or indirectly, or from the gospel of Christ in any form, would be equally prompt in giving practical evidence of their gratitude to the Giver of all good, according to their means and circumstances, remembering the apostolical injunction, "Freely ye have received, freely give."

341. The Pearl of Great Price.— A wealthy lady of Java, having been married to a European merchant, came to reside in England. She often called for her treasure-box, and amused herself by inspecting her jewels. She would first hold up a fine necklace, and then a pair of earrings, and boast of their beauty as they glittered in the sunlight. Her Scotch nurse being one day in her room, in broken English the lady said, "Nurse, this is poor place—poor place! Me look out of the window and see no woman in the street with jewels on. In my country we dig into the hills and we get gold, and silver, and precious jewels. You dig in your hills and get nothing but stones." The nurse replied, "Oh, yes, madam, we have a pearl in our country—a pearl of great price." The lady caught her words with great eagerness. "Pearl of great price! have you indeed? Oh that my husband was come home! He would buy me this pearl; me part with all my pearls when he come home to get this pearl of great price." "Oh," said the nurse, "this pearl is not to wear. It is not to be had in the way you think. It is a precious pearl indeed, and they who have it cannot lose it. They who have it are at peace and have all they wish for." "Indeed," said the lady; "what can this pearl be?" "The pearl," said the nurse, "is the Lord Jesus Christ, who came into the world to save sinners. All who truly receive this saying, and have Christ in their hearts as the hope of glory, have that which makes them rich and happy, whatever else they want; and so precious is Jesus to them that they count all things but loss for the excellency of the knowledge of Him." It pleased God to bless the words of the Scotch nurse. The lady obtained a believing view of Christ, "in whom are hid all the treasures of wisdom and knowledge;" and in whose presence this world's gems cease to shine, just as the stars lose their brightness and cease to shine before the splendour of the morning sun. Some time afterwards, the lady sickened and died, and on her death-bed she desired that her jewels should be sold and the proceeds go toward sending the knowledge of the "Pearl of great price" to those in heathen countries who have it not. She felt its value and she wished that her country-people and all the world might feel it too.

342. Laughing at Worship.— None but those who have been actually engaged in endeavouring to introduce the Gospel among an ignorant, wild, and savage people, can comprehend the numerous difficulties which have to be encountered at the commencement of the work. One of these is thus described by the Rev. William Shaw, when adverting to some of his earliest religious services with the untutored Kaffirs in South Africa in 1826.

On one occasion whilst engaged in religious conversation with a party of natives, I wished to introduce something like an act of Divine worship, in addition to my familiar talk with them concerning the Gospel; but as they had never been accustomed to any kind of religious worship,—for the Kaffirs are not even worshippers of idols,—they did not readily comprehend my intentions. I, however, desired the interpreter to explain that "I wished them all to kneel on the grass as they would see me do, as I was about to speak to God, and ask Him to do us good, and that because He is great and holy we must prostrate ourselves before Him." After some difficulty they all imitated me, and knelt down in a circle; but there was one droll fellow among them, who, on looking round and noticing the new and strange attitude which they had assumed, could not restrain his risible faculties; he began to laugh immoderately; a fit of cachinnation spread itself around the circle, and for a time worship was rendered impracticable. This sort of difficulty often occurred afterwards in various places when we itinerated among the people. But let the missionary cultivate the grace of patience; for patience and firmness will, in time, by the Divine blessing, remove any obstacle of this kind. The people soon become orderly and attentive; and when individuals who have not been accustomed to worship become noisy and ill-behaved, they are immediately taken to task and subdued into quietness, by their better instructed or better informed countrymen. I have not unfrequently, at subsequent periods, seen a plebeian Kaffir reprove a chief for disorderly conduct during public worship. The argument adduced by them on such occasions is, that even if they do not believe the Gospel, yet civility and good manners towards the teacher, who does believe, require that he should not be disturbed or affronted while engaged in the worship of God.

343. John Woolman.—When labouring in the West Indies in 1841, the writer was favoured with a visit from three Quaker evangelists from America, who manifested a deep interest in the welfare of the poor negroes, then just emerging from their long night of bondage. On their departure they presented him with a copy of the "Journal of the life, Gospel labours, and Christian experiences of that faithful minister of Jesus Christ, John Woolman." This remarkable volume has often been perused since, with feelings of uncommon interest, the more so because we were shortly afterwards privileged to visit the beautiful valley of Wyoming in Pennsylvania State, which was the principal scene of his self-denying labours among the poor Indians, with whom, as well as with the abject negro slaves, he deeply sympathised in their sufferings. A few particulars of the toils and triumphs of this remarkable man may be acceptable to the reader:—

John Woolman was born at Northampton, West Jersey, North America, in the year 1720, of parents belonging to the Society of Friends. In his own simple and charming narrative of the dealings of the Lord with him, he says, that when he was only seven years old he began "to be acquainted with the operations of Divine love. In 1743, feeling constrained to devote most of his time to itinerant evangelism, he obtained a certificate from the Burlington monthly meeting, and set out on the first of a long series of preaching tours; now amongst the scattered struggling settlers of the backwoods, now amongst the thriving traders of the ports, now amongst the wealthy planters of the South, and subsequently among the wild Indians of the forests. His tastes and sympathies were with the poor sheep in the wilderness; he loved to share their rude and scanty hospitality, or to lodge in the woods when nightfall overtook him at a distance from any settlement. He made long journeys for the express purpose of remonstrating with individual members of the Society of Friends who kept slaves, and as an abolitionist was far in advance of the times in which he lived. These evangelistic and philanthropic tours extended over a distance of nine hundred miles from his home in New Jersey.

In the year 1863, with the concurrence of his monthly meeting, John Woolman went on a mission to the Indians, having, as he records, many years felt "love in his heart towards the natives of this land, who dwell far back in the wilderness, whose ancestors were the owners of the land where we dwell, and who, for a very small consideration, assigned their inheritance to us." The night before he started, "News came from Pittsburg that the Indians had taken a fort from the English, and slain and scalped English people in divers places." But this did not delay him for a moment. He crossed the mountains of the blue ridge, and with an Indian guide, made for the native village of Wehaloosing, two hundred miles from Philadelphia. Lodging in the woods in the night, he examined himself strictly as to his motives for undertaking the enterprise, and arrived at the satisfactory conclusion that "love was the first motive, and thence a concern arose to spend some time with the Indians, that I might *feel and understand their life*, and the spirit they live in, *if happily I might receive some instruction from them*, or they be in any degree helped forward by me." He mused tenderly on the heavy hardships which colonisation had inflicted on the poor aborigines, pushing them back from the sea-board and the tidal rivers, and, while thus depriving them of the fish, destroying the wild herds on which they mainly depended for food, and poisoning them with rum—the "fire-water" of the pale-faced strangers, which has worked such mischief among the red men of the forest.

Woolman opened his commission at the Indian settlement of Wyoming, not long afterwards the scene of that terrible massacre of the whites which Thomas Campbell made the theme of his noblest poem, "Gertrude of Wyoming," and where a monument was erected to commemorate the event, on which I looked with peculiar feelings in the month of May 1844. Here news met the missionary, brought by "Indian runners," of "warriors with English scalps," prowling about the place of his destination. He says, "I grew jealous of myself, lest the desire of reputation as a man firmly settled to persevere through dangers, or the fear of disgrace arising on my returning without performing the visit, might have some place in me." After travelling sixteen days his health gave way under the hardship, exposure, and unusual diet; and an Indian informed him that he was close upon the war-trail of the savages. He, however, still pressed on with a Moravian missionary whom he had met with in the way, and the next day reached Wehaloosing. By the direction of their guide they sat down on a log, whilst he went to the town to tell the people that they were come. He says, "Great awfulness came over us, we rejoiced in a sense of God's love. After a while we heard a conch-shell blow several times, and then came an Indian, who kindly invited us to a house near the town, where we found about sixty people seated in silence. On the sides of large trees, peeled for the purpose, were various representations of men going to and returning from the wars, &c. I walked about, viewing these Indian histories which were painted in red and black, thinking on the innumerable afflictions which the proud, fierce spirit produceth." To these poor children of the forest he preached several times, "feeling the current of love running strong,"—so that one of them, named Papunheang, exclaimed, "I love to feel where words come from." He not only addressed them in their public assemblies, but visited them in their wigwams, and became much endeared to them.

After labouring long and earnestly for the benefit of the poor negroes, Indians and others in America, in 1772, John Woolman visited England where a gracious influence attended his ministry. Arriving at York he was seized with small-pox, of which he died in great peace, at the age of fifty-two. He was the author of several works on slavery, education and other subjects, and his memory is cherished with much affection by all who are acquainted with his real worth.

344. Boniface, "The Apostle of Germany."—During the dark and gloomy Middle Ages of our country's history, it is pleasant to meet with a few devoted Christian men who possessed in a remarkable degree the genuine missionary spirit, despite the ignorance and superstition by which they were surrounded. One of the most eminent of these was Boniface, who because of his abundant labours has been called "the apostle of Germany." He was an Englishman, born at Crediton, in Devonshire, about the year 680. Having received a religious training in a monastery at Exeter, he might have occupied a prominent position in the priesthood at home; but, at an early period, a desire came upon him to carry the Gospel to the pagans of his own race in Germany.

It was in 715, when he was in the prime of life, that Boniface went forth on his arduous mission, in which he was destined to spend forty years. At first he was driven back by the hostile attitude of the pagan Saxons; but nothing daunted by the opposition which he met with, he renewed the attempt with greater success three or four years afterwards. On this occasion he went to Rome to obtain for his enterprise the countenance and help of the Pope, for he was a consistent Catholic at a time when Popery was not so degenerate a system as it afterwards became. The first twenty years that Boniface and his companions spent in Germany were years of hard indefatigable work, the results of which were seen in forests cleared, idols forsaken, native evangelists trained, and schools, monasteries, and churches established in various places. All this was not achieved without much patient toil and some remarkable deeds of daring. An account of one of these has come down to us. It is said that an object of superstitious fear, far and near, was an ancient oak at Geismar in Hesse. While this stood, idolatry stood. Boniface resolved to prove that it was no god. Giving notice of his intention, on the day appointed, he advanced with his companions to the oak, axe in hand; soon the popular idol lay prostrate on the ground, and with it the faith and worship of centuries.

So rapid was the spread of the truth, and so great the demand for additional labourers, that Boniface had to appeal to the Church in England for help. The spirit and tenor of his letter can scarcely fail to command our admiration. "Pray for us," he wrote, "and pray to God and our Lord Jesus Christ, who would

John Woolman, the Quaker Philanthropist, preaching to the Indians.

have men to be saved and come to a knowledge of the truth, that He will vouchsafe to convert to the true faith the hearts of the pagan Saxons, that they may be delivered from those bonds of the evil one wherewith they are held captive. Have compassion on them, brethren. They often say, 'We are of one blood with our brothers in England;' have pity on them, your kinsmen according to the flesh, and remember that the time for working is short, for the end of all things is at hand, and death cannot praise God, nor can any give Him thanks in the pit. Aid us, then, while it is yet day."

The appeal was not in vain; but, after Boniface had been favoured to see great prosperity, his useful life was brought to an untimely end by a storm of persecution which broke over him and his associates when on a mission to the pagan remnant of Frisia. He died the death of a missionary martyr on the 5th of June 1755, and rested from his labours in the seventy-fifth year of his age.

345. Persecution in Italy.—Mr Arrighi, an Italian evangelist employed by Dr Vernon, superintendent of the Methodist Episcopal Mission in Italy, writing from Florence under date of July 6, 1874, gives the following account of his experience at the commencement of his labours, and of the opposition that he met with from his countrymen:—"Last February I was sent by the president here to open a mission, and preached my first sermon, Feb. 6, 1874, to a large audience of Italians. From that time up to the present, I have preached three sermons a week. While preaching my first sermon, a shower of stones was thrown against one of the doors of my hall; but Jesus gave me courage to go ahead. A few evenings afterwards, I was mobbed by a mob sent there by the parish priest. Whilst I was preaching to a few in the hall, one of the doors which I always kept closed, was broken down by this mob, who made a rush for me, intending to take my life. I was alone; I did not know a single soul; indeed, everything outside looked very dark; but oh, within all was joy and peace. I felt that Jesus was with me, and therefore I was not afraid. The Lord moved the hearts of two young men who were in the mob to come up to me. Another said to the mob, that the first man that dared to touch me would be a dead man. They then told me to follow them and not be afraid. I saw that they were my friends, and I followed them. They then took me into a place of security, and went after the police. When they arrived on the ground, they made a thorough examination, and next morning six of the ringleaders were arrested, and lodged in gaol, where they remained for over two months. This took place on Friday evening, and I had only Saturday to repair the hall and door; but I got things fixed up the best I could, and on Sunday I had my services as usual, and have had them ever since. Almost at every service I have had two police in the hall; but notwithstanding this, now and then stones are being thrown against one of the doors.

"Sometimes they come in front of my hall during service, and set up hallooing and hissing; but Jesus is giving me the victory, and now I have a little church of about thirty members, and among them are the two young men who so nobly defended me, and, I may say, saved my life on the night of the mob. Oh, how they love me! I have, indeed, some very interesting cases of conversion, which would do honour to any Methodist revival meetings. Almost every week some new ones are coming into the Church. The Lord is truly with me, and oh, how I thank Him for the success He has given me! I could write you a very long letter about my church and other things, but time will not permit. I have so many things that I want to write that I hardly know what will interest you most, and must now conclude for the present."

346. Progress of Methodism in Canada.—At a great representative meeting of various branches of Methodism in America, held on the 18th of July 1874, the Rev. Dr Anson Green from Canada said, "The Dominion of Canada salutes the United States of America, and the Wesleyan Church in Canada presents its greetings to all the branches of the Methodist Church on this continent. We have a peculiar filial affection for the Methodist Episcopal Church, for we owe to you our existence. Eighty-four years ago there was in this region a presiding elder's district, which extended south as far as New York, east to Boston, north as far as Montreal, and west beyond the great Falls of Niagara. A very large district, to be sure, but there were giants in those days, and among those giants, and the prince of them all, was the Rev. Freeborn Garrettson. He sent out scouts into all this region, and one came across into Canada, and reported that it was a good field for Methodism. The next Conference, sitting in Albany, 1790, sent the first appointed Methodist preachers into Canada." He then briefly sketched the growth of the work in the Dominion, and spoke of the efforts now being made to unite all the different branches of Methodism in Canada, saying that "the Canadian Conference and the British Eastern American Conference are already united, and the brethren of the New Connexion Church are expected soon to be organically connected with us. We have, moreover, had some progress. Our first little Conference of 17 has grown to a ministry of 700, and our membership has reached 75,000. More than one-fourth of all the people of Upper Canada, at the last census, reported themselves as Methodists. More than one-half of all the Church buildings are Methodist churches. I thank God for all that He has done for me personally. I have been happy in Him for fifty-four years, but I have never been so happy as I am to-day."

347. "The Seed is the Word." The Rev. E. R. Young, a missionary from the far north-west of America, gives the following striking instance of the influence of the written Word of God, in regions where the missionaries had never yet been:—"I was sitting in my study one day reading, when the door noiselessly opened, and a few Indians entered the room. I at once observed, as I rose to speak to them, that they were strangers. After a little conversation with them I interrogated them as to the object of the visit. 'Missionary,' said they, 'we have come from a far-off land to see you; and we want you to go and visit us, and explain to us the Word of God.' I replied, 'I am pleased to see you, and should like to go; but where do you live?' 'Our home,' they replied, 'is *fifteen nights* away.' This is the Indian mode of estimating distances, meaning that they had travelled sixteen days, sleeping on the river banks or rocks fifteen times.

"I answered, 'I am delighted to see Indians from such a distant place: but what put this desire into your hearts to see the missionary?' Their answer was this, 'We have read the Word of God in our wigwams, and hundreds of us can read it, but we want you to come and explain it to us.' I answered, 'You say you can read the Good Book; did you ever have a missionary among you?' 'No.' 'Why, how is this?' I asked, getting very much interested. 'How then did you learn to read?' Their answer is worth remembering. 'Missionary,' they continued, 'the hunting grounds of your Indians and ours adjoin; and when we would be out in the woods hunting the wild animals, sometimes when the days were bad for hunting, we would go and visit your Christian Indians. We found they always had with them their Bibles or Testaments. They taught us the syllabic characters, and how to read; and then when we returned to our people, we taught others, and they taught others, until now the *whole tribe* can read the Word of God; and when we carried our furs in boats down to York Factory on the Hudson's Bay, we found at the mission house there as many Bibles as we required for our people. Come, missionary, and visit us, and explain this Good Book to us. It is like a musical instrument; there are sweet sounds, but we cannot read it aright.'" Thus was the way prepared for the preaching of the everlasting Gospel to these poor benighted pagans by the silent influence of the written Word.

348. Belief in the Resurrection.

—On one occasion when a naval officer was inspecting a mission school in the Island of Barbadoes, containing about two hundred negro boys and girls, a remarkable instance of intelligence and ingenuity was exhibited, which is worthy of notice. A little boy made the usual sign, by lifting up his hand, that he wished to speak with the teacher. On going to the child, who was only about eight years of age, the teacher inquired what was the matter. "Massa," he replied, with a look of horror and indignation, which the officer said he should never forget, and pointing to a boy of the same age, who sat beside him, "Massa, this boy says he does not believe in the resurrection." "That is very bad," said the teacher; "but do you, my little fellow," addressing the informer, "believe in the resurrection yourself?" "Yes, massa; I do." "But can you prove it from the Bible?" "Yes, massa; Jesus says, 'I am the resurrection and the life: he that believeth in Me, though he were dead yet shall he live;' and in another place, 'Because I live ye shall live also.'" The teacher added, "Can you prove it from the Old Testament also?" "Yes, for Job says, 'I know that my Redeemer liveth, and that He shall stand at the latter day upon the earth: and though after my skin worms destroy this body, yet in my flesh shall I see God;' and David says, in one of his Psalms, 'I shall be satisfied when I awake with Thy likeness.'" "But are you sure these passages are in the Bible? Here is a Bible, point them out to me."

The little boy instantly turned to all the passages, and read them aloud to the surprise and delight of the distinguished visitor.

349. Mission School Children.

—The anxiety of children on mission stations to learn to read and write, when once awakened to a sense of the great advantage of knowledge, is truly remarkable, and their ingenuity in overcoming difficulties has often excited our admiration. The Rev. John Williams, when about to leave Raratonga, makes the following remarks on this subject:—
"The progress the children had made in writing was not more grati-

fying than the ingenuity they had displayed in providing themselves with a substitute for slates and pencils. We taught them to write at first by means of sand-boards, but, of course, they could not by this mode acquire any great facility in the art. They frequently expressed their regret at this, and as our supply of slates was very small, they determined, if possible, to find a substitute. Having formed the resolution, they were observed one morning, on leaving the school, running in groups up the mountains, and shortly after returning with flakes of stone, which they had broken off from the rocks.' These they carried to the sea-beach, and rubbed with sand and coral until they had produced a smooth surface. Thus far successful, they coloured the stones with the purple juice of the mountain plantain, to give them the appearance of English slates. Some of the boys completed the resemblance by cutting them square and framing them, so that without close examination you could scarcely detect the difference. The next desideratum was a pencil, and for this they went into the sea, and procured a number of the *echinus*, or sea-egg, which is armed with twenty or thirty spines. These they burnt slightly to render them soft, that they might not scratch, and with these flakes of stones for slates, and the spine of the sea-egg for pencils, they wrote exceedingly well; and hundreds of them took down the principal portions of every discourse they heard.

"The schools in most of the islands were at this time in a pleasing state of prosperity. In that of Papehia there were about 500 children, in Mr Buzacott's 700, and in Mr Pitman's upwards of 900, and on the morning of our departure, they wrote to me on their slates several hundred letters, expressive of their regret at our leaving them. One of these, written by a little boy about nine years of age, I desired him to copy upon paper. The following is a translation:—'Servant of God, we are grieved very much for you; our hearts are sore with grieving, because you are going to that far distant country of yours, and we fear that we shall not see your face again. Leave us John to teach us while you go, then we may expect to see you again; but if you take John too, we shall give up all hope. But why do you go? You are not an old man and worn-out. Stay till you cannot work any longer for God, and then go home.'"

350. Heathen Surprise at the Resurrection.—The Rev. R. Moffat gives the following graphic account of his attempt to instruct the great chief, Makaba, and his people, on his visit to them in the interior of South Africa, one Sabbath afternoon, and of their surprise on hearing of the resurrection of the dead:—

"Sitting down beside this great man, illustrious for war and conquest, and amidst nobles and counsellors, including rain-makers and others of the same order, I stated to him that my object was to tell him my news. His countenance lighted up, hoping to hear of feats of war, destruction of tribes, and such like subjects, so congenial to his savage disposition. When he found that my topics had solely a reference to the Great Being of whom, the day before, he had told me he knew nothing, and of the Saviour's mission to this world, whose name he had never heard, he resumed his knife and jackal's skin at which he had been working, and began humming a native air. One of the men sitting near me seemed struck with the character of the Redeemer, which

I was endeavouring to describe, and particularly with His miracles. On hearing that He had raised the dead, he very naturally exclaimed, 'What an excellent doctor He must have been, to make dead men live!' This led me to describe His power, and how that power would be exercised at the last day in raising the dead.

"In the course of my remarks the ear of the monarch caught the startling sound of the resurrection. 'What!' he exclaimed with astonishment, 'What are these words about? the dead, the dead arise!' 'Yes,' was my reply, 'all the dead shall arise.' 'Will my father arise?' 'Yes,' I answered; 'your father will arise.' 'Will all the slain in battle arise?' 'Yes.' 'And will all that have been killed and devoured by lions, tigers, hyenas, and crocodiles, again revive?' 'Yes, and come to judgment.' 'And will those whose bodies have been left to waste and to wither on the desert plains, and scattered to the winds, again arise?' he asked with a kind of triumph, as if he had now fixed me. 'Yes,' I replied, 'not one will be left behind.' This I repeated with increased emphasis. After looking at me for a few moments, he turned to his people, to whom he spoke with a stentorian voice:— 'Hark, ye wise men, whoever is among you, the wisest of past generations, did ever your ears hear such strange and unheard-of news?' And addressing himself to one whose countenance and attire showed that he had seen many years, and was a personage of no common order, 'Have you ever heard such strange news as this?' 'No,' was the sage's answer: 'I had supposed that I possessed all the knowledge of the country, for I had heard the tales of many generations, but my knowledge is confounded by the words of his mouth, surely he must have lived long before the period when we were born.' Makaba, then turning and addressing himself to me, and laying his hand upon my breast, said, 'Father, I love you much. Your visit and presence have made my heart white as milk. The words of your mouth are sweet as honey, but the words of the resurrection are too great to be heard. I do not wish to hear again about the dead rising! The dead cannot arise! The dead must not arise!' 'Why,' I inquired, 'can so great a man refuse knowledge, and turn away from wisdom? Tell me, my friend, why I must not add to words, and speak of a resurrection.' Rising and uncovering his arm which had been strong in battle, and shaking his hand as if quivering a spear, he replied, 'I have slain my thousands, and shall they arise?' Thus was conscience at length aroused from its long slumber."

351. **Namaqua Huts.** — The natives of Namaqualand, in Southern Africa, who belong to the Hottentot race, live a wandering kind of life, having to follow their cattle over extensive regions, wherever water and pasturage are to be found. Hence the huts in which they reside are of a very frail and unsubstantial character, and so constructed as to be readily taken down, packed up, and removed to a new site in an incredibly short space of time. We have found, however, by experience, that a Namaqua hut is not to be despised as a place of residence when a person is once accustomed to its use. To a novice, however, it seems strange, as will appear from the following account given by the Rev. Robert Moffat of his experience on first arriving in the country, on the 26th of January 1818:—

"After waiting for some time,

Christian Africaner made his appearance; and after the usual salutations, inquired if I was the missionary appointed by the Directors in London; to which I replied in the affirmative. This seemed to afford him much pleasure; and he added, that as I was young, he hoped that I should live long with him and his people. He then ordered a number of women to come; I was rather puzzled to know what he intended by sending for women, till they arrived bearing bundles of native mats and long sticks, like fishing-rods. Africaner, pointing to a spot of ground, said "There you must build a house for the missionary." A circle was instantly formed, and the women, evidently delighted with the job, fixed the poles, tied them down in the hemispheric form, and covered them with mats, all ready for habitation, in the course of little more than half-an-hour. Since that time I have seen houses built of all descriptions, and assisted in the construction of a good many myself; but I confess I never witnessed such expedition. Hottentot houses are at best not very comfortable. I lived six months in this native hut, which frequently required tightening and fastening after a storm. When the sun shone it was unbearably hot; and when rain fell, I came in for a share of it; when the wind blew, I had frequently to decamp to escape the dust; and in addition to these little inconveniences, any hungry cur of a dog that wished a night's lodging, would force itself through the frail wall, and not unfrequently deprive me of my anticipated meal for the coming day; and I have more than once found a serpent coiled up in a corner. Nor were these all the contingencies of such a dwelling, for, as the cattle belonging to the village had no fold, but strolled about as they pleased, I have been compelled to start up from a sound sleep, and try to defend myself and my dwelling from being crushed to pieces by the rage of two bulls which had met to fight a nocturnal duel."

Many years afterwards, when encamped near the place where young Moffat encountered these and other privations at the commencement of his eventful career, we have thought of him and others into whose labours we had entered, and whilst engaged in worship with a goodly number of converted natives, we have thanked God from our heart for what He had done for these poor outcasts by the renewing and regenerating power of His blessed Gospel.

352. Encouragement after Trials.—After passing through some trying circumstances in the early years of his missionary labour in South Africa, the Rev. Robert Moffat was much encouraged by the consistent deportment of the chief Christian, Africaner, who had been recently brought to a saving knowledge of the truth. The missionary gives the following account of this remarkable man:—Soon after my stated services commenced, I was cheered with tokens of the Divine presence and blessing. The chief Africaner, who had for some time past been in a doubtful state, attended with such regularity, that I might as well doubt of the morning's dawn as of his attendance on the appointed means of grace. To reading, in which he was not very fluent, he attended with all the assiduity and energy of a youthful believer; the Testament became his constant companion, and his profiting appeared unto all. Often have I seen him under the shadow of a great rock, nearly the livelong day, eagerly perusing the pages of Divine inspiration; or in his hut he would sit, unconscious of the affairs of a family around, or the entrance of a stranger, with his eye gazing on the blessed book, and his mind wrapt up in things Divine. Many were the nights he sat with me on a great stone at the door of my habitation, conversing with me till the dawn of another day on creation, providence, redemption, and the glories of the heavenly world. He was like the bee gathering honey from every flower, and at such seasons he would, from what he had stored up in the course of the day's reading, repeat, generally in the very language of Scripture, those passages which he could not fully comprehend. He had no commentary, except the living voice of his teacher, nor marginal references, but he soon discovered the importance of consulting parallel passages, which an excellent memory enabled him readily to find. He did not confine his expanding mind to the volume of revelation, though he had been taught by experience that that contained heights, and depths, and breadths, which no man comprehends. He was led to look upon the book of nature; and he would regard the heavenly orbs with an inquiring look, cast his eye on the earth beneath his tread, and regarding both as displays of creative power and infinite intelligence, would inquire about infinite space and endless duration. I have often been amused when sitting with him and others, who wished to hear his questions answered, and descriptions given of the majesty, extent, and number of the works of God; he would at last rub his hands on his head, exclaiming, "I have heard enough; I feel as if my head was too small, and as if it would swell with these great subjects." I may add that, during the whole period that I lived there, I do not remember having occasion to be grieved with Africaner, or to complain of any part of his conduct.

353. **Bushmen.**—The Rev. Mr Kicherer, a German missionary, who lived and laboured for many years as a missionary in Southern Africa, gives the following account of the lowest and most degraded tribe of the Hottentot race called Bushmen:— "Their manner of life is extremely wretched and disgusting. They delight to besmear their bodies with the fat of animals, mingled with ochre, and sometimes with grime. They are utter strangers to cleanliness, as they never wash their bodies, but suffer the dirt to accumulate, so that it will hang a considerable length from the elbows. Their huts are formed by digging a hole in the earth, about three feet deep, and then making a roof of reeds, which is, however, insufficient to keep off the rains. Here they lie close together like pigs in a sty. They are extremely lazy, so that nothing will rouse them to action but excessive hunger. They will continue several days together without food rather than be at the pains of procuring it. When compelled to sally forth for prey, they are dexterous at destroying the various beasts which abound in the country; and they can run almost as well as a horse. They are total strangers to domestic happiness. The men have several wives; but conjugal affection is little known. They take no great care of their children, and never correct them except in a fit of rage, when they almost kill them by severe usage. In a quarrel between father and mother, or the several wives of the husband, the defeated party wreaks his or her vengeance on the child of the conqueror, which in general loses its life. Tame Hottentots seldom destroy their children, except in a fit of passion: but the Bushmen will

kill their children without remorse, on various occasions; as when they are ill-shaped, when they are in want of food, when the father of the child has forsaken its mother, or when obliged to flee from the farmers or others; in which case they will strangle them, smother them, cast them away in the desert, or bury them alive. There are instances of parents throwing their offspring to the hungry lion, who stands roaring before their cavern, refusing to depart till some peace-offering be made to him. In general their children cease to be objects of a mother's care as soon as they are able to crawl about in the field. In some few instances, however, we have met with a spark of natural affection which places them on a level with the brute creation."

To the substantial correctness of his humiliating account, the present writer can testify from personal observations made whilst travelling in the interior of Africa; but he rejoices to be able to add that, degraded and miserable as is the condition of the poor Bushmen in their heathen state, they are not beyond the reach of the Gospel. He has known some pleasing instances of the civilisation and conversion of individuals belonging to this class of poor degraded outcasts, which go to prove that Christianity is a religion adapted for *all*.

354. Danger from Hyenas.—

Wild animals are very common and sometimes dangerous in the thinly populated districts of the interior of South Africa. And of those with which the missionaries and their people are brought in contact, none is more so than the hyena. This savage and voracious animal not only attacks and carries off sheep, goats, poultry and other domestic stock, but it will assail human beings, and is frequently known to disinter the dead to satisfy its craving appetite. The following instances, given by the Rev. R. Moffat, may serve to illustrate the boldness and daring of these troublesome creatures well as the superstition of the natives in allowing them to increase in the land:—

"One night we heard a woman screaming in the town, and, on inquiring in the morning, found that a hyena had carried away her child, which had happened to wander a few yards from the door. On our expressing astonishment, we were informed that such occurrences were very common, and that after nightfall the hyenas were in the habit of strolling through all the lanes of the town, and carrying away whatever they could seize. As these animals were thus accustomed to gorge themselves with human flesh, it became extremely dangerous to pass the night in the open field, especially on the confines of a town. I pointed out plans by which it appeared to me they might succeed in extirpating them; but they seemed very indifferent to my suggestions; urging as a reason, that there was something not lucky in coming in contact with the blood of a hyena.

"One evening, long before retiring to rest, we heard, in the direction of the water pools, the screaming of women and children, as if they were in the greatest danger. I sent off a few men, who ran to the spot, and found three children who had been drawing water closely pursued by hyenas, which were on the point of seizing them. The men succeeded in driving the animals away, on which they ran towards the women, whom the men also rescued. I understand that it frequently happens, that children sent to the pools for water never return. Many must thus be devoured in the course of a year."

When dwelling in or travelling through such countries, the missionaries and their families often have their faith and confidence severely tried, and all that they can do under such circumstances is to cast themselves upon the promises of the Almighty for Divine protection. Nor have they generally been disappointed. The preserving care of their heavenly Father has often been extended to them in a very remarkable manner. Surely they will not be forgotten, but affectionately remembered in prayer by the true friends of the missionary enterprise.

355. Left alone to Die.—One phase of heathen darkness and cruelty is presented to our view, in a very touching light, by the Rev. Robert Moffat, in the affecting account which he gives of a poor old woman, who had been left alone to die in the desert. The missionary and his people were on their return journey from the distant northern regions of Great Namaqualand, South Africa, and were hard pressed for want of water. Mr Moffat says:— We had travelled all day over a sandy plain, and passed a sleepless night from extreme thirst and fatigue. Rising early in the morning, and leaving the people to get the waggon ready to follow, I went forward, with one of our number, in order to see if we could not perceive some indications of water. After passing a ridge of hills, and advancing a considerable way on the plain, we discovered, at a distance, a little smoke rising from a few bushes which seemed to skirt a ravine. Animated with the prospect we hastened forward, eagerly anticipating a delicious draught of water. When we arrived within a few hundred yards of the spot, we stood still, startled by the fresh marks of lions which appeared to have been there only an hour before us. We had no guns, being too tired to carry them, and we hesitated for a moment whether to proceed or return. The waggon was yet distant, and thirst impelled us to go on, but it was with caution, keeping a sharp look-out at every bush we passed.

On reaching the spot we beheld an object of heartrending distress. It was a venerable-looking old woman, a living skeleton, sitting with her head leaning on her knees. She appeared terrified at our presence and especially at me. She tried to rise, but, trembling with weakness, she sunk again to the earth. I addressed her by the name which sounds sweet in every clime, and charms even the savage ear. "My mother, fear not; we are friends, and will do you no harm." I put several questions to her, but she appeared either speechless, or afraid to open her mouth. I again repeated, "Pray, mother, who are you, and how do you come to be in this situation?" to which she replied, "I am a woman; and I have been here four days; my children have left me here to die." "Your children!" I interrupted. "Yes," raising her hand to her shrivelled bosom, "my own children, three sons and two daughters. They are gone," pointing her finger, "to the blue mountains, and have left me to die." "And, pray, why did they leave you?" I inquired. Spreading out her hands, "I am old, you see, and am no longer able to serve them. When they kill game, I am too feeble to help in carrying home the flesh; I am not able to gather wood to make the fire; and I cannot carry their children on my back as I used to do." This last sentence was more than I could bear; and, though my tongue was cleaving to the roof of my mouth for want of water, this reply opened a fountain of tears. I remarked that I was surprised that she had escaped the lions which seemed to abound. She took hold of the skin of her left arm with her fingers, and, raising it up as one would do a loose fold of linen, she added, "I hear the lions; but there is nothing on me that they would eat; I have no flesh on me for them to scent." At this moment the waggon drew near, which greatly alarmed her, for she supposed that it was an animal. We would have taken her in, but she refused, so we collected some fuel for her fire, gave her some dried meat, tobacco, a knife, and some other articles, and travelled forward, promising to return when we had found water. On returning to the spot we found the old woman gone, and we afterwards learned that her children had returned to take her away, on seeing the kindness of the stranger.

356. **Tamatoa.**—Among a number of native converts to the faith of the Gospel in the South Sea Islands, a veteran old chief, named Tamatoa, is worthy of special notice. Several interesting particulars concerning him are recorded by the Rev. John Williams, but the following are the principal:—

He was the patriarch of royalty in the Society Islands, his eldest daughter having the government of Huahine, and his granddaughter being the queen of Tahiti. He was a remarkably fine man, being six feet eleven inches in height, and well-proportioned. In his heathen state he was worshipped as a god, and to him the eye of the human victim was presented before the body was carried to the mara to be offered in sacrifice. When visited by the deputation from the London Missionary Society, after his conversion, Mr Bennet requested me to ask him, which of all the crimes he had committed lay heaviest upon his mind; and, after some hesitation, he replied—"That of allowing myself to be worshipped as a god, when I knew I was but a man."

Before he was brought under the influence of the Gospel, Tamatoa was much addicted to the vice of intoxication, first by the use of the kava root, and afterwards by drinking ardent spirits, when introduced by vessels from England and America. When under the influence of these vile narcotics, he was like a madman, and would frequently seize his club or his spear, rush out of his house and wreak his vengeance on friend or foe, man, woman, or child whom he might happen to meet. On one occasion when thus excited, he rushed out of his dwelling, and not being able to find a weapon, he struck an unoffending person such a violent blow with his fist, that he knocked his eye out, and mutilated his own hand so much, that he lost, in consequence, the first and second bones of his forefinger. Thus he continued till he embraced the Gospel; but then he made a solemn vow to Jehovah that he would never again, to the day of his death, taste anything intoxicating. I knew him intimately for fifteen years, and I am convinced that he kept his vow most sacredly. The effect of his example upon the people was exceedingly beneficial; for whilst the stations of my brethren were suffering severely from the poison of the soul as well as the body, we were entirely free from it, and during the above-mentioned period of fifteen years, I saw but one or two persons in a state of intoxication.

Tamatoa was constant in his attendance at our adult school, as well as at the prayer-meetings and the more public ordinances of God's house. He delighted in receiving Christian instruction, and in everything calculated to benefit his people. I visited him frequently in his last illness, and found his views of the way of salvation clear and distinct, and his spirit resting on Christ alone. Just before he expired, he exhorted his son, who was to succeed him, his daughter, and the chiefs assembled on the mournful occasion, to be firm in their attachment to the *Gospel*, to maintain the *laws*, and to be kind to their *missionary*. Extending his withered arms to me, he exclaimed, " My dear friend, how long we have laboured together in this good cause ; nothing has ever separated us: and now death is doing what nothing else has done ; but 'who shall separate us from the love of Christ ?'" Thus died the chief Tamatoa, once the terror of his subjects, the murderer of his people, a despotic tyrant, and a most bigoted idolater. Here we see the wonderful power and transforming influence of the Gospel.

357. Teava's Prayer.—When a party of native teachers were about to proceed upon an important mission in the South Sea Islands, to carry the good news of salvation to tribes of people who had never before heard the Saviour's name, they met together to implore the blessing of God upon the enterprise. One of them, named Teava, offered up a prayer so appropriate and impressive, that the missionary at their head was induced to note down the substance of it, of which the following is an abstract:—

"O God, Thou art everywhere ; if we fly up to heaven, we shall find Thee there ; if we dwell upon the land, Thou art there ; if we sail upon the sea, Thou art there, and this affords us comfort ; so that we sail upon the ocean without fear, because Thou, O God, art in our ship. The king of our bodies has his subjects, to whom he issues his orders ; but if he himself goes with them, his presence stimulates their zeal ; they begin their work with energy, they do it soon, and they do it well. O Lord, Thou art the King of our spirits ; Thou hast issued orders to Thy subjects to do a great work ; Thou hast commanded them to go into all the world, and preach the Gospel to every creature ; we, Lord, are going upon that errand ; and let Thy presence go with us to quicken us, and enable us to persevere in the great work until we die. Thou hast said that Thy presence shall go with Thy people, even unto the end of the world. Fulfil, O Lord, to us this cheering promise. I see, O Lord, a compass in this vessel, by which the shipmen steer the right way ; do Thou be our compass to direct us in the right course, that we may escape obstructions and dangers in our work. Be to us, O Lord, the compass of salvation."

The simplicity and earnestness with which this prayer was offered, impressed the minds of all present, and the native evangelists proceeded in their work with good courage, and were made instrumental in the conversion of hundreds and thousands of their fellow-countrymen to the faith of the Gospel. When we remember that Teava and his companions, and the natives generally of the island to which they belonged, were but recently rescued from the deepest depths of moral degradation, we are constrained to glorify God in them, and to acknowledge that the Gospel of Christ is indeed, and of a truth, what it professes to be,—"the power of God unto salvation to every one that believeth."

358. Domestic Bereavement.—When the Rev. John Williams and his devoted wife were called to resign their *seventh* dear child, and to prepare for it a little grave in the

Island of Raratonga, their hearts were sorely wounded; but they received on that mournful occasion the most indubitable proofs of the affection and sympathy of the people among whom they laboured. Adverting to these things Mr Williams says, "We had entertained fond hopes that this dear babe would have been spared to us, but in this we were again disappointed; and, while we endeavoured to bow with submission to the will of an all-wise and gracious Father, we found it difficult to restrain the tear of parental affection, and even now, when we speak of our seven dear infants, whose little bodies are slumbering in the different isles of the far distant sea, our tenderest emotions are enkindled, but our murmurings are hushed into silence by the sweet conviction that they are gone before us to heaven. Just before the lid of the little coffin was fastened down, all assembled to take a last look, when our feelings were much excited by an expression of our then youngest child, who at that time was about five years of age. Thinking in the native language, and speaking in English, after looking intently at the beauteous form of the lifeless babe, he burst into tears, and, in accents of sweet simplicity, cried out, 'Father, mother, why do you plant my little brother? Don't plant him, I cannot bear to have him planted.' Our kind and beloved friends mingled their tenderest sympathies in our affliction, and did everything that the sincerest affection could suggest to alleviate our distress.

"I wrote a letter to inform the chief, Makea, of the circumstance of our bereavement, when he immediately collected all the people of his settlement, and accompanied them to Nagatangua to condole with us in our affliction. No individual came empty-handed; some brought mats, others pieces of cloth, and others articles of food, which they presented as an expression of sympathy. A few of the principal women went in to see Mrs Williams, laid their little presents at her feet, and wept over her, according to their custom. The affection of this kind-hearted people remains unabated. In a recent visit paid to Raratonga by my esteemed colleague, Mr Barff, he perceived that the congregation of three thousand people to whom he preached were all habited in black clothing, made from the paper-mulberry and coloured with preparations from the candle nut. Upon inquiring the reason for this unusual and dismal attire, he was informed by Mr Buzacott that, on the recent death of his little girl, the king and chiefs requested that they and their people might be permitted to wear mourning, as they did not wish to appear in their ordinary gay habiliments while the family of the missionary was afflicted. Such an instance of delicate respect could scarcely have been expected from a people who, twelve years before, were cannibals and addicted to every vice."

359. The Blind Old Warrior.— The Rev. John Williams gives the following account of a remarkable native convert in one of the South Sea Islands:—"In my own church was an old blind warrior called Me. He had been the terror of all the inhabitants of Raitea, and the neighbouring islands; but, in the last battle that was fought before Christianity was embraced, he received a blow which destroyed his sight. A few years after my settlement at Raitea, Me was brought under the influence of the Gospel, and when our church was formed, he was among the first members admitted. His diligence in attending the house of God was remarkable, whither he was guided by some kind friend, who would take one end of his stick, while he held the other. The most respectable females in the settlement thought this no disgrace, and I have frequently seen principal chiefs, and the king himself, leading him in this way to chapel. Although blind, he attended our adult school at six o'clock in the morning, and by repeating and carefully treasuring up what kind friends read to him, he obtained great familiarity with the truths of the New Testament.

"On returning home from a journey on one occasion, I missed old Me, and, on inquiry, I was informed that he was exceedingly ill, and not expected to recover. I determined, therefore, to visit him immediately. On reaching the place of his residence, I found him lying in a little hut, detached from the dwelling-house, and on entering it, I addressed him by saying, 'Me, I am sorry to find you so ill.' Recognising my voice, he exclaimed, 'Is it you? Do I really hear your voice again before I die? I shall die happy now; I was afraid I should have died before your return.' My first inquiry related to the manner in which he was supplied with food, in answer to which he stated that at times he suffered much from hunger. I said 'How so? You have your own plantations;' for, although blind, Me was diligent in the cultivation of sweet potatoes and bananas. 'Yes,' he said, 'but the people with whom I lived seized my ground, and I am at times exceedingly in want.' I asked him why he had not complained to the chief, or to some of the Christian brethren who visited him; and his affecting reply was, 'I feared lest the people should call me a talebearer, and speak evil of my religion; and I thought I would rather suffer hunger or death, than give them occasion to do so.'

"I then inquired what brethren visited him in his affliction, to read and pray with him. Naming several, he added, 'They do not come so often as I could wish, yet I am not lonely, for I have frequent visits from God;—God and I were talking when you came in.' 'Well,' I said, 'and what were you talking about?' 'I was praying to depart, and to be with Christ, which is far better.' Having intimated that I feared his sickness would terminate in death, I wished him to tell me what he thought of himself in the sight of God, and what was the foundation of his hope. 'Oh!' he replied, 'I have been in great trouble this morning, but I am happy now. I saw an immense mountain, with precipitous sides, up which I endeavoured to climb, but, when I had attained a considerable height, I lost my hold, and fell to the bottom. Exhausted with perplexity and fatigue, I went to a distance and sat down to weep, and while weeping I saw a drop of blood fall upon that mountain, and in a moment it was dissolved.'

"Wishing to know his own ideas of what had been presented to his imagination, I said, 'This was certainly a strange sight; what construction do you put upon it?' After expressing his surprise that I should be at a loss for the interpretation, he exclaimed, 'That mountain was my sins, and the drop which fell upon it was one drop of the precious blood of Jesus, by which the mountain of my guilt must be washed away.' I expressed my satisfaction that he had such exalted views of the efficacy of the Saviour's blood, and that, although the eyes of his body were blind, he could, with the '*eye of his heart*,' see such a glorious sight. He then went on to state that the various sermons he had heard were now his companions in solitude, and the source of his comfort in affliction.

"On saying, at the close of the interview, that I would go home and prepare some medicine for him, which might afford him ease, he replied, 'I will drink it because you say I must, but I shall not pray to be restored to health again, for my desire is to depart and be with Christ, which is far better than to remain longer in this sinful world.' In my subsequent visits I always found him happy and cheerful, longing to depart and be with Christ. This was constantly the burden of his prayer. I was with him when he breathed his last. During this interview he quoted many precious passages of scripture; and having exclaimed with energy, 'O death, where is thy sting?' his voice faltered, his eyes became fixed, his hands dropped, and his spirit departed to be with that Saviour, one drop of whose blood had melted away the mountain of his guilt. Thus died poor old Me, the blind warrior of Raitea. I returned from the overwhelming and interesting scene, praying as I went that my end might be like his."

360. Vara as a Heathen.—In the history of the introduction of Christianity and the triumphs of the Gospel in the South Sea Islands, we find recorded the following account of Vara, a minor chief in the Island of Aimeo:—

In the time of their ignorance, he was a procurer for the superior chiefs of human sacrifices, and on one occasion Pomare sent to him in order to obtain one immediately. Vara was rather at a loss to satisfy this imperious demand; and in going in search of a victim, his own little brother followed him at a distance, and cried after him. As soon as he saw him, he turned round, and struck his head with a stone and killed him, and, having put him in a large basket made of cocoa-nut leaves, sent him to Pomare. When his mother bewailed the death of her child, and charged him with the cruelty of killing his brother, he abused her, and said, "Is not the favour of the gods, the pleasure of the king, and the security of our possessions, worth more than that little fool of a brother? Better lose him than the government of the district!" How affectingly correct is the scriptural representation of man in his heathen state, "without natural affection, implacable, unmerciful!"

Another office held by Vara, was to rally dispirited warriors; and many a night has he walked from house to house, to rouse the savage spirit of the people by assuring them, on the authority of a pretended communication from some god, of their success in an approaching battle. Nor was he backward in actual conflict with the enemy. He was wont to lead forth those whom he animated to deeds of courage and savage daring, and as often as their spirits flagged, or they showed the least sign of giving in, he would urge them on to renewed efforts till they gained the victory. In one word, he was a man of war, cruelty, and blood.

But this implacable and unmerciful heathen was brought under the convincing, subduing, and renewing power of the Gospel. He heard the truth—repented, wept, believed, and became a consistent Christian. To the day of his death, he adorned his profession by a consistent walk and conversation. He received Christian baptism at the hands of the Rev. Mr Henry, but was for many years a member of the Church under the care of Mr Ormond. Vara's eyes being bad he could not learn to read; but, having been in the habit of treasuring up in his memory passages of Scripture, he had obtained a correct and extensive knowledge of the great and essential doctrines of the Gospel. He was, moreover, active in doing good to the utmost of his ability, and he was, for a long time, "a burning and a shining light," being as zealous and earnest in the cause of God as he had formerly been in the service of Satan.

361. Vara as a Christian.—When the missionaries returned from the Navigator Islands and visited Aimeo, to give to the Christian natives an account of the wonderful openings which presented themselves for the introduction of the Gospel to the regions beyond, none was more delighted than the converted chief Vara. At the close of an earnest address which he gave at a meeting held on the occasion, he lamented exceedingly that he was not a young man, to go on such an errand of mercy, and then, turning to his pastor, the Rev. Mr Orsmond, he said with great fervour, "Do not despise these islands because their inhabitants are not so numerous as those of the Navigator and other groups. But take great care of these churches, and let them supply brethren to bear the news of salvation to more populous lands." This was almost the last meeting that ever Vara attended, for he was then suffering under the illness by which he was soon afterwards called to his rest. He was visited many times in his dying moments by Mr Orsmond, who gives the following account of his state and prospects:—

On seeing that the end of the venerable chief was fast approaching, I said to him, "Are you sorry that you cast away your lying gods by which you used to gain so much property?" He was roused from his lethargy, and, with tears of pleasure sparkling in his eyes, he exclaimed, "Oh, no, no, no. What! can I be sorry for casting away death for life? Jesus is my rock, the fortification in which my soul takes shelter." I said, "Tell me on what you found your hopes of future blessedness." He replied, "I have been very wicked, but a great King from the other side of the skies sent His ambassadors with terms of peace. We could not tell for many years what these ambassadors wanted. At length Pomare obtained a victory, and invited all his subjects to come and take refuge under the wing of Jesus, and I was one of the first to do so. *The blood of Jesus is my foundation.* I grieve that all my children do not love Him. Had they known the misery we endured under the reign of the devil, they would gladly take the Gospel in exchange for their follies. Jesus is the best King; He gives a pillow without thorns."

A little time after, I asked him if he was afraid to die, when, with almost youthful energy, he replied, "No, no. The canoe is in the sea, the sails are spread, she is ready for the gale. I have a good Pilot to guide me. My outside man and my inside man differ. Let the one rot till the trumpet shall sound, but let my soul wing her way to the throne of Jesus." Soon afterwards Vara passed away to be for ever with the Lord. Will he not through eternity sing hallelujahs to God and the Lamb, because of the South Sea Mission?

362. Krishna Pal.—The first native convert to Christianity in India, as the result of the Baptist mission, established in Bengal by William Carey and others, was Krishna Pal, who was brought to a saving knowledge of the truth in a very remarkable manner. On the 25th of November 1800, Mr Thomas, being at Serampore, was summoned to the help of a native whose shoulder was dislocated. Binding the man to a tree, and instructing Carey and Marshman to pull his arm, he guided the joint into the socket. The man, when the arm was set, complained still of pain, but more of himself as a sinner, for he had frequently heard the Gospel preached, and now on reflection he began to see its truth and to feel its power. With many tears he cried out, "I am a great sinner; save me, sahib, save me!" Mr Thomas's zeal caught fire, and, with fervour and point unusual with him, he preached Christ to the penitent native; and, as the man afterwards confessed, and as a long life of constancy proved, he received the truth in the love of it. This was Krishna Pal, and it was arranged that he and another native who, like Krishna, had broken caste by eating with the missionaries, should be baptized during the following month. The other native drew back, but on the 26th of December 1800, Krishna Pal and Felix Carey, the missionary's son, were baptized by Mr Carey in the river near the mission-house. This first native convert became an eminent and useful labourer in the Lord's vineyard. And, being a man of considerable culture and mental power, he was a great help to the missionaries in their literary engagements. To him we are indebted for the hymn which begins and ends as follows:—

"Oh thou, my soul, forget no more
 The Friend who all thy misery bore;
Let every idol be forgot,
But oh, my soul, forget Him not.

. . . .

"Ah no! when all things else expire,
 And perish in the general fire,
This name all others shall survive,
And through eternity shall live."

363. Strange Vicissitudes.—The Rev. Felix Carey was the son of the celebrated Dr Carey, of the Baptist mission at Serampore. Having devoted himself to the same blessed work, in 1807, he was sent as a medical missionary to Rangoon, in company with the Rev. Mr Chater. In 1814 Mr Carey was summoned to Ava, the capital of the Burman empire, to vaccinate, when the brig in which he sailed, with his family, was upset in a squall. As soon as the alarm was given, he rushed to the cabin to rescue his wife and children. As he entered, the water poured in on every side and made him a prisoner. Nor could he for some time find access to his family. He heard their screams but could not reach them. At length he got to the place where they were struggling in the water, and seizing his two little girls and their mother and nurse, he thrust them all through the cabin window upon the vessel's broadside. The ship began to sink immediately on his joining them. The sea was rolling furiously, and the current was fearfully rapid. His wife and infants clung to him for a time, but as he sank, their hold was relaxed and he saw them no more. Rising to the surface Mr Carey managed to float to the shore, where he sat in the grass jungle up to the breast in water for some time, until a boat came to his rescue. This sad catastrophe bereaved the missionary of an affectionate wife and two lovely children; and, in deep sorrow, on the following day he resumed his voyage to Ava.

The narrator of this touching incident adds that Mr Carey's reception at the capital was one of cordial sympathy. Liberal presents were bestowed upon him. He was moreover appointed ambassador of His Majesty the Emperor, at Calcutta, to adjust some differences that had lately arisen between the two governments. He now received the style and equipage of a prince of the realm, with large allowances of money to maintain them. The humble and bereaved missionary thus became an ambassador from the Burman to the British Government. He submitted to these honours, and perhaps acquired a liking for them. They were not of long continuance, however, as something soon occurred to displace him from his office. He afterwards entered the service of another Indian prince, and met with a similar fate. He then lived for a time in a Bangali hut, to hide his retreat from the scenes of evanescent splendour, and in deep privation. Discovered at length by some friends, he was brought to Serampore, and employed once more in the work of the mission, as a translator or editor, having learned lessons never to be forgotten.

364. **A Word in Season.**—It is related of the Rev. Lewis Way that, in the course of one of his journeys, a little incident occurred which, in the providence of God, was productive of great and important results. He was riding by the walls of a garden, belonging to a certain lady in the county of Devon, when some one said to him, "The owner of that garden must have been a very peculiar character, for she left a request in her will that some of the trees which she had planted, might not be cut down till the Jews were restored to their own land." This circumstance led the reverend gentleman to reflect upon the subject, and to read the Scriptures with special reference to the Jews, and as he read, his mind became deeply impressed with the thought that they were emphatically *the* people of God that they were beloved for their fathers' sake, and that in the divine purposes, they were destined to exhibit the unchangeable faithfulness of Jehovah in their future restoration to their own land, and in their conversion to their own Messiah. Thus was the seed lodged in that good man's mind and heart, which took deep root, and which produced abundant fruit. He became henceforth the warm and devoted friend of the "seed of Abraham," and by his noble contribution of £10,000 was instrumental in the hands of Divine Providence, in preserving from ruin, and in placing upon a stable foundation, that excellent institution, "The London Society for Promoting Christianity among the Jews,"—a Society which is second to none in its earnest and indefatigable efforts to gather the "lost sheep of the house of Israel," at home and abroad, into the fold of the Redeemer.

365. **Missionary Aspect of the Bible Society.**—The manner in which the British and Foreign Bible Society aids the various missionary associations, whilst, at the same time, it is assisted by them in its turn—the missionaries being frequently the translators as well as the circulators of the sacred volume—will be seen at a glance if we consider the vast extent of its labours.

The number of languages and dialects into which God's Word is translated, has been raised from *fifty* to *upwards of two hundred*, while the number of versions of the Scriptures, in whole or in part, hitherto issued (there being sometimes more than one version in the same language) is about *two hundred and sixty*, the preparation of which has been promoted, directly or indirectly, by the British and Foreign Bible Society. In above *thirty* instances languages have been for the first time reduced to a grammatical and written form by the missionaries of different societies, in order to give to the people speaking them the Word of God in their own tongues.

In addition to the circulation of the English Scriptures to the extent of thirty-seven millions of copies in Great Britain, Ireland and the Colonies, the Society is prosecuting its work in all the countries of Europe, as well as among the principal Asiatic and African nations, in Madagascar, in the chief islands of the South Pacific, in South America, Mexico, Labrador, and Greenland. And it is ever ready to furnish Christian missionaries with copies of the Word of God in the languages of the people amongst whom they labour, whilst on the other hand the missionaries are equally ready to supply translations, and to aid in the circulation of the sacred volume among all nations.

366. A New Heart.—Tedynscung was a celebrated chief among the Delaware Indians of North America, in the latter part of the last century. The efforts of Christian missionaries, after many disappointments, trials, and failures, had been the means of diffusing a considerable amount of spiritual knowledge among the people of the tribe, and the doctrines which had been promulgated were frequently the subject of conversation and general discussion. One evening Tedynscung was sitting by the fireside of an English friend, who mentioned to him the golden rule of the Saviour as very excellent, " For one man to do unto another as he would the other should do to him." " That is impossible ; it cannot be done," said the Indian chief. After smoking his pipe and musing for about a quarter of an hour, Tedynscung again gave his opinion, and said, " Brother, I have been thoughtful on what you told me. If the Great Spirit that made man would give him a new heart, he could do as you say, but not else."

This is just what God has promised to do, and what the missionaries proclaim when they preach the Gospel of Christ to the poor perishing heathen. "Then will I sprinkle clean water upon you and ye shall be clean : from all your filthiness and from all your idols will I cleanse you. A new heart also will I give you, and a new spirit will I put within you : and I will take away the stony heart out of your flesh, and I will give you an heart of flesh " (Ezekiel xxxvi. 25, 26).

" A heart in every thought renew'd,
And full of love divine ;
Perfect, and right, and pure, and good,
A copy, Lord, of Thine ! "

367. Drawn out of the Pit.—The following by a converted Chinese, on the superiority of Christ and Christianity to anything to be found in the "Celestial Empire," is truly characteristic, and worthy of record here, as illustrative of the power of divine truth on the native mind, and of the tact with which it is sometimes exhibited to the view of others :—

A man had fallen into a deep dark pit, and lay on the miry bottom, groaning and utterly unable to move. Confucius, the great moralist of China, walked by, approached the edge of the pit, and said, " Poor fellow ! I am very sorry for you. Why were you such a fool as to get in there ? Let me give you a piece of advice ! If you ever get out, don't get in again." " I can't get out," groaned the man. A Buddhist priest next came by and said, " Poor fellow ! I am very much pained to see you there. I think if you could scramble up two-thirds of the way, or even half, I could reach you, and lift you up the rest." But the man in the pit was entirely helpless, and unable to rise. Next the Saviour came by, and hearing the cries, went to the very brink of the pit, stretched down His arms and laid hold of the poor man, brought him out and said, "Go and sin no more." This allegory is in perfect harmony with the joyful language of David when he realised his personal interest in the great salvation. "I waited patiently for the Lord; and He inclined unto me and heard my cry. He brought me up also out of an horrible pit, out of the miry clay, and set my feet upon a rock, and established my goings. He hath put a new song into my mouth, even praise unto our God: many shall see it and fear, and shall trust in the Lord" (Psalm xl. 1–3).

368. Kaffir Chief Kama.—Among the first-fruits of the Wesleyan mission to the wild and warlike Kaffirs of South Africa, was the young chief, Kama, whose character and course beautifully illustrate the declaration of the Apostle that, "Godliness is profitable unto all things, having the promise of the life that now is, and of that which is to come." Adverting to the early history of this remarkable man, the Rev. William Shaw says:—"On my first visit to the colony, in February 1824, I took with me the young Kaffir chief, Kama, and two or three of his attendants. It was a great proof of his confidence that he was willing to go with me; and his people consented with reluctance; but they were ashamed to express their apprehensions since I was leaving my wife and children among them. No Kaffir chief had, however, visited the colony for many years; and in no instance had a chief visited it since the arrival of the British settlers. Hence the event created considerable interest on both sides of the frontier. Kama was received by the British in Graham's Town, both civil and military, with great kindness. Many presents of clothing and other articles were given to the chief by various friends; and besides clothes, the commandant sent to Kobi, by Kama, a present of a horse. The young chief attended Divine worship in the English chapels at Graham's Town and Salem; and he witnessed, on these occasions, the administration of the sacraments of baptism and the Lord's supper. At one of these services, although not understanding our language, he had been seized with an apparently irresistible emotion and shed 'floods of tears.' After our return to Wesleyville, he narrated to the people, at the close of the first service, a few days afterwards, the various circumstances connected with his visit to the colony; speaking in high terms of the kindness and hospitality of the English, and describing the seriousness and solemnity which he had observed in their religious assemblies, showing that they consider God's worship to be a work of great importance. His statements excited no small interest among the people of his tribe."

From this time the mind of the young chief gradually opened to the reception of Divine truth, and he soon relinquished the last vestiges of heathenism, and embraced Christianity with all his heart. Mr Shaw says, "Amongst the natives whom I baptized at Wesleyville were the chief, Kama, and his wife. The latter is the daughter of the great chief Gaika, and sister of Makomo, the noted leader in the late Kaffir wars. Kama and his wife, amid many temptations and serious difficulties, designedly put in their way by the heathen chiefs, to seduce them from their steadfastness, are still members of our church, and are regular in their attendance on the ordinances." This was written in 1860, thirty-five years after their conversion, and it is a remarkable fact that Kama's tribe has continued to grow and prosper, whilst those of many other chiefs have been broken and scattered. He has, indeed, been a nursing father to his people, and has always set them an example worthy of being imitated.

369. Memorable Lovefeast.—In
the month of December 1834, three young missionaries, just about to embark for their respective stations in foreign lands, attended a lovefeast in Spitalsfields Chapel, London, which they much enjoyed, and the attendant circumstances of which will never be forgotten. The minister conducting the meeting was the Rev. Dr Jobson, then in the first year of his ministry, and, on hearing the testimonies of the missionaries as to their experience and purposes (the Lord helping them), he requested the prayers of the congregation on their behalf in a very feeling manner, and a gracious influence pervaded the assembly. The next speaker was a venerable Christian brother who gave utterance to his feelings in a tremulous voice, but with much pathos and power. Among other touching things, he said that the experience of the young missionaries had done his soul good, and that he should add their names to a list which he kept of dear friends for whom he prayed every day. This little incident made such an impression upon the minds of the young men, that they retired from the Spitalsfields lovefeast much strengthened and blessed in their souls; and when far away from friends and home, contending with the trials and difficulties of missionary life, they were often encouraged and strengthened by the remembrance of the fact that they were not forgotten at the throne of the heavenly grace by the friends of missions in England. Two of the three missionaries have long since been called to their reward in heaven, but the third is still spared, and, after the lapse of forty years, is thus permitted to record this little incident for the encouragement of others. "Brethren, pray for us, that the word of the Lord may have free course and be glorified, even as it is with you."

370. Model Branch-Missionary
Society.—If prizes were awarded to the most earnest, persevering, and successful organisations for aiding in the glorious work of spreading the Gospel of Christ throughout the world, there is no doubt but the little Bourton Branch Wesleyan Missionary Society in the Banbury Circuit would be honourably distinguished. In all our travels, at home and abroad, we have never met with a more striking display of missionary zeal than has been manifested there during the past few years. The population of the village only amounts to about two hundred and fifty, and yet this limited number of persons, together with the occupants of the surrounding farms, have, by dint of persevering efforts and by all manners of contrivances, raised upwards of £100 per annum for foreign missions. The leading spirit in this movement is Mr John Archer, a man of quiet zeal and unassuming manners, but of quenchless love for the mission cause, and of indomitable perseverance in promoting its interests.

The report of the last missionary anniversary of the Little Bourton Branch Society, published in the *Banbury Guardian* for January 1st, 1874, is full of interest and worthy of the study of all who are engaged in the noble enterprise. The public meeting was held in the Town Hall at Banbury, under the presidency of W. Mewbury, Esq., and interesting addresses were delivered by the chairman, the Revs. G. T. Perks (President of the Conference), P. B. Walmsley, Messrs J. Archer, R. Edmunds, G. S. Hazelhurst and others. The chairman reminded the audience that "this was Little Bourton missionary meeting, although they were assembled in the Banbury Town Hall. He did not think the friends at Little Bourton intended to have their meeting every year at Banbury, but this year was an exception. They were very highly honoured and favoured that night, with the presence of the President of the Conference, whom they loved and esteemed, and who promptly responded to the invitation of the Little Bourton friends. The President's coming there, in the midst of his many engagements and multifarious duties, showed the fostering care of the Wesleyan Missionary Society, in the work of which the President had taken no small share. It showed that at head-quarters they knew what was going on in little country places. Mr John Archer had always a financial statement of his own to make at this meeting, and he always made the first speech."

Mr Archer said he had not very much to say or to read, but to his thinking it was very good. He then read a list of contributions, which amounted to £101, 4s. 0d. He felt very thankful for the result. He was told by some that he did too much in the cause, but he felt he ought to do something, for it was a cause that lay very near to his heart. He felt exceedingly thankful for the help he had received. They were told last year that they might get £100, and they had accomplished this. He had met with very generous friends, and was thankful to say he had got a little towards the collection. He then handed a purse containing £8, 15s. to the chairman.

Mr Walmsley said the report read by Mr Archer showed considerable ingenuity in the way of giving, and he only wished the generosity of the Church at large had a little more of the ingenious element introduced into it. Mr Hazelhurst was the next speaker; he remarked that Mr Archer's hobby seemed to be foreign missions, in the promotion of which he had been most successful. Mr Archer had done so well, that it seemed he might almost bring in any amount they might require.

Mr Perks then addressed the meeting, and said it afforded him very great pleasure to find himself in the midst of this very interesting missionary meeting. The chairman only did him justice when he said that he (the speaker) was very busy. He travelled 400 or 500 miles and preached ten sermons a week, besides addressing numerous meetings; but he was very glad to come, if it had only been to listen to that most encouraging statement read at the commencement of the meeting; and if such a place as Little Bourton could raise £100 for missions, they had reason to thank God and take courage. If other places did the same in proportion, they would be able to multiply their missionaries throughout the whole world. He rejoiced very much in the spiritual tone of the meeting, and he hoped his address, by the blessing of God, might help to sustain the gracious influence.

Towards the close of the meeting the chairman announced that the collection, including the purse presented by Mr Archer, amounted to £22, 3s 2d., which, added to the list of subscriptions read, brought the amount contributed to the Mission Fund for Little Bourton for the year to the noble sum of £123, 7s. 3d., being an increase on the former year of £72, 19s. 9d. The complete list was as follows:—

	£	s.	d.
A. B., Grazing of Oxen	10	0	0
A Friend, Grazing of an Ox	4	10	0
A Friend, two Oxen	30	0	0
A Friend to Missions	20	0	0
Archer, Mr J., Grazing of an Ox	5	0	0
Archer, Mrs J., Bees	1	0	0
Boxes by a Friend	1	12	6
„ a Little Friend	2	5	0
„ Archer, Mrs. J.	5	10	0
„ Archer, Mrs R.	2	10	0
„ Cheekley, Mrs	2	18	0
„ Frost, Miss	2	0	0
„ Golsby, Mrs	1	15	0
„ Huckerby, Mrs	5	13	6
„ Summet, Miss	3	0	0
Prayer Meeting	3	9	4
Public Collection	22	3	11
Total for Little Bourton	£123	7	3
Total for Banbury Circuit	531	17	1

371. Regard for the Scriptures. —Whilst the Rev. W. Ellis was resident in Madagascar, two men came to him one night to confer with him on the subject of religion. They had walked two hundred miles, and were delighted to see a missionary, after the long night of persecution through which they had passed. "Have you the Bible?" asked Mr Ellis. "We have seen it and heard it read," one man said; "but we have only some of the words of David, and they do not belong to us; they belong to the whole family." "Have you the words of David with you now?" asked Mr Ellis. They looked at each other, but would not answer. Perhaps they were afraid; but Mr Ellis spoke kindly to them. Then one of the men put his hand into his bosom, and took out what seemed to be a roll of cloth. He unrolled it, and after removing some wrappers, behold there were a few old, torn, dingy leaves of the Psalms, which had been read, passed round, and re-read, until they were almost worn out! Tears came to Mr Ellis's eyes when he saw them. "Have you ever seen the words of Jesus, or John, or Paul, or Peter?" asked the missionary. "Yes," they said, "we have seen and heard them, but we never owned them." Mr Ellis then went and brought out a Testament with the book of Psalms bound up with it, and showed it them. "Now," said he, "if you will give me your few words of David, I will give you all his words, and all the words of Jesus, and John, and Paul, and Peter besides." The men were amazed and delighted; but they wanted to see if the words of David were the same in Mr Ellis's book; and when they found they were, and thousands more of the same sort, their joy knew no bounds. They willingly gave up their poor, tattered leaves, seized the volume, bade the missionary good-bye, and started off upon their long journey, rejoicing like those who had found great spoil.

372. Power of Kindness.—The celebrated Robert Southey relates a striking instance of the power of kindness on the part of a poor negro youth, which is illustrative of a favourable feature in the character of the race to which he belonged, whilst at the same time it teaches a good moral lesson to all classes.

"When I was quite a youth," he says, "there was a black boy living in the neighbourhood, by the name of Jim Dick. I and a number of my playfellows were one evening collected together at our sports, and began tormenting the poor black, by calling him 'negro,' 'blackamoor,' and other degrading epithets; the poor fellow appeared excessively grieved at our conduct, and soon left us. We soon afterwards made an appointment to go a-skating in the neighbourhood, and on the day of the appointment, I had the misfortune to break my skates, and

I could not go without borrowing Jim's skates. I went to him and asked him for them. 'Oh yes, Robert, you may have them and welcome,' was his answer. When I went to return them, I found Jim sitting by the fire in the kitchen, reading the Bible. I told him I had returned his skates, and was under great obligation to him for his kindness. He looked at me as he took his skates, and, with tears in his eyes, said to me, 'Robert, don't never call me blackamoor again,' and immediately left the room. The words pierced my heart, and I burst into tears, and from that time I resolved never again to abuse a poor black."

373. Generous Indian.—In our intercourse with various tribes of men in foreign lands, we met with some fine specimens of humanity, which may well put to shame the silly notions of certain sceptics that those to whom the Gospel is sent in heathen countries are not men of like passions with ourselves, but a lower order of beings. Take an instance from "Jefferson's Notes on Virginia," in reference to a generous Indian.

It is there stated that Colonel Byrd of that state, was sent at a certain time to the Cherokee nation to transact some business with them. "It happened," says the writer, "that some of our disorderly people had just killed one or two of that nation. It was, therefore, proposed in the council of the Cherokees that Colonel Byrd should be put to death in revenge for the loss of their countrymen. Among them was a chief called Silouce, who on some former occasion had contracted an acquaintance and friendship with Colonel Byrd. He came to him every night in his tent, and told him not to be afraid,—they should not kill him. After many days' deliberation, however, the determination was, contrary to Silouee's expectation, that Colonel Byrd should be put to death, and some warriors were despatched as executioners. Silouee accompanied them, and when they entered the tent of the Colonel, the generous and courageous chief threw himself between them and the object of their revenge, and said to the warriors, 'This man is my friend; before you can get at him you must kill me.' On this they returned without accomplishing their cruel purpose, and the council respected the principle so much as to recede from their determination." And thus the life of the Englishman was preserved through the noble intervention of an Indian.

374. Indian Honesty.—An American Indian visiting his white neighbours, asked for a little tobacco, and one of them, having some loose in his pocket, gave him a handful. The day following the Indian came back, saying he had found a quarter of a dollar among the tobacco. Being told as it was given him he might as well keep it, he answered, pointing to his breast, "I got a good man and a bad man here; and the good man say, It is not mine, I must return it to the owner; the bad man say, Why, he gave it to you, and it is your own now. The good man say, That not right, the tobacco is yours, not the money; the bad man say, Never mind, you get it, go, buy some drink; the good man say, No, no, you must not do so; so I don't know what to do, and I think to go to sleep; but the good man and the bad man keep talking all night, and trouble me; and now I bring the money back, I feel good."

375. Folly of Idolatry.—It is recorded of the eccentric but earnest

Rev. John Thomas, of the Baptist Missionary Society in India, that he made a company of Hindus ashamed of their idol-worship, on one occasion, by a very simple device. When travelling through the country in the discharge of his duties, he came one day upon a number of people waiting near an idol temple. He went up to them, and as soon as the doors were opened, he walked into the temple. Seeing an idol in an elevated position, he walked boldly up to it, held up his hand, and asked for silence. He then put his finger on its eyes, and said, "It has eyes, but it cannot see! It has ears, but it cannot hear! It has a nose, but it cannot smell! It has hands, but it cannot handle! It has a mouth, but it cannot speak! neither is there any breath in it!" Instead of being offended or doing the missionary any injury for thus affronting their god and themselves, the natives were all surprised and ashamed; and an old Brahmin was so convinced of his folly by what Mr Thomas said, that he cried out, "It has feet, but it cannot run away!" The people raised a shout, and being ashamed of their stupidity, they left the temple and went to their homes.

376. Picture Worship.

The absurdities of idolatry sometimes assume a truly ludicrous form, and might well excite our risibilities if the consequences were not so solemn and momentous. At a place called Baitenzorg, a village of Java, Messrs Tyerman and Bennet, the Deputation of the London Missionary Society, observed a street occupied exclusively by Chinese. They called at several of the houses and noticed an idol in each. In one they observed an engraving of the French Emperor Napoleon, in a gilt frame, before which incense was burning. The old man to whom the picture belonged, in their presence paid it Divine honours, bowing himself in various antic attitudes, and offering a prayer for blessings upon himself and family. When asked by the strangers why he worshipped a European engraving, the ignorant and deluded idolater replied, "Oh, we are not particular, we worship anything!"

377. Tact and Moral Courage.

A certain amount of self-respect and moral courage is absolutely necessary for a Christian missionary who has to work his way among all kinds of people in strange lands. In former times, before the questions relating to civil and religious liberty were well understood by petty aristocratic government officials and High Church clergymen, it was especially so. The conduct and bearing of the Rev. William Shaw, at the commencement of his missionary career in South Africa, strikingly illustrate this, and are worthy of the attention of those whom they may concern. Adverting to this subject, and to other interesting incidents which occurred at the time, Mr Shaw says:—

"I landed on the jetty at Simon's Town, on the 2nd of May 1820, and the next day proceeded to Cape Town. On my arrival at the Cape, I met the Rev. E. Edwards, who had just commenced preaching in this place. Having, with the aid of some pious soldiers and others, fitted up a wine-store as a place of worship, I had the pleasure of commencing my public ministry in South Africa by preaching in this building on Thursday evening, the 4th of May, to a small congregation of civilians and soldiers, on Acts xi. 23: 'Who, when he came, and had seen the grace of God, was glad and exhorted them all, that with purpose of heart they would cleave unto the Lord.'

Kama, the converted Kaffir Chief, addressing his people.

"While in Cape Town—the acting Governor, Sir Rufane Shawe Donkin, being away on the frontier—I called on the colonial secretary, and requested information as to the channel through which I was to derive the promised means of support from government, after my arrival in the new settlement. But the secretary —who I afterwards learned was a Roman Catholic gentleman—either knew nothing, or affected to know nothing of any claim on government. He said, 'All that can have been promised to you is *toleration*. You will be *permitted* to exercise your ministerial functions.' This induced me to show him a letter from the Under Secretary of State for the Colonies, in which the obligation of the Cape Government to 'provide for my decent maintenance' was distinctly stated. The secretary's tone towards me was now suddenly changed; and at length he pleasantly bowed me out saying that, on my arrival at my destination, I could address the government on the subject.

"On the 5th of May, Mr Edwards, from whom I had received the most affectionate attentions, rode with me on horseback from Cape Town to Simon's Town, and going on board, preached to the people in the evening. On Sunday the 7th, after conducting Divine service on deck as usual, I went on shore and preached in a private dwelling-house, where a few soldiers were in the habit of assembling for prayer. A small congregation of about thirty persons were present, and appeared to enjoy the opportunity. A message was subsequently sent to me on board the *Aurora* by the resident clergyman, stating that I had no right to hold religious services in Simon's Town; and if I presumed to do so again, it was hinted that certain disagreeable consequences to myself would follow. Had we been detained longer in the Bay, there is little doubt but I should have braved this petty threat, and again preached to this poor people who were anxious to hear the Gospel.

"As I had long before received, and put faith in the dictum of an eminent English lawyer, that 'the Toleration Act travels with the British flag,' I resolved to regard the matter from this point of view; and hence I never applied for any licence or permission from any functionary whatever, but at once proceeded to discharge all public duties wherever I met with any class of people willing to receive me in the capacity of a minister. I preached and celebrated the services for marriages, baptisms, and funerals, never allowing it to be supposed that I considered any man in a British colony had any right to interfere with my religious liberty as a free-born Englishman. On one occasion a gentleman high in office asked me by what 'authority' I did these things, and I simply showed him my certificates of ordination, and of the usual oaths required by the Act of Toleration which I had taken before the Lord Mayor of London. At another time, the acting colonial secretary intimated that the government conceived I should confine my labours to the locality where the settlers resided for whom I was the recognised minister; but, as I had no mind that the government should assume the authority to direct my ministerial conduct, I quietly proceeded in my own way, without taking the slightest notice of this intimation, and heard no more about it."

378. Seasonable Counsel.—When the Rev. William Shaw had made the necessary preparations to enter Kaffirland, in 1823, and was about to attempt the establishment of a mission among one of the most degraded, savage, and warlike tribes of Southern Africa, intelligence was brought that the natives had assumed a very threatening and hostile attitude towards the British settlers. It was said that, within a few days, parties of Kaffirs had carried off many cattle belonging to the frontier farmers, and murdered two or three of the herdsmen. This report naturally produced much excitement in the country, and some of his kind-hearted friends, who had often expostulated with the missionary on the rashness of his enterprise, now renewed their efforts to dissuade him from his purpose. Adverting to the reports alluded to, and to attempts made by the settlers to detain him in the colony, Mr Shaw says,—"I cannot say that these suggestions and remonstrances produced no effect upon me. I felt my mind burdened with a load of care and anxiety. But happy is the missionary who has a good and faithful wife, who sympathises in his objects and aims, and who, in addition to an affectionate heart that affords solace in sorrow, likewise possesses a sound judgment, qualifying her to offer counsel in time of difficulty. Many missionaries have been so favoured, and can understand my feelings, while I acknowledge how much benefit I derived from the self-sacrificing spirit and noble bearing of my wife at this trying crisis. When I repeated to her what our friends had urged upon me, and asked what she thought we ought to do;—entering into the whole case with calmness and clearness, she gave utterance to several pertinent remarks, saying in substance and nearly in the following words, 'You have long sought and prayed for this opening; Divine Providence has now evidently set the door open before us; expenses have been incurred in the purchase of outfit; you stand pledged to the chiefs; and the character and conduct of the Kaffirs only show how much they need the Gospel. We shall be under Divine protection;' closing with these emphatic words, '*Let us go in the name of the Lord.*' With a full heart and streaming eyes, I answered, 'That reply has settled the matter, and we will start as soon as I hear that the Great Fish river is likely to be practicable for the waggons to pass.'" They went, and the result of the mission is now matter of history.

379. **Kaffir Encampment.**—When Major Somerset, Commandant of Kaffraria, proposed to meet in conference the principal Kaffir chiefs, in 1824, with a view to promote a better understanding between the colonists and the native tribes, the latter consented only on condition that the Rev. William Shaw, who had recently commenced his labours among them, would accompany them to the place of meeting. At length the missionary reluctantly consented, although he felt very averse to mix himself up with the political questions which were being discussed. He gives the following graphic description of their encampment for the night, when on their way to the appointed place of meeting:—

"I can never forget that night. We were to sleep in a deep glen surrounded by a very wild and broken tract of country. The Kaffirs selected an extensive bush, to serve at once for shelter, and as their garrison for the night. It supplied them with sufficient firewood, and water was not far distant. Several oxen which had been brought for the purpose were killed; the butchers and their numerous assistants broiling and eating various parts of the internal viscera of the animals, while engaged in their occupation of skinning and cutting them up. These men were all entirely naked, and seemed wonderfully to enjoy their occupation, and the titbits which they were eating; for at intervals they sang and danced after their barbarous fashion, and in a manner anything but agreeable to European notions. At length, the animals being cut up, the beef was distributed to the various chiefs and their vassals. Great care was taken to observe the proper gradations of rank in this distribution. The breast portions of the animals, cut up after their peculiar method, were regarded as the prime parts, and these were reserved specially for the great or principal chiefs.

"I afterwards noticed that the chiefs were attended by their servants with some form and ceremony. Their cooks broiled their beef on the burning embers with particular care; and, when the steaks were ready, took branches from the bushes, which they intertwined, and thus formed a kind of mat or receptacle on which the meat could be placed. The flesh was cut into long strips, from three to twelve or more inches in length, and about an inch broad. The attendants likewise produced large milk sacks, which had been brought on pack-oxen; from these they poured the sour and curdled milk into vessels made of rushes or grass platted together, and then placed them at the feet of the principal persons in the group. A sort of ladle was provided, made from a calabash or small gourd. The attendant, or master of the milk sack, who enjoys certain privileges, dipping his ladle into the milk, drank a portion of it, to show that there was no poison or dangerous ingredient mixed therein. The chief then used the same instrument, and partook of the milk, passing it round the circle. In like manner, it was curious to see how they managed to eat without knives, forks, plates, or dishes. The head man of the circle, taking up one of the long slips of flesh described above, and putting part of it with his left hand into his mouth, cut off, with a javelin which he held in his right hand, as large a morsel as was agreeable to himself, or at least convenient for him to masticate. He then passed the remainder of it to the person next to him, who, having performed the same pleasant operation, passed it on in turn to his neighbour, and so on around the circle. It evidently required some tact, and was regarded as a species of polite etiquette in this style of feeding, so to adjust the morsels as there might be sufficient for each one in the party to receive a piece.

"A bountiful supply of beef from the parts most esteemed was duly forwarded to me by the chief, for myself and the natives attached to my party. The latter had brought my small tea-kettle, which, being filled with water, and boiled for my use, with some admixture of tea and sugar, and a few biscuits, together with a steak broiled before the wood fire, supplied me with an abundant meal, for which I had a sufficient appetite, having eaten nothing since an early breakfast. Having partaken of my supper I had time to look around me, and I visited various parts of the encampment, which seemed like a large sylvan city. There were between two and three thousand Kaflirs assembled, all well armed with their full complement of spears and javelins, fencing sticks and knobbed sticks, or clubs. They were distributed into parties of from twenty to fifty men. Each party had its separate fire for warmth, and broiling their beef; and the blaze of so many fires in all parts of the wood, with the naked Kaflirs flitting to and fro, the incessant noise and chatter of most of the people, contrasted with the gravity of some of the chiefs and counsellors who sat conferring together, combined to produce a strange scene.

"I felt no fear, but I was not sure there was no possibility of danger; for I could not forget that I was the only European present, an unarmed individual, amidst this great gathering of some of the wildest men, including some of the most notorious robbers in Kaffraria. When some of the chiefs came to my fire to have some talk with me as to the best course for them to pursue, I felt it my duty to advise them to take from the thieves, and restore to Major Somerset, certain cattle which had been recently stolen by a bad set of people, who had for some time detached themselves from their proper tribes, and were living as a sort of lawless banditti on the border of their lands. After the Kaffirs had finished their supper, leaving marvellously small remnants of the cattle that had been so recently slaughtered, the noise began to subside; and having prayed with the few people who were attached to me, I adjusted my saddle for my pillow, rolled myself on my sheep-skin karos, and placed myself with my feet towards the fire, and was soon asleep on the rough ground. In truth, notwithstanding the wild character of my companions, I was so wearied that I slept till sunrise as soundly as I could have done on any curtained bed of down.

"Early in the morning, certain spies sent out by the chiefs returned to our bivouack, and reported that they had seen a colonial force which had reached the western side of the Keiskamma river, near the ford that the commandant had appointed for the meeting; and in the course of the day the conference took place and terminated in a manner satisfactory to all the parties concerned; so that we eventually returned to our homes in peace and safety."

380. Small Beginnings.—Adverting to the early history of the Wesleyan mission in South-eastern Africa, the Rev. William Shaw says:—"On the 22d day of March 1825, I held the first class meeting in Kaffraria, at which six of the natives were present. We were exceedingly gratified with the truly earnest manner in which they expressed their desire to save their souls. How pleasing to hear a Kaffir say, 'I am always glad when I hear the bell ring to call us to church! I could not be at rest to live where I could not hear the great word.' A Kaffir woman said that all her sorrow and distress of mind arose from a consciousness that she was a great sinner." After the class meeting held during the following week, the devoted missionary makes this entry in his journal:—"It was a pleasant and profitable occasion; we have good reason to hope well of all who were present; but they are very weak in the faith and very ignorant, and must be treated with much tenderness and forbearance. We shall consider them on trial for an indefinite period, and when it is deemed expedient they will be baptized."

Writing at a subsequent period he says—"The first public baptism at Wesleyville was held on the 19th of August, the centenary of the day on which Wesley was ordained to the office of a preacher of God's Holy Word. On this occasion, three of the native converts were baptized in the presence of a large assembly of people. The event was a source of much encouragement to us; for we viewed these persons as the firstfruits of a great harvest, which will in time be gathered from among the various Kaffir nations. Nor has this hope deceived us. A system of quarterly administration of the baptismal rite has been introduced on all our stations, and I believe that no quarter of a year has ever passed, since that date, in which some of the adult natives have not been, in this manner, received as fully accredited members of Christ's visible Church, on one or other of our stations. The aggregate of these quarterly baptisms has been steadily and largely on the increase for some years past."

Before Mr Shaw left Wesleyville, in 1830, he was enabled to give the following account of this the first mission station in Kaffirland:— "Religious ordinances were regularly maintained, and the number of inquirers and converts steadily increased. The Sabbath was fully recognised by the people in all the surrounding country. The school was in active operation. The plough had been introduced. A store placed under the care of Mr R. Walker was established, for supplying clothing and useful articles to the natives, in return for the raw produce of the country. A very pretty village had arisen, which consisted, besides our own dwelling and the school-chapel, of a number of cottages erected by the natives, each containing two rooms, forming an immense improvement on the native huts." Such was the beginning of a good work which ultimately spread all over Kaffirland, exhibiting to the view a chain of stations stretching away from Graham's Town to Natal, which have been centres of light and blessing to all around, and the means of salvation to hundreds and thousands of the once degraded tribes of Africa.

381. First Spanish Convert.— The importance of mission schools for training up the rising generation in the knowledge and love of God, is beautifully illustrated by the following incident related by the Rev. Dr Rule, as having occurred at Cadiz in Spain, when he attempted to establish a Wesleyan mission there many years ago:—

Among the children first brought to our day-school in that city, was Enriqueta Martinez, an interesting girl about thirteen years old, eminent above her equals in age for a fine natural disposition, and successful industry in the prosecution of her studies; but, in common with all the natives of Spain at that time, a Romanist. She had not been long enrolled with our pupils, when her father died suddenly, but without any saving knowledge of Jesus Christ; and her widowed mother was left with herself and one brother, a youth of about eighteen,—heedless like the Spaniards in general of all that is good. Enriqueta then became the stay of her mother, whose whole heart seemed to be absorbed in promoting her happiness and advancement in the world.

I well remember that shortly after that event, I was one afternoon endeavouring to arouse a Bible-class, of which she was a member, to a concern for the salvation of their souls, and was dwelling with delight on the blessed work in which our heavenly Master employed Peter, when He made him "a fisher of men." "Would to God," said I, "that I could fish up some of you out of the sea of guilt and danger, where it is to be feared many of you will be lost for ever! Which of you is willing to devote herself to Jesus?" No one answered *then;* but the stirring of conscience was apparent in some of their countenances. However, as I had but too often made fruitless appeals to men, women, and children,—and that in England as well as in Spain,—I scarcely ventured to hope that the invitation would have been accepted more readily by those little girls than by others, not knowing that God had lodged that word in Enriqueta's heart, and by His Holy Spirit was pleading with her from day to day, that she would devote herself to Him.

Having consulted her mother she came to the mission house one day, after school hours, and requested an interview with me. It was some time before she could overcome deep emotion; but at last she said, "O Sir, I could wish to become a Protestant— a Methodist! might this be permitted?" After speaking of the way of salvation for the penitent by faith in Christ, I advised her to seek first the approbation of her mother that they might be of one mind in so important a matter. But she had already done so; and not only did *she* join a class, but *her mother* attended with her, first to see and hear, and then to speak for herself. Others were won by her conversation and example; and in a very short time, twenty-five native Spaniards received class-tickets, as members of our church. Here, I believe, was the first converted Spaniard who spontaneously joined us in Christian communion in Spain itself; and this a child. Men and women followed forthwith; and the Lord Himself came into the midst of our little assemblies.

382. **Kaffir Children.**—At an early period of the missionary enterprise, doubts were entertained by some as to the capability of the most degraded tribes of heathens and their children to receive instruction. But as the work advanced, facts were brought to light calculated to dispel all such doubts, and to prove that none are too deeply sunk to be elevated by the regenerating power of the Gospel. The following incidents are given as illustrations of this, and they might be multiplied to an almost indefinite extent :—

On the 13th ʻ June 1828, only a few years after he commencement of the Kaffir missio in South Africa, an interesting school examination was held at Wesleyville. The Kaffir children and a considerable number of their parents and friends assembled in the chapel about eleven o'clock A.M., when, after singing and prayer, about twenty-nine of the children recited portions of Scripture and verses of hymns in a manner highly honourable to themselves and creditable to their teacher. The first and second chapters of Genesis, part of our Lord's Sermon on the Mount, the Ten Commandments, the Lord's Prayer, the Creed, part of the Catechism, a hymn on creation, one on redemption, and another on the Trinity were successively repeated by the children in the Kaffir language. A Hottentot boy also repeated, in an interesting manner, a Dutch hymn; and three Kaffir girls, two of whom were the daughters of a chief, repeated with a correct pronunciation several verses in English. Two English youths who were attending the mission school for the purpose of being trained as government interpreters, likewise recited portions of Scripture in the Kaffir language.

The chiefs Pato, Kama, and Congo were present, and a number of the natives. When the chiefs heard their own children reciting portions of Scripture they were much affected. After the Rev. Samuel Young had addressed the children, Kama spoke to the following effect :—" The children have done well : I am glad to hear them. We must all learn to know this great word; and it is right that the children learn to read it." Congo then addressed the children, and said, "Children, learn ye, make haste to learn; do not be ashamed; it is a great thing to know how to read and write. We old people, your fathers, would be glad to learn; but we are too stupid: therefore I say, learn ye; and we shall hear from you this good news of God." Pato then concluded all in true Kaffir style, by saying "*Inkos! inkos*" (that is, thanks, thanks), I thank you that you came to me and my people: we were in the dark, but I see the light is now among us. Go on and teach; never be tired; though we are a bad people,—a people without ears. Children, you must learn; neither the tending of the calves nor anything else must hinder you."

About sixty children were present, and the missionary adds the pleasing fact, that "two of the three Kaffir girls who repeated verses in English were converted to God four years afterwards, and baptized by me at Wesleyville."

383. Popish Intolerance.—

Among other trials which Protestant missionaries in foreign lands have to experience, is the occasional advent of Romish priests in localities where they were little expected, and where their influence sometimes threatens to damage a good work of grace among a simple-minded people just emerging from the darkness of heathenism. In the early part of the year 1848, a Romish priest from Belgium found his way to the district of Somerset East, in Southern Africa, where he did all in his power to pervert the minds of the people by his pernicious doctrine; but happily other teachers had been before him and his efforts were unsuccessful; the name of this bold adventurer was Hoendervanger, which, rendered into English, would be "Fowl-catcher." In the course of his travels he called upon a respectable farmer, and having ascertained that his wife attended the Wesleyan ministry, he assured her that in such a course she would never be saved. As the poor woman made some reference to the Dutch Bible, he took it in his hands, and after examining two or three passages in it, and expressing great disgust and contempt for them, he held up the sacred volume, and entreated her at once and without delay, to throw it into the fire and burn it! The fire was burning brightly on the hearth at the time. She looked at the Bible and at the priest, and then at the fire, and, being incapable of speaking a word, shuddered with horror. Shortly afterwards the priest went out of the house for a while, and her son, a fine youth, who had stood a silent spectator, as soon as they were alone, said, "Mother, let us hide the Bible before he returns into the house, or else I see he will burn it himself." Accordingly they secreted the precious book before the priest returned to the house, lest he should proceed to commit such a sacrilegious outrage. Thus was Mr Fowl-catcher disappointed of his prey, nor did he succeed in proselyting the people of that neighbourhood.

384. Perilous River Crossing.—

Describing an extensive missionary journey which he took through the Bechuana country, Natal and Kaffraria, in 1848, the Rev. William Shaw gives the following account of an adventure experienced by him and his companions, which may serve as a specimen of many similar incidents which might be given:—

In crossing the Bashee river we sustained a perilous accident. The river was swollen with recent heavy rains, and we attempted to cross it before it had sufficiently subsided. The waggon upset in the midst of the stream, Mr Impey and I were obliged to jump into the water, and get out of the river as best we could. The stream was so strong that I should hardly have been able to bear up against it, if I had not been assisted by a Kaffir accustomed to it. Our waggon was all night in the river, all our clothes, books, bedding, &c., were completely saturated. I had to walk about naked till I could dry some clothes so as to be able to clothe myself. It occupied us two days to get our waggon out of the river, and dry the various articles contained therein. We did not lose much, but many things were completely spoiled by the water. The Kaffirs who live here were very friendly, and rendered us all possible assistance; and although the accident might have been very disastrous, yet we had reason to praise God that none of our party were drowned, nor was the waggon very materially injured. I have several times sustained accidents of this sort, in the course of my missionary career: few people but those who have to travel long journeys in the parts of Africa not occupied by Europeans, know the difficulties and dangers which often occur to travellers in crossing rivers and traversing mountainous regions, where there are neither bridges nor roads.

385. Humble Lodgings.—When travelling from station to station, in Southern Africa, in former times, the Christian missionary had frequently to "rough it" in the bush, and after a long day's journey, had sometimes to put up with very inferior lodgings. This was especially the case when travelling on horseback, which we know by experience, and which is evident from the following account communicated by the Rev. William Shaw:—

Leaving Butterworth we pursued our way towards the colony. The Kie river, however, was impassable for the waggon, and likely to be so for several days. We therefore hired some Kaffir swimmers, who had frequently taken me through the stream on former occasions. By their assistance we got safely through; we swam our horses through, and having put on our clothes on the opposite side of the stream, we proceeded to a Kaffir kraal, and after sleeping in a hut we rode sixty miles next day, and reached Mount Coke after nightfall.

It may amuse you if I tell you that the hut we slept in near the Kie was circular, about twelve feet in diameter, formed of sticks, and covered with grass, about seven feet high to the highest part of the cone; and in this space we ate our supper and slept; the fire being in the centre, and no chimney to take off the smoke; indeed no opening whatever but a hole about three feet by two feet, which served as a door. The inmates for the night were three Englishmen and our two native boys; one Kaffir woman, two girls, three children, four Kaffir men, and five goats. I, nevertheless, found space to stretch myself upon the earthen floor, and, wrapped up in my cloak, slept soundly till about an hour before daylight, when it was necessary to saddle our horses and start for our long ride. The Kaffirs were very friendly, although they belonged to the very clan which only seven months before barbarously murdered several English officers who had strayed from their camp; and were within sight of the very mountain upon which the troops afterwards attacked them and inflicted a severe chastisement upon them, killing a large number of them. When the Kaffirs fight, they take every possible advantage, and spare no one; but when peace is restored they seem ready to forget the most recent scenes of warfare, however they may have suffered in them.

386. Last days of Dr Livingstone.—Having been personally acquainted with Dr Livingstone in Southern Africa, we have a mournful pleasure, if such a phrase may be allowed, in recording in this place a few particulars in reference to the closing scene of his life and labours, as given in one of the notices of his newly-published journals. Most of the facts were taken down from the lips of his faithful attendants, who accompanied the remains of their lamented master to England.

The country was desolate: there was no game, it was thinly populated. Sometimes the cooing of doves, the screaming of the francolin, or the music of the singing birds, announced that a village was near; but the people, supposing the great explorer to be a slave-hunter, concealed their food, and deserted their village as soon as he approached. Others, pretending to act as guides, misdirected him, and on one occasion he lost his way for a fortnight. This terrible kind of life soon began to tell upon a constitution already enfeebled by disease. He offered up prayers that he might be allowed to finish his work, and return and be at rest; but first he must find the four fountains. "Nothing earthly," he says, "will make me give up my work in despair." On the 19th of April he writes—"I am exceedingly weak; but for the donkey could not move a hundred yards. It is not all pleasure this exploration." On the 21st he started in the morning from a small village where he had slept; but before he had gone very far he fell from the donkey, and was taken by his men back to the village. They now made a litter and carried him from village to village. On the 25th he was brought to a hamlet from which the people had not run away. He called them, and asked them if they knew of a hill on which four rivers took their rise. They replied that they were not in the habit of travelling. On the 27th he made the last entry in his diary. "*Knocked up quite, and remain—recover—sent to buy milch goats. We are, on the banks of the Molilamo.*" He was now unable to stand upright. He often implored his bearers to place the litter on the ground. Sometimes a drowsiness came over him; and the men began to be frightened, for they knew that death was drawing near. They arrived at Hala, and laid him in a hut on a native bed, raised above the ground. Beside him was placed a box with the medicine chest upon it; outside near the door was lighted a fire, and around it sat the watchers, waiting for the end. A boy lay within the hut, to be ready at the call of his master.

It was on the night of the 30th of April. At 11 P.M. he sent for Susi, and asked whether those were his men that were shouting. Susi replied that it was the natives scaring away a buffalo from the fields. He then asked how many days it was to the Luapula, and soon afterwards sighed as if in great pain, and said, "Oh, dear, dear!" and then dozed off.

At midnight Susi was sent for again, and Livingstone took a dose of calomel. He then said in a feeble voice, "*All right, you can go now.*" These were his last words. At 4 A.M. the boy ran to Susi and said, "Come to Bwana. I am afraid, I don't know if he is alive." Susi called Chumah and four other men, and they entered the hut. Their master was not on the bed, but kneeling beside it; a candle, stuck by its own wax to the top of the box, shed a light sufficient for them to see his form. His body was stretched forwards, his head buried in his hands on the pillow. One of the men approached softly, and put his hands to his cheeks. They were cold. Livingstone was dead. A little while afterwards the cock crew. It was the morning of May 1st, 1873.

> "Servant of God, well done!
> Rest from thy loved employ,
> The battle fought, the victory won,
> Enter thy Master's joy."

387. Power of the Gospel.—The success of the gospel in most of the South Sea Islands, when once introduced by the missionaries or native teachers, was very remarkable; but there were individual instances of determined opposition and obstinacy which sorely tried the faith of those who laboured among the people. And yet in many striking instances the power of divine truth mightily prevailed. On one occasion, at the close of a faithful sermon preached by the missionary in Raiatea, an old man stood up and exclaimed, "My forefathers worshipped Oro, the god of war, and so do I; nor shall anything that you can say persuade me to forsake this way. And," continued he, addressing the missionary, "what do you want more than you have already? Have you not won over most of the chiefs, and even Pomare himself! what want you more?" "All—all the people of Raiatea, and you yourself I want," replied the missionary. "No, no," cried the old man; "me—you shall never have me! I will do as my fathers have done; I will worship Oro. You shall never have me, I assure you." Little, however, did this man understand the power and love of God. Such was the effect of the gospel upon his heart shortly afterwards, that, within six months from that time, this inveterate adherent of Oro, the Moloch of the Pacific, abandoned his idol, and became a consistent worshipper of the true and living God.

338. Two kinds of Idolatry.—It is stated by those who have had opportunities of observing, that the more intelligent Chinese and Hindus object to many parts of the Roman Catholic system, because of their resemblance to the worst features of their own religion. They charge the missionaries of the Church of Rome with "preaching down Chinese or Hindu idolatry, and preaching up European idolatry," for they say they have more reason to worship their own saints than those of Europe, of whom they know nothing. They are willing, in some instances, to lay aside the worship of their own images, but not to exchange them for those of Europe. They are also offended at the indulgences sold for money, for this they say is priestcraft. "I know a native merchant," says a gentleman who resided among the Chinese, "who threw off the Romish religion in consequence of being denied the privilege of eating pork in Lent, without paying the Church, which he was not then disposed to do; and without it he understood he was to be damned, which startled him. Upon this he inquired why he might not as well eat the flesh as the fish fried in fat pork, which all the Christians in Macao were allowed to do. He therefore told the Padre that if his salvation in the Romish Church depended on so nice a point as the difference between fat and lean, he should no longer be of that religion, and so returned to paganism. He often asked why the English did not send Padres to China who worshipped no images, to teach their religion, for it would be better approved by the people. Since then missionaries of a different kind have gone to those countries, and many of the natives have been induced to receive the truth as it is in Jesus."

389. Gentle Missionary.—In reference to an encounter which he had with certain Brahmins on the banks of the Ganges, the Rev. Henry Martyn writes in his journal as follows:—"I walked into the village where the boat stopped for the night, and found the worshippers of Kali by the sound of the drums and cymbals. I did not speak to them, on account of their being Bengalees; but being invited to walk in by the Brahmins, I went within the railings, and asked a few questions about the idol. The Brahmin, who spoke bad Hindoostani, disputed with great heat, and his tongue ran faster than I could follow, and the people, who were about a hundred in number, shouted applause. But I continued to ask my questions without making any remarks upon the answers. I asked, among other things, whether what I heard of Vishnu and Brahma were true, which they confessed. I forebore to press him with the consequences, which he seemed to feel, and so I told him what was my belief. The man grew quite mild, and said it was *chulabat* (good words), and asked me seriously at last what I thought—'Was idol-worship true or false?' I felt it a matter of thankfulness that I could now make known the truth of God, though but a stammerer, and that I had an opportunity of declaring it in the presence of the devil. And this I also learned, that the power of gentleness is irresistible."

390. Praying Mothers.—The following incident may be given as a specimen of thousands which might be adduced, in illustration of the benefits which result from the faithful, fervent, and persevering prayers of pious mothers:—

A gentleman entered the Fulton Street prayer-meeting, at New York, one day in 1858, when the exercises were about half through, and laid a sealed letter on the desk of the leader. He then turned round to the audience and said, "I am a Methodist minister, and I am appointed to a special service which will require me to be travelling most of the year in California. Hearing of this, a devoted Christian mother came to me, and putting this letter into my hand, requested me to carry it to California, and to inquire everywhere for her son, and, if I should find him, put this letter into his hand, and tell him it was from *his mother*. I lay this letter before you, and ask you to pray that I may find this son, and that God will make this letter the means of his salvation. Till now that mother has been an entire stranger to me; but I feel that there is a solemn and special providence in this matter." The effect which this little incident produced upon the meeting was most touching. Men wept like children during the prayers which followed — prayers which were exceedingly earnest, and which appeared to go up from the meeting as from the heart of one man.

A person who was present on the occasion alluded to, happened to attend a similar meeting in Philadelphia the following year, when the same minister stood up and related how he had found the praying mother's son in California. He said he carried the letter in his pocket for nearly a year, everywhere inquiring for the young man to whom it was addressed. "At last," said the preacher, "I found him. He was at a gambling saloon in Sacramento. I had him pointed out to me, and walking up to him, and putting my hand upon his shoulder, I told him I wished to have a few minutes' conversation with him outside. 'Wait,' said he, 'till I have played out this game, and I will go with you.' He was with me in a few minutes, and when by ourselves, he said, 'What is it?'

'Here is a letter,' said I, 'from *your mother*, which I have carried almost a year to give you. I was directed to give it you with my own hand. And here it is.' The young man turned deadly pale. 'Oh,' said he, 'don't give it—I can't take it.' 'Yes,' said I, 'you can, and you shall take it. I am not to have a year's work for nothing. Please take it and read it, and see if there is anything more I can do for you.' The young man read the letter, and seemed overwhelmed with deep and sudden distress. 'Oh!' he groaned out, 'what can I do? What shall I do? I am a poor undone wretch. What shall I do?' 'Do?' said I, 'we must begin somewhere, and do as fast as we find anything to do. And, in this very moment, and as the first thing to be done, I want you to kneel down, and on your knees sign this temperance pledge.' The signing was soon done, for I found him willing to do anything. 'Now,' said I, 'are you willing to kneel right here, and now pledge yourself to Jesus Christ that you will be His now, and for ever.' 'Yes,' he answered, 'I am willing.' We knelt together, I prayed, and he prayed, and the result was most affecting. Suffice it to say that the Holy Spirit seemed to do His special official work on his heart, in answer to his mother's prayers, and perhaps in answer to the prayers of the Fulton Street prayer-meeting. Subsequent days and weeks of acquaintance proved that the lost and ruined young man had really passed from death unto life.

391. Joseph Skunk.—The following account of the conversion and happy death of a young North American Indian was communicated by the Rev. Joseph Stinson, and clearly shows the blessed results of religious instruction among a people who have sometimes been considered the most unpromising subjects of missionary labour:—

"Joseph Skunk was one of the first scholars of the Indian school at Grape Island, in the Bay of Quinte, Western Canada. His disposition was lively and daring, and his talent for the acquisition of knowledge being quick and vigorous, he obtained in our Sabbath and day schools a very fair English education, and was a great favourite with his teacher, the Rev. Silvester Hurlbert. At an early age he became the subject of powerful religious impressions. He felt that he was a guilty, polluted, and lost sinner; and with a penitent and believing heart he sought the mercy of God. Nor did he seek in vain: he found redemption in the blood of Christ, even the forgiveness of his sins.

"After his conversion Joseph Skunk not only endeavoured to make himself useful to his youthful companions, but his benevolent zeal took a wider range; he longed to be extensively useful to his Indian brethren generally. He therefore offered himself as a teacher, and was employed in a school far away from his native tribe. On that distant station he had laboured with fidelity and success for about two years, when his health failed. He was attacked by a disease which baffled all human skill, and compelled him to leave a work in which he delighted, and to return home. He suffered greatly for a few months, and then sank into an early grave.

"During the whole of his affliction, although destitute of many of the comforts which his melancholy condition required, he evinced a degree of patience, meekness, and resignation which afforded ample evidence that, while he was but young in years, he was a mature Christian. He frequently expressed his firm confidence in Christ as his all-sufficient Saviour, and closed his short but useful life in the peace and hope of the gospel."

392. Jack Spense.—Such was the name of a converted Indian youth, whose simple piety and love for the Word of God are worthy of record here. The missionary in charge of the station in the Hudson's Bay Territory where he lived, gives the following account of his character, sickness, and death :—

"I found him dying of consumption, and in a state of the most awful poverty and destitution, in a small birch-rind covered hut, with nothing but fern leaves under him, and an old blanket over him which was in a condition not to be described. After recovering from my surprise, I said, 'My poor boy, I am very sorry to see you in this state: had you let me know, you should not have been lying here.' He replied, 'It is very little I want now, and these poor people get it for me; but I should like something softer to lie upon, as my bones are very sore.' I then asked him concerning the state of his mind; when he replied that he was very happy; that Jesus Christ, the Lord of glory, had died to save him, and that he had the most perfect confidence in Him. Observing a small Bible under the corner of his blanket, I said, 'Jack, you have a friend there: I am glad to see that: I hope you find something good there.' Weak as he was, he raised himself on his elbow, held it in his attenuated hand, while a smile played upon his countenance, and slowly spoke, in precisely the following words:—'This, sir, is my friend; you gave it me. For a long time I read it much, and often thought of what it told. Last year I went to see my sister at Lake Winnipeg (about two hundred miles off), where I remained two months. When I was half-way back through the lake, I remembered that I had left my Bible behind me. I directly turned round, and was nine days by myself tossing to and fro, before I could reach the house; but I found my friend, and determined that I would not part with it again; and ever since it has been near my breast, and I thought I should have it buried with me; but I have thought since I had better give it to you, that when I am gone it may do some one else good.' During this conversation he was often interrupted by a sepulchral cough, and sunk down exhausted. I read and prayed with him, the hut hardly affording me room to be upright when even kneeling, and the poor sufferer soon afterwards passed away to his eternal rest."

393. The City of Melbourne.—In his interesting narrative of his Deputation visit to Australia, the Rev. Dr Jobson gives the following graphic account of the capital of Victoria, where he arrived on the 14th of December 1860 :—

"Melbourne, for the period of its existence, is undoubtedly the most wonderful city in the world. It is the growth of a single generation: indeed, mostly of the last ten or twelve years. Earlier it was only a long straggling village, or embryo town, with stumps of felled forest trees in its streets. Now it is a large city, extending two and a half miles in length, and one and a half in breadth. On all the land sides,—amid park-like scenery,—it is surrounded with thickly-populated and richly-ornamented suburbs. It has at present 120,000 inhabitants, and its number is constantly increasing. The streets are wide, well paved, and well laid out; and you see in them stores, shops, and houses of good architectural style: some resemble what are seen at the West End of London; but for the most part they resemble those of a good second-class city or enterprising English town. The city is already rich in public buildings, and these are continually on the increase. Some of them, for government and legislative uses, are even sumptuous in their character and decorations. Many of the shops and warehouses are of grey-white grit stone, clean and ornamental, as in the best streets in Manchester and Liverpool.

"The first Gospel sermon preached in this section of the island-continent was by the Rev. Joseph Orton, a Wesleyan missionary, who had accompanied the enterprising Bateman from Tasmania, across Bass Straits to Port Philip. It was preached in April 1836, beneath the shadow of the forest trees on the crest of Bateman's Hill. The service was attended by the colonist and his household, and by a goodly number of the aborigines, who, attracted by the novel scenes and sounds, crowded near to learn what was meant. The text was, 'Except a man be born again, he cannot see the kingdom of God,' and the sermon has been described by one that heard it, as being most powerful and impressive: so that all, including the poor ignorant aborigines, were awed and bowed under it. This was the first Methodist seed sown in this region of Australia, and it has issued already in an abundant harvest. Within the colony of Victoria there are at present 44 Wesleyan ministers, 249 chapels 5909 church members, 13,631 Sabbath scholars and 43,627 attendants on public worship. Melbourne has its proportionate share in these Methodist efforts and distinctions. The best and most imposing ecclesiastical structures of Melbourne belong to the Methodists; and in character and size are like the large Gothic chapels recently built by the Wesleyans in London and Liverpool. One of them, a large imposing building in Lonsdale Street, is of grey granite with free-stone dressings: it has a tower and spire and transepts, and is in appearance the cathedral of the city."

394. Australian Colonists.—

The manner in which Methodism provides for persons belonging to its communion, who emigrate to the British Colonies, is beautifully illustrated by Dr Jobson's description of the first service in which he engaged on his arrival in Victoria, in 1860. The following is a brief extract from his interesting narrative:

"My first sermon in Australia was preached in Lonsdale Street Wesleyan Church, Melbourne, which was densely crowded. And never shall I forget that wedged mass of living beings, nor that sight of them, when, after the reading of the Liturgy from the desk by the Rev. James Waugh, the resident superintendent, I went up the spiral staircase of that beautiful cedar pulpit, and in giving out the hymn beginning 'God of my life, through all my days,' looked forth upon that sea of upturned eager faces, browned with the Australian sun. They were nearly all persons in middle life; many of the men with stiff furze-like beards and long hair, while some of the women appeared worn and subdued by the heat, and the vast assembly was sprinkled all over with countenances familiar to me from having seen them in congregations to which I had preached in different parts of England. On a careful computation afterwards made, it was reckoned that I knew one-third of the whole assembly, either in their own faces or in their family likenesses. The effect of a voice familiar to so many of them, and calling up at a moment, as by a single link, a host of home associations, was indescribably exciting. In all directions eyes gushed full of tears; faces flushed and quivered with emotion; and a sigh of deep feeling heaved and swayed the mighty mass, until it waved before and around the preacher like the swelling billows of a sea.

"With imposed restraint upon a soul moved to its utmost depths at the sight, I preached from the 103d Psalm, on the grateful remembrance of divine mercies, and found that the spirit and tone of my audience were in full accordance with the theme. In the evening of the Sabbath the large building was still more densely crowded; and our subject of meditation was the Lamb in the midst of the throne. The collections proved the strength of gratitude and love influencing the congregations; and it may be humbly hoped that the services of that day in the Lonsdale Street Church were not in vain."

395. **Palankeen Travelling.**—In his interesting narrative of his missionary travels and labours in India, the Rev. Dr Hoole gives the following account of the method in which rivers are crossed in palankeens:—

"I rested the first night in a choultry or *chattram*; an edifice of one story, constructed of brick and chunam, or of granite, presenting no other accommodation than bare walls and a roof. One of my attendants, whose business it was to cook for me, kindled a fire outside the choultry, and prepared for me a cup of tea. I then lay down, and slept undisturbed till three o'clock in the morning.

"The moon shone beautifully clear; I roused my men, who were sleeping on the ground around me, that we might continue our journey before the heat of the day. We had not proceeded far before we came to the banks of a river, much swollen by the late rains, but which, like many on the same journey, had to be passed without either bridge or boat, in the manner that I shall now describe.

"On these occasions the palankeen-bearers take off the greater part of their clothing, and fold it on or about their heads. They advance till about knee-deep in the water, bearing the palankeen in the ordinary mode; when they stand still, and, by a joint effort, raise it on the heads of six of them (the traveller of course remaining in it the whole time); they thus proceed to the opposite bank, sometimes up to the neck in water, the hands of those who are bearing the palankeen being held and supported by their companions. This plan of crossing rivers may appear dangerous; but the men are so careful, that it is seldom that any serious accident occurs. I have, however, heard of instances in which a sudden rush of water from the mountains has overwhelmed the whole party, and washed them into the sea."

396. **Singhalese New Testament.**—The Rev. Thomas Kilner gives the following account of the good which resulted from reading the New Testament Scriptures in the vernacular tongue of the far-distant East:—"A young lad, having been for some time in one of the Wesleyan mission-schools in Ceylon, obtained a Singhalese New Testament as a reward for good conduct. When he left the school he promised to read it at home with great care, which he did with the most blessed results. Some time after this he entered into the service of an English officer of the army, to whom he gave great satisfaction. But it was not long before the officer had to remove

from Ceylon to Bombay, on the continent of India, and he wished the young man to go with him. His parents were consulted, and their consent obtained. In packing up his boxes for the journey, he did not forget to take his New Testament with him. They had not, however, been long in Bombay before the young man sickened and died. The officer immediately sent a letter to his parents, giving them an account of the last hours of his faithful servant. Among other things he stated in his letter, that frequently during his affliction he found the young man reading his Testament, which he begged leave now to send back to them, hoping that it might afford the parents some consolation to possess the book which had imparted so much peace and comfort to their beloved son in the immediate prospect of death. The British officer further stated that he often found his servant at prayer in his native language, with the book in his hands; and that whenever he thus found him, he appeared to be exceedingly happy; that the truths of the New Testament appeared to be his only, and yet sufficient, support and happiness in his dying hour."

The interest of this incident is enhanced by the fact that the young man was not sufficiently acquainted with the English language to enable him to express his religious feelings to his master, nor did the officer know anything of the native tongue of his servant, whilst the language of Bombay was equally foreign to them both. And yet, under these painful circumstances, a stranger in a strange land, without any one with whom he could hold Christian intercourse, this devoted Singhalese youth derived consolation from the Word of God in his dying moments.

397. Little Ango.—The Rev. Elijah Toyne gives the following account of a little Indian girl named Ango, a scholar in the Wesleyan mission-school at Point de Galle, in the island of Ceylon, and it strikingly illustrates the benefit resulting to heathen parents from their children being trained up in the fear and love of God, and in the knowledge of His Holy Word:—

"Little Ango's father was dead, and her mother was in the habit of acting as *ayah*, or nurse, in respectable families, that she might earn the means to support her fatherless children. Although, in the East, poor people's children are required very early to do something towards maintaining themselves and their parents, on hearing of a native or Singhalese school being commenced in the neighbourhood, her mother resolved to spare Ango, although the eldest of the family, to attend the school, in order that she might receive Christian instruction, and be taught to read and sew. Ango was quick and intelligent, and remarkably neat in her person. She was very regular in her attendance at school, and applied with so much eagerness and diligence to her lessons, that she was soon ready to enter the Testament class. It was a rule in the school that those children who could read the New Testament in the vernacular tongue should, as a reward, be taught English and ornamental needlework, so that they might be qualified for becoming servants in English families, as there were always a number of military officers there whose ladies were glad to have female servants who knew something of the English language, and who had been trained in the mission-schools.

"On entering the school one day, I found that little Ango was absent, and instantly concluded, from her former punctuality, that something was the matter, and that perhaps she was unwell; so I resolved without delay to go to her house and make inquiry respecting her. On going to her abode, I found that not Ango but her mother was sick. Everything about the house was as comfortable as Ango could make it; and she was busy in attendance on her afflicted mother, who it was evident was seriously ill. She was reclining on a mat spread on the room floor, with a hard pillow to support her feverish head. I sat down and entered into conversation with her, relative to the concerns of her soul. I had previously observed her at the mission-chapel, where she had been induced to attend through the invitation of her little daughter. During my interview with her, I found the poor woman possessed some knowledge of her sinful state by nature, and of the way of salvation through faith in our Lord Jesus Christ. I observed a copy of the New Testament in the room, and perceived it to be the one that little Ango used in the mission-school, but which she had brought home, in order to read to her afflicted and dying mother about Him who died on the cross for sinners of every colour and clime. At every subsequent visit, it seemed that she gained clearer views of the nature of true religion, and of the character and offices of the Saviour. I frequently selected portions of Scripture, suited to her case, to be read to her by Ango in the interim of my visits; till in the course of a few weeks her spirit took its flight, I humbly trust, to the paradise of God. Thus little Ango, by being able to read the Word of God, contributed greatly to the comfort and instruction of her dying parent, and had the happiness of soothing her passage through the dark valley of the shadow of death. It is only necessary to add that the blessing of God rested upon this dear little orphan girl, and she was henceforth enabled to look to Him as her Father, and to feel that she was His child, having a blessed hope of meeting her dear mother in heaven."

398. The Sabbath in Africa.— One of the first and most striking indications of a good moral impression having been made by the preaching of the gospel in heathen lands is to be seen in the regard which is generally paid to the holy Sabbath in the neighbourhood of our mission-stations. And as the good work advances, and native churches are organised, the Lord's day is kept with a sacredness and reverence which might well teach a lesson to some professedly Christian countries. But even before this is the case, the heathen in the vicinity of mission-stations frequently show marked respect for the day of God, and will sometimes reprove ungodly European traders for its wanton violation. In illustration of this, the following incident may be given:—

In South Africa a Kaffir chief, on one occasion, sent one of his men a journey of fifteen miles to ask a missionary if the word he had taught him about the Sabbath was the "fast word;" that is, whether or not it came from God, and was a command that they must strictly keep; for an English trader had brought his waggon near their village, and was asking his people to trade with him, although it was the Lord's day; and the trader said he had no Sunday, which greatly astonished the Kaffirs. The chief, however, replied that the missionary should decide the question, and sent to him accordingly, telling the trader that, in the meantime, he might let his oxen graze, and make himself comfortable, until the messenger returned with an answer.

On reaching the station, the messenger related the story to the missionary, exclaiming, "How can this be? The man is a white man. Where was he born, that he has no Sabbath?" The missionary expressed his sympathy with the chief and his people, and sent word by the messenger that the command was a "fast word," for it was God who said, "Remember the Sabbath-day to keep it holy," and that this word was binding upon all men of every nation. The man thanked the missionary in the name of the chief, and said that he must never be tired of teaching the Kaffirs; for their minds were very dark, and they needed telling the same things over and over again. He then returned to his tribe, and found the chief and a large assembly waiting to hear the "great word" which should decide the question between the trader and themselves. When the chief received the message, he cried, "Do you hear that now? The missionary must be right, because he has the 'book,'" meaning the Bible. The trader was then told that he must wait until the next morning, when they would be glad to trade with him; for they would have nothing to do with him on the holy day.

Of the same people the missionary says, "It is truly pleasing to see them on the Lord's day, dressed in neat and clean European clothes, forming a contrast to the filthy dresses which they wore in their heathen state. They meet together in the house of God, and their worship begins with singing a hymn: they then join in solemn prayer. A text of Scripture is read, and a sermon is preached; when the minister tells of the fallen state of man, and speaks of the death of Jesus as the only means of pardon and peace with God. There is also a school for the little black children; and at the close of the Sabbath may be heard in many of the huts the voice of prayer and praise for the mercies and blessings of the gospel which they are favoured to enjoy."

399. Spontaneous Testimony.—The Rev. James Smeeth records the following spontaneous testimony to the usefulness of mission-schools at the Cape of Good Hope, which is valuable, inasmuch as it shows the estimation in which the work is held by those who reside in the country and witness its progress:—

"After I arrived in South Africa, a Sunday-school was commenced in a village about four miles from Cape Town. One Sunday, while engaged in it, Her Majesty's Attorney-General, the Honourable William Porter, called to see what we were doing. He attended to the children in their classes, and remained while I addressed them at the close. The next morning he wrote to the Rev. T. L. Hodgson, the superintendent minister, to express not only his satisfaction but his delight with all that he had witnessed at our school on the previous day, and begged him to accept a donation of two guineas, and to consider him an annual subscriber of one guinea per annum as long as he should remain in the colony, in addition to his usual subscription to the general Mission Fund."

That Mr Porter faithfully kept his promise, and continued a steady friend to the mission, in all its interests, the present writer can testify from personal observation, having, in after years, regularly received his contributions in aid of the work, which were always tendered with a cheerfulness and hearty good-will worthy of the highest commendation. Nor was Mr Porter alone in his generous patronage of the missionary enterprise at the Cape of Good Hope. He was nobly seconded by many other gentlemen in high official positions, from the Governor downwards, who were ever ready to assist us in the erection of new chapels, the establishment of schools, and in the general spread of the gospel in various parts of the colony, and among the degraded tribes of the interior.

400. Josiah Tanui.—The Rev. T. Padman, writing from Hobart Town, Tasmania, on the 13th of September 1843, says:—"Josiah Tanui, the son of a New Zealand chief, has arrived here from London. He slept in the same room with me, and as he was with us about a fortnight, I had many opportunities of conversing with him. I found him to have a very superior mind, and also very pious. I took him with me to the class-meeting. The following is what he said:—

"'I feel thankful to God He open my heart to receive gladness of salvation. I feel thankful Jesus Christ died for me. I feel thankful I take my sins to Him; He take them all away. I feel thankful I feel peace, happy. I feel thankful God love me, I love Him. I feel thankful I go on my way rejoicing.'"

401. Happy Blind Negro.—The Rev. Jonathan Cadman says:—"I remember attending a love-feast at Dieppe Bay, in the Island of St Christopher, when, among others, a blind man rose and said, with much feeling, 'I bless God for the Methodist missionaries: before I heard them preach, I was very miserable. Being blind, the time used to hang heavy, and did not pass away fast enough. I could not really enjoy anything. I would sit down and ponder, till the thought of my affliction was almost more than I could bear, and I was strongly tempted to destroy myself. But I went to hear the missionary. The word came to my heart. I sought the blessings of salvation, and was made happy in God. Now I can thank God for my affliction. I can enjoy the society of my fellow-Christians. I can sit and think of the goodness of God all day long; and I am willing to stay here till the Lord takes me home to Himself.' Verily, 'If any man be in Christ, he is a new creature; old things are passed away, and all things are become new.'"

402. Jews' Wailing-place.—On the 17th of May 1861, when on a visit to Jerusalem and the Holy Land, Dr and Mrs Jobson inspected the Jews' Wailing-place, of which they give the following description:—

"Ascending the valley north-westward, we passed the lower pool of Gihon, with its aqueduct at one end, through which, most probably, water was brought to the temple from Solomon's large pools beyond Bethlehem; and, re-entering Jerusalem by the Jaffa Gate, we dismounted our horses, and walked forth, it being Friday, to see the Jews' 'Wailing-place.' It is a short space, like a narrow courtyard, paved with flat stones, but not a thoroughfare, lying under the high wall which forms a part of the western boundary to Omar's mosque, or temple site. The huge stones, for about half-way up, with their bevelled edges, would seem to be of Jewish masonry, and this is very credibly believed to have been part of the ancient temple wall. The Jews are not allowed to enter the temple area, but they are permitted to come here once a week, and wail for the ruined city of their prostrate nation. They do so by reading and repeating, with sobs and tears, passages from the Psalms and Prophets, expressive of deep lamentation over the ruin of their holy city, and its holy and beautiful house in which their fathers praised God. And it was, indeed, a tender and moving sight to see ancient long-bearded men, and women shrouded in long white robes, enter the area, walk along the sacred wall, kiss its stones, and pouring into its crevices their lamentations and prayers! It was a scene confirmative of the truth of Christianity; for it brought forcibly to mind Christ's own lament over Jerusalem before its fall, and His prophecy on its coming desolation."

403. Unexpected Testimony.—The *Times* publishes an extract from a private letter from Ningpo, dated October 20, 1874, in which the writer says:—

"I heard a remarkable testimony the other day to the power of Christianity, from the mouth of a heathen. He came into our little preaching-room while I was waiting for a person whom I had appointed to meet. He was a respectable man, in easy circumstances, and very courteous. He had never heard the gospel, he said, but had seen it. He began extolling its power and excellency. 'I know a man,' he said, 'who used to be the terror of his neighbourhood. If you gave him a hard word, he would shout at you, and curse you for two days and two nights without ceasing. He was as dangerous as a wild beast, and a bad opium-smoker.' (I have since heard that he was involved in two quarrels in which blood was shed.) 'But,' he continued, 'when the religion of Jesus took hold of him, he became wholly changed—gentle, not soon angry, moral in his conduct, left off opium-smoking, and was in every respect a new man. Truly the doctrine of Jesus is good.'"

Such a testimony from one who had never heard, but who had only *seen* the gospel, may well afford encouragement to those who are engaged in circulating the Scriptures, inasmuch as it shows how God can cause the written word to make a deep impression upon those who read it, and induce them to seek for further information as to the way of salvation from those whose special office it is to explain and apply the teaching of the sacred records.

404. Memorable Missionary Meeting.—When the writer was about to leave his native land, as a Christian missionary, for the third time, a little incident occurred which made a pleasant and lasting impression upon his mind, and which is worthy of record here. He had embarked on board the good sailing ship *Emperor*, in company with his devoted wife and the Rev. John and Mrs Thomas, on Tuesday, the 19th of November 1850, and the vessel was lying at anchor off Gravesend. In the course of the afternoon we incidentally heard that a Wesleyan missionary meeting was to be held in the town that evening, and as we found that our ship would not sail till the next morning, we resolved to go on shore that we might once more share in the joy of such a gathering. On entering the meeting, just after the proceedings had commenced, it was no sooner known that we were missionaries, and that one was leaving his native land for the *second*, and the other for the *third* time, than both ministers and people gave us such a hearty reception, that we were in danger of feeling proud that we were missionaries. Among the foremost to congratulate us were the Rev. Benjamin Gregory and the Rev. James Gillings, the honoured members of deputation, who generously made way for us, and gave us the time and opportunity, which of right belonged to them, to state at considerable length, before an enthusiastic audience, the particulars of our past missionary experience, and our hopes and prospects with regard to the future. Before the meeting closed, the chairman requested the congregation to remember us at the Mercy-seat in future, and then and there to join in devotion, whilst the Rev. Mr Tippett commended us in prayer to God, which he did with much feeling, and a gracious influence descended upon the assembly. The next morning we weighed anchor, and proceeded on our voyage towards the Cape of Good Hope, cheered with the thought that we should not be forgotten at the throne of the heavenly Grace. More than twenty-four years have passed away since, but we have never forgotten that memorable missionary meeting.

405. Buddhism in Japan.—The following brief extract from an able article, communicated by an intelligent gentleman resident in Japan to the *New York Independent*, in 1874, may serve to convey some idea of the extent to which Buddhism has spread in that country:—

According to the best received authorities, Buddhism entered Japan through Corea about A.D. 552. In forty-two years it had made such progress, that the Buddhist priests, or bonzes, presumed on making the Emperor Suiko a present of some of the canonical books and images of Buddha. The followers of six sects of Buddhists entered the south of Japan, and speedily overran the country, advancing northwards with the victorious armies of the Japanese conquerors, who drove the Aino, or aborigines, northward to Yesso, where they now remain, or tranquillised them and the places where their submission was received. At the end of the seventh century there were in Japan 46 Buddhist temples, 1816 priests, and 569 novices. In the sixteenth century, Buddhism was most probably co-extensive with the Japanese language.

In 1869 there were 168,000 priests and 460,244 temples in Japan, of which about 3000 were in Kioto, the sacred capital of the empire. After the overthrow of the Tokugawa dynasty, in 1868, and the reinstatement of the Mikado to his ancient power, a purification of all the mixed Shinto temples was begun. A rage for pure Japanese ideas and institutions, and a desire to purge the nation from all ideas derived from India and China, seized the authorities in power. In many places which Buddhism had anciently entered, instead of destroying it had added to or coalesced with the prevailing superstitions, and patronised the ancient deities and local spirits. There were "union" temples, with both Shinto and Buddhist shrines and priests. These were now purged, leaving only pure Shinto symbols and priests. Besides this, the Buddhists were stripped of much of their landed property and revenues, and were further commanded to pay a sum of ten million dollars to the Government for being permitted to continue their existence.

That Buddhism is tottering, and that Shinto is powerless to replace it, are truisms that no careful observer need repeat. Buddhism is tenacious of life, and may linger in Japan for centuries to come ; yet, for years past, the number has been daily increasing of those who no longer use the vain repetition, "Save us, Eternal Buddha!" but for themselves, and their fellow-countrymen, utter that prayer in which all Christians should join — "That they might know Thee the only true God, and Jesus Christ whom Thou hast sent."

406. Population of the Globe.—
The following facts from the "Student's Handbook," respecting the present state of the human race, and the mortality of man, will not be read without interest by genuine Christian philanthropists and by the true friends of the missionary enterprise :—

Division.	Sq. Miles.	Population.
Europe	3,787,469	301,600,000
Asia	17,326,794	794,000,000
America	15,813,592	84,524,000
Africa	11,556,298	192,520,000
Oceania (Australia, &c.)	3,425,156	4,365,000
Total		1,377,000,000

The population is thus divided in point of religion :—

Christians— Protestants	76,000,000
Romish Church	170,000,000
Greek Orthodox Church	89,000,000
Total	335,000,000
Jews	5,000,000
Mohammedans	160,000,000
Heathens, or Pagans	200,000,000
Asiatic Buddhists	600,000,000

Dietrich thus distributes the population of the globe according to races :—

Caucasian race		369,000,000
Mongolian	„	552,000,000
Ethiopian	„	196,000,000
American	„	1,000,000
Malay	„	200,000,000
Total		1,318,000,000

The inhabitants of our globe speak 3064 now known tongues, in which upwards of 1100 religions or creeds are preached. The average age of life is 33½ years. One-fourth of the race die before they reach the age of 7 years, and a half before the 17th year. Out of 100 persons, only 6 reach the age of 60 years and upwards, while only one in 1000 reach the age of 100. Out of 500 only one attains 80 years; out of the thousand million living persons 32,000,000 die annually, 91,000 daily, 3730 every hour, 60 every minute, and, consequently, one every second. The development of medical science and the diffusion of a knowledge of the laws of health have tended wondrously to advance the average duration of the life of men. At Geneva, in the 16th century, 1 individual in 25 died annually; in the 18th century 1 in 34; at the present time 1 in 46. In the British navy, amongst the adults, the annual average of mortality (during peace) is one in 100; in 1808 it was one in 30; in 1836 that mortality had diminished to less than one-seventh of what it was in 1770. In the American army the mortality is stated at 1 in 300 a year. In London in the middle of last century it was 1 in 32 per annum; in 1828 it was 1 in 36. Within the last 20 years the mortality in Russia has been 1 in 27, Prussia 1 in 36, France and Holland 1 in 30, Belgium 1 in 43, England 1 in 53, Sicily 1 in 32, Greece 1 in 30, Philadelphia 1 in 42, Boston 1 in 45, New York one in 37.

407. Solemn Thought.—
If it be true, as we believe it is, that, notwithstanding all that has hitherto been done to propagate the gospel of Christ in heathen lands, a large proportion of the human race still remains ignorant of God and His salvation; and that one immortal soul is passing out of time into eternity every second, 60 every minute, and 3730 every hour; what a solemn responsibility rests upon professing Christians to hasten to the rescue of their perishing fellowmen. No time is to be lost, what we do we must do quickly, or the help we propose to send to the perishing heathen may arrive too late. We must "work while it is day, for

the night cometh when no man can work."

It is related of a mission-station in India, that shortly after the introduction of the gospel among the people, a school anniversary meeting was held, when a most affecting incident occurred. The little Hindu children who had been trained in the mission-school, sang several beautiful hymns most sweetly, and went through their catechetical and other exercises, to the great delight of their parents and friends who were present. Among the spectators was a poor heathen mother, who had no child in the school, and who was seen in the course of the exercises to burst into tears, and to give vent to her feelings in loud and impassioned lamentations, crying, O my child! my child! When the missionary came to her to inquire what was the matter, she confessed with shame that she had destroyed with her own hands her only child, a lovely little boy, because he was troublesome to her at a crowded heathen festival. When she had finished her mournful story, she continued her lamentation as before:—"O my child! my child! Why did you not come *sooner* with the good news, that my child might have lived and stood among the school-children to-day? O my child! my child!"

In view of the wants of the world, the dangers to which the poor heathen are exposed, the shortness of time, and the solemn realities of eternity, let us address ourselves afresh to the important duty of sending the "glorious gospel of the blessed God" to every nation and people and kindred and tongue. If we with our prayers, and influence, and offerings, and such service as we can render, come up *promptly* and *perseveringly* to the help of the Lord against the mighty, we shall not labour in vain or spend our strength for nought. The kingdom of God will come with power and great glory, and ultimately all shall know the Lord, from the least even unto the greatest."

"From all that dwell below the skies,
Let the Creator's praise arise:
Let the Redeemer's name be sung,
Through every land, by every tongue.
Eternal are Thy mercies, Lord;
Eternal truth attends Thy word:
Thy name shall sound from shore to shore
Till suns shall rise and set no more."

408. Powerful Motives to Effort.

—Whatever view we take of the claims of dark, benighted, heathen nations upon our sympathies, prayers, and benevolence; whether we look at their numbers, degraded condition, or final destiny in the world to come, we see numerous and powerful motives to prompt and persevering efforts on their behalf. The venerable Dr Somerville, in one of his excellent lectures on missions, puts the matter before us in a very striking light, in the form of a solemn and impressive simile. With evident emotion and under a deep sense of the importance of the subject, he says:—"Suppose a precipice, at the foot of which the deep ocean is foaming; and suppose a procession, consisting of men, women, and children, moving on, night and day, two abreast, and at the rate of two miles an hour; and suppose that when they reached the precipice, they threw themselves over, and were engulphed in the devouring waters; and suppose that you inhabited a cottage near the precipice, and heard the ceaseless scream, and shriek, and loud agony of those perishing amid the billows—could you dwell in that house? Would it be possible to remain quiet? Would you not rush forth, and endeavour to arouse the neighbourhood to prevent those deluded persons from destroying themselves?"

The application of this forcible and touching figure is plain and easy. The poor degraded heathen, by hundreds and thousands, are "perishing for lack of knowledge." They are hurrying on to ruin at a rate more rapid, more awful, and as certainly fatal, as the living stream of human beings plunging over the frightful precipice in the simile of the learned doctor. And shall we who know the truth, and who have ourselves been rescued from sin and guilt, and death and hell, not make haste and try to save them before they are lost for ever?

> "Shall we, whose souls are lighted
>   With wisdom from on high,
> Shall we to men benighted
>   The lamp of life deny?
> Salvation! O salvation!
>   The joyful sound proclaim,
> Till each remotest nation
>   Has learnt Messiah's name!

409. The Grand Consummation.—The grand end and aim of the missionary enterprise is to win souls for Christ, to gather wandering sinners into the fold of the Redeemer, and thus to prepare the way for the peaceful reign of Messiah in every land and in every heart. In prosecuting the blessed work, we may meet with discouragements; but if we continue faithful to the end, we shall not labour in vain. We may "go forth bearing precious seed, weeping;" but if we faint not, we shall doubtless "come again with rejoicing, bringing our sheaves with us." Jehovah Himself has said, "As the rain cometh down and the snow from heaven, and returneth not thither, but watereth the earth, and maketh it bring forth and bud, that it may give seed to the sower, and bread to the eater; so shall my word be that goeth forth out of my mouth; it shall not return unto me void, but it shall accomplish that which I please, and it shall prosper in the thing whereto I sent it. For ye shall go out with joy, and be led forth with peace: the mountains and the hills shall break forth before you into singing, and the trees of the field shall clap their hands. Instead of the thorn shall come up the fir-tree, and instead of the briar shall come up the myrtle-tree: and it shall be to the Lord for a name, for an everlasting sign that shall not be cut off' (Isa. lv. 10–13). For this glorious consummation every true friend of Christian missions will faithfully labour, and devoutly pray that the word of prophecy may be fulfilled, and that every nation and people and kindred and tongue may be brought to a saving knowledge of Christ.

> "Oh, multiply the sower's seed!
>   And fruit we every hour shall bear,
> Throughout the world Thy gospel
>   spread,
> Thy everlasting truth declare."

INDEX.

(The figures indicate the numbers of the Anecdotes, and not the pages of the book.)

ADDRESS of an African chief, 293
Affecting funeral, 139
Affection and gratitude, 309
Affection, paternal, 192
Africa, Sabbath in, 393
Africa, South, change in, 156
African converts, 189
African fevers, 104
African shepherd-boy, 283
Africaner, 188, 323, 351
Africans, account of, 24
Africans, elevation of, 155
Africans, kindness of, 280
Aged convert, 195
Agreeable surprise, 300
Aitutaki evangelised, 326
Alarm produced by a cat, 325
Albrecht, Rev. Mr and Mrs, 323
Amelia, the Indian convert, 216
America, Methodism in, 77
American Indians, 11.
Americans, South, 18
Answer, long-expected, 84
Answer to prayer, 321
Archbell, Rev. John, 187
Archer, Mr John, 311, 370
Arthur, Rev. William, 320
Arrighi, an Italian evangelist, 345
Assam, openings in, 88
Assyrians, ancient, 4
Astronomer, self-taught, 60
Athenians, ancient, 2
Atkin, Rev. Mr, murdered, 148
Australian colonists, 394
Australian settler, 198
Australasia, 83
Ayliff, Rev. John, 228.

BABE in Bethlehem, 284
Baboo, Christian, 231
Baboon annoyance, 117
Badge of Christianity, 329
Bailie, Rev. John A., 229
Baker, Rev. T., murdered, 147
Barbadoes, incident in, 348
Barbarous practices, 32
Bartimeus, the blind preacher, 69
Barry, Rev. John, 218
Beans, missionary, 256
Beaumont, Rev. Dr, 288
Benevolence enjoined in Scripture, 276
Bereavement, domestic, 358
Bereavement overruled for good, 86
Bermuda, 302
Bernau, Rev. Mr, 214, 215
Bible Society, missionary aspect of, 365
Bishop Crowther, 67
Blind colporteur, 175
Blind Mamotlobogi, 225
Blind old warrior, the, 359
Boardman's deliverance, 96
Boniface, the apostle of Germany, 344
Borneo, the Dyaks of, 55
Brahmins, perpetual fires of, 50
Branch Missionary Society, a model, 370
Brave Christian youth, 202
Britons, ancient, 5
Brooking, Rev. Mr and Mrs, 317
Brown, Catherine, 180
Bulu, Joel, 206
Bumby, Rev. J. H., drowned, 145
Bushmen in Africa, 353
Burmah, success in, 168
Burman girl, happy death of, 234
Burning thirst, 118

U

Burning widows, 47
Burns, Rev. William, 135
Buteve, the spiritual beggar, 2.

CADMAN, Rev. Jonathan, 401
Cameron, Betsy, 122
Canada, progress of Methodism in, 346
Cape of Good Hope, 82
Cardwell, Rev. Mr, 136
Carey, Dr, and his son Felix, 362
Cat, alarm produced by a, 325
Cato Madan, 184
Cats, missionary, 262
Catherine Brown, 180
Chapman, Rev. Mr, 280
Charles Raven's last contribution, 254
Cherry-tree, missionary, 264
Child redeemed by a missionary, 157
Child's self-denial, 267
Children saved by the gospel, 161
Children maimed in honour of idols, 40
Children, methods of destroying, 42
China, missions in, 169
China open for the gospel, 89
Chinese infanticide, 54
Chinese temple service, 51
Chinese threatening his god, 53
Chip, the talking, 297
Christ precious, 233
Christian Baboo, 231
Christianity, badge of, 329
Christianity in Fiji, 165
Christie, James, 340
Cleansing blood of Christ, 210
Closing scene, the, 213
Cocoa-nut trees, missionary, 263
Coke, Dr, 78, 219, 285
Colmeister, Mr, 312
Comfort, Rev. Mr, 209
Converted Indian's testimony, 318
Convert, Romish, 173
Cook, Rev. Emile, shipwreck and death of, 320
Cornelius, the negro preacher, 181
Cornforth, Rev. Mr, 317
Crocodiles, danger from, 124
Crocodiles, sacred, 29
Cross, Rev. Mr and Mrs, shipwreck of, 44
Counsel, seasonable, 378
Crowther, Bishop, 67
Cruel practices, 12
Cruelty, heathen, 38, 46
Curious incident, 287

DANGERS and deliverances, 91
Danger, double, 121
Danger from a deceiver, 110
Danger from crocodiles, 124
Danger from drinking poisoned water, 115
Danger from dogs, 130
Danger from fire, 98
Danger from hurricanes, 107
Danger from hyenas, 354
Danger from lightning, 109
Danger from lions, 120
Danger from puff-adder, 123
Danger from serpents, 114, 125, 126
Danger from snow, 100
Danger from thunderstorms, 102
Danger from wicked men, 125
Danger from wild beasts, 116
Death averted, 106
Degradation of Hindu women, 44, 45
Deliverance, remarkable, 96
Deputation, singular, 328
Destitution, spiritual, 22
Difficulties of translation, 312
Discomforts and privations, 303
Dispensations, mysterious, 131
Division of labour, extraordinary, 296
Domestic bereavement, 358
Domestic worship in Fiji, 330
Double danger, 121
Draper, Rev. Mr and Mrs, drowned, 142
Drawn out of the pit, 367
Drowning, saved from, 124
Ducks, missionary, 259
Dying Hindu, 232
Dying Namaqua, 229.

EARNEST inquirer, 199
Edwards, Rev. Mr, 191, 225, 377
Egyptians, ancient, 3
Elephant's sagacity, 289
Eminent negro characters, 59
Encouragement after trials, 352
Erromanga, martyrs of, 146
Escape, ingenious, 63
Esther Jones, 228
Europe, openings in, 73

FAITHFUL unto death, 333
Farthing movement, 274
Father Grassi, 174
Feast of Arafat, 9
Female agency, 279
Female degradation in India, 44, 45
Fever, danger from, 104

INDEX. 307

Fiji, Christianity in, 165
Fiji, missionary martyrs, 147
Fiji, missionary meeting in, 242
Financial progress, 278
Fire, danger from, 98
Fire, Wesley's rescue from, 95
First-fruits, 224
First penny, my, 271
Fish-pots, missionary, 261
Fox, Rev. William, 223
Franklin, Sir John, 15
Franzen, the convert, 215
Friendly Islands, heathen customs in, 40
Friendly Islands evangelised, 163
Funeral, affecting, 139

GARROWS of Assim, 88
Gauls, ancient, 6
Gentle missionary, 389
Gentile nations, 1
George, King of the Friendly Islands, 205
Ghost story, 10
Giving, a good reason for, 268
Giving, intelligent, 252
God, heathen notions of, 15
Gods made of paper, 52
Good reasons for giving, 268
Gordon, Rev. J. D., murdered, 146
Gospel in Madagascar, 165
Gospel, power of the, 387
Gospel promotes peace, 158
Gospel, success of, 310
Gospel, truth and power of, 184
Grand Consummation, 409
Grassi, Father, 173
Gratitude, practical, 340
Green, Dr Anson, of Canada, 346

HADARA, the Abyssinian convert, 196
Hamilton, Rev. Mr, 290
Happy blind negro, 401
Happy Indian boy, a, 214
Harper, Rev. Mr, 285
Harrop, Rev. Mr and Mrs, death of, 137
Hazark, village of, 76
Heart, a new, 366
Heartfelt testimony, 313
Heathen estimate of life, 37
Heathen cruelty, 38
Heathen customs in the Friendly Islands, 40
Heathen darkness, 1

Heathen systems, similarity of, 56
Helping others we help ourselves, 306
Hens, missionary, 258
Hervey's Islands, heathen, 43
Hill, Rev. W., murdered, 143
Hindu, the dying, 232
Hindu female convert, 208
Hinman, Rev. Mr, 13
His promise cannot fail, 285
Hoole, Rev. Dr, 395
Hospital converts, two, 211
Human instrumentality, 235
Human sacrifices, 31
Humble lodgings, 385
Hunt, Rev. John, 207
Hurricanes, danger from, 107
Hyenas, danger from, 354

IDOLATRY, two kinds of, 388
Idolatry, folly of, 375
Idols, rejected, 299
Ignorance, extreme, 14
Ignorance of God and spiritual things, 36
Incident, curious, 287
India open for the gospel, 87
India, success of the gospel in, 166
Indian, a generous, 373
Indian honesty, 374
Indians at Rice Lake, 317
Indian's offering, the, 16
Indian's idea of Christ. 281
Indian's testimony, 318
Infanticide in China, 54
Infanticide in the Friendly Islands, 28
Infanticide in Polynesia, 124
Ingenious escape from slavery, 63
Ingenious missionary, 339
Inquirer, earnest, 199
Instant in season and out of season, 291
Instrumentality, human, 235
Intelligent giving, 252
Intolerance, popish, 383
Israelites, liberality of the, 237
Italy, persecution in, 345

JACOBS, Peter, 179
Jager, Johannes, murdered, 140
James Ah Ling, 212
Japan, Buddhism in, 405
Japan open for the gospel, 90
Japan, commencement in, 170
Jenkins, Rev. W., shipwrecked, 97
Jews' wailing-place, 402

Jobson, Rev. Dr, 369, 393, 394, 402
Joel Bulu, 206
John Barry, 218
John Sunday, 173
Johnson, Rev. W., 322
Jones, Esther, 228
Jones, Peter, 177
Joseph Qualaka, 226

KAFFIR chief, Kama, 368
Kaffir children, 382
Kaffir encampment, 379
Kaffir native minister, 34
Kaffir superstitions, 68
Kama, a Kaffir chief, 368
Kay, Rev. Stephen, 139
Keane, Robert, 219
Kendal, Berbice, 220
Kilner, Rev. Thomas, 396
Kindness, the power of, 176, 372
King George Tabou, 205
King George's speech, 331
Kirkland, Rev. Mr, 281
Krishna Pal, the convert, 362

LAUGHING at worship, 342
Lawes, Rev. G. W., 160
Leal, George, 316
Lees, Mr John, 167
Left alone to die, 355
Left for dead, 93
Legacy, a seasonable, 266
Legend, South African, 33
Leonora, the Indian convert, 217
Liberality of an emancipated slave, 247
Liberality of the Israelites, 237
Liberality of the Macedonians, 238
Liberality, unexpected, 251
Life, heathen estimate of, 37
Light in the valley, 230
Lightning, danger from, 109
Links, Jacob, murdered, 140
Lions, danger from, 119, 120
Little Amelia, 216
Little Ango, 397
Little Benome, 27
Little Burman girl, 135
Little Mie David, 227
Little and little, by, 270
Little missionary, 305
Little trials, 304
Littles, importance of, 275
Livingstone's, Dr, last days, 386
Lodgings, humble, 385

Logic of the negroes, 62
Lolohia, poor, 203
London, steamship, loss of the, 142
Loss of the *Maria* mail-boat, 136
Lost in the desert, 113
Ludicrous mistake, 286
Lutgens, Sophia, death of, 230

MACEDONIAN liberality, 238
Madagascar, the gospel in, 166
Mala of Divi Pathan, 46
Mann, Rev. James, deliverance of, 101
Mantatee convert, 193
Maria mail-boat, loss of, 136
Martyrs of Erromanga, 146
Martyrs of Fiji, 147
Martyrs of Melanesia, 148
Mary and her Bible, 204
M'Donald, Rev. B., 134
M'Muilen, Rev. James, 132
Meeting, the unexpected, 82
Melbourne, city of, 393
Memorable love-feast, 369
Methods of destroying children, 42
Methodism in Canada, progress of, 346
Mexicans, account of, 17
Mexico, Methodist mission in, 80
Mexico, openings in, 79
Miscellaneous incidents, 207
Missionary aspect of the Bible Society, 365
Missionary contributions abroad, 241
Missionary beans, 256
Missionary bees, 260
Missionary bullocks, 311
Missionary cats, 262
Missionary cocoa-nut trees, 263
Missionary cherry-trees, 264
Missionary ducks, 259
Missionary fish-pots, 161
Missionary, gentle, 389
Missionary hens, 258
Missionary intelligence, value of, 277
Missionary martyrs, 140
Missionary meetings, good, 338
Missionary meeting in Fiji, 242
Missionary meeting, memorable, 404
Missionary meeting in Namaqualand, 243
Missionary meetings in the West Indies, 244
Missionary murdered in prison, 143
Missionary orphan, 132

INDEX. 309

Missionary overboard, 133
Missionary pigs, 257
Missionary plundered, 135
Missionary prisoner of war, 134
Missionary's farewell, 308
Mission-school children, 349
Missions, objects of, 172
Missions, temporal benefits of, 149
Mistake, a ludicrous, 286
Mites, the widow's, 239
Mites, two, 240
Model Branch Missionary Society, 370
Moffat, Rev. R., 112, 188, 224, 290, 291, 292, 294, 350, 351, 352, 354, 355
Mohammedan convert, 183
Moral courage, 377
Moreau, poor, 182
Morrison, Dr, and the little girl, 336
Moses, poor old, 313
Mothers, praying, 390
Mothibi, the chief, 191
Motives to effort, 408
Murder of the Rev. J. S. Thomas, 141
Music, mysterious, 323
Mysterious dispensations, 131

Namaqua huts, 351
Namaqua, the dying, 229
Namaqualand, missionary meeting in, 243
Native genius, 57
Native poets, 61
Native reasoning, 295
Negro bishop, 67
Negro boy and his Bible, 324
Negro boy, happy death of, 223
Negro's defence, 58
Negro girl, happy death of, 222
Negro, happy blind, 401
Negro logic, 62
Negro love-feast, 154
Negro missionary-meeting, 215
Negro preacher, 481
Negro post-boy, 64
Negro shrewdness, 302
Negro slaves learning to read, 153
Negro, the faithful, 283
Negro witchcraft, 21
New disciple, a, 209
New heart, a, 366

Objects of worship, 28, 39
Offering, the Indian's, 16
Openings in sundry places, 72

Opposition subdued, 85
Orphan girl's offering, 253
Orsmond and Henry, Messrs, 360

Palankeen travelling, 395
Paper gods, 52
Parkinson, death of Mr and Mrs, 138
Parting prayer, 201
Patagonians, 19
Pattison, Bishop, murder of, 148
Paul stoned, 93
Paul's shipwreck, 92
Paying rent to the Lord, 269
Pearl of great price, 341
Pence, take care of the, 273
Peregrine, the Mohammedan convert, 183
Perilous river-crossing, 384
Perishing in the snow, 307
Perpetual fires of the Brahmins, 50
Persecution in Italy, 345
Perseverance rewarded, 194
Peter's escape from prison, 94
Peter Jacobs, 179
Peter Jones, 177
Pettit, Rev. Mr, 288
Petty annoyances, 290
Picture worship, 376
Pigs, missionary, 257
Pitman's, Mr, narrow escape, 129
Pleasing surprise, 162, 282, 300
Poets, native, 61
Poisoned water, drinking, 115
Poor Lolohia, 203
Poor old Moses, 314
Popish charms, 8
Popish intolerance, 383
Population of the globe, 406
Porter, Hon. William, 399
Power of gospel truth, 185
Powerful motives to effort, 408
Practical gratitude, 340
Prayer answered, 108, 321
Prayer, the parting, 201
Praying mothers, 390
Privations and discomforts, 303
Providence of God, 71
Progress, financial, 278
Progress in India, 167
Prudence in collecting, 248
Punishment of sin, 332

Qualaka, Joseph, 226

Raiatea, account of, 319

Rain contribution, 255
Rain-makers and witch-doctors, 35
Rarotonga, change in, 159
Rasalama, the Madagascar martyr, 197
Reconciled, way to be, 322
Rejected idols, 299
Remarkable deliverance, 96
Repeating the sermon, 292
Restitution, 111
Resurrection, belief in the, 348
Resurrection, surprise at the, 350
Retrospect, the, 171
Rice Lake Indian mission, 317
Ridgill, Rev. R., 194, 195
Rigg, Rev. Dr James H., and Rev. John, 132
River-crossing, perilous, 384
Roasting stones, 298
Rome, openings in, 74
Romish convert, 173
Romish infatuation, 7
Ross, Captain, 14
Rudolph, Rev. C., shipwrecked, 100
Rurutu, how the gospel came to, 319

SABBATH in Africa, 398
Sabbath in Tonga, 164
Sacrifices, human, 31
Savage Island Christianised, 160
Schmidt, Rev. George, 189
Schools on mission-stations, 70
Scott Chin's speech, 246
Scott, Rev. James, 221
Scott, Mrs, in India, 209
Scriptures, regard for the, 371
Seasonable counsel, 378
Seeing Jesus, 221
Self-consecration, entire, 247
Self-denial of a child, 267
Self-denial for Christ, 335
Self-taught astronomer, 60
Serpent, missionary attacked by a, 114
Serpent, bitten by a, 124
Shaw, Rev. Barnabas, 82, 113, 229
Shaw, Rev. William, 342, 368, 377, 378, 379, 380
Shepherd-boy, African, 283
Shipwreck and robbers, 97
Shipwreck of Mr and Mrs Cross, 144
Shipwreck of Paul, 92
Shipwrecked among the ice, 100
Shrewdness, negro, 302
Sierra Leone, mission in, 81
Similarity of heathen systems, 56
Singhalese New Testament, 396

Singular deputation, 328
Skunk, Joseph, 391
Slave, liberality of a, 247
Slave-hunting, 26
Slavery and the slave-trade, 25
Small beginnings, 380
Smeeth, Rev. James, 399
Smith, Rev. Gervase, 317
Snow, danger from, 101
Snow, perishing in the, 307
Soga, Rev. Tiyo, 68
Sokappa Reddy, 315
Solemn thought, 407
Source of light and comfort, 294
South Africa, change in, 156
South African legend, 32
South America, 118
Southey, Robert, 370
Spanish convert, the first, 381
Spense, Jack, 392
Spiritual destitution, 22
Spontaneous testimony, 399
St Eustatius, 285
Stinson, Rev. Joseph, 391
Story of Jung Chuo, 54
Strange superstition, 23
Strange vicissitudes, 363
Success of the gospel, 310
Sunday, John, 178
Superstitions of South Sea Islanders, 39
Superstitions of Hindus, 46
Supply, timely, 112
Surprise, agreeable, 162, 282, 300

TACT and moral courage, 377
Talking chip, the, 297
Tamatoa, a converted chief, 356
Tanta Mariann, 187
Tanui, Josiah, 400
Tasmania, snakes in, 126
Taylor, Rev. Mr, 219
Teava's prayer, 357
Temporal advantages of missions, 149
Testimony, spontaneous, 399
Testimony, unexpected, 403
Testimony, heartfelt, 313
Testimony to the value of missions, 301
That's my penny, 272
The seed is the Word, 347
Thirst, burning, 118
Thomas, Rev. John, 203, 332, 362
Thomas, Rev. J. S., murdered, 141
Threlfall, Rev. W., murdered, 140

Thunderstorms, danger from, 102, 103, 109
Timely supply. 112
Tindall, Rev. Henry, 125
Tonga, Sabbath in, 164
Toyne, Rev. Elijah, 397
Tract, usefulness of a, 334
Translation, difficulties of, 312
Tranter, Rev. William, 327
Trials, little, 304
Try again, 249
Turkey, openings in, 75
Turkey, progress of the gospel in, 150
Turner, Rev. Mr, 206
Twentyfold, 316
Two mites, 240

UNEXPECTED liberality, 251
Unexpected fruit, 190
Unity of the human race, 57
Useful lesson, 337

VANDERKEMP, Dr, 189
Vara as a heathen, 360
Vara as a Christian, 361
Varani, a chief in Fiji, 207
Vernacular Education Society, 315
Vernon, Dr, in Italy, 345

WATCHFULNESS of God, 91
Ways and means, 265
Way to be reconciled, 322

Way to succeed, 250
Way, Rev. Lewis, 364
Wesley overboard, 99
Wesley rescued from fire, 95
West Indians, 20
West Indies, change in, 152
West Indies, mission to, 78
Western Africa, 155
Wharton, Rev. Henry, 186
Whither shall I go at last, 48
Wicked men, danger from, 125
Widows, burning of, 47
Widow's mites, the, 239
Williams, Rev. John, 128, 129, 146, 349, 356, 358. 359
Williams, Rev. Joseph, death of, 139
Witchcraft, negro, 21
Witch-doctors and rain-makers, 35
Witty retort, 288
Woolman, John, 313
Word in season, a, 364
Worship, objects of, 28, 29
Worship, picture, 376
Worshipping the peacock, 49
Wreck of the *Haidee*, 105
Wrigley, death of Mr and Mrs, 137
Wyandot Indians, 151

YOUNG, Rev. E. R., 347
Youth, brave Christian, 202

ZULUS in England, 66

www.ingramcontent.com/pod-product-compliance
Lightning Source LLC
Chambersburg PA
CBHW021156230426
43667CB00006B/424